HUNGRY BEAT

About the authors

Douglas MacIntyre was a key part of the Scottish postpunk scene and since 1994 has operated the Creeping Bent Organisation, the Scottish independent label viewed as a successor to Fast Product and Postcard.

Grant McPhee is director of the film, Big Gold Dream, interviews for which have been revisited to partly contribute to the book.

Neil Cooper is an arts journalist and has chronicled Scottish postpunk manoeuvres.

HUNGRY BEAT

The Scottish Independent Pop Underground Movement (1977–1984)

Douglas MacIntyre & Grant McPhee with Neil Cooper

WHITE RABBIT

First published in Great Britain in 2022 by White Rabbit
This paperback edition first published in Great Britain in 2023 by White Rabbit,
an imprint of The Orion Publishing Group Ltd
Carmelite House, 50 Victoria Embankment
London EC4Y 0DZ
An Hachette UK Company

1 3 5 7 9 10 8 6 4 2

A CIP catalogue record for this book is
available from the British Library.

ISBN (Mass Market Paperback) 978 1 3996 0025 5
ISBN (eBook) 978 1 3996 0026 2
ISBN (Audio) 978 1 3996 0027 9

Typeset by BORN
Printed and bound in Great Britain by Clays Ltd, Elcograf S.p.A.

www.whiterabbitbooks.co.uk
www.orionbooks.co.uk

To the memory of

Gordon Dair, Billy MacKenzie, Alan Rankine,
Paul Reekie, Jock Scot, Ian Stoddart,
Thomas McLaughlin (aka Rev Volting),
Stuart Wright – the hungriest Beats of all.

Contents

List of Illustrations   ix
Foreword by Ian Rankin   xiii
Preface: Vertical Integration   xvii
Introduction   1
Dramatis Personae   3

Chapter 1: 1977 – We Oppose All Rock 'n' Roll   7

Chapter 2: 1978 – Ambition   29

Chapter 3: 1979 – Everyone Is a Prostitute   71

Chapter 4: 1980 – Parallel Lines   123

Chapter 5: 1981 – Chasing the Chimera   195

Chapter 6: 1982 – Split Up the Money   295

Chapter 7: 1983 – Empty Shell/Make Me Sad   347

Epilogues: 1984 – Exit: No Return   383

Text Permissions   425
Sources   427
Reading List   429
Thanks   431
Index   435

List of Illustrations

p. 7   Subway Sect: Paul Myers, Vic Godard and Rob Symmons (Getty / Gus Stewart)

p. 13   The Slits: Ari Up (Shutterstock / Ian Dickson)

p. 27   The Rezillos: Fay Fife (Harry Papadopoulos, courtesy of Street Level Photoworks)

p. 29   Bob Last (courtesy of Paul Research)

p. 35   The Mekons: Andy Corrigan, Mark White and Tom Greenhalgh (Getty / David Corio)

p. 39   Geoff Travis (Getty / Estate of Keith Morris)

p. 43   The Dirty Reds: Andy Copland, Russell Burn, Tam Dean Burn and Dave Carson (courtesy of Heather Findlay / Alistair Littlejohn Archive)

p. 49   Talkovers: Angus Groovy and Davy Henderson (courtesy of the Angus Whyte Archive)

p. 71   Scars: John Mackie, Robert King, Calumn MacKay and Paul Research (courtesy of Hilary Morrison)

p. 74   The Pop Group: (foreground) Gareth Sager and Mark Stewart (Getty / Dave Corio)

p. 95   The Human League: Martyn Ware, Philip Oakey, Ian Craig Marsh and Adrian Wright (Topfoto / Photoshot)

p. 98   Gang of Four: Jon King and Andy Gill (Harry Papadopoulos, courtesy of Street Level Photoworks)

p. 105   The Flowers: Hilary Morrison and Andy Copland (courtesy of Michael Barclay)

List of Illustrations

p. 123   Orange Juice: James Kirk, David McClymont, Edwyn Collins and Steven Daly (Harry Papadopoulos, courtesy of Street Level Photoworks)

p. 128   The Flowers: Fraser Sutherland (courtesy of Peter Tainsh)

p. 139   Alan Horne and Edwyn Collins (Harry Papadopoulos, courtesy of Street Level Photoworks)

p. 152   Josef K: Ronnie Torrance, David Weddell, Malcolm Ross and Paul Haig (Harry Papadopoulos, courtesy of Street Level Photoworks)

p. 160   Jaine Henderson and David Henderson (courtesy of Carole Moss)

p. 169   The Go-Betweens: Robert Forster (courtesy of Simon Clegg — Dark Live & Sweaty Archive)

p. 183   Boots for Dancing: Jamo Stewart, Jo Callis, Dave Carson, Mike Barclay and Douglas Barrie (courtesy of Hilary Morrison)

p. 189   Altered Images: Clare Grogan and Caesar (Harry Papadopoulos, courtesy of Street Level Photoworks)

p. 195   Fire Engines: Russell Burn, Davy Henderson, Graham Main and Murray Slade (courtesy of Hilary Morrison)

p. 212   Restricted Code: Kenny Blythe, Tom Cannavan, Frank Quadrelli and Stephen Lironi (Harry Papadopoulos, courtesy of Street Level Photoworks)

p. 223   Article 58: Gerri McLaughlin, Ewan MacLennan, Douglas MacIntyre and Robert McCormick (courtesy of Robin Gillanders)

p. 263   Orange Juice: James Kirk and Edwyn Collins (Harry Papadopoulos, courtesy of Street Level Photoworks)

p. 295   Hilary Morrison (courtesy of the Angus Whyte Archive)

p. 303   Jazzateers: Colin Auld, Alison Gourlay, Keith Band and Ian Burgoyne (Harry Papadopoulos, courtesy of Street Level Photoworks)

p. 312   The Bluebells: David McCluskey, Robert Hodgens, Ken McCluskey, Russell Irvine and Lawrence Donegan (Harry Papadopoulos, courtesy of Street Level Photoworks)

p. 316   Associates: Billy MacKenzie and Alan Rankine (Harry Papadopoulos, courtesy of Street Level Photoworks)

p. 320   Allan Campbell (Simon Clegg — Dark Live & Sweaty Archive)

p. 343   The French Impressionists: Malcolm Fisher (courtesy of the Malcolm Fisher Archive)

p. 347   Aztec Camera: David Mulholland, Campbell Owens and Roddy Frame (Harry Papadopoulos, courtesy of Street Level Photoworks)

p. 355   Paul Quinn (Simon Clegg — Dark Live & Sweaty Archive)

p. 366   Strawberry Switchblade: Jill Bryson and Rose McDowell (Alamy / Mirrorpix)

p. 371   The Pastels: Brian Superstar (Harry Papadopoulos, courtesy of Street Level Photoworks)

p. 383   Alan Horne and Jazzateers (Harry Papadopoulos, courtesy of Street Level Photoworks)

p. 389   Bourgie Bourgie: Keith Band, Ian Burgoyne, Paul Quinn and Mick Slaven (Harry Papadopoulos, courtesy of Street Level Photoworks)

p. 393   Stephen Pastel (Harry Papadopoulos, courtesy of Street Level Photoworks)

p. 400   James King (Simon Clegg — Dark Live & Sweaty Archive)

Foreword

by Ian Rankin

My band was called the Dancing Pigs. Every town seemed to have a band in the late 1970s and early 1980s. We practised in a room above the YWCA hall in Cowdenbeath, a stone's throw from a football stadium that got its biggest crowds when it was being used for stock-car racing. Our first gig was in that same hall, to a busload of kids with special needs who were on a day out. They thought we were The Ramones, which was fine by us. Not that we were a punk band — punk had burned brightly but was already dimming fast. We had a synth player who built his own machines from diagrams and wanted to look like David Sylvian. Me, I probably wanted to be Ian Curtis. I think we were playing a pub in Cowdenbeath the night his death was announced. It felt like another big moment.

The Dancing Pigs weren't exactly front-page news in Fife, where the local heroes were the Skids. Guitarist Stuart Adamson had been a couple of years above me at school. A bunch of us travelled to most of the more easily reached Skids gigs. They played regularly at the Pogo-A-Go-Go in Kirkcaldy, which was actually the ballroom of the Station Hotel. There was no stage, which seemed amazing to me. I'd become used to gigs by rock and prog bands in Edinburgh, where the audience was kept at a safe distance from the performer. Punk had broken down those walls, along with a lot of other things. You no longer needed a battery of Moogs and a dazzling light show. You just needed the confidence that you had something worth hearing. Clubs were springing up everywhere. Bruce's, the record shop in Kirkcaldy, had its own free fanzine called *Cripes*, which looked home-made because it was. Soon its owner, Bruce Findlay, would start a record label and become manager of Simple Minds. Everything was in flux; anything was possible.

I reached Edinburgh and university in good time to watch local bands such as Josef K and the Scars. They often took the support slot when bigger groups from elsewhere swaggered into town, filling the likes of Clouds and Valentino's. And when we weren't there, we were huddled around our bedroom radios tuning into the nightly *John Peel Show*, hoping to hear the next big thing. He even namechecked my band, after I'd put in a request, though alas this happened in the days before we'd settled on an actual name, so that we became 'the as-yet unnamed band from Cowdenbeath'. But hey, he'd wished us luck and that was good enough. Later we sent him a demo tape, but to no avail. Other bands were doing better. By coincidence, between term times at university I'd found a job in a chicken factory in Kinglassie, working beside a local lad called Michael Barclay. He was in a band called Thursdays and before long they appeared on one of Fast Product's *Earcom* compilations, though Michael soon decamped to another band called Boots for Dancing. Back at uni, a fellow student played bass in the band the Delmontes, while Rab, singer with the Scars, headlined at my poetry group one night, reading us his lyrics. If you didn't know someone in a band, there had to be something wrong with you. Music no longer belonged to London or Los Angeles or New York — things were happening right here in Scotland, exciting things, unpredictable things, and nothing would be the same again.

Foreword

It was a time when record companies sent scouts north in the expectation of discovering fresh and radical talent, but punk had taught a whole generation of home-grown fixers and entrepreneurs that you could keep things local. London needed you, you didn't necessarily need London. Enter two brilliant mavericks — Alan Horne and Bob Last — and their record labels, Postcard and Fast. Postcard ruled over the Glasgow scene, while Fast belonged to Edinburgh. They were magnets for the young, mercurial talents they would nurture. More than that, however, they created a vibrant counterculture that drip-fed into areas such as film-making, literature (including publishing) and graphic design. The possibilities seemed endless. Scotland was suddenly cool and almost achingly hip. It was a time when The Bluebells could appear on the cover of *Melody Maker* before they'd even made a record, a time when an Edinburgh label could put out music by Joy Division. Punk had, in its short life, ripped up the rule book so that the musicians who came after could create their own alternative, leading to some of the most exciting (and sometimes challenging) music imaginable. You could be dancing to Orange Juice or Aztec Camera one minute and nodding along thoughtfully to Josef K or the Fire Engines the next. Not that it was all about the Scottish bands. From Gang of Four and the Human League to the Go-Betweens, these labels and others like them opened my ears to music from around the globe.

It couldn't last of course. Wondrous things seldom do. Hilary Morrison, one of the scene's prime movers, sums it up when she says that 'once you get into the belly of the beast you have to be awfully careful that the beast doesn't start pouring its digestive juices all over you'. The music industry can be greedy, chaotic, blinkered and unforgiving. *Hungry Beat* is the story of an all-too-brief era where the short-circuiting of that industry seemed viable. But hell, the times were luminous, as was the music these artists made. The songs and many of the players remain, and here they tell their story and lick their wounds. I hold my memories dear — of sweaty gigs in packed clubs, Saturday afternoons mooching in record shops, bedsit listening parties poring over picture sleeves and constant proximity to so much talent, unsung and sung alike. So what if the Dancing Pigs didn't make it? We were around to witness many other bands who did, their hungry beats making our hearts race and our spirits soar.

It's high time the tale was told . . .

Preface: Vertical Integration

May 7, 1977 was the Year Xerox moment for the teenage revolution that begat Scotland's independent record label explosion. That was the night Subway Sect and the Slits fired a generation of young punks attending the Edinburgh leg of the Clash's White Riot tour at Edinburgh Playhouse. As with Subway Sect and the Slits, Buzzcocks impacted more than the headliners. The Manchester quartet connected the power lines with the audience, who would burn the past from their minds and start a new fire.

This would manifest itself eight months later when Fast Product put Edinburgh, art, consumerism and primitivism on the map with their first release, 'Never Been in a Riot', the debut single by the Mekons — catalogue number FAST 1. Media attention and the long-term critical and commercial success of the Fast Product roster highlighted how the strategic intervention by the label put post-punk Edinburgh on the world map in the process.

By 1980, the new decade brought a west coast retaliation to east coast pop culture supremacy, when Postcard Records of Scotland launched with an equally intelligent but inherently more melodic noise, primarily by way of Orange Juice. Where Fast Product looked to the future when they unleashed the Human League, Postcard and Orange Juice kept a sly eye on the past with their clear admiration of Dylan, the Byrds, the Lovin' Spoonful and Stax Records. Within eighteen months, however, Postcard had changed the face of independent pop culture. By the end of 1981, it looked set to become one of the most important record labels in the world. Then they stopped.

Hungry Beat aims to tell a different story to the one regularly regurgitated. This bookends a period starting at the White Riot concert through to the age of entryism that culminated in 1984 with mainstream chart success for many of the protagonists.

Introduction

I first met Grant McPhee at the start of his long process of bringing the story of Fast Product and Postcard Records to cinematic fruition. His lauded documentary, *Big Gold Dream*, opened the 2015 Edinburgh Film Festival and toured the international film festival circuit to much acclaim. The film was wonderfully narrated by Robert Forster of the Go-Betweens and reframed the post-punk period in Edinburgh and Glasgow, shining the spotlight on these iconic labels for a new generation when it was screened by BBC Television. Somewhere along the line I started constructing an oral history (in cahoots with Grant and his interview archive). I would not have been able to write this book without the considerable input of Grant.

I was at a perfect age (sixteen) for the emergence of Fast Product and Postcard. I'd been turned on by punk, particularly by the BBC Radio 1 John Peel sessions by Subway Sect and the Slits. I wasn't the only one. The impact made on those Scottish punks who attended the Clash's White Riot tour in Edinburgh in 1977 was acute and resulted in many of them starting groups and labels. As Fast Product and Postcard made their presence felt I was ripe for it, and as an underage teenager gained entrance to the clubs and bars that were promoting concerts by Scars, Josef K, Orange Juice and Fire Engines. The excitement of this period was the spark that ignited me to start up my own Scottish independent label in 1994, The Creeping Bent Organisation.

Grant and I both knew arts culture journalist Neil Cooper, largely through being interviewed by Neil over the years. We felt his overview of what we were trying to achieve with the book would prove invaluable — it did. Neil interviewed Geoff Travis for *Hungry Beat* to get his viewpoint on the significance of Fast Product and Postcard from a Rough Trade perspective. Neil also spoke to Bob Last and Hilary Morrison to corroborate our thoughts on the Fast Product story.

The immense cultural contribution made by Bob Last and Hilary Morrison in Edinburgh, followed by Alan Horne and Edwyn Collins in Glasgow, cannot be underestimated. They helped create a confidence in being Scottish that hitherto had not existed in pop music (or the arts in general in Scotland). Their fierce independent spirit helped stamp a mark of quality and intelligence on everything they achieved with their labels over a very short period of time. Fast Product and Postcard had more in common with art movements than the commercial music industry. The aesthetic of their packaging and design drew from the past but propelled them forward. Fast Product and Postcard remain touchstones for anyone involved in the arts in Scotland.

Working on *Hungry Beat* with Grant and Neil has been an inspiring process; hopefully our different disciplines (film director, journalist and musician) resulted in a considered overview of an exciting and important period of Scottish cultural output. We hope you enjoy the book and are inspired to listen to the incredible artists involved with the Fast Product and Postcard movement.

Douglas MacIntyre

Dramatis Personae

In order of appearance:
Bob Last: Fast Product/pop:aural
Hilary Morrison: Fast Product/pop:aural; the Flowers (vocalist)
Davy Henderson: Fire Engines (vocalist/guitarist)
Angus Groovy (Whyte): Fire Engines manager; Codex Communications
Vic Godard: Subway Sect (vocalist)
Paul Research: Scars (guitarist)
Tam Dean Burn: Dirty Reds (vocalist)
Dave Carson: Boots for Dancing (vocalist)
Robert King: Scars (vocalist)
John Mackie: Scars (bassist)
Russell Burn: Fire Engines (drummer)
Fay Fife: the Rezillos (vocalist)
Jo Callis: the Rezillos (guitarist); the Human League (synthesiser)
Jon Langford: the Mekons (drummer)
Mark White: the Mekons (vocalist)
Geoff Travis: Rough Trade
Graham Main: Fire Engines (bassist)
Grace Fairley: writer
Michael Barclay: Thursdays/Boots for Dancing (guitarist)
Fraser Sutherland: the Flowers (bassist)
Innes Reekie: writer
Simon Best: Fast Product/pop:aural; the Flowers (drummer)
Martyn Ware: the Human League (synthesiser)
Jon King: Gang of Four (vocalist)
Gareth Sager: the Pop Group (guitarist)

Mark Stewart: the Pop Group (vocalist)

Murray Slade: Fire Engines (guitarist)

Ian Curtis: Joy Division (vocalist)

Peter Hook: Joy Division (bassist)

Sandy McLean: Fast Product Distribution

James King: Fun 4/the Lone Wolves (vocalist/guitarist)

Jill Bryson: Strawberry Switchblade (guitarist)

Edwyn Collins: Orange Juice (vocalist/guitarist)

Brian Superstar (Taylor): the Pastels (guitarist)

Stephen Pastel (McRobbie): the Pastels (vocalist/guitarist)

Alan Horne: Postcard Records/Swamplands

Rose McDowell: Strawberry Switchblade (vocalist)

Robert Hodgens: the Bluebells (guitarist/vocalist)

Ken McCluskey: the Bluebells (vocalist)

Steven Daly: Orange Juice (drummer)

Paul Haig: Josef K (vocalist/guitarist)

Malcolm Ross: Josef K (guitarist)

Ronnie Torrance: Josef K (drummer)

Allan Campbell: Josef K (manager); Rational Records

Stefan Kassel: Marina Records

Caesar (Gerard McInulty): Altered Images (guitarist); the Wake (vocalist/guitarist)

Malcolm Fisher: the French Impressionists (piano)

Robert Forster: the Go-Betweens (vocalist/guitarist)

Jacquie Bradley: The Hellfire Club

Jaine Henderson: the Hellfire Club

David Henderson: the Hellfire Club

Paul Morley: writer

Tom Cannavan: Restricted Code (vocalist/guitarist)

Frank Quadrelli: Restricted Code (guitarist)

Kenny Blythe: Restricted Code (bassist)

Campbell Owens: Aztec Camera (bassist)

Gerri McLaughlin: Article 58 (vocalist)

Ewan MacLennan: Article 58 (bassist)

Roddy Frame: Aztec Camera (vocalist/guitarist)

Billy Sloan: Writer/DJ

Stephen Lironi: Fast Product Distribution; Article 58/Restricted Code/Altered Images (drummer)

Alan McGee: Creation Records

Clare Grogan: Altered Images (vocalist)

Russell Irvine: the Bluebells (guitarist)

David Weddell: Josef K (bassist)

Phil Oakey: the Human League (vocalist)

James Locke: Heartbeat (drums/production)

Ian Burgoyne: Jazzateers/Bourgie Bourgie (guitarist)

Keith Band: Jazzateers/Bourgie Bourgie (bassist)

Alison Gourlay: Jazzateers (vocalist)

Alan Rankine: Associates (guitarist/keyboards)

Colin Auld: Jazzateers (drummer)

Grahame Skinner: Jazzateers (vocalist)

Paul Quinn: the French Impressionists/Jazzateers/Bourgie Bourgie (vocalist)

FAST PRODUCT / POP:AURAL / BOB LAST / HILARY MORRISON / THE MEKONS / THE HUMAN LEAGUE / GANG OF FOUR / SCARS / THURSDAYS / THE DIRTY REDS / THE FLOWERS / BOOTS FOR DANCING / FIRE ENGINES / RESTRICTED CODE / POSTCARD RECORDS / ALAN HORNE / ORANGE JUICE / JOSEF K / THE GO-BETWEENS / AZTEC CAMERA / THE BLUEBELLS / JAZZATEERS / THE FRENCH IMPRESSIONISTS / THE REZILLOS / THE POP GROUP / JOY DIVISION / ROUGH TRADE / GEOFF TRAVIS / ALTERED IMAGES / ASSOCIATES / THE PASTELS / STRAWBERRY SWITCHBLADE / ALLAN CAMPBELL / RATIONAL RECORDS / ARTICLE 58 / BOURGIE BOURGIE / SWAMPLANDS / JAMES KING & THE LONE WOLVES / WIN / PAUL MORLEY / VIC GODARD & THE SUBWAY SECT

CHAPTER 1

1977 – We Oppose All Rock 'n' Roll

Subway Sect: Paul Myers, Vic Godard and Rob Symmons

Year Xerox

The Clash rolled into Edinburgh on their White Riot tour on 7 May 1977 to be met with an audience that was ready, primed and on a self-created cultural launch pad. Punk had been a spur, a call to action, but in Scotland the young people who would go on to create the Scottish independent music landscape a few years later were less interested in absorbing the punk polemic of the Sex Pistols or the Clash. Instead, those in the crowd at the White Riot concert in Edinburgh were tuned in to the scrambled frequencies and messages being broadcast from the stage by opening artists Subway Sect and the Slits, whose new ideas stimulated the artistic awakening of a new breed of entrepreneurs, schemers, musicians, artists, conceptualists and chancers living in Scotland. These young people would go on to create and participate in the two record labels that were central to the Scottish independent music movement: Fast Product in Edinburgh and Postcard Records in Glasgow.

The energies unleashed by punk soon assumed a suffocating orthodoxy, an identikit punk sound and look that had emerged after the initial explosion which quickly became a dated straitjacket. The aspects of punk that stimulated the people that formed Fast Product in Edinburgh were arguably more in tune with the ideas Malcolm McLaren, Jamie Reid and Bernard Rhodes were repurposing. McLaren and Reid were heavily influenced by the situationist movement, particularly French Marxist theorist Guy Debord, a founding member of Situationist International. Jamie Reid's artwork for the Sex Pistols' singles, album and attendant advertising posters were viewed in some quarters as being more exciting than the music released by the Sex Pistols. Situationist concepts relating to interventions in media through the use of pamphlets and art, allied to critiques of advertising and consumerism, held great appeal to Fast Product.

BOB LAST: I started Fast Product in 1977 very self-consciously as a brand. I wrote a statement of brand values though at that point I didn't know what I was going to apply that brand to. However, I liked the idea of the mass market. We weren't a record label — I started it as a logo that I designed and I had no thought about making records. The very first thing that Fast Product did was create a sarcastic sticker saying that we guaranteed 100 per cent pure art. We put these stickers over a lot of Edinburgh Festival posters that had been supported by the Arts Council. We were messing around with these provocations about challenging classical notions of fine culture, so I guess when punk started emerging it was naturally appealing to Fast Product.

HILARY MORRISON: When the White Riot tour came to Edinburgh on 7 May 1977 it was one of those moments where you realised that all the things you were feeling about being disenfranchised, young, poor and confused were reflected back at you. Seeing the Subway Sect and the Slits was absolutely extraordinary, the bands came down and mixed with the audience and chatted and that was just unheard of, absolutely unheard of.

BOB LAST: I was at Edinburgh University studying architecture but dropped out. One of the reasons I took a year out from my architecture course was they did not like postmodernism, and I was really into Charles Jencks and thought I was a postmodernist, so I left the course. I guess I was an aspiring entrepreneur or impresario. I enjoyed music and film very intensely, and although I didn't see myself as a musician or a film-maker, I wanted to facilitate, so I set up the Fast Product brand to do that without knowing the specific medium. I watched an awful lot of films at that time. I would sit and watch the end credits and have no idea that these were jobs that you could actually do. It never occurred to me that you could go and do one of these things, so I made the assumption that if I want to be involved in making stuff, I'm going to have to do it for myself.

HILARY MORRISON: I bought my then boyfriend [Bob Last] a copy of Buzzcocks' *Spiral Scratch* EP, which was released on their own New Hormones record label. Everyone was listening to John Peel on BBC Radio 1, buying the music press, going anywhere you thought there might be something happening and chatting to anyone who appeared like-minded. That's how we all met each other.

BOB LAST: I remember my girlfriend at the time and subsequent partner [Hilary Morrison] bought me Buzzcocks' *Spiral Scratch* and that was the key moment. I listened to *Spiral Scratch* and thought, 'OK, this is what Fast Product should do,' and went out to find my *Spiral Scratch*.

DAVY HENDERSON: The first punk gig I saw was the White Riot tour. It was a real year-zero moment, I mean it was incredible. I used to go and see bands a lot prior to punk – I'd seen AC/DC, Cockney Rebel, Be-Bop Deluxe when I was a kid, I'd go to see anything. You knew you'd never see Bowie because Bowie had retired. Suddenly, with punk that excitement was there in the shape of the Slits, because bands before that were like divinities almost, you know, they were rock stars, separate, they weren't connected in any way to the people who were out front in the audience. They cultivated that because they wanted to be stars, and people wanted them to be stars, and that completely changed the very first time the Slits walked onstage. They were young girls, the singer was exactly the same age as me actually, she was sixteen. Ari Up walked onto the stage and said, 'Has anybody got a comb?' She asked the audience if anybody had a comb and came down into the audience, so she had broken that barrier right away by coming down into the audience and getting a comb off somebody and started back-combing her hair. It was unbelievable. I have a vivid memory of seeing the Slits, followed by the Subway Sect, who were like a Dada-esque performance like Hugo Ball, the first Dada performance, it was incredible. Buzzcocks followed, just an amazing energy, it was around the time of *Spiral Scratch* and I became a total Buzzcocks fan. They had a great bootleg around at the time called *Time's Up*, which captured that moment before they became an ultra pop band. The Jam came on after that, that was all right, and the Clash were just incredible, their performance, the way they connected to the audience. Joe Strummer tuned into the local radio station on a hand-held transistor radio as they had this song called 'Capital Radio', and Radio Forth were playing 'Knowing Me, Knowing You'. Strummer started singing along with his little yellow transistor, singing, 'Knowing me, knowing you, ah ha,' and it was just connecting, completely iconoclastic. It was breaking down everything that went down before and trashing it, but in a performance with energy, melody, ingenuity and also just complete newness.

The Slits: Ari Up

ANGUS GROOVY: The White Riot concert was a formative experience. I was seventeen and it was the second gig I had been to
after moving into Edinburgh. I went on my own and with some
trepidation, as it was my first experience of punk, except for Eddie
and the Hot Rods at the same venue six months earlier. Much as

I had enjoyed that, this was something that felt completely new and revolutionary. The crowd was exciting, it felt like a coming together of like minds. A sound system playing thick heavy dub added to the sense of anticipation. Then the Slits and the Subway Sect and Buzzcocks looked just like they could have stepped out of the crowd, but confident enough to scratch out something. At first I wasn't quite sure whether I was into it until the Subway Sect played 'Chain Smoking'. Then I felt this sense of hilarity and growing excitement, which the Slits then whipped up inspirationally. The Jam seemed to me like a Who tribute band and left me cold. The Clash were thrilling, but more validatory than revelatory. Buzzcocks on the other hand, like the Subway Sect and Slits before them, were a revelation and inspiration. I felt instantly that this was something I wanted to be part of.

VIC GODARD: I took the name Godard from Jean-Luc. I used to go and see his films with Rob Symmons before we started Subway Sect. We'd often go to see late-night films by Godard, Truffaut, Malle. I was at school with Rob and we decided to start a group, though we weren't a group as such, Subway Sect was really just a name. Originally we mucked about in a youth club then we bought a drum kit on hire purchase but we didn't know anything about drums. We thought a bass drum was purely for displaying your name. Malcolm [McLaren] saw us at Sex Pistols gigs and asked Rob if we were a group, so of course we said yes, and he asked us to start playing gigs. Bernie Rhodes then invited us to rehearse at his place, Rehearsal Rehearsals. He said he wouldn't charge us but we had to mop the place out, which of course we didn't do. Malcolm McLaren then asked us to play at the 100 Club Punk Festival, so that was really the beginning of Subway Sect. Bernie Rhodes started managing us so we were invited to play on the Clash's tour in 1977, the White Riot tour. Subway Sect were more into non-punk music, though we liked the Buzzcocks, but we got fed up with punk really quickly. That's when we started listening to Tamla Motown and soul music, Frank Sinatra, Tony Bennett. I hated punk really, and after we'd learned to play our instruments I wanted to do something different as soon as possible, and that's when the northern soul influence became strong on the Subway Sect sound.

The period from the White Riot concert in Edinburgh in May onwards saw an upsurge in groups who had formed as a direct consequence of punk. Scars had been formed in Currie on the outskirts of Edinburgh by brothers Paul and John Mackie, who recruited vocalist Robert King from an advert in an Edinburgh record shop. The Dirty Reds were another group formed in the wake of the sea of possibilities opened up by punk. A lot of the activists involved in the burgeoning punk scene in Edinburgh congregated in the local record shops.

PAUL RESEARCH: We put an advert in a record shop window called Hot Licks, looking for a singer for Scars, which is how we got Robert. Shortly after that I saw a postcard in the same record shop in which a girl singer seemed to be advertising for like-minded musicians. I thought the postcard was really well designed and it turned out to have been designed by Bob Last. It did actually look recognisably like his style. So it was Bob Last's girlfriend Hilary Morrison who was looking for the band and I phoned the number. I was deliberately reaching out and trying to make friends with other bands, and suggested to Hilary if she had her band together we should do a gig. She didn't have a band, but she came to see Scars play our first gig, which was in Balerno in late summer 1977. Everything happened so quickly at that time — Hilary introduced us to Bob Last shortly afterwards and then he started putting out records on Fast Product.

TAM DEAN BURN: There was a Virgin record shop in Frederick

Street in Edinburgh, and we'd go there every lunchtime to listen to albums. I knew a guy that worked in Virgin called Dave Carson, who had been at the same school as me.

DAVE CARSON: I had started working in the Virgin record shop which made me aware of music like Can and Neu! There were a plethora of record shops: I was working in Virgin, and there was also Bruce's, Listen, Hot Licks and others. We had the Sex Pistols come up to do a record-signing session — Rotten, Jones and Cook, but Sid wasn't there.

HILARY MORRISON: There used to be a little independent record shop in Lady Lawson Street, and I remember going out and buying 'Anarchy in the UK'. I met Davy Henderson, Rab King and Dave Carson when the Virgin record shop in Frederick Street had a personal appearance by the Sex Pistols. I got John Lydon to sign a Sex Pistols single I'd just bought, and as I handed it to him to sign it he said, 'I despise you.' We were all like, 'Johnny Rotten despises us!' It was so silly. We all started hanging out together, there was a sort of buzz.

ROBERT KING: Access to music was limited by *Top of the Pops*, though as a teenager I'd go into record shops and look at record labels and sleeves. Anything I thought was aesthetically pleasing I'd investigate: David Bowie and Roxy Music, things like that.

DAVY HENDERSON: I'd go into a record store and spend hours and hours at the racks, that's how I'd spend my Saturday afternoons. A lot of my pals would do the same thing. There were lots of record stores in Edinburgh, loads — down in Stockbridge, in St Mary's Street, in the Royal Mile, also places like Hot Licks, as well as the big places like Boots. You'd go into these record stores and scour the racks and just make connections, see who played on what — 'oh, Alice Cooper's guitarist played on *Rock 'n' Roll Animal* or whatever.

It was just joining the dots, pretty much what people probably do now on the internet, but in a different way. Record shops were also selling magazines like *ZigZag* and there were fanzines like *Sniffin' Glue*, which was obviously the first one, that Mark Perry started.

ANGUS GROOVY: The White Riot concert was indirectly my first encounter with Davy Henderson, at the time an androgynous-looking wraith with long black locks like Patti Smith. He introduced himself a week later in the Hot Licks record shop in Cockburn Street and started chatting about the White Riot concert as he'd seen me at the Playhouse. We hit it off, and started meeting up every weekend in the Wig and Pen at the foot of Cockburn Street, which famously tolerated underage punks. I first met Bob and Hilary weeks rather than months after White Riot at the Playhouse. I had noticed a Warm Jets flyer Hilary had posted up in the Hot Licks shop and was really intrigued by the graphics, the Eno reference, the mention of polymorphous sexuality. Davy said he'd seen it too and it was he who phoned Hilary, who had posted the flyer. We arranged to meet Hilary at the Keir Street flat to discuss what became the Warm Jets idea.

Record shops were the epicentre of most local music scenes in towns throughout Scotland. They were influential in shaping tastes, they brought people together. During punk the record stores provided an outlet for fanzines and self-released 7-inch singles, and helped to galvanise a communication system for outsiders to connect. Before punk most people consumed music brought to their attention by John Peel's BBC Radio 1 programme and the weekly music papers. The charts and daytime BBC Radio 1 were also a magnet for young ears — *Top of the Pops* provided BBC Television performances by the pop, soul, glam and rock artists who had reached the heady heights of the top 30 singles chart. *The Old Grey Whistle Test* promoted artists on major record labels aimed squarely at the album market and featured live performances on late-night BBC 2 for heads. Often derided as being the refuge of boring singer-songwriters, it should be noted that artists as eclectic as Bowie, Roxy Music, Bob Marley and the Wailers, the Sensational Alex Harvey Band, Curtis Mayfield, Can, Captain Beefheart and, most notoriously, the New York Dolls all appeared on the *OGWT*. The Edinburgh movers inspired by punk obviously had a record-buying past, though most would deny they were fans of bands like Yes or ELP once the punk putsch kicked in.

BOB LAST: As a kid I travelled with my parents all around the globe. I lived in Sudan for a while, New Zealand, the States, but probably in Sussex more than anywhere else. My parents moved up to Scotland at the beginning of the seventies, so I did my last two years of school in Scotland and that's how I came to find myself in Edinburgh. Before punk I was listening to some things that in retrospect seem significant, I had a copy of the Kingsmen doing 'Louie Louie' — how I came to have it I have no idea. I was also listening to Miles Davis, Funkadelic, then Parliament and Bootsy — that was probably my musical immersion. I wasn't brought up on pop music at all or classical music really, and although I love that kind of music, I didn't see myself as immersed in the musical world at that point.

HILARY MORRISON: Prior to punk I listened to Bowie, T. Rex, soul and lots of funk: artists like Parliament, Funkadelic, Sly and the Family Stone. We all grew up with the Rolling Stones and the Beatles, but that was our big brothers' and sisters' music.

TAM DEAN BURN: I got *Ziggy* [*Stardust*, Bowie's album] for my fourteenth birthday and to be into Bowie and get that degree of sophistication at fourteen years old, I thought, stood me in good stead. I was also really into Mick Ronson, Dr. Feelgood and Patti Smith, just prior to punk.

ROBERT KING: I grew up in a large family and most of my cousins were into soul. They were all older than me so I kind of grew up knowing quite a lot about the soul and funk scene, and through that I was also interested in reggae.

PAUL RESEARCH: Glam was a big influence. I was absolutely mad about T. Rex when I was about twelve, and then Ziggy-period David Bowie, *Aladdin Sane*, Roxy Music — all of the glam bands were a massive influence.

JOHN MACKIE: I was a Bowie and T. Rex fan and used to watch *Top of the Pops* every week. Being a bass player I loved that home-grown funk thing as well, like the Average White Band. The Sensational Alex Harvey Band were fantastic theatre. I saw them live on a number of occasions and they always really impressed me.

DAVY HENDERSON: Prior to punk, around '75 and '76, I loved Patti Smith's *Horses*. I also got switched on to Kevin Ayers when he brought out a single called 'Stranger in Blue Suede Shoes', which John Peel used to play. I was a David Bowie fan from the age of about ten because my big brother got *Hunky Dory* when it came out. I loved Cockney Rebel and I also loved Lou Reed's *Transformer*, after hearing 'Walk on the Wild Side' in the charts. I used to listen to the radio a lot, to the charts and to John Peel, where I first heard Roxy Music. I loved Eno's voice, it was so unusual. His first solo single 'Seven Deadly Fins' was like nothing else, it sounded like it had just landed.

As 1977 developed and the major punk groups (Sex Pistols, the Clash, Buzzcocks) released records on major labels and were played by John Peel on BBC Radio, local punk groups formed throughout the UK. The Edinburgh groups grounded in punk that eventually transitioned to Fast Product in future mutations were Scars, the Dirty Reds and the Flowers.

TAM DEAN BURN: When punk came along I was just completely ready for it and able to dive right in, initially just by myself. I think one of the most significant points that informed me and led to eventually forming the Dirty Reds was in April '77, when I went down to London with three mates from Clermiston to the Roxy to see Johnny Thunders and the Heartbreakers, and Siouxsie and the Banshees. The next night we went to see the Damned at some university, then Iggy at the Rainbow.

DAVY HENDERSON: I never thought it seemed possible, the idea of making music, even though every person I knew wanted to be in bands. It just never seemed possible because you had to be almost a virtuoso musician, I mean that's how it appeared. I tried a neighbour's guitar and right away I felt deflated and just thought, 'That's complex, I'll never be able to manage that.' It seemed being a musician was almost like an elite that you would never be welcomed into, it never seemed possible that you could teach yourself how to play guitar.

There weren't a lot of punk records about at all, it took the Slits aeons to make records, but Peel would then have these groups on his radio show, recording sessions. So it was the Peel sessions that were explosive, incendiary really, because you'd see these names of groups in the music papers and only hear them on Peel sessions. They existed at Maida Vale, the Subway Sect's incredible sessions, the Slits sessions, these are artworks. They're more than just young people making music, they are a heritage of British art. They're incredibly important and I still don't think they've been consumed by the masses at all in any way, apart from aficionados, so they're in a pristine state.

ROBERT KING: It was reading about the Sex Pistols in the music papers that led to starting a band at school with my friend Callum, who was later to become the first drummer of the Scars.

The epiphany moment for me was when I started to buy punk records and one day I was in Hot Licks. I was looking at the ads for band members and I saw an advert by a band called the Scars, looking for a singer. So I decided to phone them up and did an audition rehearsal with them. They wanted me to join and I convinced them that the drummer who was in my previous band was good, so Callum also joined.

PAUL RESEARCH: I was in the school band from about age fifteen. I was always really keen to play the electric guitar and my brother John made an electric guitar and a bass — those were the Scars' first instruments. Things really kicked off when the Ramones released their first album, which was fantastic, and when the Sex Pistols started appearing in the music press, I realised this is our chance. Punk coincided with me leaving school, so I realised that I was going to have to do something in the world and in life, and this was what I really wanted to do.

JOHN MACKIE: We'd put an advert for a singer in Hot Licks record shop and Robert answered. When he auditioned he just opened out, I think it was 'Anarchy in the UK' that he did, and the other guy auditioning was so frightened by Robert's performance that he just got up and left. Paul and I looked at each other and realised that Robert was exactly what we needed. So Robert had the gig and he knew a drummer he was at school with, Calumn MacKay, so he became Scars' drummer, the best drummer I've ever worked with. Robert had an enormous amount of energy and also a left-field approach. He was into some things that I hadn't been exposed to, so there was a lot of cross-fertilisation of ideas that came into our songwriting very quickly. We let all our influences bleed into each other and found we had a lot of common ground in terms of influences, so it worked in a strange and unpredictable way.

PAUL RESEARCH: Robert was very articulate, energetic and quite sort of tough, a resilient type of character and very imaginative. He was into a lot of art-oriented things, including Japanese literature.

HILARY MORRISON: I remember going on the bus all the way out to Ratho to see the Scars practise in some youth club or barn. We became a bit like a gang, and then started meeting other people in Edinburgh who were into punk. People started saying they were in a band even if they didn't have a musical instrument, and I remember Davy Henderson and I formed a band the day after we first met after the Pistols signing in Virgin record shop. We discovered we were into Roxy Music and Eno, so we thought we'd call ourselves the Warm Jets — we didn't want an identikit punky name. It had to be something a bit glam, so we were Warm Jets, but we had no instruments, nowhere to practise, nothing. It was about a pose — the idea was very much about making yourself look as cool as possible, because we'd all been into Bowie. We immediately started calling ourselves glam punks, buying second-hand clothes, and we were very young, unemployed, short on money. What was a wake-up call for me was, on my birthday, Rab of the Scars and Davy Henderson gave me a guitar and informed me I had to start learning to play, which made me think, right, this is serious.

TAM DEAN BURN: Dave Carson was a friend of mine from Craigmont school. Dave was really into the US garage punk scene so we started to look at the idea of starting a band. He was learning bass and my wee brother Russell had always been interested in playing drums. Dave Carson had a mate called Andy Copland, so we got together with me singing as a band called the Dirty Reds. I've always looked on the idea of the Dirty Reds as a sort of little gang, the archetypal four young guys.

DAVE CARSON: I was listening to chart stuff, glam, soul, some prog. I remember listening with Tam Dean Burn to *Horses* along with the garage punk compilation *Nuggets*. The Ramones' first album was the moment where I felt I could maybe be in a band, so Tam fancied being the lead singer and I took up learning bass, with my friend Andy playing guitar. Tam said his wee brother was going to take up drums, so that's how we got Russell in the band. We started practising in my dad's garage, mainly cover versions of the Stooges, though we did a version of the Seeds' 'Pushing Too Hard'. We started writing our own songs, one of which was called 'Here Come the Rich Reds from Underneath Their Waterbeds' — we were called the Dirty Reds by then.

RUSSELL BURN: I started playing drums with the Dirty Reds when I was still at school. I think the very first song we practised in Dave's dad's garage was 'Stepping Stone' by the Monkees, and we also did 'Pushing Too Hard' by the Seeds, which was great. Practices got a bit heavy because Tam and Andy Copland were at loggerheads all the time, which was a bit frustrating as they ended up always arguing. Tam decided to go to drama college to pursue his acting career and Hilary Morrison came in on vocals. The Dirty Reds became the Flowers.

TAM DEAN BURN: When the first album by the Clash came out there was a budding of politics in me and that's why I wanted to call our band the Dirty Reds. I was definitely gearing towards an anti-authoritarian stance and I wanted to look for politics in punk. The Dirty Reds Mk 1, with myself, Russell, Dave Carson on bass and Andy Copland on guitar, only lasted one gig. We supported the Rezillos, at the drama college at Queen Margaret in Edinburgh where I'd just started studying drama. We had that one gig but we never really hit it off. Andy and I in particular had big musical differences. So Davy and Andy went with Hilary Morrison, she joined them as singer, and they became the Flowers.

ROBERT KING: I had been at the White Riot concert so had an idea about how punk bands performed onstage and how they presented themselves, so obviously I was taking a leaf out of what I'd seen from their performance onstage in addition to using what interested me. We had a similar ethos about what we wanted the Scars to be. We wanted to be punk but also wanted to move away from punk in the sense that we wanted to have our own identity, and a lot of that came from glam bands who would like to present things in a way that was individual to themselves. In order to emphasise my difference I would change my name every couple of weeks. I called myself Bobby Charm in an attempt to be the opposite of a carbon-copy punk outlook.

PAUL RESEARCH: Glam was quite sparse music actually and that's inspiring for people who are just learning to play, because it is something that you can latch on to and play yourself. My guitar style was all about the limitations of technology really. I think one thing that differentiated Edinburgh from other punk movements in the country was the fact that people wanted to move on from punk really quickly and make their own original music.

JOHN MACKIE: We were going to see a lot of punk bands. We decided that the do-it-yourself approach could work for us — get up and do it, make it yourself. Ours was a DIY ethic. We started hearing all these new punk sounds — there was no polish to it but there was an energy, and out of that grew a whole new generation of musicians, that was the entry point. Have something to say and you can get up and create. Make it happen.

ROBERT KING: The first Scars gig was in September or October of 1977, literally just a few weeks after we formed. It was at Balerno town hall. We hired the hall ourselves, got the PA and the lights and did all the promotion ourselves, and we managed to fill the place and get a couple of encores. By that time we had responded to another advert in Hot Licks that was put there by Hilary Morrison. She was looking for talent that was different, so we responded to that and she came along to the gig and took some photographs of us. That debut gig was a great success and from there we started to get a small following until it was time for us to release a single.

Robert King met James Oliva through Oliva's big brother, and they quickly bonded over punk. Attending early punk concerts led to meeting like-minded aficionados on the scene, Angus Groovy and Davy Henderson. Oliva accompanied King when he successfully auditioned for the role as Scars' vocalist, and later met Hilary Morrison and Bob Last at the debut performance by Scars.

PAUL RESEARCH: Scars felt like a gang, especially in the early days when the original line-up first got together. We used to go out together quite a bit and there was a group mentality. People would collectively refer to us as the Scars and that's how it all started off, but we all went to different schools, the other guys were from different parts of Edinburgh and had their own different experiences to deal with.

ROBERT KING: As soon as we met anybody that was in another band we'd support each other, borrow equipment from each other and share PAs, put on gigs together so that we could get to play live. Eventually we became part of a scene, we all clung together and met each other at record shops on a Saturday afternoon. If you were in a band that was affiliated with the punk movement you were part of the scene and you were welcome. We did feel that we were outside of society because of the way that the press was presenting punk. So that helped us cling together and our fans would become our friends, there'd be no discrimination between the bands and the fans in that respect. We were against fascism and any forms of discrimination, we'd go to gay bars and gay clubs. Scars played there as well and nobody really cared.

JOHN MACKIE: We all let our influences bleed into each other and found we had quite a lot of common ground in terms of influences, so it worked in a strange and unpredictable way. Robert was much more sub-cult driven, he was listening to more obscure music and artists, some of which I thought were pretty interesting, but ultimately he had a pop sensibility about him as well, which is very much where Paul and I were coming from. We wanted to write pop songs and we wanted them to be different. We didn't want to sound like anyone, so we promptly set about inventing ourselves as a live band — we weren't thinking about recording. At that time Edinburgh was the sort of place where everybody knew each other, they were either drinking together or playing together. I suppose you could say it was incestuous in some terms, but I never felt it was overbearingly so.

Edinburgh had been put on the punk map by the Rezillos and their independent single 'Can't Stand My Baby'. Bob Last had tour-managed (then managed) the Rezillos as they performed around the UK, and picked up ideas along the way from the punk cognoscenti in receptive cities like Liverpool and Manchester.

FAY FIFE: The Rezillos were very much in our own pod, we started off very early. We were not part of a scene at all, we were totally alien. We came out of nothing really. Then a punk scene started up and that was interesting, but when we started we were more like an artistic, conceptual thing. I do remember I went to see the Damned play their first gig in Clouds [Edinburgh] and punk became an influence, but at the same time we recognised that we seemed to be part of punk in an obscure, off-kilter sort of arty way.

The Rezillos: Fay Fife

JO CALLIS: I started writing material in the Rezillos. I was influenced by glam rock, the New York Dolls, the Shangri-Las, and developed from there. Prior to recording our first single we were getting good feedback, then we recorded 'Can't Stand My Baby' which was obviously a great turning point for us. That song was really pivotal and changed the musical direction of the Rezillos, I think. We moved from being a bit of a sixties kind of retro showband into being something contemporary.

FAY FIFE: The first single by the Rezillos, 'Can't Stand My Baby', came out independently on Sensible Records, then we signed with Sire, a US label who went through Warner Brothers. We became part of the punk movement, although we were like creative outliers, so that brought lots of attention. I heard through the grapevine that Elton John told Seymour Stein, the head of Sire Records, that he should check us out, that the Rezillos were great. There were major record labels interested in the Rezillos at the time. I think being part of a movement it was easy to draw that attention, but we decided to go with Sire. We thought that Sire would actually be able to understand where we were coming from artistically, the evidence for that being when I went to Sire Records' offices in New York I saw a shelf filled with Shangri-Las master tapes. So that was vindication.

JO CALLIS: After the attention gained from the independent release of 'Can't Stand My Baby', the Rezillos signed to Sire in 1977, and released another single, '(My Baby Does) Good Sculptures'. By this time Bob Last was managing the business side. Bob was one of those people who used his own initiative quite a bit. It became evident from him setting up amps, changing guitar strings, he could competently fulfil the road manager role for the Rezillos, and from there he was the obvious choice to manage the group.

FAY FIFE: I really can't remember how Bob Last got involved with the Rezillos, but I remember he wore an orange boiler suit and he was on the road crew. Bob became part of the big Rezillos conglomerate, though obviously he had ideas of his own, some of which were spot on for us and some of which were incongruent. Bob went from tour manager to managing the Rezillos, which just seemed to happen by osmosis. I always thought Bob was very creative and had a lot of ideas, though maybe a tad pretentious here and there.

CHAPTER 2

1978 – Ambition

Bob Last

As '77 became '78 and the Sex Pistols fell apart on their USA tour, the ripples of the Pistols' previous sixteen months as music press phenomenon, through to their four singles, album and accompanying artwork and advertising, had reached all corners of the UK. Nineteen seventy-eight saw debut gigs by Joy Division, the Durutti Column, debut albums by Pere Ubu, Throbbing Gristle, Alternative TV, and debut singles/EPs by Siouxsie and the Banshees, Subway Sect, the Fall and Cabaret Voltaire. The transmogrification of Johnny Rotten into John Lydon, and the debut single, album and concert by his new group in cahoots with Keith Levene and Jah Wobble— Public Image Ltd — were truly seismic, and would be deemed more influential than the Sex Pistols in the new musical landscape. PiL seemed like the absolute definition of post-punk and its oft-mentioned possibilities, a touchstone for artists in terms of their sound and presentation.

The music papers and John Peel's broadcasts to the nation on BBC Radio 1 spread the spores of new ideas in this period beyond punk, and 1978 would see the inauguration of new independent labels like Rough Trade, Mute and Factory. But the first of the new labels that encompassed new ways of seeing was Fast Product with the release of FAST 1 in January 1978, 'Never Been in a Riot'.

Edinburgh groups used the initial impetus of punk to develop their own modernist view on how to move punk forward. Scars, the Dirty Reds Mk 2 and the Flowers all absorbed the initial punk explosion and transposed the energy transmitted by Subway Sect, the Slits, Buzzcocks, via their John Peel sessions broadcast on BBC Radio 1 in 1977. Bob Last had already initiated a brand, Fast Product, and now had a mission. Bob and Hilary (Morrison) officially started work on the Fast Product label in December 1977 and gave Edinburgh a focal point that harnessed the punk spirit. However, the first single release on Fast Product was not by an Edinburgh group but by a group of University of Leeds art students, the Mekons. Last had approached the Mekons when they supported the Rezillos at the F-Club in Leeds in October 1977, and they became the first group to sign to Fast Product.

BOB LAST: I was interested in Mao's military strategy. I mean God knows why, but that was the sort of stuff I was reading. I actually read quite a lot of military strategy books around that time and I was very interested in how the British army was trying to operate in Northern Ireland for example. The intelligence involved in punk was interestingly at odds with the apparent visceral simplicity of the music, and some of the most intellectual punks made the crudest music, which was an interesting tension. It was the possibility of having that visceral connection, but also strategically using it to unsettle things, that interested me. I think I was always quite strategic, interested in what that moment offered, and in retrospect, I can see there were things that happened that would not have happened if I hadn't been involved and done them. It could have been somebody else, but when you're channelling things that are happening, you don't sit down and plan them. It was this combination of very simple visceral pieces of music combined with a really intelligent understanding of music. I mean, from day one, I thought I was making hit records, though obviously I wasn't. I believed I was engaged in a strategy to get Fast Product in everyone's face, but it was, if you will, an art brand. It also came from me reading a lot of theoretical stuff. I read more Herbert Marcuse than anything else. I was also very interested in leftist propaganda as a cultural form. I read a lot of political texts and was very interested in Althusser's ideological state apparatuses, and, to a degree, I thought Fast Product at times was an ironic capitalistic version of an Althusserian ideological state apparatus. That's the kind of thinking that we were doing.

HILARY MORRISON: Bob and I had both been working in theatre, at the Traverse, and through that we got hold of lighting equipment that we were loaning to the Rezillos when they were touring. We went along on their tours doing lighting and helping them put on a more professional show, and through that we started to see these other bands all over Britain. It felt like a good idea to do a record label. A lot of the bands we saw supporting the Rezillos were as good as any that were putting out records, so it seemed the obvious thing. I had several skills: I could type, and I had done an unemployment course where I had learned phone skills, you know, how to talk on the telephone. So I could phone up people, type letters and put logos together, and make things look really professional even though we were only operating Fast Product from a tiny little flat.

BOB LAST: To make a living I had been a road manager for the Rezillos. I met Jo Callis when I was working at Traverse Theatre, so there were an odd set of coincidences that took me round the UK. I was particularly driven by Jo's love of a good chord here and there and a good thrash. The Rezillos were part of the punk scene and it was a very small scene. So you go around the UK and you play a gig and meet everyone who's in a band for fifty miles around, whether it's Middlesbrough or Liverpool or Sheffield or wherever, so that's how I encountered other bands.

JON LANGFORD: I met Mark 'Chalkie' White and Andy Corrigan [who would be the singers in the original Mekons] on my first day in Leeds in October 1976. They were my freshers' group leaders and were supposed to show a group of us new students around the art department. We got about as far as the pub. They told me they had a mate who was forming a band that was a cross between Dr. Feelgood and the Velvet Underground — that was Andy Gill of the Gang of Four. I got my drum kit brought up from Wales as fast as I could 'cause it was obvious something was afoot — rumblings in the tabloids and Ramones on Peel etc. By the end of the school year the Pistols, Clash, Damned tour had been through town and I was pretty fed up with art school. Tom Greenhalgh was in the same year as me and mates of the Gang of Four and other Mekons from school in Kent. He asked me if I wanted to be in a band where nobody could play. There was quite a tight-knit community amongst other local bands such as Gang of Four and the Delta 5 which was very different from what was happening in London, who seemed very antagonistic towards each other.

MARK WHITE: All those Leeds bands tackled similar themes but in different ways, different forms. Gang of Four had a plan for example, but the Mekons were not like that at all. The Mekons tended towards a 'this is a team effort, that means we will now say a lot before we do anything' approach. There were a lot of Mekons for a start, usually ten working together, it was important to us that the decision making, songwriting and economic arrangements etc. should follow the political constructions that we were trying to develop. To criticise monopoly capitalism by producing a superior and unique monopoly commodity (successful band) that featured a single figure standing above all others (lead singer) condemning patriarchy by a lofty male voice, to reproduce the hierarchy of the family onstage, to pay different levels of wages to equal members of the group, all of this seemed unethical.

JON LANGFORD: We were a social group first of all, mostly art students, but the Gang of Four were always gonna be a proper band. We were very committed to the idea that we were not a real band and we would only ever support the Gang of Four or make a record. I missed the first gig in the summer of 1977 [Andy Gill played drums] but the first proper gig was opening for the Rezillos at the Ace of Clubs on Woodhouse Street [Leeds] a few days after my twentieth birthday. That's where we met Bob Last and all the bullet points in our manifesto started to evaporate!

The Mekons: Andy Corrigan, Mark White and Tom Greenhalgh

BOB LAST: I approached the Mekons about recording a single for Fast Product but they tried to dissuade me from making a record with them. I remember them telling me about Gang of Four and at that time I wasn't interested, so that's how I encountered the Mekons, from that touring connection, and they were an exemplar of having a world of ideas and absolutely no interest in musical competence for its own sake. I mean you could not have had a more extreme example of that, which was part of what appealed, but there was also clearly a real insight and thoughtfulness layered into that noise that they made. We went and recorded the Mekons single in a cottage down in the Scottish Borders. 'Never Been in a Riot' was basically a live recording.

HILARY MORRISON: We had nowhere to record the Mekons single and weren't sure of the process. Then one of the Rezillos told us their uncle had a place in the country, a cottage down in the Borders, and that we could record the single there. So we went down to the cottage and it was all locked up, the uncle only stayed there sometimes. So, the long and short of it was the Mekons' first record started by me breaking into this house out in the middle of nowhere. I was quite small, so I was put through a window and let everyone into the cottage and we took over the house for the weekend and recorded the Mekons single, the first release on Fast Product.

BOB LAST: I then went to the bank manager of the Bank of Scotland and I told him I wanted to borrow 400 quid to put a record out, and he said OK. I had no idea about business. My understanding of business was based on reading the back cover of Marxist books — I didn't understand it, I hadn't a clue. However, I thought the Mekons had made a hit and therefore it deserved to get out there, but nobody would stock it.

Rough Trade had been established as a record shop by Geoff Travis in 1976 in Ladbroke Grove, London. The shop stocked dub, experimental German music, and Velvet Underground and Stooges rarities — records that were not always easy for fans to track down. They also supported new artists with information and advice about the distribution of records into other retailers throughout the UK and beyond. Rough Trade was the obvious first stop for Fast Product to approach for distribution of 'Never Been in a Riot'.

GEOFF TRAVIS: Rough Trade was a shop first, then mail order, and then distribution. Distribution became the all-consuming idea at Rough Trade, and that was the political ideal, to get this distribution network organised.

HILARY MORRISON: I got sent on the overnight bus to go down to London to try to talk Rough Trade into distributing the Mekons single and get it into record shops, but they thought the record was incompetent and hated it. I went to see TV and radio producers to hustle them, convince them to take the Mekons record and play it. I was walking in cold off the overnight bus, going to see BBC Radio 1 producers, and it was kinda horrible.

BOB LAST: Famously Rough Trade said it was the worst record they'd ever heard and they weren't stocking it. Which of course we absolutely loved, it was exactly the correct wrong thing for them to say. That Geoff Travis from Rough Trade would not distribute our first record on the grounds of it not being musically competent was the perfect kind of tension and irony that we were playing with. It was in fact musically extremely competent in the sense that it did what it needed to do to get across the point that they wanted to make, and that's what was interesting about it. We didn't have a clue how to put a record out and promote it. I just assumed I'd made something fucking great so I'm going to find a way to reach out and there are going to be people who will want to buy it. I had no clue how we were going to find those people. We just went out and hustled people. It is cool to leap off a cliff sometimes, provided you know it doesn't always work out, but I think we started getting somewhere because we had that kind of front and belief in Fast Product. There's always an element of luck and I don't think we started really selling the Mekons single until it got reviewed in the *NME* when Tony Parsons and Julie Burchill did this joint review and made it single of the week. That was when it really started working, that was the first external attention that Fast Product got.

HILARY MORRISON: I think there was a lot of wishful thinking involved. We were slightly naive because we were young and thought there was a mini sexual revolution going on. When I got off the overnight bus from Edinburgh to London and went to see Rough Trade, I thought I would be welcomed in as an equal, rather than being met by dismissive grumpy hippies.

GEOFF TRAVIS: I became aware of Fast Product when Hilary came down from Edinburgh and gave me the first Mekons single. And this is a disaster really, in terms of history, because, instead of embracing my comrades in spirit from the northern climes, I just didn't really get the Mekons' first single when Hilary played it to me. Despite her protestations that this wasn't just a racket, but a serious record that Rough Trade should really be pouncing on and grateful to be involved with, I just didn't get it, to my shame. I came to appreciate the virtues of 'Never Been in a Riot' as time went on, but Hilary probably thought I was a complete cretin for not appreciating what was going on. I hope she forgave me over the years. Bob certainly forgave me, and we did become distributor for Fast Product and the Mekons.

Geoff Travis

BOB LAST: I converted the attention the Mekons single was receiving on the back of being the *NME* single of the week into a strategic trap. We'd intended of course to call Rough Trade's hippy bluff and prove that their understanding of punk was flawed, and that's how the process worked. There's that military saying, 'no plan survives first contact', but then what really counts was how you responded to things. So being rejected by Rough Trade was a badge of honour, and we did start selling it into some independent record shops, of which there were a lot at that time. There was this small and fanatical underground who were seeking out new things that they hadn't heard of, so there was a bit of an undertow of activity when the *NME* review came along. There was very little context to what Fast Product were aiming to do, in that there was only a handful of people doing it themselves and making records on their own or starting independent labels. I suppose everyone had that same glorious ignorance that allowed them to try doing it, we were doing this in a void. There are weird ways in which things emerge from the ether, but we found out step by step by phoning people up and learning on the fly. I mean we were very connected to the scene, but had no real meaningful connection with any of the other labels. Subsequently there were people who came and asked us for advice and there were bands that were self-releasing rather than people operating as labels. I think that's why we stood out early on because I always wanted to build a Fast Product identity, not because it was more important than the bands, but because I had this brand thinking. I felt the brand was what would give us power to introduce music to people that they wouldn't otherwise hear, that was the point of accumulating power to the brand itself. Our disappointment that 'Never Been in a Riot' wasn't in the top 10 was to some extent rhetorical, but I did believe that it was pop music and that therefore it had that potential to find a bigger audience.

HILARY MORRISON: To a certain extent we wanted to pull the curtains back and show the mechanism behind the process, to demystify it. Even in the way that we put the artefacts of a record together, we would try and show how it had been done, that it wasn't just a mass-produced thing that was beyond people's abilities or capabilities, and that became quite important.

ANGUS GROOVY: I was aware of 'Never Been in a Riot' before its release, and a big fan of the Mekons. The support that the single got from the *NME* and John Peel made a huge difference to sales, letting Bob and Hilary spend more time on the label. Bob spent quite a lot of time in Leeds and Sheffield. I think the connection to the Mekons was via Simon Best, as he was a friend of the Mekons' manager. I remember Hilary took a bunch of us down to Leeds for a week or so. Davy, Russell Burn, James Oliva and I stayed with the Mekons in a house in Chapeltown, before Talkovers played at Leeds Polytechnic, supporting the Mekons at an Anti-Nazi benefit.

The impact made by FAST 1 when released in January 1978, and the subsequent media interest in Fast Product, was astutely capitalised on by Last and Morrison. 'Never Been in a Riot' achieved the twin peaks of being awarded *NME* single of the week *and* being regarded by Rough Trade as the worst thing they'd ever heard. A perfect punk storm. *NME* journalist Paul Morley coined the phrase 'post-punk', which seemed a reasonable way to describe the adventurous new sounds that started to emanate from various towns and cities across the UK during 1978. Decentralisation and regionalisation were beginning to be viewed as an attractive counterpoint to the previously held belief that artists had to move to London to be active participants in the culture.

GEOFF TRAVIS: We knew about Métal Urbain because John Peel was playing their first single, 'Panik', on the radio, and when we heard it we really liked it. Then we wrote to them in Paris and asked if we could get some copies for the shop. I think we were thinking more about distribution, which we were working on. That was really the main thing. So the idea of having the label wasn't really a plan or an ambition, but the people working in the Rough Trade shop had a lot of knowledge about the history of record labels. When the guys from Métal Urbain unexpectedly arrived at the shop to give us a tape of their new recording and told us they had no money to release it, we wanted to help them. The Rough Trade label was born in that instant. This was post-Desperate Bicycles, they'd showed everybody that you could just do it yourself, as Scritti Politti also later talked about on their first single. So that was an impetus, the culture of DIY was starting to be in the air. I gravitated towards doing the label because my invoicing skills as a distributor were so poor, because no one could read my writing. I was demoted from invoicing duty, so I decided I would be the A & R person for the label.

BOB LAST: I was pissed off that Métal Urbain didn't call me and went straight to Rough Trade.

FAST 2 had already been lined up, a single called 'All Time Low' by a group from Sheffield called 2.3, though in truth it felt like a backward step in the aftermath of the attention gained by 'Never Been in a Riot'. This would be the only slip in the inspired Fast Product trajectory that would follow through the rest of 1978 into 1979.

BOB LAST: I think learning lessons was not our strength; we thought we were teaching people. I'm not sure what we learned from our first release with the Mekons. I mean, the next single by 2.3 was perceived as us trying too hard, relatively speaking. The 2.3 single was recorded and produced with great sophistication compared to what we had done with 'Never Been in a Riot'. That was partly an adjustment to the difficulty of trying to get the Mekons to be a hit. We were figuring out what you're supposed to do, and it didn't work. 2.3 didn't have the provocative value of the Mekons.

PAUL RESEARCH: I remember being in Bob and Hilary's flat and hearing a tape of the song sent up by 2.3 that they proposed as the follow-up to their Fast single, and Bob was very dismissive of their efforts.

HILARY MORRISON: Once we'd done the Mekons and 2.3, and through the Mekons connection we'd lined up Gang of Four for later in the year, I told Bob we needed to find Scottish talent and that I knew the same vibrancy was happening in Edinburgh. He agreed and I was told to go out and find it, which I very quickly did in the form of the Scars, although they wouldn't release a single until 1979.

ROBERT KING: Scars were offered the opportunity to record a debut single for Fast Product and it was one of the coolest, if not the coolest, independent labels in Britain, because at that time Factory Records and Rough Trade Records didn't exist.

JOHN MACKIE: We attracted the interest of Bob Last and Fast Product, and we really liked his whole left-field approach. He was interested in art, which also interested us.

The Dirty Reds: Andy Copland, Russell Burn, Tam Dean Burn and Dave Carson

DAVY HENDERSON: The Dirty Reds Mk 1 were going around playing gigs in Edinburgh. I saw them supporting someone, and I knew these guys from Clermiston. I didn't know them personally but I recognised the singer, I knew him as Tam, Tam Burn, and his wee brother Russell was playing the drums. They were playing with Dave Carson on bass and Andy Copland was playing guitar, they were the Dirty Reds and it was brilliant that they were from Clermiston. Tam never had a top on and he was wearing gloves, ladies' gloves, and I thought 'who is this guy, what's he up to, man?', and that was Dirty Reds Mk 1.

GRAHAM MAIN: Russell introduced me to Davy, early '78, and not long after Tam and I moved into a west end flat, with Davy and Russell joining us later.

HILARY MORRISON: When the imaginary band I had with Davy Henderson, the Warm Jets, failed to do anything, I was asked by Dave Carson to come and do vocals in his band called the Dirty Reds. We changed the name to the Flowers and got started. I had written a lot of lyrics that were angry young woman lyrics, but it wasn't a totally enjoyable experience because I was the only girl in the group. It was fun, it was interesting, but it made me sick with nerves half the time.

DAVE CARSON: Tam decided to focus on drama college, so we recruited another singer for the Dirty Reds, Hilary Morrison. We changed our name to the Flowers, which we copped from 'The Flowers of Romance' [the name of an early punk group in London that featured Viv Albertine of the Slits and Sid Vicious of the Sex Pistols]. We spent a lot of time working on songs for the Flowers at Hilary and Bob's flat in Keir Street, which was the centre of operations for Fast Product. I played around ten gigs with the Flowers before I decided to leave the band. Russell Burn left around the same time to join the Dirty Reds Mk 2, which ultimately became the Fire Engines.

GRAHAM MAIN: Hilary was putting the Flowers together with the bassist and guitarist from the Dirty Reds Mk 1, Dave Carson and Andy Copland. Russell was the tug-of-love child, torn between going with Hilary or with the Dirty Reds Mk 2 which was Tam, Davy and I. After a few gigs with both bands he decided to stay with us, and Simon Best, a Mekon pal, took the stool for Hilary.

TAM DEAN BURN: Hilary [and Bob Last] were the two older heads in the Edinburgh punk scene, the equivalent of Malcolm McLaren and Vivienne Westwood. I wanted to get back into singing, so the Dirty Reds Mk 2 got together with myself on vocals, my brother Russell on drums, Davy Henderson on guitar and Graham Main on bass. Our first gig was for the Edinburgh University Communist Society, and right at the start of the gig I noticed that Hilary Morrison was in the audience, so I started singing 'where have all the flowers gone'. She went fucking apeshit and jumped up onstage and was fighting, pulling, banging away at me, so that augured the way the gig was going to go.

DAVY HENDERSON: We were all sort of pals — the Dirty Reds, Hilary, Scars — then I got really friendly with Rusty [Russell Burn] after he joined the Flowers and we had the common bond of being from Clermiston. We really hit it off and became great friends. I mean, the guys in the Flowers could play — Andy had an original guitar style — but around that time I think there was a bit of tension with Rusty, which resulted in a falling-out because Rusty had come over and joined the Dirty Reds Mk 2, so we'd taken the Flowers' drummer.

GRAHAM MAIN: I knew Tam Dean Burn from the age of seven, so when he started the Dirty Reds with his wee brother Russell, I thought they were amazing.

TAM DEAN BURN: I was at drama college by this time and I knew that Davy Henderson was going to be a much better singer than I would be and write better songs, so I pulled out, but it was all amicable. We all stayed in a flat together by then, but the Dirty Reds were a Clermiston band, we were a real little community that developed and the rest of the guys became the Fire Engines. We used to have a photo, we never knew who took it, but somebody wrote on a wall up to the High Street — 'The Dirty Reds: Edinburgh's only true punks', and that's good enough for me.

DAVY HENDERSON: I remember when I played in the Dirty Reds Mk 2, that was the second group I was in. The first group I was in was a group with Angus Groovy, who became the manager of the Fire Engines. We were called the Talkovers, [along with] Robert King, aka Robert Allen, Rab, Bobby Charm and Strolch (when he was in his Anthony Burgess phase, which was one of his great phases). Rab used to play the drums for the Talkovers and he used to play like Palm Olive, so we had our own Slits drummer in the form of Bobby Charm. So the Talkovers was my first group and I found chords really difficult to play. Playing one barre chord was just really difficult, especially with Rusty creating the tempo on drums. It was really sore, so there was one stipulation when we started the Fire Engines, and it was we don't play any chords — no chords, OK?

The Fast Product flat in Keir Street was in close proximity to the Wig and Pen pub, and became the after-hours hangout for musicians and artists, effecting a Warhol-esque environment in which teenage Edinburgh discovered their own strategies and methods with which to interact and participate.

BOB LAST: I heard an excitement in *Spiral Scratch* in particular, but also in some of the other music that was going on in 1977/'78 that I had liked. I was always very responsive to that sense of visceral noise, that's why I like Funkadelic. I suppose punk as we now think of it prioritised that kind of visceral impact, and it was something that I immediately responded to. We were running the label out of a flat in Keir Street, which was just round the corner from the Wig and Pen pub, and as is always the case in big cultural movements, the local bar has an important role to play. A bunch of these really young kids were hanging around in the flat — I mean I was young myself at the time, but they were even younger. Some of the Scars were part of that, some of what subsequently became the Fire Engines, these kids were just hanging around, shooting the breeze and listening to stuff. I suppose the fact that they were hanging around there had an impact in making them believe things were possible, which was great because that was the whole idea of the label, we were saying things are not as you assume.

GRACE FAIRLEY: I had come down to Edinburgh from Fife as a student and ended up spending a lot of time in Keir Street at the Fast Product flat. We would tend to go there after the Wig and Pen pub closed for the night. Davy Henderson was a force of nature from the word go. I think he was sixteen when I met him and he came up with idea after idea after idea, you were never bored. I can remember the first time Davy picked up a guitar at Bob and Hilary's flat. He had huge energy and huge charisma. I met Paul Reekie from Thursdays at the flat. Paul said to me, 'Rab King asked me to play guitar on something he was doing, and when I told him I can't play guitar he said he just wanted my attitude.' Paul then told me his reply to Rab, which was, 'What am I going to do, plug my attitude into an amp?' My first impression of Rab from the Scars was that I didn't like him. I thought he was really obnoxious. However, we quickly became close friends. He had massive charisma and huge intelligence.

MICHAEL BARCLAY: I was at university in Edinburgh. I'd come down from Fife, and over that 1977/'78 winter Bob and Hilary were hanging out and we'd go round to the Fast Product flat all the time. Bob and Hilary were gathering and collecting people, collating ideas and defining creative principles. We were all really into the aesthetic of Richard Hell and the Voidoids.

BOB LAST: I would have loved Richard Hell and the Voidoids to be on Fast Product. Bob Quine is still my favourite ever guitarist, and also James White and the Blacks.

DAVY HENDERSON: We all went to see Richard Hell and the Voidoids when they played Clouds and after they came offstage me and my friends went back into the dressing room. The Voidoids were all ripped, the smell of grass was unbelievable. Richard Hell said he was going out to the car and I asked if I could join him. So I walked to the car park in front of Clouds in Tollcross and he was wearing his original red T-shirt, the cut-up T-shirt that's ripped to shreds that Richard's wearing on the back of the *Blank Generation* LP cover. I had a home-made Voidoids T-shirt on and I asked if he wanted to swap T-shirts, and he said yes. So he took his T-shirt off and we swapped T-shirts in the middle of Tollcross car park, and it's the actual T-shirt that is on the album cover. I mean that's pretty generous, man, that's his first album, his T-shirt, it's got lots of biblical terminology on it, so I'm very fond of him. That's an indicator of the sort of generosity of the people who were making punk music and it's indicative of how things had changed from the rock divinities of the seventies. Everything had changed. There was a complete cultural shift in the people who were involved in making music. They responded to the people who bought or consumed their music, there was a real connection.

GRAHAM MAIN: Davy was wearing Richard Hell's genuine torn red T-shirt from the cover of the *Blank Generation* LP for most of that year until his mum spotted it in his room and threw it out because she thought it was a rag!

GRACE FAIRLEY: I remember Davy, Rab and Angus Groovy getting together and doing a song at the Wig and Pen. They called themselves the Talkovers. Nobody was thinking they were going to be a musician as a career, people were just playing, making things up spontaneously, so Davy, Rab and Angus formed this band called the Talkovers and did a gig in the Wig and Pen, playing for about fifteen minutes. We would all go back to Bob and Hilary's flat all the time — you were always aware of Bob in particular working very seriously in his office.

Talkovers: Angus Groovy and Davy Henderson

ANGUS GROOVY: Talkovers was I suppose where the early Fire Engines aesthetic germinated. Hilary's Warm Jets incarnation left her a little frustrated at the messy rehearsals and she left Davy and myself to it, with him as guitarist and vocalist and myself as bass player. Talkovers was mostly talk, most of it in the Tap o' Lauriston [a pub across from Edinburgh Art College], and a vehicle for a platonic relationship. I was working at the Virgin Records store at the time, and introduced Davy to albums coming from the New York punk scene. We loved the style of the Subway Sect, Slits and Buzzcocks. We had ideas about using performances to create chaos, and decided that we would only use photo booth photos for publicity shots and dictaphone tapes for communiqués as if we were musical terrorists. Some of this stuff later fed into Fire Engines' aesthetic and lyrics. What we lacked was songs. Davy was starting to write them — 'A Weekend in Paris' I recall being one of them — but was hampered by my lack of musical ability.

BOB LAST: I would argue that all the work we'd done to create the Fast Product brand was about this brand not being about what you expect, about giving you opportunities to think and experience things differently, to change your mind and revise and rethink. We'd created a space where we could all do that and it actually got a reception that it might not otherwise have done. I think Fast Product was a verification that we'd created a group of people who trusted us and therefore looked at it openly and embraced it. We had been careful with the brand to set up this space where it was about being open and curious. We were like explorers. I set up stall, said here's the attitude and it just dropped into my lap.

JOHN MACKIE: Fast Product and the whole approach of Bob was very art orientated. He definitely wasn't interested in what external people thought, he was just going to do what he was going to do, he liked what he liked. That's one of the things we really liked about him, he didn't follow any kind of pattern at all, it was all straight from the cuff. It was refreshing, and I think everybody would tell you the same thing.

PAUL RESEARCH: Myself and the other guys from the Scars would go round to the Fast flat. Davy Henderson would be round there a lot with Russell Burn, as would the Flowers.

FRASER SUTHERLAND: I first met Dave Carson and others from west Edinburgh such as Tam and Russell Burn, and Davy Henderson, either on the last bus home from gigs at Clouds, or hanging out at Virgin Records, I can't recall which came first. Paul Reekie [vocalist in Thursdays] and I became friendly when we discovered that our fathers had grown up together in the same stair in Leslie [village in Fife]. I'd seen the Scars perform a few times before I got to know them. By that time people were meeting in the Tap o' Lauriston, a pub over the road from both Fast Product and Edinburgh College of Art. These places became a kind of creative trinity, where ideas were exchanged, unified and put into action. The art college put on live bands at their dances, and their organisers were usually quite relaxed about who took the stage, so there would be impromptu performances by folk who'd hatched a plan in the pub over the road that night. There was a real atmosphere of experimental and creative adventure, so much energy, exchanges of ideas and encouragement to try things out.

GRAHAM MAIN: Davy was acquainted with Bob Last and Hilary through Rab Scar and had made a few visits to their flat which was next to Edinburgh College of Art. I tagged along with Russell and Tam into what was a new world to me. It was like an exhibition opening with interesting artwork on the walls, sculpture and paintings. There would be members of bands like the Rezillos, Human League, Gang of Four, Mekons, Scars, all hanging out chatting, drinking, passing through socially and on business. It was a world away from my suburban upbringing and I liked it!

DAVY HENDERSON: Hilary would invite everybody up to her house for a cup of tea. It was a great pad. I automatically fell in love with it, it had an aroma of feline urine and a great kitchen just full of art posters, like situationist posters. They had this great living room that had a bed in it that you could sit on, and a jukebox, and in white and yellow on the walls Bob Last had written 'This is luxury.' That just seemed so radical, so that's how we became friends and that became the hangout really. I don't know how they could put up with people weekending in their house, like young people that they barely knew, but we all got pretty close. Everybody was pretty passionate about what was happening there and then, and we were making things up. When I first met Hilary, I think Bob was away on tour with the Rezillos, but I met him a couple of weeks later. He was the first real artist I'd ever encountered and he was very serious about executing his ideas. Bob used the young group members that hung out at Keir Street as a kind of focus group, but he was using the medium of music to put his ideas across, and that was a total gas.

BOB LAST: FAST 3 was thought of as a fanzine but it was really some photocopied pieces of artwork in a plastic bag along with some rotting orange peel. *The Quality of Life* was done because I was getting worried that we were starting to get a bit too settled in our ways already, people were possibly starting to get expectations of what we were going to do next and that's not helpful. So FAST 3 was produced partly for that reason and also because we were seen as being political but not political. Punk took a lot of agitprop art as a reference point, I mean it was a commonly used reference point, and *The Quality of Life* was partly a gesture about using those techniques but using them enigmatically. It is actually quite enigmatic, it's not hectoring with some obvious message, and the reference points were similar people. I was interested in the work of John Heartfield, who'd done stuff during the Second World War about the Third Reich. I was interested in the constructivists at the time of the Russian Revolution, I was interested in all this kind of work, but the other point about all of that is that this is also when the notion about postmodernism became part of the contemporary dialogue. I came out of an architecture background, although I was a drop-out, and was aware this sort of cultural theory first evolved in architecture, so I was particularly aware of that and it was partly why I dropped out of architecture. There were notions about playfulness — in fact we talked about theory and how it can be boiled down to a very simple idea about the importance of playfulness in cultural work, whether it's serious or trivial. So we made FAST 3. It was also about playfulness, it was us saying that just because we are a record label doesn't mean that is what we have got to do.

ROBERT KING: Fast Product was quite revolutionary because Bob Last would release small works of art, little posters in cellophane bags. Later on he would sometimes get me to make something, and he would sell that and it would become a release on Fast. So there was a kind of excitement around Fast — we weren't just making music, we were also making visual art and expressing statements based around advertising. We would generate work where we would cut images, slogans out of magazines, anything that we saw that caught our eye, and would use them. Fast Product was taking inspiration from everywhere — Dada, surrealism, pop art, it was all definitely allied to the notion that the current consensus needed to be challenged and that in itself is always worthwhile.

INNES REEKIE: The second time I met Davy Henderson, he was wearing black impenetrable fifties wraparound sunglasses, a ripped pink T-shirt with the word Voidoid scrawled in black across the chest. He was standing in a bath clutching a large plastic flower, carrying on an in-depth conversation about William Burroughs and Brion Gysin. He looked like a young Lou Reed. The location was Bob Last's apartment, conveniently situated in the shadow of Edinburgh College of Art. Bob and Hilary's flat had become a creative hub for the city's more discerning, disenfranchised, punk rock cognoscenti. It was in this Keir Street tenement that the seeds of Edinburgh's contribution to the post-punk era germinated and finally came to full bloom.

DAVY HENDERSON: I never really questioned or asked Bob what the concept behind Fast Product was, but he was putting the ideas together simply and quickly, putting them into production. There were *The Quality of Life* fanzines that went along with it — I don't know what motivated him to make it all up but I do know that for me it was like an art project. I was asking Bob about something that he'd made related to the posters and fanzines, *Wild, Wild, Wild Youth*, which is from a Generation X song, and there was a picture of a baby with a plastic bag over its head, and I was like, 'What's that, what have you done that for? What does that mean?' He said, 'It doesn't matter what it means as long as it looks good.'

JOHN MACKIE: [Bob and Hilary's flat had] big high ceilings and huge windows, and it was full of art, a lot of which Bob had created himself. He used to wander around in an orange boiler suit. It was a place where ideas hatched. The atmosphere and approach of Fast and Bob was inspiring to the Scars, it made for quite a fertile environment for ideas to be hatched and started. That was very much the feeling at the time: 'Forget what's just happened, move forward.'

HILARY MORRISON: I was mostly involved in the photography, but in the design too to a certain extent. People aren't even aware of Letraset any more, but we would go out and buy Letraset and drop down each letter. We'd insert a deliberate error in our art to show the process by which it was done. Both Bob and I were quite keen on doing that because it was a fun element.

GRACE FAIRLEY: Hilary was a really powerful presence. I think Hilary was the heart of Fast Product. I can remember being in awe of her because she was a little bit older and appeared to be incredibly confident, she knew what she was doing or appeared to know what she was doing. I think that was probably the first time I'd come across a woman like that who was so strong. Hilary embodied that attitude: if she'd decided she'd wanted to do something, she would just do it. Politically as well she was very savvy, which I suppose I wasn't.

DAVY HENDERSON: Hilary Morrison and Bob Last were creative partners, they were collaborators, absolutely 100 per cent. Fast was an inspiring environment. I was never out of the place, I used to be in their house all the time, I loved being there. The fact that he was putting records out and the records were getting reviewed and getting played on Peel was amazing. It was just incredible that somebody in your immediate vicinity, that you could have a conversation with in a kitchen, was putting vinyl out.

INNES REEKIE: Bob and Hilary would spend time at Keir Street formulating ideas, taking photographs, designing packaging and ultimately planning. They appeared to welcome guests with attitude and vision, hence their home became a veritable post-punk creative workshop. The Human League's Phil and Adrian, Gang of Four's Jon and Andy, Mekons, Simon Best, Tim Pearce, Scars, the Dirty Reds, the Flowers, Thursdays and Talkovers would all regularly visit.

ANGUS GROOVY: Davy and I met quite frequently with Hilary at Keir Street before I moved in at some point in late '77, when one of her and Bob's flatmates moved out. The flat was part of a housing co-op and they let out a couple of rooms. If I remember correctly Bob was just getting Fast Product off the ground, and he used a cupboard as an office. There was a lot of his artwork around, and recycled parts from stage sets he was designing at the time, like a full-size Dalek. I had dropped out of Edinburgh Uni but still hung around with a handful of students, like Innes Reekie and Mike Barclay. There were frequent visits from Bob and Hilary's friends Simon Best and a guy called Tim Pearce, who was a roadie for the Rezillos and rolled huge spliffs.

MICHAEL BARCLAY: Fast was a constantly evolving, interesting period. I was in the flat when he received a cassette from a band accompanied with a letter on silver foil. It was the Human League and the track was 'Being Boiled'. It sounded phenomenal, like a primitive pop version of Kraftwerk.

GRACE FAIRLEY: I can remember Bob playing us a tape that he'd just received through the post from America and it was 'Human Fly' by the Cramps, and he was thinking about taking them on for Fast Product. I remember saying I thought the track was amazing but Rab hated it, he thought it was just rock 'n' roll, he didn't see it, and for whatever reason Bob decided not to take them on. There was a constant flow of stimulation at the Fast Product flat.

SIMON BEST: I can vividly remember hearing the first tape sent to Fast Product by the Human League. Fast used to get between twenty to thirty cassette demos a week, and Bob and I, along with Hilary, used to meet every Sunday afternoon with a six-pack and go through them. Most of these were regulation punk and quickly rejected. Even before listening to the demo of 'Being Boiled', we knew that the League were something unique – their cassette came with fully developed artwork with much of the imagery that we subsequently used on the cover already in place and a one-page Philip K. Dick-inspired introductory cover story about the League.

DAVY HENDERSON: The Human League hadn't thought of their name yet and I don't think they'd even met Bob – their relationship with Fast happened by mail. I'm not entirely sure about the genus of that particular situation, but Bob responded to the music that they sent up on a cassette and then they started corresponding. It was getting close to the time Bob wanted to put a record out. I still don't think they'd met, but they hadn't decided on a name. They'd sent up four suggestions for a name – one of the four nominations was the Human League. Bob asked the people that were in the Fast kitchen. Bob would involve you in everything and it was amazing to be taken seriously, that he respected what we thought of ideas.

ANGUS GROOVY: The big kitchen table at Keir Street was the scene of a lot of creative encounters, I guess, though I mostly remember vegetarian meals, spliffs and much listening to the Bowie/Iggy albums recorded in Berlin. Following the success of the Mekons single, Bob started getting tapes through the post, and he and Hilary would often play them and ask what I thought of them. I don't recall all of them, but I remember him playing a demo by the Cramps, who we agreed were 'not really Fast', and the Human League. Bob was unsure that the Human League would appeal widely enough to get money in, and needed a bit of convincing that it would be worth borrowing more from the bank. Hilary was more influential on what to release than I ever was.

MARTYN WARE: Sheffield in the late seventies was not a great place to be growing up as a teenager, as all the traditional heavy industries were shutting down. However, this meant that the closed-down industrial warehouses became available for musicians and artists to use, so that's where we rehearsed. We felt we had something in common with Andy Warhol's Factory, creating art in various rooms, with Cabaret Voltaire and Martin Fry's pre-ABC group, Vice Versa, working on experimental electronic music. We all grew up with glam like the New York Dolls, but punk seemed a bit pub rock, although groups like Suicide were great. I met Paul Bower, who had a group called 2.3, and he heard 'Being Boiled' and thought we should send it to Bob Last, who had just released the 2.3 single on Fast Product. Bob absolutely loved 'Being Boiled' and wondered if we had any artwork, so I sent him some Letraset artwork I'd put together, which Bob used for the single design when he released the track as a single on Fast Product. Once the single came out we were suddenly picking up lots of play on John Peel and music press features, and before long major labels started getting interested.

BOB LAST: I don't know how the Human League heard of me or the label but they sent 'Being Boiled' and a bunch of incredible things through on a cassette in the post. Interestingly enough, it had two bits of paper in it which I remember very clearly: one was a sheet of Mylar, which is that shiny kind of silvery material, with some statements or lyrics felt-penned on it, and then it had a bit of that old-school computer printout with a kind of manifesto typed on it. So they were kind of already in the area of what we were doing. I was already intrigued. Then when I listened to the material, particularly 'Being Boiled' and I guess probably 'Circus of Death', I suddenly thought I was listening to a Parliament record. That's where what I was listening to before punk suddenly kicked in, in that it had that massive big fat bass which drove the whole thing and I kind of got that, but I got that through the filter of Bootsy Collins rather than being a Kraftwerk fan. The other thing that intrigued me about the tape was the very strange combination of apparently incredibly significant and important lyrics that also insisted on being completely meaningless and poppy at the same time. I loved that tension, so they had me straight away and I'd put a record out before I'd ever met them. I don't know if we even spoke on a phone. I wrote back and said, 'Yeah, great, want to put it out now.'

The initial impact made by FAST 1 resulted in further media attention for the Mekons to follow on from their *NME* single of the week. The group were invited to record a session for the John Peel show, broadcast to the nation on BBC Radio 1 on 14 March 1978. 'Never Been in a Riot' had drawn extreme responses, something that greatly pleased Bob Last. The 'All Time Low' single by 2.3 had failed to register, but had allowed Fast Product to gain more experience recording, designing, manufacturing and promoting a release. There was a confidence at Fast Product about the next single, 'Being Boiled' by the Human League. FAST 4 was released in June and it felt there was now a forward-looking group for the forward-thinking Fast Product to develop. Musically, lyrically and visually, the Human League embraced the now, inspired by science-fiction writers, surrealist art and experimental German electronic groups. The Human League were sonically antithetical to FAST 1 and the Mekons' aesthetic — the Leeds/Sheffield divide had never been so audibly wide.

MARTYN WARE: The Human League never thought anyone would be interested in releasing any of our music; as far as we were concerned we were doing art. We were just as interested in graphic visual design, science-fiction literature, art, electronic music. More surrealist art seemed to be in the air with the idea of collectables being incredibly desirable to us. We were interested in the experimental German groups like Neu!, Can, Tangerine Dream, along with Philip Glass and Steve Reich, but we also loved pop.

I regarded the visual aspects of what the Human League did [as being] connected to the fanzine culture and the confidence that emanated from within that scene.

BOB LAST: Partly through my own ignorance I thought Fast Product was releasing pop music, yet at the same time it was clearly insurrectionary. If you take that fascination with strategy, and my own belief that 'Being Boiled' was pop music, those are the things that just gelled in that moment. The most important thing about any brand or concept is that it's at its most effective when it's no longer necessary to understand it. I think what's very interesting is that most of what we did cut through a requirement to have some understanding, but actually the only significant thing about Fast Product from a conceptual or theoretical point of view was to say that all that you believe about the value in anything is slippery and provisional. We famously released and successfully sold bits of rotting orange peel as part of *The Quality of Life*; the point about that was to make a point that if you put it in a different context even rotting orange peel may have a value.

MARTYN WARE: Bob had an aura around him, and although he was a similar age to ourselves he was like your dad or something! He was really authoritative, and we really liked the way he approached business and the fact he knew Malcolm McLaren, so we felt he'd be a perfect Machiavellian manager for the Human League.

BOB LAST: The punk ethic really fitted with our cause in that it was musically simplistic but had a real value and strength. If Fast Product had an ideology, it was that we believed the end user of a piece of cultural product is the person that determines the meaning, not the author. It is the end user who determines the meaning and they determine that meaning as a result of all sorts of things, including in our case the packaging. We put a huge amount of importance on the packaging, but not because we thought it was more important than the music. Sometimes we used the packaging to directly contradict what the music seemed to be saying, because we thought that was part of the end user experience and we were very interested in the way all these different elements created meaning. One of the oddities of the time is that many people involved in punk thought that they were against packaging, viewing it as some sort of grubby marketing process. I took the opposite point of view. I was excited about doing this because I like deploying packaging and marketing in the name of this visceral and unsettling music.

HILARY MORRISON: I think there was a pop sensibility with the Human League right from the start, from the first time we heard 'Being Boiled' on the cassette they posted to Fast Product. I thought it was pop music, I thought it was like Donna Summer and Giorgio Moroder, I thought it was great immediately and felt we should do a single. So there was always a pop sensibility, I suppose, and it was quite nice to have my sensibilities suddenly come to the fore, which I reckon went well for us.

SIMON BEST: The Human League's music spoke for itself as home-grown electronic music with intriguing lyrics from a band with clear ambitions to be a pop group. We couldn't resist the challenge and Bob upped the Fast overdraft with the bank so we could press up a bigger than usual first batch. John Peel loved it and as I recall, we eventually sold 80,000 copies which was a huge number for an independent label. There's no question that 'Being Boiled' was a ground-breaker and it was a bonus to find that the League had also already worked out a very original and compelling live act with the added dimension of Adrian Wright's slide show. Adrian's slides were already part of the show when I first saw the League live. However, we were able to fund him scaling up from a couple of projectors and screens to I think nine mounted in a major scaffolding frame by the time we tried out their new show for the first time in late '78. There really wasn't anything else like it at the time in pop music, although the Andy Warhol Factory shows with the Velvets were a prototype. Audiences loved it.

MARTYN WARE: Fast Product was a conceptualist project. It was deliberately obtuse.

The Human League single and artwork worked hand in glove with Fast Product to establish an aesthetic that drew equally from J.G. Ballard and German electronic music, but was also pop in its outlook. The group immediately attained critical kudos from both the weekly music papers and Peel, whose support of the new electronic sounds being created in Sheffield showed how quickly people had moved on from the rock 'n' roll tropes of so-called punk groups like Sham 69 and the UK Subs. The Human League recorded a Peel session, broadcast on 16 August 1978, which included a cover version of the Righteous Brothers' 'You've Lost That Loving Feeling', further proof of their interest in pop. By the end of 1978 the Human League were described as being 'trendy hippies' by Johnny Rotten, while Bowie declared to the *NME* that in seeing the Human League live in concert in London he 'had seen the future of pop music'. Bowie contacted Bob Last via letter, praising the artistic endeavours of Fast Product.

Bob Last's old employers the Rezillos also had a hit single from their New York-recorded debut album. Their 'Top of the Pops' hit single was performed by the Rezillos on the titular television chart show.

FAY FIFE: We were aware of the irony and strangeness of us singing a song called 'Top of the Pops' whilst being on *Top of the Pops*. I remember being very interested in the other artists on the show when we were on. Boney M. and Chic were on with us, and the guy from Boney M. said to our singer Eugene he thought he was dressed up in cool gear, which I thought was hilarious. It didn't seem extraordinary, it just seemed normal, and maybe that's a mark of my abnormality. I remember recording our debut album in New York, it was an amazing experience to be there at that time. I met Lux and Ivy from the Cramps and saw them at CBGBs — I hung out with them a lot. The Cramps took me to see the B-52s, who Lux and Ivy said were kind of interesting but they didn't like them because they dressed in normal clothes during the day. At that time New York was a grungy hellhole, which was fantastic. I soaked up the way that it looked, the way it smelled, the dirt — I just loved it, basically. CBGBs was fun and the Rezillos played there. Something about the aesthetic of New York at that time was just so spot on for myself and Eugene, that's where we were coming from.

JO CALLIS: The Rezillos signing to Sire and recording an album in New York was a fantastic experience. We knew about the Talking Heads and the Ramones being on Sire so we quite liked that thought of being the only new-wave band in Britain that were signed to an American label. That gave us a bit of uniqueness, and I think it was Seymour Stein's idea to take us out of our own environment and record in New York for six weeks to get a bit of that vibe.

Fast Product was being noticed, making its mark and moving forward with a certain brio. The speed of life with the Keir Street young team during the second half of 1978 was such that the surfeit of creativity didn't have enough outlets to be fully realised. Noises were also heard about why Scars hadn't made a record yet. The media was willingly being massaged, and bought into Fast and the Leeds/Sheffield dynamic, with interest in the label about to be torqued further by a brace of releases by the Mekons and their fellow Leeds University comrades, Gang of Four. Although they shared political interests, the Mekons and Gang of Four could not have been further apart in terms of musical competence. The primitive abilities of the Mekons were poles apart from the taut funk bass lines and beats of Gang of Four, over which agitprop vocals collided with slash-and-burn guitars that were one part Jimi Hendrix, two parts Wilko Johnson.

JON KING: There wasn't a scene in Leeds at all, though the local polytechnic put on a night featuring Sex Pistols, the Clash, Johnny Thunders and the Heartbreakers and the Damned on the Anarchy tour. It was fantastic for a quid, and it was pretty much empty. With the Gang of Four we just invented our own thing, we wanted our sound to get more empty. It was the north rebelling against this very southern-centric thing, and so when Gang of Four and the Mekons emerged with what seemed like fully formed world views it seemed to come from nowhere.

FAST 5 was another 7-inch blast of raw power — the Gang of Four debut EP, *Damaged Goods* — on which the song titles alone gave a good indicator of the band's political perspectives feeding through Gang of Four: 'Damaged Goods', 'Love like Anthrax', 'Armalite Rifle'.

JON KING: The first proper Gang of Four song was 'Anthrax'. We mapped it out without having played any of it. We realised we could do something thrilling and really different. We used a load of feedback, some really funky, heavy repetitive drum and bass parts, and then chanted over the top of it. If we had been in London and somebody had come along and seen us playing a song like 'Elevator', they'd have said it was a derivative version of Dr. Feelgood, which of course it was. We were learning how to be in a band then learning about what we actually wanted to do. This was mixed in with determination to do something that was worthwhile, because we were pretty unforgiving with each other. If anybody did something that was not the right thing it would be stamped on by everybody.

While the Mekons' second single, 'Where Were You?', was hardly polished, it was a commercial step up from the clattering racket that was 'Never Been in a Riot', and it captured media attention again. The public were now buying into the Fast Product ethos more than ever — 'Where Were You?' sold out its initial 27,500 pressing and gained a degree of popularity the Mekons/Gang of Four collective crew had not anticipated. The Mekons initially insisted on no surnames or photographs, an anti-image stance and co-operative outlook that was soon tested by the demands of commerce.

GEOFF TRAVIS: I made up for my lack of appreciation of 'Never Been in a Riot', I think, by loving 'Where Were You?', the Mekons' next single. I went to visit the Mekons in the studio at Spaceward in Cambridge when they were recording 'Where Were You?', and was very impressed by the sound they got. That is one of the reasons why we went there to record the Raincoats album, which Mayo Thompson and I produced. Mayo and I produced the Stiff Little Fingers album at Spaceward as well, so Rough Trade has lots of things to thank the Mekons for.

FAST 5 — Last deployed Brechtian alienation techniques with the Gang of Four packaging when he subverted the precise printed instructions the group had sent in a letter to the label for how they wished the EP cover artwork to look. The group wanted their single cover to be a photograph they'd ripped out of a newspaper of a female matador and a bull. In conjunction with this photograph they wanted the following statement to be captioned with the matador explaining, 'You know, we're both in the entertainment industry, we have to give the audience what they want. I don't like to do this but I earn double the amount I'd get if I were in a 9-to-5 job', to which the bull retorts, 'I think at some point we have to take responsibility for our actions.' Last reproduced the typed-letter instructions and ripped-out newspaper cutting with the photo of the matador and the bull, but on the back of the sleeve (with Last's own design featuring on the front cover). The group were miffed at this deconstruction of their original concept, but it was yet another example of the playful, cutting subversion that was now synonymous with Fast Product packaging.

The Gang of Four sound approached a more conventional rock guitar attack, albeit a sound that stripped the component parts down to their punk-funk essence. Allied to a lyrical approach that highlighted their understanding of Gramsci, Brecht and Marxist critical thinkers, Gang of Four were the academic music journalists' dream ticket and reviews were superlative. Peel got on board and played all three tracks on the *Damaged Goods* EP with equal fervour. While the sound and vision of the Human League single tuned in perfectly with Fast's consumerist aesthetic, it could be argued that Gang of Four's hardcore Marxist political theory was key to their Fast appeal.

BOB LAST: My family was not political but it was politically aware, and you have to remember at that time that a conventional sense of politics was very much in the foreground. We'd come through periods of time where the rubbish didn't get collected on the streets, where power cuts were things that one expected. There was a sense of instability and opportunity, but as to where I got that rebelliousness from, I guess some of us are like that and some of us aren't. We were trying to teach people that things were not as they seemed. Don't be certain, don't be sure. We were trying to teach people to ask questions both political with a small 'p' but also kind of culturally and also even musically.

HILARY MORRISON: I suddenly had a wake-up call. I began to think sexual equality was not happening fast enough. Boys liking the Slits, starting to wear a bit of make-up and borrow our clothes, is not a sexual revolution. Not to put too fine a point on it, but the music industry was a big, bad, sexist world full of really horrible people that when a young woman turned up from Scotland trying to persuade them to play the Mekons on the radio they were like, 'Come here little girl, sit down next to me.' What the fuck!

GRACE FAIRLEY: I was so naive politically: if it's left wing then it's good was the extent of my political awareness and a kind of feminism that had been based on articles from *Cosmopolitan*. The politics that were around at the time had been really worked out by some of the people hanging around Fast, I think, probably a lot of it at the time completely went over my head. The Mekons would come up to Fast and they were very, very politically aware, it was just a matter of soaking it up and listening to it really.

TAM DEAN BURN: I can vaguely remember the three-day week, but we never really paid much attention to politics in any real way, it was more a matter that we were rejecting what was going on. It was still feasible to sign on the dole and not be pressured into getting a job, so the attitude towards politics was that we largely ignored it.

ROBERT KING: Punk offered a lot to people that were disenchanted with this whole non-opportunity situation, the idea that if you left school before you went to university you either worked in a bank or office or a factory or a building site, and depending on which job you did, you lived in a certain type of house, you lived a certain type of life and you had a certain type of future, it was all mapped out for you. I mean ultimately the punks did change the world just by making people question themselves.

DAVY HENDERSON: I have a letter that Paul from the Scars wrote to Siouxsie Sioux and delivered to her backstage: 'I hate you, I hate your band, I've seen them only once and I would never go to see you again, you were shit, boring derivative music has always made me sick and you're the worst. You supported the Heartbreakers at Edinburgh, you're great at being clever but when Rab asked you why you wore a Nazi eagle, all you could say was "I just liked it, that's all". And then you got up on stage and tried some crap type of Nazi salute, I hate people like you.'

BOB LAST: As a teenager I was intensely politicised, but perhaps a little differently from others in that I read a lot of analysis and I was very interested in cultural theory, but I did not translate that into taking a clear political position. Neither myself personally or Fast Product ever took a clear political position on a lot of issues that other people did, for example Rock Against Racism or anti-Thatcherism. It's ironic that we were very political in some senses and people were aware of that, but we were not in the business of taking or promoting specific political views. We were in the business of asking people to ask questions, and I suppose my understanding of what I was doing was very political. Musically there were inherent contrasts or conflicts between and within the music that we put out, and I liked the challenge of that, that sense of it opening up spaces for people to think and do things.

HILARY MORRISON: In a way we were pop-Marxism in that we took the means of production and wanted to show you could control it yourself and influence it yourself, but also to show how ephemeral it was. That yes, it mattered, but it mattered for a moment, so when you had that moment, make it matter, make it say something, because tomorrow it might mean nothing.

MARTYN WARE: We really liked Hilary and the other people at Fast Product. We felt a strong affinity with Scottish people, I guess, because we share socialist beliefs.

Fast Product explored other ideas to visually represent Gang of Four: Hilary Morrison created stickers from photographs she took of James Oliva and three friends at the St James Centre in Edinburgh. Morrison's notion was that her photograph of the four boys could represent Gang of Four. To that end she reversed her photograph, made it a negative image of four males standing still while all the shoppers in the St James Centre provided movement.

HILARY MORRISON: I can remember when we were putting out the Gang of Four record that they phoned up Fast Product and started complaining down the phone and shouting at me. They clearly thought we had an office and possibly all the accoutrements that went with an office, but it was just me.

BOB LAST: We would do the packaging, sometimes directly in opposition to the band's expressed wishes. This was obviously borne out most dramatically with the Gang of Four, who were very precise about what they wanted on the cover of their *Damaged Goods* EP. We ignored their wishes and deconstructed the information and image they wanted as the front cover of the EP; the newspaper cuttings and typed instructions the group sent to me, they appeared on the back of the cover instead, and I designed the front cover.

GEOFF TRAVIS: Honestly, those records were just fantastic, 'Being Boiled' and 'Damaged Goods'. I mean, what was great is that this is your peer group, and this is what they're doing, and they're putting out fantastic records. That's what you want, you want to be in a milieu where what you're doing can stand next to the best of what other people are doing. So it's great, and I think it's a kind of competitiveness, and that's what you want it to be. I guess it's like if you write your first novel, and you want it to be compared to other things that you admire. I mean, we didn't feel inferior, but it was a fantastic standard to set. The first Fast Product records were fantastic.

Fast Product started 1978 with its first statement in January via the Mekons, 'Never Been in a Riot', which sounded apposite and signalled an intention to provoke. The brand exuded a spirit of invention and playfulness that unfolded as the various Fast artefacts were released throughout 1978. The groups that had been launched — the Mekons, the Human League, Gang of Four — had all attained a critical mass that could not have been predicted by the protagonists. Fast Product had created an Edinburgh scene by not releasing any music by an Edinburgh group, though that would come soon as Scars, the Flowers, Fire Engines, Thursdays et al. percolated concepts for the year to come. Fast Product released five singles throughout the year, but arguably more importantly had also packaged and sold rotting orange peel and two discursive fanzine interactions, FAST 3 — *The Quality of Life* and FAST 6 — *SeXex*.

Nineteen seventy-eight also saw Joy Division release their first music, initially on their own label before they released a track as part of the first record launched by Factory — a luxuriously packaged (by Peter Saville) double single (*A Factory Sample*) released at the end of the year that also featured tracks by Cabaret Voltaire and the Durutti Column. The year saw debut singles by Scritti Politti, the Cure, Subway Sect, the Fall, Swell Maps, Public Image Ltd, all of which signalled a change in the musical landscape (as did the initiation of Rough Trade, Mute, then Factory as independent record labels). Bob Last now had sparring partners in Geoff Travis, Daniel Miller and, in particular, Tony Wilson.

CHAPTER 3

1979 – Everyone Is a Prostitute

Scars: John Mackie, Robert King, Calumn MacKay and Paul Research

Nineteen seventy-nine opened with Fast Product at peak power as post-punk facilitators, as evidenced when Bob Last appeared on the front cover of the *NME* on 13 January in tandem with Ian Curtis. The lead article — 'Nationwide Ethnic Credibility Special '79' — highlighted Fast Product as being at the epicentre of the explosion in independent record labels and associated artists. Fast was regarded as the leading light in this new independent terrain as the year began to career forward. Gang of Four had their debut John Peel session broadcast on 18 January (Peel sessions by the Mekons and the Human League had already been broadcast in 1978). The chasing pack of independent labels Rough Trade, Mute and Factory were ready and primed for engagement. New ways of responding to punk's stimuli continued apace, and in February the inevitable response from Liverpool to Factory resulted in a new label called Zoo. They signed and released a brace of bands that connected with media and the public alike. Debut singles by the Teardrop Explodes and Echo and the Bunnymen were released in quick succession, which put Liverpool, Zoo and Bill Drummond in the public eye.

Zoo's singles were well received in Scotland. However, the group that made the biggest impact with the Edinburgh cognoscenti since Subway Sect and the Slits played on the White Riot tour released their debut single in March. The Pop Group's 12-inch, 'She Is beyond Good and Evil', on the new Warner Brothers-funded Radar label, was produced by UK reggae producer Dennis Bovell and sounded utterly unique; it was as if the free-thinking essence of punk had been distilled in these teenage Bristolians. The dissonant noise made by guitarist Gareth Sager and the other musicians was complemented perfectly by the unique lyrical and vocal delivery of Mark Stewart and deconstructive production by Bovell. The Pop Group already had a Peel session broadcast in August 1978 that signposted their punk-funk intentions, but 'She Is beyond Good and Evil' was the ultimate year-zero moment for many.

GARETH SAGER: I grew up in Currie, which is about six miles from the centre of Edinburgh, and lived there until I was nine before ending up living in Bristol. The first gig I did with the Pop Group in Edinburgh was supporting Patti Smith at the Odeon on her first British tour. The last time I had been in the venue was when I was a kid and I saw *The Sound of Music* at the Odeon cinema. I think two of the Scars, the Mackie brothers, also came from Currie.

The Pop Group: (foreground) Gareth Sager and Mark Stewart

MARK STEWART: Bowie was really important. Through him we found out who William Burroughs was, who Jean Genet was, who Luis Buñuel was. A lot of punk was just glam fans with different clothes on. When we first saw the Clash at the ICA in London, I was sixteen. Paul [Simonon] had stickers on his bass to show him where to put his fingers, and we thought 'we can do that', and that was the central idea of punk.

GARETH SAGER: I see nobody as our peers. We were really influenced by the Subway Sect, but apart from them there was nobody that we felt any kinship with. I feel with the Pop Group, when you are outriders you don't really look over your shoulders.

MARK STEWART: Vic Godard is the man, he is a visionary. Subway Sect supported the Clash when they came to Bristol, and hearing 'Nobody's Scared' and seeing Vic perform live was crucial, as was hearing early tracks by Television — both were very important for the Pop Group.

JOHN MACKIE: The thing I liked about the Pop Group was the inherent chaos of it all — there was a big kernel of chaos at the centre of everything they were doing. They were quite happy to let it spill out, you know. Now that's attractive because it's not scripted, that's who they were, that's who they are.

MARK STEWART: I think punk was so important, it blew everything up and knocked down the doors, therefore what came immediately after is separate and I think post-punk is a valid term. Punk was quite simplistic musically, but the Pop Group felt we could do anything — free jazz, dub, experimental, literature, political — we were given that freedom to explore and create with the Pop Group and we just ran with it. What was influential for me living in England in the early seventies was the Angry Brigade — I took a lot of information from their manifestos and put them into lyrics.

GARETH SAGER: Davy Henderson told me the Fire Engines were influenced by the Pop Group, and I think we were the first group after the Pistols to take the punk ethos and move everything forward. We were on the front cover on the *NME* when we were eighteen, so the groups that were influenced by us like Fire Engines and Scars were only a couple of years younger than us. Because we were so young, people don't realise we were out there before Joy Division and other groups associated with what's now known as post-punk.

DAVY HENDERSON: I mean the thing about the Pop Group is that they're a Bristol-based band and there's a massive Jamaican influence in that town, and they loved reggae and brought that same energy fuelled by what was happening in 1977, which was like punk.

BOB LAST: Part of the Fast Product modus operandi was to be contentious. I passionately believed in what the bands were doing and I never ever thought that anything the label did itself was more important than what they did. The only reason the label existed or I was doing what I was doing was because of what these bands did, but following on from our sense of how the audience enjoyed them was mediated by all these other elements. That could be our packaging or the marketing or what we said to the press — these elements all mattered and were a part of the process, we didn't think that a respect for what the band did meant that we didn't bring something else to the table in that chain. There would be huge ideological battles in the studio about whether or not there should be reverb on something and whether that was selling out; however, I just didn't care about any musical points of view from a production perspective. I would argue that from a musical point of view I was probably more of a punk than half our bands, in that if it somehow worked or had an attitude that I thought was interesting I absolutely didn't care about what rules it transgressed.

Very rapidly punk itself settled into an incredibly antiquated and geriatric set of rules about what was and wasn't punk, which we were already completely uninterested in.

MARK STEWART: I thought the point of punk was that everyone was equal, the audience was as important as the people on the stage and it was a levelling thing. Guy Debord put it best with *Society of the Spectacle*, the idea that the spectacle is a distraction, and what happened with punk is that it became part of the distraction. Punk became part of the problem and became the new orthodoxy.

GARETH SAGER: I was aware of the Gang of Four, who to my mind had a far straighter rock 'n' roll approach than the Pop Group. They shared our office in London around their Fast Product period, but within a year it would be the Pop Group that ended up supporting the Gang of Four. That was a bit of a downer.

MARK STEWART: The packaging on the Fast releases was amazing. What Bob Last did with that was the template for all the cool independent labels. Fast Product influenced the Pop Group's label, Y, and it really really influenced Tony Wilson and Factory. The idea that Fast Product gave a catalogue number to a bag of orange peel — that was a complete and utter situationist kind of thing. The ideas of the situationists influenced all of us, especially the idea they had of having a book cover made of sandpaper so it would rip the covers of all the other books in the book shelf. This obviously influenced Factory with their LP cover for the Durutti Column.

The social and economic climate in the UK in 1979 was far from healthy. Newspaper headlines proclaimed an impotent Labour government hamstrung by union demands. Headlines like 'Crisis? What Crisis?' and 'Winter of Discontent' defined the era, which allied with public fatigue and endless strikes paved the way for the Conservatives to win the general election in May. Margaret Thatcher became prime minister and polarised a generation as she repositioned the country on a right-wing trajectory. Scotland voted for a Scottish Assembly by a large majority during the Scottish devolution referendum; however, this was not implemented due to a condition that at least 40 per cent of the electorate must support the proposal.

The far right were mobilised on the streets and a culture of violence hung heavily in the Scottish air. Anyone who dared to look different and didn't wear denim or burgundy-coloured shoes was asking for a kicking off any neds they had the misfortune to come across in the street. Bob Last was on the receiving end of a battering one evening on his way back to the Fast flat when he was jumped by two guys who caught him unaware, shouting as they punched and kicked him, 'You're an arty cunt, you're arty wankers, we fucking hate you, we fucking hate what you're doing.'

TAM DEAN BURN: In Clermiston there was a sectarian situation; there was a gang of really neo-fascist types that were into Loyalism. They were supporters of football teams like Hearts and Rangers, whereas we were all Hibs supporters by and large. They were a bit nasty and aligned themselves with organisations like the National Front. In the lead-up to punk the BNP never really had any impact up here, mainly because there were very few black folk. We did get politicised when punk came along and when the Anti-Nazi League and Rock Against Racism mobilised with their big gigs with the Clash. These were amongst our first trips to London and they definitely politicised us.

ROBERT KING: Scars did an Anti-Nazi League gig where we had a few run-ins with some elements of the crowd that shouted abuse at us because of the way we were dressed. Everybody else was dressed up in an aggressive way, so we would dress up in a feminine way, and we'd come onstage and people would shout at us, call us poofters and whatever. So I started the gig by saying, 'Anybody that wants to fight us, you're welcome to meet us backstage after the gig.' Nobody ever came backstage.

MICHAEL BARCLAY: Thursdays' gigs used to commence with our singer Paul Reekie starting the set with a Nico lyric, 'Frozen Warnings', in poem form, and we would get angry audience reaction. In Glasgow there were bottles thrown as we walked on. Paul just stood there reciting this poem and then we joined him onstage ducking bottles, so gigs were quite tense. That was good because all the audiences there had to pay attention because they weren't getting what they expected. It led to quite difficult situations, one gig in particular where Paul had to actually get involved with the main aggressor in the audience and I ended up jumping on this guy, rolling around the floor, and there was a big fight. I thought we were going to get our heads kicked in because our backs were to the wall and the audience were going to tear us apart. Then the main aggressor who we'd been fighting with reappeared and he was clearly the main gang leader, but he was grinning from ear to ear. He told us he'd had a brilliant night and that it was fantastic that the lead singer in the band had decided to have a scrap with them.

PAUL RESEARCH: I never saw *A Clockwork Orange*. Kubrick actually barred it from the cinemas long before I was old enough to go and see it. Obviously we heard about it but it's one of those things, a kind of taboo, a forbidden subject that is therefore extremely exciting and attractive. Something about the Scars seemed to attract that kind of particularly violent or aggressive edge from audiences, and sometimes from the band towards audiences.

HILARY MORRISON: I was the only girl in the Flowers and that was difficult, though it was interesting at times. We occasionally got booked into places where we shouldn't have been playing that would have audiences full of bikers. God knows why we were booked to play for bikers who wanted to hear bands playing heavy rock. We were about to get seriously done over when I told our guitarist to play 'Smoke on the Water' by Deep Purple. As he did that, I made an appeal to the girls in the audience, 'Look, come on, I'm just trying to do a thing', which worked and we got the bikers on our side and they stopped trying to attack us and listened to us, so we got out alive. At another concert in Ferguslie Park in Paisley we only got out alive once the police had been called. The locals were hard men, they turned on all the punks, and we were playing with a local punk group called the Fegs who tried to help, but we had to get out under police escort.

TAM DEAN BURN: The Dirty Reds Mk 2 played a gig at the [University] Communist Society, who had all these big banners of Marx and Lenin on the walls, and I started shouting from the stage that we were anarchists, pull these fucking posters down. So people in the audience are going up and pulling the fucking posters and banners down, then the students are coming up onstage and grabbing the microphone from me. The next thing I saw was this fucking hi-hat cymbal coming flying past me. Russell threw the cymbal and it was flying through the air, which if it had hit somebody, it would have been death, but it clattered off the back wall, and that was typical of how Dirty Reds gigs turned out.

GRAHAM MAIN: Our first Dirty Reds Mk 2 gig was total mayhem. Amps and equipment was getting thrown all over the stage, it was wild. I couldn't believe what was happening, it was madness, it was great. However, Tam left to go to college to focus on his acting.

DAVY HENDERSON: I think the Dirty Reds Mk 2 isolated a lot of people, there was polarisation. I think we kind of enjoyed that and there were lots of eventful gigs or performances, involving lacerations and near decapitations.

Societal tension was obviously visible throughout the UK. Within the Fast Product petri dish at the Keir Street flat different kinds of tensions were evident in the kitchen conversations between all the Fast-related protagonists. The Dirty Reds Mk 1 had already become the Flowers, which had become in turn a vehicle for Hilary Morrison's musical ambitions. The Dirty Reds Mk 2 mutated into Fire Engines, and other Fast habitués brewed ideas for new groups like Thursdays and Boots for Dancing. The big news within the Fast microsystem was that finally Scars were going to record their Fast Product single in January.

GRACE FAIRLEY: Keir Street and Fast Product was a complete hotbed of action — you cannot understate the energy of everybody involved at that point. Bob provided that space and also that belief in people. I can remember at the time people going, 'Why hasn't Bob put out a record by the Scars yet?' I think he was just waiting until they were ready.

PAUL RESEARCH: Everything happened so quickly at that time. For example, it was late summer 1977 that we did our first gig in Balerno and Hilary Morrison was there, then we met Bob shortly afterwards and he started putting out records on Fast Product. A whole year passed and singles by the Mekons, Gang of Four, the Human League all came out and it felt like we were never going to get our chance to make a record. I was thinking, Fast is getting really hip and really big; Bob's probably not going to be interested in the Scars any more. But he did finally do it, lucky for us.

DAVY HENDERSON: When I first met Rab he told me he was in a band called the Scars and someone in Edinburgh was going to release his record, on a label called Fast Product. I was a Scars fan after meeting Rab, and he told me he was playing in the Wig and Pen. I met him in town and we went to look in the record shops. So I became really good friends with the Scars. They had a regular gig in the Wig and Pen in Cockburn Street and they were pretty phenomenal; it was incredible to think that somebody was the same age as you and writing these super-original songs. They weren't just three-chord songs, they were really original and individual. John and Paul were the Mackie Brothers (there was loads of tension there) and they had an amazing drummer called Mac, an incredible drummer. They could all play and they had this attitude where everybody was pretty pretentious, and I mean that in the sense of virtue. By then I'm thinking I'd love to do this, I'm going to do that, be in a band. 'Love Song' was Bobby's pop song, it was a bit like the Buzzcocks. Paul and Rab were seventeen, you know what I mean, and nobody could touch them, there was nobody actually making music at that time in Edinburgh like the Scars.

Bob Last and Hilary Morrison had taken note of the work James Oliva had been doing as Scars manager. He'd started off as their drum roadie before becoming their manager, and impressed Last and Morrison with his proactive, pragmatic approach. They offered him a job at Fast Product — it didn't take long for Oliva to accept and he packed in his job as a civil servant to work on Fast's mail order.

BOB LAST: I think in the case of the Scars, there were certainly things that they had that were perceived as contrary to orthodoxy, as punk very rapidly became a set of orthodox ideas, so their whole idea of being attractive, sexy and glamorous was something that I absolutely encouraged. I can clearly remember seeing Roxy Music on *The Old Grey Whistle Test*, and when I first saw the Scars play live with Paul Research wearing ladies' pink leather boots, that's when

I really got the Scars. I guess early Roxy Music was my reference point for Scars, in much the same way that 'Being Boiled' immediately made sense to me because I'd been listening to Bootsy and Parliament.

JOHN MACKIE: Bob Last took us to Rochdale to record our first single and it all happened really quickly. It was quite raw. Rochdale in the rain — grim. I remember it very well and it was a seminal moment for us. We thought being in the studio was great. It was an awakening actually doing that recording, we were desperate to record the single.

ROBERT KING: Bob Last was very driven — he knew exactly what he wanted for Fast Product. He was quite diplomatic, but always managed to get someone like myself, who was a confident and sometimes chaotic teenager, to sit down and do the kind of things he would prefer me to do.

PAUL RESEARCH: Fast Product packaging was good, but to me that was normal as they were the only record label I'd known and I thought all labels were like that, to be honest. I also thought all record labels would be run by someone with a vision who realised that the whole thing was a product. It just seemed natural and sensible to me and I would apply that to myself in any kind of undertaking involving the Scars. We cared about what we looked like, where we played, not just what the songs were like, and it was the same for Fast Product.

GARETH SAGER: I was aware of the Scars single on Fast Product, they'd obviously created some great songs.

FRASER SUTHERLAND: Scars' early performances were often confrontational. Audiences could be hostile to the fact that the band would not conform to the punk uniformity that seemed to be developing by

'78. There also seemed to be a tension within the band, oppositions that gave their performances a real edge. I had a cassette of a show they did, in Grangemouth I think, that typified this, which I'd play all the time. That tension and energy is there in the Fast single, which remains one of my favourites from around then.

GRAHAM MAIN: We were envious of the Scars when they got a deal with Fast to record 'Horrorshow'/'Adult/ery' at Cargo studios in Rochdale.

BOB LAST: I think the fact that the Scars, Flowers, Thursdays and Fire Engines were hanging around at the Fast flat so often probably had an impact in making them think things were possible, which was the point of Fast Product, to impart that things are not as you assume. It was extraordinarily exciting to see kids that had been lurking around in the Fast flat take some of the ideas we were playing with to a whole other level. I really love the Scars single, it was an underrated release, I think.

Scars' debut 45 was released in March; as the first Edinburgh group to be released on Fast Product they didn't disappoint. Bob Last's production and packaging, Hilary Morrison's photographs of the group on the back cover, the songwriting, the component parts of the group, the Anthony Burgess-inspired lyrics and Paul Research's high-concept/high-treble guitar sound all combined to make FAST 8 the equivalent of Scotland's 'Anarchy in the UK'. This was a pivotal event, which effectively ignited the Scottish independent music explosion. Fast Product and Scars captured a moment in time in Scottish pop that was never to be repeated. Scars' 45 was noticed not only by the next wave of groups to emerge through the Fast scene, but also by their future west coast rivals and contemporaries.

ROBERT KING: We recorded 'Adult/ery' and 'Horrorshow' for our debut single on Fast Product. The songs were interesting; 'Horror-show' was essentially a synopsis of *A Clockwork Orange*, because I'd always been fascinated by *Clockwork Orange* as had the other members of the Scars. I think most teenagers of our generation were fascinated by *Clockwork Orange* because only a few people had ever seen it, so it held a strong hold over the psyche of the British youth, particularly because it was based round gangs and also the way the guys dressed. It was really striking so it caught the public imagination. I remember reading 'Horrorshow' was called 'possibly the most violent song ever written', just because of the nature of the lyrics, which were about real ultra-violence. I mean I was seventeen when I wrote the songs, so they're quite straightforward in their lyrical endeavours.

PAUL RESEARCH: My relationship with Bob Last was a good one and I thought he was a good guy, he's humorous. I was impressed by his canny business sense, as I saw it at the time, although I didn't really know anything about business. He seemed to be looking after our interests and his interests and not just selling things too cheaply.

ANGUS GROOVY: I think the 'Horrorshow' single was a major achievement, both for the Scars and for Fast, although it seemed slightly anomalous for Fast at the time. I had become friends with Rab Allen (as he was then) around the same time I met Davy. I introduced Rab to Hilary and Bob and encouraged them to take an interest, but I don't think he was particularly impressed with them until receiving a demo tape a year or so later. Bob's focus was more on the Leeds and Sheffield scene at the time, and there was no sense in which he saw Fast as a 'local label'. Hilary paid more attention to the Scars and I recall her being around more local band performances than Bob was. On reflection I think that single captured a time when a lot of creative contradictions came together — between several clashing personalities in Scars, and between Fast's transition from a quite 'arty' orientation to embracing pop music. I think both Rab and Bob would have liked Scars to have become pop stars, but neither had the measure of each other's talent.

Scars were finally launched on Fast Product and Scotland finally came alive. The intelligence, playfulness and business-art ethos of Fast had antecedents in Andy Warhol's Factory of superstars in New York. Paul America, Bridget Polk, Rod la Rod, Nico, Billy Name, Edie, Lou, Candy Darling — they all sounded like musicians in Fast Product groups (or vice versa). The group Warhol sponsored, the Velvet Underground, were the defining influence for underground pop groups in Scotland.

FAY FIFE: When I auditioned to sing with the Rezillos I was a very young person from Fife, and I was doing things like dancing around my handbag, very nervous. At the audition I sang the Velvets' 'Sweet Jane' and a Shangri-Las song, so the direction where I was coming from with the band was there right from the start.

GARETH SAGER: The Velvet Underground were one of Vic Godard's biggest influences, which is borne out by Vic's very literate lyrics. I love his Subway Sect lyric 'we oppose all rock 'n' roll', it sounds like a manifesto. I would say Subway Sect obviously influenced the Fire Engines and the Scars.

DAVY HENDERSON: From buying *Transformer* I became intrigued about the Velvet Underground. I remember seeing their albums in Cockburn Street Market, which was a sort of a hippy market. Listen to a Lou Reed song, it's up there with the greatest American songwriting, lyrically, and as a personal vision. Lou Reed was able to write these incredible songs that were apparently very straightforward and simple. Lou and Dylan had these unclassical voices, they sound like a normal person in a lot of ways, and that's maybe why, subtly, people respond to it. The thing I loved about the Velvets was their absolute vibrant raw nature, the use of sixties classic pop symbols and the fact that they had a Welsh guy who was ultra exotic with an incredible voice that played the viola, writing the music along with Lou Reed. They had Nico as well, this girl who sang part of the songs who was meant to be a film star.

GARETH SAGER: I think the Velvet Underground were the most important group to every Scottish band that followed after the Pop Group. My theory is that Scottish people are brought up with drones through being exposed to bagpipes, and the Velvet Underground used a lot of drones in their music.

The Keir Street gang fermented their own artistic vision, facilitated and encouraged by Bob Last. The Flowers had sprouted from the Dirty Reds Mk 1 and harnessed Hilary Morrison's musical vision — they were ready for action. Thursdays prepared themselves too as they absorbed the Fast Product aesthetics and threw poetry into the mix. The Dirty Reds Mk 2 had spawned Fire Engines, who worked off a rigid musical manifesto that they rigorously adhered to.

HILARY MORRISON: After my pretend band with Davy Henderson, Warm Jets, failed to do anything other than be a pretend band, I was asked in by Dave Carson to sing in the Dirty Reds. I was asked to come in and do something with them, then we changed the name and started the Flowers. I had already written a lot of lyrics that were angry young woman lyrics, though the Flowers was fun, it was interesting. But it made me sick with nerves half the time, when I see photographs of me from that period I'm always looking numb.

SIMON BEST: I was a founding member of the Delta 5 and wrote their best-known song, 'Mind Your Own Business', but left before they signed to Rough Trade, when I moved from Leeds back to Edinburgh in early 1979. I was drummer in the Flowers. Bob Last and I had been best friends at my school, which he joined aged fourteen. We were both interested in cultural politics and I introduced Bob to the early albums of Frank Zappa and the Mothers which challenged the US status quo and consumerism. When punk came along in 1977, we recognised that it was another wave of challenge, initially straight from the mouths of kids from all backgrounds, and we wanted to make sure that as many of them as possible had a voice.

MICHAEL BARCLAY: Thursdays were formed due to complete boredom. I had moved from Fife and had been in Edinburgh for a year. I met Bob Last and Hilary Morrison, Davy Henderson, the Scars and some amazingly exciting creative young people. I bought a guitar but didn't know anything about it, I couldn't play anything on it. I couldn't get a grasp on any of us ever doing gigs or making records, but Rab from the Scars changed my mind about that because he had so much creative energy. I was introduced to a poet called Paul Reekie; without much discussion we understood each other musically, though I remember when I asked Paul about his lyrics he told me it was none of my business. Thursdays hired a hall in Glenrothes and invited the Fast Product gang up to Fife to see us perform live. One of the songs we performed in our set was a cover of 'Dock of the Bay', and that's when Bob Last got it, that's when he got Thursdays. We were very shambolic — I knew just enough and no more to get through the song structures in the songs we were trying to play.

HILARY MORRISON: Going to Glenrothes and getting to see the Thursdays perform, signing them to Fast Product, watching a guy singing 'Dock of the Bay' in a howling Fife accent. That was a moment. You know, when Paul Reekie did that, it was amazing.

DAVY HENDERSON: I never thought that I could play music, but I always wanted to be in the band. I mean there was nothing more joyful than getting an album that had a lyric sheet so you could sing along to everything and take great pride in learning every single word. I can still sing the whole of *Ziggy Stardust* from start to finish. The Dirty Reds Mk 2 were cultivated isolation. Tam's a natural method actor and had studied the Lee Strasberg/James Osterberg method – he was a big Iggy fan. Tam was looking for a cathartic experience every time he performed and it was pretty explosive. It was really exciting and adrenaline-fuelled, and getting that kick from being in the band, that's what I was looking for. However, Tam was starting to get acting work and I think we just wanted to change. I wanted to be the singer in the band and, to be frank, Graham and Russell did as well. We told Tam that's what we were going to do, and he acquiesced. It wasn't like we fell out with Tam – we remained pals and all still lived in the same flat together. So we started looking for a guitar player, and were into Murray Slade's guitar playing in a band called Station 6. Murray was my friend – I was at secondary school with Murray and we were both into music. I switched him on to the Voidoids and we were into Television. I remember him coming up to my house to listen to the Voidoids during our break from exams and he really dug it, and we went to the White Riot tour together, and were influenced by it. We asked Murray to be our guitar player and asked him not to play chords.

RUSSELL BURN: Davy suggested working with Murray Slade, so we started rehearsing in the basement of his parents' house and it all got tighter. Murray came up with a new name, Fire Engines, because we were listening to 13th Floor Elevators a lot.

MURRAY SLADE: Our plan was that it couldn't be laid back. Thatcher was kicking about so there was a lot of anger around too. It had to be upbeat and in your face, it was more about energy. I enjoyed life in the seventies in Scotland, mine was perfectly fine, perfectly comfortable. I quite enjoyed school actually. It was at school that I met Davy Henderson. We were starting off at secondary school and pupils brought LPs in, and there was obviously punk rock records at the time, certainly a music culture was going on in our school. Personally I still think the seventies was a pretty good period for growing up. I was still at school when Davy left, sixteen, and he soon put a proposition to me to join his band, this bunch called the Dirty Reds. That's when I was aware of Davy's current friends and confidants at that time, then one day in a record shop uptown I met Davy after school and he asked if I wanted to come around to the Dirty Reds' flat, he had a proposition to put to me. When I went around he told me Tam Dean Burn was leaving the Dirty Reds to become an actor, and did I want to do something new?

RUSSELL BURN: When I started playing drums I wondered why drummers always used all parts of the drum kit, always played the hi-hats. I wanted to try something different — I wanted to feature the cowbell and not use hi-hats or cymbals, strip everything back. Fire Engines were really into New York 'no wave' — that sound was clinical, stripped down and basic.

GRAHAM MAIN: Davy, Russell and me started Fire Engines with new guitarist Murray Slade. I was really taken by Dave Alexander's bass playing on the Stooges albums and George Scott from James White and the Blacks. Big bass riffs was my way forward. We lived together in a flat, staying up all night listening to the Fall, Captain Beefheart, taking do-dos and creating music and getting our thing together. We were like brothers — we still are — we were all singing from the same sheet. It was all about musical discovery. We all contributed to the songs.

MURRAY SLADE: Davy was enigmatic, enthusiastic and funny. Once I met Angus Groovy, Russell Burn and Graham Main, I could see why he thought I would fit in with this new group. I was brought up in Clermiston initially, and Davy was brought up in Clermiston too, our mothers knew each other before we did. When I went to secondary school I had moved to a bigger house, which was described as a Thunderbird stackhouse by the band, and we practised there. I technically came from what I suppose you could call a middle-class background. I hate classist expressions of any sort but I suppose at the time the group was really from a working-class background. However, it never occurred to me, me being middle class, it was never an issue — I play guitar, they play guitar. They introduced me to new ideas, and I could actually tune my instrument, which was a help.

RUSSELL BURN: I think the new mood seemed to be inspired by the rawer elements of the Velvets, but we really liked the poetry of Patti Smith and Television, and the noise of James Chance and Lydia Lunch.

DAVY HENDERSON: There was a real novelty and also fear of not being able to express ourselves articulately on our instruments. So it was really a challenge all the time, day by day, to make something up, and it was a really difficult language. That's why we liked things that sounded uncontrollable, like the Pop Group and James Chance, kinetic, frenzied, frantic, chaotic sounds, that was always appealing to the Fire Engines when we were starting off.

MURRAY SLADE: Fire Engines was a very manifesto-driven idea. We'd all seen punk bands retort that you didn't have to be a great musician to make music together as a band, and our main agenda was to not be laid back in any way — laid back was just bad. We possibly had a lack of technique, but we also thought that would give us a good edge. Possibly we took influence from the New York no-wave scene we were into, like what James Chance played on saxophone with the Contortions. Getting into Captain Beefheart and the Magic Band was another impetus in getting us started. Each of our song ideas emerged from that kind of mix, jamming these different angles.

RUSSELL BURN: Captain Beefheart and the Magic Band were a different sort of group sonically, and he had this amazing voice. The Magic Band was basic blues overlapping these intricate ideas, and the cowbell rhythms were amazing. There's a track from their album *Clear Spot* which has these intense rhythms, an unbelievable track called 'Circumstances', which was an influence on Fire Engines' initial sound.

MURRAY SLADE: The fact that we used to play with lots of treble on our amps gave us a really jarring, sharp, tinny edge. What Davy and I were playing on the guitar gave us an angle, I suppose, as did the sound of Davy's voice. You can also take it right down to Russell's drumming, which was a kind of chopped angularity. I don't mind that description of Fire Engines, but descriptions can be bad because it starts to narrow options. From the start I knew I had to provide a guitar line that was playing the whole time. I've got nothing against playing chords, but the type of music we played suited riffs better, somehow. Davy played lead, and that meant there would be a hook that came in when he wasn't singing. It was a formula that was quite simple but seemed to work fairly well.

DAVY HENDERSON: At the start of Fire Engines' rehearsals we listened to 'She's beyond Good and Evil' and 'We Are All Prostitutes' by the Pop Group followed by 'Designed to Kill' by James Chance. Thinking about it, maybe we were trying to steal the riffs, but it was also to vibe us up, which it did.

RUSSELL BURN: I think I got a lot of drum ideas from James Chance and the Contortions. That music was so extreme, but it was always on it and had a craziness and certain type of funky groove.

MURRAY SLADE: Being young and nervous, I never really took on what the crowd thought about us when we started playing Fire Engines gigs. In a way this is what true artists are supposed to do, they don't give a monkeys about the crowd, but I think once we played several gigs the crowds were supportive. The fifteen-minute shows came about for a couple of reasons really. The main one being we would go out to gigs and the bands will be on for an hour and a half, which we thought was boring. I mean, I thought Joy Division were great, but an hour of Joy Division in the middle of the night isn't necessarily what you're looking for. So we thought, why not come on for couple short bursts and that way, if people don't like it, they're not getting their evening wrecked. We only performed what we thought was our best stuff, which is what any artist would want to do, and of course there's the Andy Warhol 'fifteen minutes of fame' thing.

RUSSELL BURN: Fire Engines' fifteen-minute concerts were like a short, sharp shock. We'd take a break and show films and visuals, then do another fifteen minutes. It was a nice atmosphere, we'd be playing all our favourite songs between our sets, doing DJ sets.

DAVY HENDERSON: The idea for fifteen-minute Fire Engines sets wasn't through design but because we only had a few songs. I suppose it came from the first gig that we played. We had four songs and, depending on how Russell was feeling on the kit, on his adrenaline, it would affect the length of the songs. Something we'd been rehearsing that was two and a half minutes would never be two and a half minutes long when we played it live. How Rusty was feeling and the tempo of his count-in would then determine the length of the song, so at our first gig there was a lot of adrenaline, even though it was a Sunday afternoon in Leith Community Centre. People would say we only played for fifteen minutes and we were like, well you're only famous for fifteen minutes, who wants to play any longer than fifteen minutes?

The new breed of young Edinburgh-based groups developed under the aegis of Fast Product and cut their formative master plans. Bob Last plotted a conceptual course of action that would shift Fast out of kilter with their independent contemporaries. The Human League had followed the obscurist electronic pop of 'Being Boiled' with a 12-inch EP, *The Dignity of Labour* (FAST 10). It was a bold stroke: an instrumental work in four parts, with obvious traces of systems music influences and heavy Philip Glass overtones. There was an overall feel of *musique concrète* that permeated throughout the EP's four tracks. *The Dignity of Labour* didn't inhabit the space-age pop of 'Being Boiled'; instead it pointed to the academic world of serious music, and included a flexi-disc which was in essence a discussion between Bob Last and the Human League about the making and rationale of *The Dignity of Labour*.

SIMON BEST: After the release of the 'Being Boiled' single it was decided that Fast Product would release *The Dignity of Labour* as a more experimental 12-inch in June 1979. Phil Oakey was impatient for the League to become a fully fledged pop group; however, artists like Bowie, Lou Reed and Eno, all of whom the League admired, had a track record of issuing interesting side projects which were less obviously commercial.

BOB LAST: Fast Product was about not being certain. *The Dignity of Labour* seemed to be instrumental and loaded with all sorts of references. My recollection of the conversation released as a flexi-disc with *The Dignity of Labour* is that it was a real conversation.

Was it done so it could be policed, so that we could all go, 'No, I said that'? That feels believable. Then I decided to have some fun and be meta and release it.

MARTYN WARE: We were terribly postmodern, the design approach to Fast Product was postmodernist.

BOB LAST: Fast Product was, from my point of view, self-consciously postmodernist. A lot of what I did with Fast Product graphics was edit what the bands brought to me.

The Human League: Martyn Ware, Philip Oakey, Ian Craig Marsh and Adrian Wright

If the Human League set out to make the point with *The Dignity of Labour* that they could deliver the same strand of instrumental electronic composition as fellow Sheffield sound collage experimentalists Cabaret Voltaire, then they succeeded. It felt like the Human League needed to get *The Dignity of Labour* out of their artistic system in order to move forward with pop song-based electronic tracks, albeit songs that were lyrically heavily influenced by science fiction writers like J.G. Ballard and Philip K. Dick. The Human League's juxtaposition of influences created music that sounded new, original, synthetic, and was garnering the kind of critical kudos that had major record labels pricking up their ears.

The independent music landscape developed an eclecticism in both output by artists and labels, and acceptance by fans. People who had initially been moved by punk rhetoric and the guitar-based rock 'n' roll of the Pistols and the Clash moved on and actively sought out the new exciting experimental music by artists who used guitars: Wire, the Pop Group, Gang of Four, Joy Division. There was also demand for new music by artists who instead of guitars used synthesisers and tape manipulation. The Human League were flying this flag for Fast Product, but other electronic-based music also made its mark via independent releases. These included records by the Normal (Mute), Throbbing Gristle (Industrial), Cabaret Voltaire (Factory and Rough Trade), and Thomas Leer and Robert Rental (Industrial, Rough Trade, Mute). These artists and labels also acutely understood the importance of artwork.

BOB LAST: Fast Product packaging and artwork were largely the result of me using elements that other people brought to the table. Certainly in some of the later ones I used photos that Hilary took, but packaging was my bag. We would often wrestle with some of our bands around that time because although some of them were aligned with our thinking, equally there was that punk thing of it being about self-determination, and that wasn't a notion that we bought into as a label. We thought notions of self-determination were illusory, including our own. We were labelled as an independent record label which I always thought was very funny because in reality we were an under-capitalised small business, a lot more dependent on bank loans than a big multinational. I saw Fast Product as a dependent record label, not an independent. So that idea of self-determination didn't wash with me.

Revolution and independent ideology was thick in the air throughout 1979, as was the notion that decentralised distribution and controlling the means of production could challenge the accepted status quo of multinational corporation practice within the music industry. Marxist critical theory and disruptive political discourse as practised by Situationist International were guiding principles for Cambridge University alumni Geoff Travis and Tony Wilson, and their labels, Rough Trade and Factory. Travis and Wilson were broadly in tandem in their belief that the independent route was best for their labels and artists to pursue. Rough Trade and Factory were strongly aligned in their belief that their business model and practices would result in them achieving their commercial and artistic ambitions without compromising their integrity. In short, Geoff Travis and Tony Wilson believed in independence as a route to market; while it was now apparent Bob Last believed that Fast Product artists should sign to a London-based major label, utilise multinational capital and infiltrate the mainstream.

GEOFF TRAVIS: Well, that was probably Bob's intention, you know. I mean, thank God Joy Division didn't sign to a major, they only didn't because of Rob Gretton. Tony Wilson and Ian Curtis were quite happy for Joy Division to sign to a major; Ian wanted to be on RCA because of Iggy and David Bowie. It was only the fateful day when Rob Gretton said, 'Let's not sign to a major, let's get Rough Trade to distribute our records,' that they didn't sign. I think their history could have been very different if they had signed to a major.

The Human League made a business agreement with Bob Last to become their manager, a decision that would have significant ramifications later in their career.

Gang of Four: Jon King and Andy Gill

A live concert at London's Lyceum Theatre dubbed 'The Gig of the Century' highlighted the breakthrough independent groups of 1979: two Rough Trade groups (Stiff Little Fingers and the Fall), and three groups on Fast Product — the Mekons, the Human League and Gang of Four. It was inevitable the strong media reaction to this concert would result in major-label interest in the participants, and it wasn't too long before offers were being received by Fast Product for its groups. All three groups were duly encouraged by Bob Last to sign to major labels and the Mekons and the Human League signed recording contracts with Virgin Records while Gang of Four signed to EMI. Gang of Four signed a publishing deal with EMI Music and the Human League signed a publishing deal with Virgin Publishing.

GEOFF TRAVIS: I loved the Gang of Four record on Fast Product. The first album is pretty good, but I don't really care about them beyond that point. That's not because they're on a major — it's the music, really. I think it does have an effect on your psychology, being on a major, but it doesn't always have to. Obviously, some of the best records ever made have been on majors. So, it was a different philosophy, really. I'm sure Bob didn't have any qualms. He probably thought we were just a bunch of amateurs playing at being in the record business. Which would have had some truth.

JON KING: There's a romance and an idealisation of indie record labels. *Damaged Goods* had sold 60,000 copies, more than enough to recoup the record's £80 recording costs, but we never got paid a penny, literally nothing. All we wanted to do when we put out the *Damaged Goods* EP was get on the John Peel show, that was our main objective. Our reason for signing to EMI was we wanted to make sure there was effective distribution and accounting.

SIMON BEST: We recognised that the Human League were serious about being a major-league pop group and needed the resources of a major label to achieve this.

BOB LAST: We were managing the Human League and signed to Virgin and encouraged Gang of Four to sign to a major label. Our groups signing major contracts was largely about being an insurgent in the mainstream. So that whole strategy was kind of done and it would have seemed like going back if I'd continued working in the independent sector. I had no ambition to have my own major label.

MARTYN WARE: Bob liked to play his cards close to his chest, but to be honest we weren't really interested in business strategy at that time and were quite happy to let him get on with negotiating with major labels. Virgin Records was always top of our list of preferred labels to sign to, so we jumped at it when they wanted to sign the Human League.

Factory largely worked as a collaborative collective: Tony Wilson was the public face of Factory, Martin Hannett produced the artists, Peter Saville designed the artwork, with Alan Erasmus and Joy Division manager Rob Gretton also in the mix. They had released the debut single by A Certain Ratio just prior to the debut album by Joy Division, *Unknown Pleasures*, being released. This album defined and encapsulated everything that was associated with post-punk; the austere stark production by Martin Hannett was matched by the iconic artwork by Peter Saville. Joy Division hated the production and the strong sonic imprint of Martin Hannett when they heard the album; nonetheless it was the perfect record for the times — lyrically stark and dystopian with strong William Burroughs overtones.

Unknown Pleasures sold extremely well and gave Factory a strong financial base from which they continued to put Manchester on the map in much the same way as Bob Last had done with Fast Product in Edinburgh.

The new exploration and movement away from the punk sound was perhaps best exemplified by Mark Perry and his group, Alternative TV. Singles like 'Action Time and Vision' had laid down a marker during the punk revolution as had their May 1978 debut album, *The Image Has Cracked*. Their second album was released in March 1979, and *Vibing Up the Senile Man* had shown how much Perry had responded to broadening his musical palate by listening to improvised free jazz over the ten months since the release of the ATV debut album. When the group toured with the Pop Group and Manicured Noise it was obvious ATV's punk followers were not ready or appreciative of the group's move away from the rock 'n' roll orthodoxy into freeform experimentation — audience disaffection with the new ATV musical direction resulted in Perry being knocked out onstage after a punk threw a glass bottle and hit him on the head, which rendered him unconscious.

Debut albums by the Fall and the Pop Group carried on the exploratory guitar-and-bass template laid down by PiL on their 1978 debut album; it was now clear the rock 'n' roll modes appropriated by the Pistols from Johnny Thunders and the Heartbreakers already sounded dated. The musicians involved in the new Fast Product groups were clearly indebted to funk, and the new albums that influenced the Keir Street musicians were the Contortions' *Buy* and their alter egos', James White and the Blacks' album, *Off White* (both albums were composed by no-wave pin-up James Chance, and released simultaneously on ZE Records). But the primo album on the new breed's diet was Y, by the Pop Group.

MARK STEWART: The Pop Group name was a situationist thing, giving the name of the area we were working in. We wanted to be the 'pop group' and create an explosion at the heart of the commodity, and use pop music as a tool to communicate radical concepts. Bristol is quite a classless and faceless society, the whole thing was mixed up so you couldn't be put in a box.

GARETH SAGER: The Pop Group were all really into funk and soul clubs, and that definitely influenced our use of funk bass lines to underpin our sound. We then did a split single with the Slits, which came about because we shared the same management, Dick O'Dell. He started the label and named it after our first album, Y. We also used to tour with the Slits and both worked with producer Dennis Bovell.

The Fast groups developed their sound and worked out their strategies, albeit they never strayed too far from the ideas they picked up from Bob Last. The Flowers and Thursdays prepared to release material, while Fire Engines drilled themselves through disciplined rehearsals and worked on their repertoire. Bob Last had licensed a single by a California-based group after he heard their single on John Peel. 'California Über Alles' by the Dead Kennedys would be the last single released on Fast Product — FAST 12.

BOB LAST: Fast Product had an international network of like-minded and interested people. We would regularly receive strange missives from Tokyo or Sydney or Paris or Berlin, all over the world. I mean people sought each other out. I thought of our audience much more like a magazine would think of its readership, that's how I thought of them, rather than as our market. Our network was global from a very early stage, particularly college radio in the States, and maintaining those connections was also a part of what Hilary brought to the table. The Dead Kennedys single, which I think technically was our last release, it kind of bookended Fast Product, and had already been released in the States on another independent label. Obviously by that time we had a relationship with John Peel. He was crucial in this world in terms of exposing this music and I heard him play 'California Über Alles', and got on the phone to him before the last chord died away. Actually I was sort of outraged, sort of, 'hang on, somebody is putting out a Fast Product record without asking me' — that's what it felt like when I heard it. So I thought

Fast Product immediately needed to put the single out in the UK. 'California Über Alles' had intensity but also a kind of provocative playfulness about it, so much so it felt like somebody had cheekily put out a Fast Product record without asking us.

Last's intervention in the corporate music industry extended to establishing a music publishing wing of the Fast Product organisation, Sound Diagrams, to handle the publishing rights of both sides of the Scars single. Sound Diagrams also had a publishing interest in the Dead Kennedys single, and publishing would prove to be a cornerstone of Last's future business activities. His suggestion that Fast groups should sign to major labels for financial advances and subvert the mainstream from within also got Last a foothold in the major-label music industry. He produced the Mekons' album at Virgin's residential Manor studio and developed strong bonds with Virgin Records' hierarchy. The support he would build from within the label would prove invaluable throughout his management of the Human League.

After the Human League supported Iggy Pop on his European tour, they entered the studio to record their first single for Virgin, but immediately learned the reality of working with a big label (and the realities of promised creative freedom). Virgin demanded a more commercial sound using female backing vocals and conventional disco instrumentation in addition to their synthesisers, which the group reluctantly agreed to. Martyn Ware insisted the band used a pseudonym for the single 'I Don't Depend on You', which came out under the name the Men. Throughout this sorry episode Last's canny managerial nous placated both label and artist, with the end result being a failed attempt at a hit by Virgin, and a positive creative outcome for the group as they were now allowed to record their debut album in their original style without interference from Virgin.

MARTYN WARE: When we signed to Virgin we were thinking we wouldn't compromise our electronic, experimental approach, but in spite of the positive media reaction to our Fast Product singles we had to compromise with Virgin with 'I Don't Depend on You'.

SIMON BEST: The first Human League tour of Europe with Iggy Pop was fantastic. Phil was an Iggy fan and they shared a similar range and some aspects of phrasing. If you close your eyes listening to 'Nightclubbing' you can imagine Phil singing it.

While Gang of Four, the Human League and the Mekons all recorded their debut albums for major labels, Fast Product launched a new concept with new groups. *Earcom* was described by Fast as 'a comic for the ears', and three releases constituted the *Earcom* series: FAST 9a, 9b, 9c. These releases were arguably the high-water mark of Fast's high-concept packaging and featured additional content, heavy with slogans. It could equally be argued that some of the musical content fell below the previous Fast standard in terms of both provocation and aural stimulation.

Earcom 1 (FAST 9a) was a 12-inch package that featured Fast friends Simon Bloomfield and Tim Pierce doing an electronic version of the Rezillos' '(My Baby Does) Good Sculptures'; the Blank Students' two songs felt like 2.3 part 2; Graph (2) were an interesting low-fidelity noise from Sheffield (best known for featuring future Human League member Ian Burden), and their track 'Drowning' was good enough to warrant further investigation.

The Prats epitomised the provocation often mentioned by Bob Last. They were from Oxgangs in Edinburgh and were all still at school. They were aged between twelve and fifteen, couldn't play or sing, weren't in tune, but sounded like a punk mission statement. Last believed anyone could contribute to the medium and that attitude was more important than ability; the Prats were proof of this. Their three tracks — 'Prats 2', 'Inverness' and 'Bored' — laid down a gauntlet of what constituted competence on a far greater level than anything on the label since 'Never Been in a Riot'. John Peel loved the Prats and had them in session; he also financed a single and was largely responsible for the group continuing to release records. The Prats released further material on Rough Trade and existed as a group until they left school.

The Flowers: Hilary Morrison and Andy Copland

The overall punk-inspired sounds on *Earcom 1* were most clearly highlighted by the long-awaited recording debut of Hilary Morrison's group, the Flowers. Both of their tracks, 'Criminal Waste' and 'After Dark', captured Morrison's exciting sound and vision — lyrically and musically they were obviously Fast. All this augered well for the new breed of artists that hatched through Keir Street (the Flowers, Thursdays, Fire Engines). That none of this trio of new groups were contractually signed to Fast Product was the antithesis of normal industry practice; however, they were clearly developed within the Fast ideas hotbed.

The packaging for *Earcom 1* featured visual references to *The Quality of Life* and *SeXex*, and Bob Last's Fast packaging style developed further. A two-colour poster was included in the package as was a micron-cut disc, *Flesh*, the technical details of which were listed on the artwork (it was also credited on the back cover as an 'extra track': 'Flesh' by the Products). The slogans were an important part of the art concept: 'something nice for you to buy', 'dare to struggle, dare to win', 'difficult fun', 'mutant pop'. It was ever apparent that the conceptual weight accorded to the packaging and slogans was of equal importance to the music released by the artists (if not more so).

BOB LAST: Being very meta, I referenced the 'Being Boiled' salmon-pink Pantone colour again when we released *Earcom 1*, which contained an unplayable 7-inch cardboard disc (*Flesh*). Fast Product was saying it was OK to have strongly held views and still have fun.

Earcom 2: Contradiction (FAST 9b) was a six-song 12-inch release (playing at 45rpm) that featured three groups who contributed two songs each. Basczax were a Teesside-based group who had supported Gang of Four. They incorporated saxophone and synthesisers in their guitar-based sound, but it was all rather pedestrian. The real interest in *Earcom 2* centred around Keir Street kids Thursdays and Factory luminaries, Joy Division.

MICHAEL BARCLAY: Bob Last asked Thursdays to do *Earcom 2* and to record our cover version, 'Dock of the Bay'. Bob galvanised Thursdays and we did concerted work on the group for a few months, but to be honest, I have no idea what happened to the band after that initial impetus.

The artwork for *Earcom 2* was possibly Bob's best work for Fast Product. The cover featured a rock climber with guiding ropes and slings on a sea cliff, viewed from above with the sea below. The inner sleeve featured a photo of a woman Sandinista guerrilla who cradled an assault rifle. Undoubtedly the major coup on *Earcom 2* was two previously unreleased tracks by Joy Division, who at that point were by far the most critically and commercially successful group in the independent sector. Factory had released *Unknown Pleasures* in June and the two Joy Division tracks donated to *Earcom 2*, 'Auto-suggestion' and 'From Safety to Where?', had been left over from the *Unknown Pleasures* recording sessions with Martin Hannett. Obtaining these tracks proved to be another astute business strategy by Bob Last, who had known Joy Division and their manager Rob Gretton from when the band were known as Warsaw and supported the Rezillos.

BOB LAST: From the very earliest days of Fast Product there was an ongoing relationship with the guys in Joy Division and their manager Rob Gretton. It was a chaotic time for me — one minute I was the Rezillos' roadie and the next minute I was managing them. Rezillos guitarist Jo Callis and me were huge fans of Warsaw, the precursor of Joy Division, and we would give them support slots whenever we could. Apparently at one of those support gigs Peter Hook alleges I dragged some skinhead backstage by the scruff of his neck and made him apologise to Peter Hook for making menacing advances. I don't remember that, but we'd always given Warsaw support gigs, and I loved Warsaw, and we had discussions about releasing them. I can remember a particular occasion when they had changed their name to Joy Division where some of the group and Rob Gretton came up to the Fast flat in Edinburgh to have a big discussion about the group being involved with Fast Product.

HILARY MORRISON: Fast Product didn't sign Joy Division because I turned them down. I knew what the name meant, and I was uncomfortable. Ian Curtis then came up to visit us at Fast. He was a lovely guy, he liked cats, it was all fine. So they did something later on for *Earcom 2* after they were on Factory and their album had been released, but you know, I had reservations.

BOB LAST: In the end I didn't release those early tracks because I was uncomfortable with the name Joy Division. The name Joy Division is a reference to the corps of prostitutes the Nazis created for their military and although I didn't ever think that they had any Nazi sympathies and were playing with iconography, the same way we did, being provocative, in the end I was uncomfortable with that. For whatever reason it was a bit of playfulness that I wasn't comfortable with, but we always loved their music and I loved what they did, so we always maintained a connection with Joy Division and Factory.

IAN CURTIS: Bob Last wanted Joy Division to do a single for Fast Product early on, but that didn't happen and Factory signed us. Fast was becoming busy with the Gang of Four and the Human League, so it never happened with Joy Division. After we did *Unknown Pleasures* we had a few tracks left over from the album sessions, and Bob mentioned his idea for *Earcom*, so we agreed to give Fast two tracks.

PETER HOOK: I'd heard the first *Earcom* and thought it was great, so when Bob Last asked if Joy Division would be interested in including a couple of songs on *Earcom 2* I was interested, and we gave Fast Product 'Auto-suggestion' and 'From Safety to Where?'. I first became aware of Bob when our pre-Joy Division group Warsaw supported the Rezillos. I was a fan of all the groups Bob signed to Fast Product, I liked the fact that both Bob and Fast Product were open and diverse. We were particularly impressed by the Gang of Four single on Fast, so much so that Joy Division chose to record in the studio that the Gang of Four used. The idea that we could give these tracks to Fast Product impressed us. Joy Division liked the idea we could release tracks on other labels — we also did a single on French label Sordide Sentimental.

BOB LAST: We always had that ongoing relationship with Joy Division, so that's how it arose that they gave me the tracks for *Earcom 2*, because I asked them, and you don't get something if you don't ask for it. When Tony Wilson started setting up Factory, he called me up many times to ask about, 'Well, how do you do this?' There are some things about what he did that come from a similar place to what we were doing. Tony Wilson himself publicly recognised that Fast Product was an influence on the creation of Factory. Much of what Tony did, he did because it arose from similar cultural roots, experiences, reading and knowledge as I'd had, so I'm not going to claim that Factory took these ideas from Fast Product. Much of what Factory did emerged in parallel, but again I think the fact that Fast Product had already stood up and done this stuff was obviously something of an inspiration in creating this space where Tony thought Factory could do it too.

Factory followed the socialist profit-split principles engineered by Rough Trade and Mute, whereby artist and label received 50 per cent each of profits once all recording and manufacturing expenditure accrued by the label had been recouped. When an artist sells as many copies of an album as Joy Division did with *Unknown Pleasures*, a considerable amount of income flows to both label and group.

BOB LAST: Tony Wilson was tapping into the same intellectual and cultural flows that I was in terms of the theory and the books he'd read and so forth. According to Tony, Fast Product influenced Factory a lot, and we'd talk often. Obviously we'd both read Marcuse and Foucault and Althusser, and he'd read a little less Mao Zedong than I had. I read *The Military Thoughts of Mao Zedong* line by line more than once. Tony saw himself more explicitly as a situationist, but yes, I think we were an influence on Factory in that sense of making Tony think he could do it. Joy Division were an amazing band, they were very much about looking into the darkness. If 'California Über Alles' was the final Fast Product release, I could have given Factory the catalogue number FAST 13 — that was how I saw Factory, that's my view. I just never told them that they had a catalogue number.

Earcom 3 (FAST 9c) deviated from previous *Earcom* releases in that it consisted of two 7-inch singles. It featured five artists that further highlighted Fast's international connections. Side one featured Noh Mercy (USA); side two featured Stupid Babies and From Chorley (UK); side three had Deutsch Amerikanische Freundschaft aka DAF (from what was then West Germany); and side four had the Middle Class (USA). Across the five artists the quality was variable. The pre-teenage Stupid Babies (who featured Adamski, a future number 1 single artist) bemoaned their babysitters on the titular track. Noh Mercy were genuinely exciting and underrated — two women from San Francisco that made a primitive noise allied with lyrics that railed against political correctness. Their best track, 'Caucasian Guilt', is classic Fast provocation. From Chorley had an unadventurous name that belied their lo-fi sonics that perhaps owed something to Cabaret Voltaire. That DAF were an important group was obvious from the first bars of 'Ich und die Wirklichkeit'. It was no surprise that the group would go on to have a successful career of electronic agitation at a big independent (Mute) then major (Virgin). The Middle Class were probably the most recognisably traditional punk sound released on Fast Product. Their contribution, 'Out of Vogue', is widely regarded as the first US hardcore punk record, which made them appear more akin to the Dead Kennedys' variant of punk.

The artwork for *Earcom 3* featured found advertisement art similar to that featured in *The Quality of Life* (FAST 3) and *SeXex* (FAST 6), with further information that related to 'the forthcoming Fast Product film'. This alluded to a film called *Always Something There to Remind Me*, the tag line to which promised 'Sex, Violence, Romance, Action, Cash, & History'. It was clear the *Earcom* releases were more about provocation and actions. Allusions to a Fast film were in tune with the concept of *SeXex* being viewed as an advertising campaign for a product that didn't yet exist. Fast did however produce a postcard for *Always Something There to Remind Me*, which utilised a Hilary Morrison photograph of James Oliva walking past two big billboards at Fountainbridge. The billboards were cut out and a photograph of Oliva's open wallet was juxtaposed with the image of him walking.

SIMON BEST: The *Earcom* series compilations on Fast released tracks by artists as diverse as the Prats, who were a bunch of schoolkids from a tough Edinburgh neighbourhood called Oxgangs, on *Earcom 1*, through to unreleased tracks by Joy Division on *Earcom 2* and Krautpunk from DAF on *Earcom 3*.

MICHAEL BARCLAY: Thursdays' cover of 'Dock of the Bay' along with one of our own compositions, 'Perfections', featured on *Earcom 2*. The fact that Joy Division also featured on *Earcom 2* meant there were huge sales of that record. This resulted in Thursdays receiving offers for lots of gigs. We played the art college and also supported the Fall at Valentino's, which was a difficult evening, trying to get a decent soundcheck and getting reluctant responses from Mark E. Smith, allied with a lack of communication amongst ourselves. By that stage, I was at art school and I was more into that. Paul was talking about his own ideas and we were trying to have an emotional impact on people but not necessarily make people feel comfortable. Thursdays was my creative stint, but I didn't have the technique or maybe the commitment to keep going with it.

The collectivist approach at Fast Product, whereby Last, Morrison, Oliva and the musicians and team would all contribute and work on all aspects of releases, was highlighted with the *Earcom 3* release. The manufacturers were late getting the vinyl and double 7-inch gatefold packaging to Fast. This resulted in all hands to the pump, trying to package the vinyl into the sleeve, box the product, then get the stock to the courier by 11 p.m. to ensure it was at retail in time for the release date. They missed the 11 p.m. deadline, so it was decided to hire a van and load the stock. James Oliva and Davy Henderson journeyed down to London and stopped off at retail sites and distribution points en route to London and their final distribution destination, Rough Trade.

Edinburgh's first punk-pop stars from the period, the Rezillos, split up with a final gig at the Glasgow Apollo on 23 December 1978. Their meteoric rise since they released their debut single, 'I Can't Stand My Baby', on the independent Sensible label in August 1977 had taken them to a major deal with Seymour Stein's Sire label in New York (with whom they recorded their only album). They toured regularly and had a hit single, appeared on *Top of the Pops* and *The Old Grey Whistle Test*, then fell apart in time-honoured fashion − all in the fifteen-month period from the release of their debut single. Bob Last had witnessed the Rezillos' rise and fall in his capacity as their roadie, then manager; he learned his music industry chops along the way (in cahoots with Rezillos guitarist and songwriter Jo Callis). The relationship between Bob Last and Jo Callis provided the future lodestar for Last's infiltration of the mainstream.

JO CALLIS: Everything Bob had created since moving on from the Rezillos with Fast Product was exciting, with Edinburgh groups like the Scars and Fire Engines developing under his wing. The DIY movement had really taken off, that was happening everywhere all across the country. Everyone was doing their own fanzines and sitting up folding the paper, folding 7-inch single sleeves together, making their own badges and things like that. But I think the aim was still to get a cover article in the *NME* and get signed to a major label. Obviously that was beneficial for both artists and managers, having the funding that a major label can provide.

Rough Trade had been set up by Geoff Travis on the same principles as a kibbutz (Travis had worked on one in his younger years) after he had travelled in America (during which time he had bought a substantial number of albums). On his return to London, he shipped the vinyl home and set up a record shop, Rough Trade, in Ladbroke Grove in west London in 1976. The shop quickly became a magnet for record buyers, particularly those that bought albums by artists outwith the mainstream. The large Jamaican population in west London bought 12-inch dub plates from Rough Trade and once the first punk singles appeared the shop was also frequented by punks. The culture clash of punks, Rastas and heads was a complementary mix and Rough Trade went from strength to strength as a record retailer, community hub and information centre. The expansion from retailer to record label was natural and Rough Trade Records released their first single in 1977, a distorted electronic punk track by French group Métal Urbain. The single, 'Paris Maquis', had the catalogue number RT001 and made an immediate impact on John Peel and the music papers. This was followed by singles by reggae artist Augustus Pablo, Sheffield distorted noise overlords Cabaret Voltaire, and the punk sound of Ulster, Stiff Little Fingers (who went on to give Rough Trade a number 14 hit in the album charts with their debut).

Rough Trade followed their successes in retail and as a record label by becoming a record distributor in 1978, which effectively meant they bought singles from independent labels and distributed them to independent retailers. As documented earlier, Hilary Morrison attempted to get Rough Trade to distribute FAST 1 only to be told 'Never Been in a Riot' was too bad to release. There were probably other tensions at play; Rough Trade's collectivist approach was poles apart from Fast Product's interest in branding, marketing and capitalism as oppositional forces. However, after the Mekons received their single of the week in the *NME* and Peel plays, Rough Trade got on board and started to distribute Fast Product releases. Bob Last recognised there was common ground between himself and Geoff Travis, and equally saw the important part Rough Trade could play in distributing Fast (although he acknowledged their relationship was an uneasy one). Richard Scott became the driving force at Rough Trade Distribution and eventually succeeded in setting up a co-operative distribution network which became known as the Cartel, made up of a collection of regional independent record retailers. The idea was to pool resources from independents throughout the UK including Probe (Liverpool), Nine Mile (Leamington Spa), Revolver (Bristol), Backs (Norwich), Red Rhino (York) and Rough Trade (London).

GEOFF TRAVIS: What Hilary and Bob were doing at Fast Product was exactly the kind of thing that we wanted to encourage. It was such a fertile time. The emergence of the distribution network came about because we started getting records into the shop that other people didn't have. So we'd get these records, like Television's first single, 'Little Johnny Jewel', or Alex Chilton's 'Bangkok' single on Terry Ork's label, or the first Pere Ubu singles which came out of Cleveland. We'd write letters to the address on the single, and we'd have to address it to Crocus Behemoth, which would turn out to be David Thomas, and we would buy these records and send postal orders and pay for them up front, and they would send the records. People knew that we had these records, and so shops started getting in touch — Geoff at Probe in Liverpool, Lloyd at Revolver, Tony K at Red Rhino, Pete Stennett at Small Wonder — because they were interested in the same kind of music that we were. So in a way, the people that were interested in the new music, the people who were interested in the Velvet Underground bootleg EP, or an Iggy Pop single, 'I Got a Right', they all wanted to have these same records for their shops because they loved them, and they knew that their clientele would be interested. So that was a spark that made us think about starting a national distribution network and we also knew that if we could build a distribution network that worked, then we could have a parallel system to the major labels, and it would mean that bands wouldn't have to sign to the majors. We were disappointed that the Clash and the Pistols signed to major labels, we just couldn't really see the point of it. That generation, Bernie Rhodes and Malcolm McLaren, were older than us and they really had a different mentality. They weren't interested in building any system to help people. They were interested in becoming interventionist stars in their own right. This was a vehicle for them, more than it was a vehicle for the groups. They were old-fashioned carny showmen from a different kind of tradition, whereas we were a bunch of socialists that wanted to change the world in our own way.

Fast accepted an offer to join the Cartel as its most northerly member, primarily handling distribution in Scotland, which complemented Bob Last's business agenda of encouraging Fast Product groups to sign to major labels. While Last had no interest in purely being a distributor, being part of the Cartel did allow Fast Product (and other comparable independents) to operate in the market at the level below major labels, which in turn allowed more interesting strategic interventions. Bob Last was aware the independents were indeed dependents and that they always required capital investment and borrowing to fund creativity and marketing. Flowers drummer Simon Best became part of the Fast distribution wing.

SIMON BEST: Bob Last and I had been best friends at my school, which he joined at age fourteen. We were both interested in cultural politics and I introduced Bob to the early albums of Frank Zappa and the Mothers which challenged the US status quo and consumerism. When punk came along in 1977, we recognised that it was another wave of challenge, initially straight from the mouths of kids from all backgrounds, and we wanted to make sure that as many of them as possible had a voice. However, as I got more involved in the music business in the late seventies and early eighties, I found I was naturally talented at some aspects and increasingly interested in the industry aspect, which was becoming disrupted by independent start-up companies like Fast Product.

SANDY MCLEAN: When I first arrived in Scotland, in Glasgow, in October '77 I didn't know anything about Scottish music. I knew a lot about British punk rock, 'cause I was really into that when I lived in Canada and I used to read a lot of music papers and had been down to New York a couple of times and bought loads of records. So I knew about the Pistols and the Clash and the Stranglers. I had no idea about any Scottish bands. Within a few weeks of arriving in Scotland I got a job at Bruce's record shop in Edinburgh and it was so much fun that I really didn't want to go back to university. Bruce's was an absolute focus for the punk movement, certainly in the east coast of Scotland, Bruce just loved the music. Bruce is a big music fan and he started his indie label in '77, Zoom Records, so he already had two Valves records out by the time I arrived. I grew up with the Edinburgh scene and the east coast scene, but at the same time we used to go to a lot of Glasgow gigs as well, so I got to know a lot of people in a pretty short space of time. I'm really a huge music fan. I guess the young punk hipsters at the time were buying a lot of New York punk — they were buying things like Richard Hell, the Ramones, Mink DeVille. There was a lot of interest in the CBGBs scene as well, with groups like Television and Talking Heads who were so different and interesting. My first week in Bruce's, the Ramones did an in-store, so I went from this little geeky guy in Nova Scotia and all of a sudden being behind the counter speaking to the Ramones.

GEOFF TRAVIS: Distribution was critically important to Rough Trade, and we did devote a lot of years of our life to building that up. And of course that made all the difference to Fast Product, Factory and Mute, and to all the independent labels. It is probably our greatest achievement of that particular time, that we were able to set that up.

The importance of record shops in the story of Scottish independent labels is crucial: these were the places musicians met each other, gossiped, bitched and formed new bands. The Cartel, under the initial direction of Rough Trade, helped enable communities within which labels and artists thrived creatively. There was an audience, there was market demand, there was now a distribution network, and there was a plethora of new groups in Scotland interested in setting up their own independent record labels, inspired by the national attention received by Fast Product.

Bob Last had actively been urging Fast Product groups to sign record deals with London majors; on his advice the Mekons, the Human League and Gang of Four had signed deals and released debut albums. Gang of Four released *Entertainment* in October, the Human League released *Reproduction* in October and the Mekons released *The Quality of Mercy Is Not Strnen* in November. Last's fingerprints were all over these debut albums, especially as manager of the Human League and producer of the Mekons. It could be argued that the records made by the Mekons, the Human League, Gang of Four and Scars that were produced by Bob Last on Fast Product were these artists' defining statements.

FAST 11 — *The First Year Plan* — was a compilation of the Fast Product singles (excluding *The Dignity of Labour* and 'California Über Alles'), and was licensed by Bob Last to EMI. The album was the perfect summation of the Fast Product mission statement through 1978 to 1979. The cover art featured all the original artwork for the featured singles along with elements from FAST 3 (*The Quality of Life*) and FAST 6 (*SeXex*). The *Wild, Wild, Wild Youth* image of the child with a plastic bag over their head was accompanied by the statement: 'EMI wish to point out that it is dangerous to put a plastic bag over your head', which in some respects highlighted the subversive nature of the collision between art and commerce. Fast Product slogans adorned the EMI packaging — it was in essence a Fast album, and having the slogans incorporated into the packaging gave it the feel of a Fast greatest concepts hits as well as including the actual Fast recordings: 'Instead of Sex: SeXex', 'Fiction Romance', 'Hardcore Fun', 'Difficult Fun'. The fetishising of consumerism and advertising was completely at odds with the worthiness being dished out by Fast's contemporaries (apart from Factory). FAST 11 also featured slogans included on early press releases: 'interventions in any media', 'we're probably posers, it's just that this is our pose', 'this is a PRODUCT'.

After he sold the label's catalogue to EMI, Bob Last closed down Fast Product.

SIMON BEST: The timing of the groups signing to majors and closing down Fast Product was just a coincidence. It was a natural progression for the groups to sign major-label deals. Bob deciding to close Fast was more to do with the waning of punk as a politically and socially challenging phenomenon and increasingly becoming a self-parody.

SANDY MCLEAN: Fast Product, Bob Last and Hilary Morrison were right there at the start of the independent-label movement, hand in hand with Rough Trade. Fast Product existed before Factory and pretty much at the same time as Rough Trade. Bob put out FAST 1, 'Never Been in a Riot', very early on. He brought that into Bruce's personally — basically he would bring them in from the pressing plant, a box of twenty-five to start things off with, so we always had Fast Product releases on day one. Bob Last really was just a guy on the scene, he was very distinctive because he had his orange boiler suit, and the best punk name — Bo Blast.

ROBERT KING: Bob Last was quite a quiet person — you always knew he was thinking about things. He was very good at getting you to do things that would benefit you, help you, as an artist or as a person. He was very supportive of the Scars. In a sense releasing our Fast Product single felt like an ambition achieved and in another sense it was an anticlimax, because as soon as it was released you wanted it to suddenly be super successful and then you wanted to do another one, or maybe an album. But at the same time it was tremendously exciting to suddenly see your song on posters advertising your new single and reading reviews in the music papers where journalists were saying nothing but good things.

PETER HOOK: Tony Wilson was very much of the same ilk as Bob Last, and looked towards Fast for information regarding Factory. Nothing at Factory was really done for the money, everything was about communicating, and Tony and Bob were great friends. There was a definite link between Factory and Fast. Joy Division was lucky because we made great music and were on Factory Records, with people like Tony and Bob changing the world and making great records on great labels, Factory and Fast Product. Tony Wilson and Bob Last have an aura about them. During that period the people were bigger than the music. I'm still making music because of people like Bob Last.

GRACE FAIRLEY: The environment of the Fast Product flat in Keir Street had a jagged energy; there were ideas darting around the whole time. I think Bob was good at steering people a little bit, you know, 'Well that idea's quite a good one' — he had the ability to spot the talent in everybody. There is an authenticity about what was going on at Fast, you know, even mad things like putting out rotting orange peel in Fast packaging, that sort of thing. I remember Angus Groovy proudly wearing his orange peel and it looked great. Everything that Fast did, whether it was music or a bit of orange peel, it had an effect and people would react to it in the streets. There was kind of a glamour about it, even though it was a bit of orange peel.

BOB LAST: I stopped releasing records under the Fast Product brand, but a part of me thought that I would use Fast Product to release something else. Again I had no idea, but I never did. Many of those bands had extraordinary careers post-Fast Product but some part of me, some instinct, I knew that nothing we would do after that, in that particular context, could be as extraordinary or special. Now whether that was just a mood I got up in one morning or whether it was some more meaningful insight, I don't know, but it wasn't an accident in that sense and in particular it was already clear that we had created a relatively extraordinary set of work. Fast Product operated in a cultural underground around the world, it was one of those moments where things really do shift and at the same time you have changing cultural ideas and practices, a change in political circumstances and a change in basic social fabrics. Those moments don't happen very often — 1968 was one of those moments in different places, but 1976 to 1979 was also one of those moments.

Battle lines had been drawn with Bob Last getting into bed with the majors. The work he had done in cahoots with Rough Trade and the Cartel to set up a distribution network within the ever-growing independent sector had helped provide a platform from which labels like Factory, Mute, Zoo and future labels could continue to grow and sell substantial amounts of records. The groups that had absorbed the culture from within the Keir Street petri dish were still developing. The Flowers had announced themselves on *Earcom 1*, Thursdays had been released on *Earcom 2* before they fell apart, Fire Engines continued to hone their disciplines, and former Dirty Red and Flower, Dave Carson, formed a new group, Boots for Dancing. Plans were afoot for a post-punk, post-Fast future, as Bob Last and Hilary plotted a new future with a new label for the Keir Street kids.

BOB LAST: Fast Product exists as a body of work that was very diverse, work collectively that everyone had done, which I think is what's interesting about Fast with the passing of time. If you think of it as one body of work that collectively anybody and everybody that ever walked in the flat collectively made together, anyone who beat me up 'cause I didn't release their single, all those people were part of a collective body of work that we all did together. So somehow or other I knew that it had finished — I can't remember exactly how I knew, but it was done. We wanted to go on doing things and trying out new ideas, so rather than muddy the waters of what Fast Product had done, we invented a new brand, pop:aural.

Meanwhile, in a small studio called Emblem Sound in a small rural market town called Strathaven in South Lanarkshire, a group recorded their debut single, a record that would herald Glasgow independence and respond to Fast Product's hitherto unrivalled dominance of the Scottish post-punk landscape. The single recorded in Strathaven was the opening salvo of a self-styled movement that became known as 'The Sound of Young Scotland'. The record was 'Falling and Laughing' b/w 'Moscow', the songs were written by Edwyn Collins and James Kirk, the group was called Orange Juice, and their label was called Postcard Records, run by someone called Alan Horne.

CHAPTER 4

1980 – Parallel Lines

Orange Juice: James Kirk, David McClymont, Edwyn Collins and
Steven Daly

Fast Product had kicked Scotland into life from punk to post-punk. Their short two-year existence had created a movement in Edinburgh that was conceptually part Warholian business art, arts lab and youth club. Bob Last and Hilary Morrison had inspired a frenetic sense of purpose throughout Scotland and Fast was admired, reviled and loved in equal measure within certain quarters. The initial slew of Fast Product groups had now signed to major labels and released their debut albums as Last's insurgency within multinational commerce continued. Fast Product had released FAST 1 at the start of 1978 and completed the mission with FAST 12 in 1979. Their speedy trajectory was over.

BOB LAST: It was about being Fast, it was about being intense, and we were done.

It had largely gone unnoticed that apart from *The Quality of Life*, *SeXex* and the *Earcom* series, something associated with Fast Product called pop:aural had issued the debut single in 1979 by the Flowers, 'Confessions'/'After Dark', catalogue number POP 001.

BOB LAST: There are times when there is an occurrence of intersections of cultural and political energy, and quite often there is some entity or person who happens to be there at that intersection who helps facilitate ideas, whereby it all feeds on itself and becomes something. It felt right that Fast Product had stopped and pop:aural had started.

HILARY MORRISON: There was a vibrant scene in Edinburgh within our Keir Street community of groups. We wanted to inject little bits of glamour into it. We had seen elements of what was called punk, but we were trying to remodel our scene on our terms with photography, glamour and a distinct style. Punk with a capital P had been commodified and sold back to kids, so by starting doing our labels we got to do our own thing, which was no longer Fast Product but pop:aural.

BOB LAST: I would argue that all the work we'd done to create the Fast Product brand was about confounding expectations: this brand is not about what you expect, this brand is about giving you opportunities to think differently. We'd created a space where you could do that and actually it got a reception.

HILARY MORRISON: Fast Product had been about showing the means of production and experimenting, and pop:aural was an attempt to take it seriously and develop careers as a professional record company would do. It was like a training school: be professional and get a good lawyer, get a very good accountant, find yourself a manager. But not everyone responded to this.

BOB LAST: We were like explorers. I set up stall, said here's the attitude and it just dropped into my lap. We embroiled anyone who wanted to be involved in whatever the job was at hand, but it was very informal and I think there was a sense that just by turning up at the Keir Street flat you were part of Fast and you were involved.

HILARY MORRISON: I used to deal with the pile of tapes that came into Fast Product and pop:aural. We were sent so many after the first few Fast records. We'd be sitting listening to them on this old reel-to-reel, or little cassettes, trying to find people for future releases and so on. pop:aural was a natural follow-on from *Earcom*, which was a concept I really liked, the idea being an aural music magazine where you got a taster of different things. *Earcom* were difficult and time-consuming projects to put together, having to phone up artists in Germany, like DAF, and Noh Mercy in California.

BOB LAST: I believed that changing our mind was important, and with pop:aural the artists dropped into my lap. We had a global network through Fast Product, so it was interesting how news of pop:aural spread out incredibly quickly.

As news of Fast Product's transmogrification into pop:aural filtered through the fanzine circuit and local scene, the first voices of discontent started to be heard. The fact that Hilary was Bob's girlfriend seemed to annoy some bands.

BOB LAST: Accusations of nepotism regarding the Flowers being signed to pop:aural were bizarre, and actually quite disorientating. I got jumped a couple of times — we assumed by groups who were disgruntled because we didn't sign them.

HILARY MORRISON: Things changed, we all got a little bit tougher, and more girls started to get involved in bands. We were trying out new stuff and standing up and saying like it or lump it, and that was good. There were a lot of things going on, some of which was young men who were slightly insecure, though they probably grew up to be charming men with broad-minded views. At that period they seemed to like challenging women, but didn't like women who challenged them.

BOB LAST: It was a male-dominated world. You had people like the Delta 5 and Au Pairs among others that were battling that same perception, but that's what the dynamic probably looked and felt like. To the extent that Fast Product and pop:aural was serious and ideological and felt it was something we had to fight, it wasn't something that we felt comfortable with; there was never any question of us taking affirmative action of any kind, because we were so much about a visceral response. But at the same time the Slits in particular were an absolutely crucial part of giving us permission to do what we did, and giving all those boys in those Fast Product bands permission to do what they did.

pop:aural was formulating a new approach and tried to establish strategies that differentiated it from Fast Product. They built a new roster of groups to join the Flowers, the first of which was Dave Carson's new group, Boots for Dancing. Bob Last restructured his independent-label imprint. At the same time he manoeuvred and negotiated his way through the boardroom politics of the major-label sector.

The Flowers: Fraser Sutherland

FRASER SUTHERLAND: It was Dave Carson who introduced me to Hilary, when Flowers were looking for a new bass player to join her, Andy Copland and Simon Best. Dave had been one of the original members, along with Russell Burn, and was at that time working at Virgin Records and formulating his new group, Boots for Dancing. I first met Bob following my Flowers audition. This would have been after the Gang of Four and Human League singles came out, when Davy, Rab etc. were hanging out at Keir Street. Flowers found a rehearsal space which we shared with the Associates, then started doing gigs fairly quickly, mostly in England with Human League and Mekons, before doing a few of our own shows in Scotland. We would often use the Mekons' squat in Leeds as a base when gigging in England — I think Scars did the same initially. There was a good spirit of camaraderie, not just among the Fast bands. Fees for gigs were small, and we were often out of pocket, even with only our travel to cover, so a lot of bands relied on reciprocal hospitality. The first Flowers single for pop:aural was recorded at Cargo in Rochdale, where many of the Fast releases had been recorded, and Bob had got to know the owner/engineer John Brierley well. We each had recording contracts with the label (which my father had to sign as I was underage), and there was a clause which stipulated that all recordings would be produced by Bob Last, so yes he was certainly actively involved. Bob I think had a clear idea, conceptually, of what he was trying to do differently with pop:aural, which was consciously crafted, subversive pop music hewn from raw talent, whereas the Fast releases had a more visceral energy. I remember a long time being spent in the control room, after the tracks had been recorded, where Bob would attempt to articulate his ideas in a way that the engineer could technically translate, but I don't think any of us were very happy with the outcome. The single version of 'After Dark' sounds quite lumpen to me in comparison to the one on *Earcom 1*. The Peel session was much more enjoyable to do, with songs recorded and mixed quickly, sounding much fresher as a result. No one was thinking too hard.

DAVE CARSON: One of the epicentres of the punk scene in Edinburgh was the Tap o' Lauriston bar near the art college. After the Dirty Reds and the Flowers, I had been working on some more extreme music with some friends from Glenrothes, Paul Reekie and Douglas Barrie, who had been in Thursdays. Our main influences were Throbbing Gristle and Cabaret Voltaire. We ended up doing an improvised fifteen-minute version of a song called 'Boots for Dancing', and a tape of it made its way to Hilary and Bob, who phoned me and asked if I'd be interested in recording a disco 12-inch-single version of the song. I took over vocal duties and we called the group Boots for Dancing, which was actually the name of one of Paul Reekie's poems, and recorded the song for Bob's new label, pop:aural. My understanding of the change from Fast Product to pop:aural is that Fast Product was documenting whereas pop:aural was trying to manipulate the multimedia outlets.

FRASER SUTHERLAND: The Flowers all came from different backgrounds, with different tastes that intersected in places, and never had that strong bond that other bands had, such as Fire Engines for instance. I think that intersection made Flowers quite interesting musically, in that we all had different ideas about how things should sound, and sometimes that fused well in the material, I think, but perhaps there wasn't a strong enough identity for it to endure.

Fast Product had established a monopoly within the post-punk landscape of Scotland, something Last expected pop:aural to continue to do unchallenged. However, something was brewing on the west coast. Glasgow readied itself for an assault on the independent crown as a clutch of punk-imbued young pretenders got ready to take on Bob Last. Postcard Records was the self-styled 'last of the punk independents'. It established itself in 1979 and recorded its first release, 'Falling and Laughing', in a country and western studio in Strathaven called Emblem Sound. The single was written and sung by Edwyn Collins and his group, Orange Juice. Postcard's 'Bob Last' figure was a young man with plenty to say for himself and for Orange Juice, someone who was a true believer, someone who was ready to take on the world as a punk version of Andrew Loog Oldham: Alan Horne.

JAMES KING: The first time I met Alan Horne he was hanging about Bruce's record store in Glasgow during the punk period. He'd hang about the shops not speaking to anyone until the stores were closing and he'd be asked to leave. You'd also see people like Jill and Rose from Strawberry Switchblade, Edwyn Collins, all hanging out in these record shops around St Vincent Street and Renfield Street, so there was a scene where you'd hang around record shops forming bands. I used to go to record stores six days a week.

JILL BRYSON: I think I first met Alan Horne and Edwyn Collins at a Josef K gig in the Mars Bar, when Josef K were still called TV Art and Orange Juice were called the Nu Sonics. Alan was really interesting, different and had real drive.

EDWYN COLLINS: The first time I met Alan, which was when Bowie played the Glasgow Apollo in 1978, I had on a pair of Levis, motorbike boots and a plaid shirt. The very first words Alan said to me were, 'Look at that fucking lanky wimp, you're John-Boy Walton.'

BRIAN SUPERSTAR: I met Alan Horne at uni, though we were both from Saltcoats in Ayrshire. I shared a few flats with Alan, ending up at 185 West Princes Street with Alan and Krysia, who did artwork on some of the Postcard artwork.

As in Edinburgh, record shops were the central meeting places for people inspired by punk. They were spaces of fermentation where new friends and enemies were made, and new groups were formed.

JAMES KING: In Glasgow you had three main record shops: Graffiti, Bruce's and Listen, and from around Jan 1977 people started congregating around these record stores. Mostly I'd hang around Bruce's, and people hanging around record shops is largely how people got to form bands. Graffiti started stocking *Punk* magazine, a US fanzine that I used to have to buy mail order from Compendium bookstore in London. Fanzines then started in Glasgow: *Ripped and Torn*, *Trash 77*, among others. People who went on to play in bands worked in the record shops: Steven Daly (Fun 4/ Orange Juice); Big John (the Exploited); Brian Superstar (the Pastels) and Micky Rooney (the Primevals) − these guys were very aware of what was happening in the punk scene worldwide.

BRIAN SUPERSTAR: Steven Daly and I both worked in Listen record shop, so we were friends. It was probably the main record shop street and the main hangout.

STEPHEN PASTEL: I was a bit of a dreamer, really naive, quite abstract. I was trying to put a group together but it wasn't clicking. I was thinking how to go from A to B and decided that Brian Taylor [Superstar] might be a good option as a collaborator. Why, I'm not quite sure − I'd read about him in a fanzine and slightly knew him from record shops.

The punk cognoscenti spent time in the record shops as they tracked down old records and tuned in to new releases − singles and fanzines were still very much the currency of the post-punk atmosphere. There were some pubs like the Mars Bar that would put on punk groups and sometimes the bandstand at Custom

House Quay allowed punk groups to play on afternoons at the weekend.

ALAN HORNE: In 1977 we *were* the Glasgow scene, there were about thirty people who were interested and wanted a scene.

ROSE MCDOWELL: It wasn't until punk and seeing loads of bands playing at the Glasgow Apollo like the Ramones that I felt if they could do it then so could I.

ROBERT HODGENS: I was really interested in punk, but the only band I saw was the Damned, because they supported one of my favourite groups, T. Rex.

KEN MCCLUSKEY: There weren't really any big punk bands from Glasgow, though there was a punk scene. However, it soon became very traditional and didn't like anything that challenged the orthodoxy. I saw Suicide supporting the Clash at the Glasgow Apollo, and Alan Vega was hitting himself with his mic and throwing himself to the ground, all to a hail of audience boos. They were bottled off because they sounded different and didn't have guitars.

JILL BRYSON: Glasgow in 1976 was an austere place, but when punk happened a small scene started quickly. We'd get a coach out to the Silver Thread in Paisley where a lot of punk bands played, and because you knew everyone in the audience it was a small scene. The city fathers banned punk for some reason — I think they considered it antisocial and aggressive, which was rubbish. Most of the people involved in the Glasgow punk scene felt that it was over by 1978.

ROSE MCDOWELL: Within Glasgow there were so few punks that you knew everybody. It was hard not to know somebody who was a punk because they gathered in the same record shops, the same places. The punks had to stay together, which might have seemed 'cliquey', but that's what movements are like. You hook up with people who are like-minded and inspire each other, which is good because if you were doing all that on your own it would be a very lonely place to be, whether you're a loner or not.

Glasgow District Council had banned the Sex Pistols' Anarchy in the UK tour from the Glasgow Apollo on 15 December 1976. The mainstream media feeding frenzy that followed the Pistols and the punk trajectory continued through 1977, when the city fathers decided they should attend a punk concert to find out what the furore was all about. The 22 June concert at Glasgow City Hall by the Stranglers ended in stage invasions and confrontations with the stewards as they tried to restore order, which was enough for the council to decide that punk concerts should be banned in Glasgow.

The Glasgow punk gig vacuum was filled by the Silver Thread Hotel, then the Bungalow Bar, both in Paisley. Glasgow punk group Johnny and the Self Abusers had created enough of a stir to get themselves a record deal. Chiswick Records released their debut single, 'Saints and Sinners', in November 1977. But in an exemplary punk statement, Johnny and the Self Abusers split up on the same day they released their debut single. The Glasgow punks that provoked the most extreme reactions were Rev Volting and the Backstabbers and the Nu Sonics. The Backstabbers featured James King (or Jimmy Loser as he was known at that time) on guitar, while the core of the Nu Sonics were three school friends from a leafy suburb of Glasgow, Bearsden: Steven Daly on vocals, James Kirk on lead guitar and Edwyn Collins on guitar. (Edwyn wrote the majority of the material and James supplied the rest.)

STEPHEN PASTEL: I grew up in Bearsden and always had a bit of a love and hate relationship with it. I stayed near Kilmardinny

Loch which could be beautiful on a summer's night. I missed a large chunk of first year at school due to illness and never quite managed to pick it back up, eventually becoming a bit of a classic underachiever. Music became my thing from about age fifteen, sixteen, and I was aware of James and Steven, and Edwyn too. I thought they all looked so cool. I eventually got on to smiling terms with James but they were all at least a couple of years older than me. They were mysterious.

Edwyn, Steven and James had all been present on 7 May 1977 at the White Riot concert in Edinburgh and were inspired by Subway Sect in particular. The Nu Sonics played one of their final gigs at Satellite City when they supported reggae group Steel Pulse. Somewhere in the crowd that night was a person who would loom large in their lives in the near future, Alan Horne.

ALAN HORNE: When I first saw the Nu Sonics and they opened their set with 'We're Gonna Have a Real Good Time Together' by the Velvets, I thought it would be important to make a record with this band.

EDWYN COLLINS: The Nu Sonics played in the original Silver Thread Hotel in Paisley. The first time we played was around the end of 1977. We were the only proper punk group, all the rest were old session men who had been playing for years. Nu Sonics supported Steel Pulse when Steven had only been playing drums for about four weeks and it was the first time that I had been singing and playing guitar.

In the meantime, a meeting between two young men at design college in Glasgow was to prove the pivot that changed the Nu Sonics into something completely fresh and new.

EDWYN COLLINS: The Nu Sonics used to listen to the Buzzcocks and Subway Sect. I met David McClymont at the Glasgow College of Building and Printing where I was studying on an illustration course. We had renamed ourselves Orange Juice. I was particularly influenced by the Beatles and early Lennon solo material.

David McClymont left the west coast village of Girvan when he was sixteen and moved to Glasgow to study graphic design. As a teenager he had been a fan of Bowie and glam rock before he moved on to Krautrock and prog rock. He introduced himself to Edwyn Collins when he saw him at college carrying an amplifier, guitar and the first Subway Sect single. The pair hit it off and within a couple of hours Collins asked McClymont if he wanted to join his band as a bass player, something he agreed to with gusto. David McClymont's meeting with Edwyn Collins provided the final element in the Nu Sonics' transmogrification into Orange Juice, with Edwyn now on lead vocals, James on lead guitar and Steven on drums. David underwent a crash course learning bass guitar under Edwyn's tutelage, though Steven would archly comment that Edwyn thought David had the right face for the part. McClymont felt Daly was suspicious of him as he hadn't fought the punk wars or attended the year-zero White Riot concert in Edinburgh. McClymont preferred Todd Rundgren and Steve Hillage. As the Nu Sonics morphed into Orange Juice, Alan Horne became to all intents and purposes the de facto manager of Orange Juice.

ALAN HORNE: When they told me they'd changed the name to Orange Juice, I just went, 'Yesss, that's wild.' It was such a contrary and strange name, so ahead of everything else at the time. They were always fighting and bickering, but I knew that what they were doing was revolutionary and I don't mean that lightly. They were so ahead of what was coming out of London at that time in 1978.

The only group at that time who made me remotely jealous was the Pop Group with that record they made, 'Beyond Good and Evil'.

No major punk group had broken big from Glasgow. Johnny and the Self Abusers were the only group to release a record and had now regrouped as Simple Minds. The Backstabbers reassembled as Fun 4 and now featured Steven Daly on drums (who had temporarily left Orange Juice). Steven was involved in the recording and setting up of a label (NMC) to release the Fun 4 single, 'Singing in the Showers', which was released in 1979. The group had recorded the single at Emblem Sounds in Strathaven.

JAMES KING: The Fun 4 never rehearsed other than in my bedroom – this was prior to playing in front of 900 people at the Satellite City. So we had no professional rehearsals. It wasn't like London where Bernie Rhodes had Rehearsal Rehearsals for the Clash and Subway Sect to rehearse. Eventually we found a place in Glasgow to rehearse, the Mad Buyer, the owners of which used to laugh at us because we were punk. However, they weren't laughing very long because punk soon took over in terms of popularity. I actually got the idea to put a record out when I met Edwyn Collins crossing St Vincent Street. Edwyn told me Steven Daly had left his group and was looking to start a label, so he put me in touch with Steven with a view to putting out a single by my band, the Fun 4. Steven was into groups like Subway Sect and ATV, which were the kind of things I liked along with the Stooges. Fun 4 put out the 'Singing in the Showers' single, which was really meant as a one-off release, after which our vocalist Rev left the band and we became the Fun 3. I took over on vocals and guitar, with Colin on bass and Steven on drums, and as the Fun 3 we recorded more songs at Emblem Sound studio – in fact Alan Horne drove us out to Strathaven. Steven took these recordings down to London to play to labels, but didn't get much interest. He then took the tapes to Fast Product and Bob Last said he'd put a single out if we got our original singer Rev back in the band, which I declined.

Steven Daly not only managed to co-ordinate the Fun 4 single, but also initiated another label, Absolute Records. He discovered an Edinburgh group called TV Art that he wanted to release a single by. Steven had one condition before he signed the group — they had to change their name, which they did, to Josef K. They recorded their single, 'Chance Meeting', which Steven released on his Absolute label in late 1979, to some acclaim.

Orange Juice were both impressed and inspired by Steven's ability to get singles by Fun 4 and Josef K recorded and released on his own labels, and decided to use the same studio in Strathaven and record a track for possible release as a debut Orange Juice single. The other members of Orange Juice had got to know Steven's new friend Malcolm Ross (who played guitar with Josef K) as both groups had organised and played gigs together in Edinburgh and Glasgow. When Alan Horne came in as Orange Juice manager, Steven left the group to drum with Fun 4. However, he came back into the fold to drum when Malcolm joined Orange Juice in Strathaven (along with Alan Horne) to help them produce their single. They'd decided this would be an Edwyn composition, 'Falling and Laughing', with an instrumental written by James on the B-side, 'Moscow', and its dub, 'Moscow Olympics' (featuring 'vocals' by Alan Wild, as Horne styled himself in homage to his short-lived group with Brian Superstar, Oscar Wild). Orange Juice sent tapes of their single to major labels but received zero interest, while another tape was sent to Zoo Records. Alan Horne suggested they set up a label to release the Orange Juice single, and after Horne borrowed money from his parents and Collins and McClymont pooled their savings, they set up a label. They decided to call the label Postcard Records.

Alan Horne and Edwyn Collins

STEVEN DALY: Alan Horne was sufficiently enthused to enter into a relationship with Orange Juice, first as manager, then as proprietor of Postcard Records.

EDWYN COLLINS: Along with Alan Horne, we decided to set up Postcard Records with Orange Juice and release 'Falling and Laughing'.

ALAN HORNE: Postcard Records is the only punk rock label, we're not new wave. The whole music business is pathetic and washed up, and Postcard is going to do a few nice things before it goes under, but we're going to do it with integrity.

Paddy's Market was situated in an alley near the Clyde and sold anything, literally anything. Second-hand clothes, shoes, books, records, cutlery, crockery, toasters, saucepans — everything and anything in any state of disrepair was available for sale at a bargain price. It was a regular haunt for musicians and artists, who would pick up cheap items of interest, and it was here that Edwyn Collins found and bought an old children's book that featured Louis Wain artwork of cats (which were accompanied with related nursery rhymes). He also bought some postcards featuring images of Scottish scenes, embossed with grooves like a flexi-disc — in effect, postcard records.

The recording session in Strathaven was deemed a success, and plans were made to release the tracks as the first single by Orange Juice and the debut release on Postcard Records. Alan Horne became the self-appointed figurehead of Postcard, basing its centre of operations at Horne's west end flat at 185 West Princes Street. Peter McArthur took the cover photograph of Edwyn, James and David (Steven still absented himself from Orange Juice in spite of playing drums on the single). The single also included a free postcard and flexi-disc, which featured a live recording of a song by James, sung by Edwyn, 'Felicity', which Malcolm Ross had made a tape recording of at a gig in Edinburgh. The flexi was originally meant to be an insert in a Postcard fanzine called *Strawberry Switchblade*, named after another James Kirk song. The fanzine never materialised but the name went to good use after James donated it to Rose McDowell as the name for the group she had started with Jill Bryson. The logo for Postcard – a kitten banging a drum – was taken from the Louis Wain book. Alan Horne's friend Brian Superstar moved into 185 West Princes Street as David McClymont departed, making it Alan, Brian and Krysia Klasicki sharing the flat that doubled as Postcard Records HQ. 'Falling and Laughing' was released in February 1980 and the Postcard story went overground.

EDWYN COLLINS: The first Orange Juice record was actually a flexi-disc of 'Felicity' that Malcolm Ross recorded on a tape recorder at a gig we were doing in Cheviots [Teviot] Row in Edinburgh. We had this idea to start a fanzine called *Strawberry Switchblade*, named after one of James Kirk's songs, and intended to give the flexi away with it. The fanzine never appeared because it was shit.

STEVEN DALY: We recorded our debut 45 in the only studio we could afford – a profoundly modest facility in a quaint, shortbread-tin village called Strathaven. 'Falling and Laughing' was a fairly ambitious choice for the Orange Juice debut; the song offered clear and early evidence that Edwyn's songwriting was developing. Remarkably enough, the first person to understand was a prominent journalist on the rock weekly *Sounds*, who anointed our idealistic effort single of the week.

EDWYN COLLINS: We recorded 'Falling and Laughing' in eight hours in a small 8-track studio and when we finished it, we felt, well, that it was rather good. The reason it sounds a bit out of tune is because we couldn't afford a guitar tuner and James was convinced that he had perfect pitch, so it's understandable that the tuning was sometimes a bit out.

BRIAN SUPERSTAR: We listened to a lot of sixties music in 185, lots of Motown, Byrds, Creedence, Lovin' Spoonful. There were always lots of people hanging around. Edwyn from Orange Juice was there most of the time, Jill Bryson from Strawberry Switchblade and her boyfriend Peter McArthur who was a photographer. It was a busy place.

STEPHEN PASTEL: I was totally stuck and decided starting a group with Brian Superstar was the best way forward. I asked him, he said yes, and that was the start of the Pastels. He was actually a really great guitar player and de facto teacher too even though I acted like I was the leader.

JILL BRYSON: I was at art school and we'd make our own clothes. When we started Strawberry Switchblade people would shout or throw things at us. Paddy's Market was a good place to get second-hand clothes. We used to go there with Edwyn Collins and Alan Horne, and I remember Edwyn picked up a second-hand copy of the original pressing of the Velvets' Andy Warhol banana album for ten pence. When Orange Juice first started playing I remember seeing them at the art school and they were badly received. We loved them, but most people were into that dark post-punk sound and Orange Juice seemed strange as they were pop. James Kirk was very encouraging — he helped me learn the basics of playing guitar, and gave us the name Strawberry Switchblade. We spent a lot of time at the Postcard flat. Alan and Orange Juice were always really cutting and camp, putting people down in an amusing way, especially Alan.

Alan's belief in Orange Juice was devotional, but he felt having another group signed to Postcard would give the label more clout, perhaps inspired by the attention Zoo Records in Liverpool had received from the national media for their post-punk brace of groups, Echo and the Bunnymen and the Teardrop Explodes. The success in the press of the Josef K single Steven Daly had released on his Absolute label had been noted, which in tandem with the reciprocal gigs Orange Juice and Josef K had organised for each other and Malcolm's helpful involvement in the recording of 'Falling and Laughing', all seemed to point to Josef K being invited to join Postcard.

ALAN HORNE: Steven Daly arranged that Orange Juice would play their first headline gig, with TV Art as support, at the Glasgow School of Art. The method in this madness was to get Orange Juice to Edinburgh, for a performance in Edinburgh on the following night supporting TV Art. As it turned out, the Art School performance justified the general belief that Glasgow was not attuned to the Orange Juice sound. Edwyn had beer thrown over him, fights broke out and the audience's behaviour was so bad that it was decided to ban groups henceforth. TV Art were very half-baked — Malcolm would be playing 'Dock of the Bay' at the soundcheck, which I thought was great, but then they'd do a Roxy Music song and I thought, 'oh God'. TV Art had one song that stood out though, 'Chance Meeting', which became their first single when they changed their name to Josef K.

FRASER SUTHERLAND: I first heard 'Falling and Laughing' on John Peel, loved it immediately, bought it the following day, and spent far too many hours trying to work out the bass parts! I saw them when they played at the Aquarius in Edinburgh, as part of a series of gigs that Allan Campbell put on there. I really liked what they were doing, even if early shows seemed to feature more tuning up of their fancy guitars than playing songs. I'd known Josef K well since TV Art days, and was a big fan, helping with their backline at gigs when I could. I wasn't aware at all at the time of this so-called rivalry between Postcard and Fast, other than what was written in the music press, so I'm not sure to what degree it's been constructed.

PAUL HAIG: We'd all come from punk, but we'd all changed. I chucked all my old records and loved the whole impact of the Pistols and punk, but as soon as I heard Television or Wire, and slightly later the *No New York* album, it all seemed to take the essence of punk to the next stage. I'd been playing guitar and mucking about with Ronnie [Torrance] on drums in his parents' attic, but I don't think we got serious until I met up with Malcolm and we started hatching some ideas.

MALCOLM ROSS: I'd started playing the guitar before punk rock happened and had a guitar. I used to like things like the Stones and the Faces. The Faces were my favourite band. But mainly, the music I liked best was Bowie, Lou Reed, Roxy Music. I couldn't really play that material, so the great thing about punk was anyone can do it, and it did feel like anyone can start a band.

RONNIE TORRANCE: I went to primary school with David [Weddell] and Malcolm, and Paul was my next-door neighbour, so I kinda grew up with them. I was into Alice Cooper and Mott the Hoople, then as teenagers Paul and I got into the Velvet Underground. Paul and I got guitars at the same time but he went for lessons and I couldn't be bothered, so I persuaded my parents to get me a drum kit for Christmas and I started practising with Paul.

MALCOLM ROSS: All the members of Josef K went to Firhill High School in south Edinburgh. By the time I met Paul, he had left school along with Ronnie. Paul and Ronnie left after fourth year when they were sixteen, while David Weddell and I stayed on to do our Higher exams. Ronnie had an attic with his drum kit set up, and it was known around school that he was a drummer, so we just started going up to Ronnie's, though David wasn't really musical when we first started. The Velvets were good to do cover versions of because you could play their songs easily – anyone can play 'Sweet Jane'. There wasn't anything to punk musically; if you look at the Sex Pistols it was just good songs, good simple songs. But how do you develop that? I think the interesting thing about post-punk music was the board has been wiped clean, so it was a question of starting again, trying to develop.

RONNIE TORRANCE: There was a meeting between Malcolm and Steven Daly and Steven kindly offered to fund the release of a single by us. TV Art had been playing gigs and Paul was writing material with Malcolm.

PAUL HAIG: Steven Daly wanted to set up a label called Absolute. He'd had experience helping James King release the Fun 4 single. Steven had met Malcolm at a gig and told him he was in a new band called Orange Juice. We released 'Chance Meeting' on Absolute and played our first gig as Josef K supporting Adam and the Ants, then the Clash shortly afterwards. We then started playing with some of the post-punk groups like the Cure, Echo and the Bunnymen, the Fall – it all happened so fast.

MALCOLM ROSS: I remember we were always looking for places to play and we started promoting our own gigs. We put on some gigs at the Netherbow Theatre and brought Orange Juice through from Glasgow. Allan Campbell used to put events on at Valentino's on a Sunday, and Tiffany's was where Regular Music first promoted gigs, so they used to do Monday nights there. We started to get supports with touring bands from England, for example we supported Magazine and Psychedelic Furs, and for a while we were the main Edinburgh support band, which was good for exposure.

ALLAN CAMPBELL: In the late seventies obviously there was a tremendous flowering of Edinburgh bands and at club level there weren't enough gigs for people to play. So, in what seemed a completely mad move I decided to set up a small live event on a Tuesday night, at a place called the Aquarius in Edinburgh, and it took maybe a couple of hundred people at the most. Once the Aquarius gigs started some acts became better known, for example Another Pretty Face, and it immediately became apparent there was a whole other culture and group of acts doing exciting things. It's a predictable thing to say but there are certain periods like the late sixties or early era of hip-hop where there seems to be a whole group trying to express themselves differently or struggling to do something interesting culturally. Something like that was certainly happening in Edinburgh, I was putting on really just quite small shows including the first ever show by the Associates, who played to maybe about thirty people, but something was happening and you could feel it.

MALCOLM ROSS: The first Josef K single had come out in 1979 and was the only release on Absolute, which was run by Steven Daly, the drummer in Orange Juice. Steven had a kind of love/ hate relationship with Orange Juice at the time — sometimes he would be in Orange Juice, sometimes he wouldn't. He also played with this Glasgow punk band called the Fun 4. Steven was a good organiser and had arranged for a single release by the Fun 4. He could see what was happening with independent record labels. So he approached us and we agreed to do a single on Absolute. At the same time Orange Juice were going to be putting out their first single on Postcard, 'Falling and Laughing'. The name change from TV Art occurred when we were going to release the first single on Steven Daly's label, and he said to us that he didn't think TV Art was a very good name. Looking back he was quite right. Paul and I had gone through to Glasgow to see him and at first we were kind of like, 'Oh, you know, how dare you?' but then we sort of thought, well he's quite right, it's a bit of a crap name. I think we drew up a shortlist and I remember I wanted us to be called Strawberry Switchblade, which was the name of an Orange Juice song, but I don't think Paul and Ronnie liked that so much, so we went for Josef K. The single on Absolute, 'Chance Meeting', came out before 'Falling and Laughing' in late 1979, and I remember thinking we were at the end of a decade. At the time it was only the second decade I'd lived in, so it seemed quite important that change from 1979 to 1980, and I remember really looking forward to it and thinking things would be different in 1980. Steven Daly's initial idea was to put Josef K on the same record label as the Fun 4, NMC Records, as in 'No Mean City'. Steven was very good at organising things, but in the end Postcard Records happened.

ALLAN CAMPBELL: Like everybody else my impetus was music. I did little bits of local music journalism and I went to university and did some reviews for the student paper. I was maybe slightly older than a lot of the young musicians coming through and could remember back to things like the MC5 and the Stooges. I wasn't quite a paid-up member of the Sex Pistols fan club, 'cause I felt they were just doing what the Stooges had done better. I can recall the first time I saw Josef K (I think they were still probably called TV Art then), playing a small place called the Netherbow Theatre, which was seated but only took about eighty people. The four guys came out wearing dark suits and played with an incredible intensity and I just thought 'wow'. They really were something and I remember thinking at that point I don't know if I can help, but this feels exciting and it feels like somebody should be doing something about these guys. At that point I was putting on local shows and I guess that's how we started to at least know each other and examine the possibility that we might be able to do something together.

PAUL HAIG: We helped Fast Product package their *Earcom* release, we'd go round to the Fast flat and help them package orange peel and stuff, but other than that we weren't really involved in the Fast clique. I think we felt like outsiders everywhere, with both Fast and later Postcard. I don't think we thought anyone would like what we were doing, but we were so consumed getting our sound and idea together and pursuing it.

RONNIE TORRANCE: Allan Campbell was a really good guy to have as a manager, speaking up for us and getting gigs.

MALCOLM ROSS: I met Allan Campbell through a guy called Johnny Waller who used to write for *Sounds* as their Scottish correspondent. Johnny shared a flat with Allan, and Allan started promoting gigs under the guise Psychotic Reaction. Allan was sound. He started managing Josef K and was great to work with.

PAUL HAIG: The photograph of Television rehearsing on the inner sleeve of *Marquee Moon* was a big influence — we thought we had to get those guitars, those amps, those shoes. Other big influences were Pere Ubu, Chic, James Brown, Teenage Jesus and the Jerks, who were amazing with their discordant guitar solos. I think in a way all the new Scottish bands had the same influences and they were all quite apparent, for example with Josef K I thought if I wanted to craft a sound it would be based on records like *Marquee Moon* and *Talking Heads: 77*. Probably us not being great musicians and adding our own glitches made it all come out a bit different, which resulted in the Josef K sound. I seem to remember hearing that Alan Horne and Edwyn Collins wanted to start a label and were interested in releasing something by Josef K, so it just seemed like the next stage for us. We had been doing quite a few shows with Orange Juice, so it made sense to be on the same label.

The media response to 'Falling and Laughing' was extremely positive, and proved useful when Alan Horne and Edwyn Collins drove to London to try to sell the singles to record shops. They also doorstepped all the music weeklies, the youthful naiveté of which worked in their favour and resulted in good reviews of the single. Less successful was the meeting with John Peel at BBC Radio 1.

EDWYN COLLINS: We came down to London to see Rough Trade and John Peel. Alan marched into the foyer in Broadcasting House and just demanded to see him. Alan is a bit arrogant, and when Peel appeared he said to him, 'All these Liverpool groups you're playing are shit, Glasgow is the next place where it's going to happen!' Then we heard Peel on air saying how he'd just been confronted by a 'truculent youth' who said that the Liverpool thing was over, and then he proceeded to play Echo and the Bunnymen. Peel didn't like our record — he only played it once.

Horne's confrontational approach to radio promotion had limited success. However, the importance of John Peel in spreading the news about Fast Product and Postcard in the UK and internationally via his BBC World Service radio programmes cannot be underestimated. Pockets of support grew internationally for the labels, particularly through sessions recorded for Peel's BBC Radio 1 show.

STEFAN KASSEL: I became aware of Fast Product and the singles by the Mekons, Gang of Four, the Human League and Scars as a teenager living in Hanover through John Peel, who had a weekly radio show on BFBS [British Forces Broadcasting Service] in Germany. His show was always a delight. Even if I did not like, let's say, 80 per cent of the stuff he played, those other 20 per cent just blew me away.

CAESAR: I read about the first release by the Mekons in the music press. I remember instantly liking the 'Never Been in a Riot' title's apparent dig at the Clash. I had already decided, rightly or wrongly (let's face it, rightly), that the Clash were pretend rebels. I didn't buy the Mekons single though, so I must have heard it later in 1978 at a friend's house or maybe on the radio — John Peel, I guess. It didn't appeal to me much. It came across as too knowing and would-be satirical, I felt there was something insincere to it. I preferred the directness, experimentation and passion of Alternative TV at that time in my life, and still do. However, the point is, I didn't even pay attention to the label in the moment, and, although born and raised in Glasgow, had no notion of Fast's existence in Edinburgh, such was the dearth of media interest in anything creative happening in Scotland before Postcard. I listened to the Human League, Gang of Four, as well as the next Mekons records without being personally affected in any meaningful way. I thought there was an element of tribute, mock protest and parody to it all and it passed me by. It was the appearance of the first Scars single 'Horrorshow'/'Adult/ery' that inspired me to pay attention to where these songs were coming from. That FAST 8 release is definitely, to this day, my favourite.

Rough Trade had gone from strength to strength since they'd refused to stock Fast Product's first release, 'Never Been in a Riot' by the Mekons. The independent scene had grown rapidly, and commercially successful releases on Fast, Mute, Factory and Rough Trade's own label helped create a financially buoyant sector. Rough Trade's record shop was hugely influential with tastemakers, while its distribution network was the means by which the new independent movement flourished. Horne and Collins met with Rough Trade's Geoff Travis and hoped to encourage him to order copies of 'Falling and Laughing', which he did, with a promise to discuss a possible manufacturing and production deal for future Postcard releases. However, there was an immediate enmity between Horne and Travis, proof positive that opposites don't attract.

GEOFF TRAVIS: Alan Horne came down to Rough Trade with 'Falling and Laughing'. I thought, yes, it's pretty good, but I didn't really think it was the Second Coming, which obviously Alan did.

Another positive from this trip to Rough Trade was the purchase of a single both Horne and Collins had heard and liked on Peel: 'Lee Remick' by Australian group the Go-Betweens. As fate would have it an employee at the Rough Trade shop mentioned that she knew the Go-Betweens and that they were currently on holiday in London, so she gave the Postcard boys the address of the hotel they were staying in. Alan and Edwyn visited but found no Go-Betweens present, so slipped a copy of 'Falling and Laughing' under their hotel room door with a note that invited them to come up to Glasgow and record. Postcard was building a roster to complement Orange Juice, with Josef K and now the Go-Betweens set to join the label.

ALAN HORNE: Initially Postcard was formed simply to put out Orange Juice singles. I wanted the best band from Glasgow, obviously Orange Juice, and the best from Edinburgh, which is Josef K. Basically I just want to reach the widest possible market with their music, while keeping it totally independent of the music industry's businessmen.

PAUL HAIG: I think Alan Horne wanted Josef K on Postcard to balance things out with Orange Juice, taking things to a darker extreme, a bit more abrasive. However, I don't think he particularly liked Josef K — he might have liked the odd show and thought we had a few decent tunes with commercial possibilities, but on the whole I don't think he did like us, but I didn't care about that at all.

Josef K: Ronnie Torrance, David Weddell, Malcolm Ross and Paul Haig

MALCOLM ROSS: Alan Horne realised he didn't want Postcard Records just to be a vehicle for Orange Juice, so although he had serious reservations about Josef K, he asked us to be on Postcard Records. Steven Daly was back in the fold with Orange Juice by this time so he'd given up the idea of having a record label of his own and was concentrating on being the Orange Juice drummer again. Alan was a larger-than-life character that used to hang around with Orange Juice. Alan could be very rude sometimes and he could be very funny, and you didn't really want to disagree with him. He was a strong personality, and for a while it worked really well for Postcard Records, he really got people to sit up and take notice.

RONNIE TORRANCE: I didn't really have much time for Alan Horne. I can't be bothered with people like that.

ALLAN CAMPBELL: I got to know Josef K a bit better, and from their point of view they wanted to develop further and felt maybe I was just the nearest person to them that seemed to have a vaguely sympathetic take on what they were doing, that might be able to get them to the next stage in a managerial capacity. When you see a band for the first time that's genuinely exciting, you very often can't quite articulate what it is. The first time I saw Josef K at the Netherbow Theatre, I felt an intensity, a commitment you can feel in your molecules. Josef K had something and you wanted to find out more about it and experience it again. So in many ways working with Josef K wasn't a grand master plan, it was just a crab-like moving towards each other and realising that we work together. It was never a formally signed management contract, just the idea that there's something good here that can move on to something better. I was happy to help and they were happy to use me in any way they could. When I began working with Josef K they had just put out their first single ('Chance Meeting') on Absolute Records, so I got on board before Postcard were involved with Josef K.

'Falling and Laughing' had definitely made an impact and as a calling card for Postcard it couldn't have been more successful. It sold its initial run, after which Alan Horne decided to disregard Geoff Travis's request to re-press the single and deleted 'Falling and Laughing'. Instead, he used the income to record new singles by Orange Juice and Josef K. Steven Daly and Alan Horne had been back down in London in March, ostensibly for Steven to try to sell stock of Fun 4 and Josef K singles he'd released on his NMC and Absolute labels. They had also arranged to meet the Go-Betweens, who they now knew were called Robert Forster and Grant McLennan. The plan had been to hook up at a Subway Sect concert in the Music Machine in Camden.

Robert and Grant didn't show up (they'd already left London for Glasgow), but the Postcard posse's frustration was alleviated by seeing Vic Godard and the Subway Sect perform a new set of songs written by Vic that were heavily influenced by northern soul. The concert was bootlegged by Horne and was the only performance of the northern soul set, which again highlighted the contrary nature of Godard in that he'd already moved on from the sonic stylings of his still-unreleased debut album. Vic Godard had been punk's *éminence grise*. Subway Sect recorded legendary Peel sessions in 1977 and 1978, and their defining second single, 'Ambition', had been released on Rough Trade. Vic was friends with Sid Vicious and Keith Levene and shared the same leisure activity, which perhaps skewed his judgement when he allowed his manager Bernie Rhodes to talk him into sacking the original members of Subway Sect after their attempts to record a debut album at Gooseberry studios. Rhodes split the Sect and put Vic on a weekly wage to write songs, largely taking control of Vic's career. Rhodes directed the recording of Godard's debut album, *What's the Matter Boy?*, which was released on MCA in April.

VIC GODARD: We thought our best song was 'Rock 'n' Roll Even', which we recorded as a single, but Bernie Rhodes thought our proposed B-side, 'Ambition', was better, so decided that should be the A-side. Bernie didn't like the name 'Rock 'n' Roll Even', and decided without telling us to change it to 'A Different Story', which we only found out when Rough Trade released the single. We never felt that 'Ambition' sounded like a single, but it didn't really matter because people liked both sides. Alan Horne and others from Postcard had come along to the White Riot gig in Edinburgh, and seem to have been inspired by Subway Sect and the Slits much more than the Clash. It was possible to go down to Oxfam and get a bunch of grey jumpers like the Subway Sect and get onstage. Alan and Steven from Orange Juice came to see Subway Sect in London when we played the Music Machine and did our northern soul set. They recorded the concert, which is where they heard our song 'Holiday Hymn', which Orange Juice later recorded for a John Peel session on the BBC. The Music Machine was a great venue — two of my favourite gigs took place there in 1977, Richard Hell and the Voidoids and Dillinger. Subway Sect played the Music Machine a couple of times, it was an amazing atmosphere.

DAVY HENDERSON: The Subway Sect were a giant, the whole group, not just Godard — the whole feel of them; their haircuts, T-shirts, sloppy joes, their guitars, the way they worked those guitars, that 'Ambition' single.

ALAN HORNE: Vic Godard is the most interesting and intelligent person in punk.

STEVEN DALY: Alan Horne and I were lucky enough to catch one of the Subway Sect's rare London concerts, which Alan taped on a bulky single-speaker boom box. I think the Orange Juice cover version of 'Holiday Hymn', an unreleased song from Vic Godard's sadly undocumented northern soul phase, must have done some kind of justice to the uplifting spirit of Vic's song, because he later became a friend of Alan's and Edwyn's, collaborating musically with both.

By the time Horne and Daly had returned to Glasgow, Alan had convinced Steven to return to the Orange Juice fold as a full-time member. Plans were hatched to record the new singles by Orange Juice and new additions to the roster in a higher-spec studio on the outskirts of Edinburgh, Castlesound studios. It was also decided to approach Alternative TV guitarist Alex Fergusson to help out with Orange Juice and Go-Betweens production duties, ATV being big favourites of the Postcard groups who had seen them play the Silver Thread Hotel.

ROSE MCDOWELL: Nobody would put punk gigs on, so basically the place for Glaswegians to see bands was the Silver Thread Hotel in Paisley. We saw loads of groups there like Generation X and the Rezillos. That's where I first went to see Alternative TV and saw Alex Fergusson. I was transfixed by his guitar playing. That was an amazing period. Every Tuesday night at the Silver Thread was where all the punks gathered — the scene was amazing because it was people who didn't really belong anywhere else.

185 West Princes Street was becoming a magnet for people that responded to the Postcard signals, and a positive aesthetic had developed that was the antithesis of the austere tones being beamed out of Rough Trade, Mute and Factory. The Postcard cult was attracting followers, the central interest of which was Orange Juice, but that would grow to include Josef K and the Go-Betweens.

ROBERT HODGENS: I started up a fanzine, *Ten Commandments*, out of boredom and to have something to do, get into some gigs for free. I was putting *Ten Commandments* in record shops in Glasgow around February 1980 when I first met Orange Juice, who were putting their first Postcard single 'Falling and Laughing' in the same record shops. I hit it off with them straight away, and we decided to do something for the fanzine.

JILL BRYSON: Alan Horne was so young when he was running Postcard, yet he had such a cynical attitude. He was really well read, clever and encouraging. Horne and Edwyn Collins had a great dynamic; I always thought of them as a duo, an odd couple, I couldn't imagine one without the other and I think Alan had a lot of influence on Orange Juice. Whilst punk was thought of as being resolutely working class — ripped clothes, leather jackets — Edwyn, Alan and James Kirk cut a bizarre look, all floppy fringes, like something from *The Famous Five*.

MALCOLM FISHER: Well before we actually spoke to one another we knew of each other's existence as I lived in the flat above Alan Horne and David McClymont. I used to see Orange Juice from my window clambering out of taxis with guitar cases, and this aroused my interest. David and Alan certainly heard me since I pounded the piano upstairs for hours every day, and it was this pounding which above all must have aroused David's curiosity since I was in a George Gershwin phase and he would have heard me experimenting with jazz chord combinations. The other song I played continuously was a manic Bertolt Brecht/Kurt Weill-esque composition I was putting together for the fun of it. I think David and I first met on the stairs and had a brief exchange and became friendly, after which he came to my flat and noticed a Max Ernst book that caught his eagle eye, along with a Paddy's Market suit I was wearing. Through David I met Alan and after that the rest of Orange Juice.

ROSE MCDOWELL: I was drumming in the Poems with my husband at the time Drew McDowell. We were all mates with Orange Juice and Alan Horne. The Poems supported Orange Juice at Glasgow College of Technology. Part of the night saw both bands merge onstage and it was the Poems and Orange Juice as one band. We just swapped around instruments. I remember I was on keyboards and I think James Kirk was on drums.

The Go-Betweens arrived in Glasgow from London to be welcomed warmly, albeit with the caustic fisheye lens of Alan Horne on them trying to determine if they were in fact long-haired, dope-smoking hippies (which they were not). Steven Daly had volunteered to drum on the two tracks they were going to record at Castlesound for their Postcard single, with Robert on guitar and vocals and Grant on bass and vocals. The music press acclaim accorded the first Postcard single had created media expectation for follow-ups.

ROBERT FORSTER: The city of Glasgow wasn't overwhelming in size or scale. London and Paris, the two cities Grant and I had spent time in over the previous five months, were big and sprawling. Arriving at Glasgow Central Station in late March 1980 and taking a taxi to 185 West Princes Street, the city instantly felt manageable and looked beautiful. I'd never met people, certainly not musicians, like Orange Juice. Very funny, very camp, witty, wise, talented and completely confident in their talents. Josef K were a little more serious, but still very approachable and funny too.

ALLAN CAMPBELL: When Alan Horne signed Josef K he was slightly [ambivalent] about them and I think this is something that Paul Haig feels. He was closer to Malcolm and not so close to Paul and he had, predictably, a grand plan. He was going to have Orange Juice as Postcard's version of the Lovin' Spoonful and Josef K were going to be his Velvet Underground, and of course he was Andy

Warhol sitting there right in the middle, looking through the tambourine. He liked that idea, the symmetry of a west coast and an east coast band, and sometimes he liked Josef K and sometimes he didn't. He'd disparagingly compare them to Joy Division rip-offs and then another day he'd think they were great.

Alan Horne decided to reinvest profits from 'Falling and Laughing' and recorded the new singles by Orange Juice, Josef K and the Go-Betweens at Castlesound studios – a definite step up from recording with John McLarty at Emblem Sound studio in Strathaven. ATV guitarist Alex Fergusson had agreed to produce the tracks by Orange Juice, 'Blue Boy' b/w 'Love Sick', and the Go-Betweens, 'Stop Before You Say It' b/w 'I Need Two Heads', while Josef K would produce 'Radio Drill Time' b/w 'Crazy to Exist' themselves. Orange Juice and the Go-Betweens rehearsed the songs at the Hellfire Club in Glasgow, a rehearsals and recording facility set up by David Henderson and Jacquie Bradley (who went on to become the drummer in all-female Glasgow group Sophisticated Boom Boom) in Carnarvon Street in Glasgow's west end (just around the corner from Postcard HQ).

JACQUIE BRADLEY: I left my job in Bruce's record shop to set up the Hellfire Club with David Henderson. We had talked about it for ages beforehand.

JAINE HENDERSON: My brother David was working in Graffiti [record shop] but was also doing live sound for Johnny and the Self Abusers and then Simple Minds. I started doing their lights and David managed to build a lighting rig which was an upgrade from what they had been using. He was creative and quick to learn on the job. After a while I think he wanted to have a place where he could make recordings and these premises became available. The name, the Hellfire Club, came to me in a dream – in a way it sounds a bit decadent but it just felt right.

Jaine Henderson and David Henderson

JACQUIE BRADLEY: The Hellfire Club was David's idea and he had all the knowledge and skill to record bands. Simple Minds gave David a Teac 4 track tape recorder, and with some financial help from David's mum we got another. Jaine worked part-time and came up with the name — a great name! I was the tape op on every single recording that was ever done in the Hellfire right up to the last day. Together we set it up and worked in it virtually every day.

DAVID HENDERSON: The Go-Betweens arrived in Glasgow and stayed in the west end, coming into the Hellfire Club to rehearse around the same time as the Orange Juice sessions.

The Postcard recording sessions in Castlesound at the end of April were run with military precision to keep within the tight budget. Prior to the Castlesound sessions all three Postcard groups were showcased at shows in Edinburgh and Glasgow. Named by James Kirk, the Funky Glasgow Now concerts at the Nite Club in Edinburgh on 11 April and Glasgow College of Technology on 24 April were trailed by Funky Glasgow Now posters, and the shows cemented the interest generated by the media acclaim for Postcard's debut single 'Falling and Laughing'. Everyone on the scene now realised there was a Glasgow independent label gunning for Bob Last's crown. The Go-Betweens staying in Glasgow and recording for the nascent Postcard gave the label an exotic interest. Glasgow, Edinburgh, Brisbane – it was a good strapline.

ROBERT FORSTER: I didn't write anything in Glasgow. I wrote one song in the six months I was in Europe from November '79 to May '80, and that was 'I Need Two Heads'. Orange Juice and Josef K affected us deeply – we were watching and learning.

DAVID HENDERSON: The Go-Betweens coming to Glasgow and recording on Postcard was another breath of fresh air. They were quite different from Orange Juice but shared the same attitude. I did live sound for the Go-Betweens in the Vic Café at the Glasgow School of Art.

MALCOLM FISHER: I remember seeing the Go-Betweens live in Edinburgh with the Postcard gang for their Funky Glasgow Now concert. There was always one song being touted as their best song, the one worth buying the single or album for — I think it was 'Karen' — and that made the gig worth the ticket price. So even if they weren't quite ready to record for Postcard they did at least have one sure-fire song which passed the Postcard song test — 'Karen'. The Go-Betweens were two very relaxed Australian guys who always had their noses in books. Definitely indoor guys, not the stereotype Aussie outdoor jocks or avid clubbers, no Maestro's nightclub for them. Outdoors activity would be a rare outing to that infamous café in Sauchiehall Street, Equi's, or the Postcard scene centre of gravity, 185 West Princes Street. So I imagine that they preferred to stay put in our friends' flat nearby, waiting, and reading, for something to happen.

ROBERT FORSTER: Alan wouldn't let me meet or go to see gigs by other non-Postcard groups from Glasgow. I only saw two shows in Glasgow at the time, both in rock show venues at the bottom of Sauchiehall Street. The first was a double bill of Magazine and Bauhaus, the first band good, the second silly theatre rock. I also saw the Slits there — Viv Albertine's guitar playing was magical. But no Glasgow groups.

MALCOLM FISHER: Alan Horne of course asked everyone else if the Go-Betweens were right for Postcard, what to do with them and so on, with the consensus being they were a fit. You have to remember that every band had to pass the Velvet Underground litmus test — if they weren't at least 60 per cent Velvet they could never record for Postcard. For Alan, or 'Andy', Horne, the Velvet Underground was the common denominator for every Postcard band — no yellow banana, no Postcard. The Go-Betweens were another Velvet variation so they got their record and a drummer on loan, Steven from Orange Juice.

PAUL HAIG: We did a recording session in late April where Orange Juice, Josef K and the Go-Betweens recorded singles in the same studio, with Orange Juice and Josef K recording on the same day — one session in the morning, the other session in the afternoon.

ALLAN CAMPBELL: Although I was aware of Postcard Records starting and releasing 'Falling and Laughing', my more intimate knowledge of Alan Horne and Postcard happened when the next two singles happened, Orange Juice with 'Blue Boy', and Josef K with 'Radio Drill Time'. That's when I started getting to know Alan Horne a bit better. Josef K and Orange Juice had formulated what they were doing in the studio at that stage.

Orange Juice developed their songwriting and arranging abilities and created a sound that would liberally borrow from disparate American sources: West Coast folk rock (the Byrds/Buffalo Springfield), soul (Stax/Steve Cropper), New York (the Velvet Underground/the Lovin' Spoonful) and disco (the Chic Organization). Throw into this pot-pourri punk influences such as New Hormones-era Buzzcocks (Manchester), Subway Sect and the Slits (London), and the Pop Group (Bristol), and you had a mine of influences hitherto untapped — this was not the cultivated gloom of Factory Records. The component members of Orange Juice were the essential elemental force that created their unique and original sound, but the guiding star of the group was Edwyn Collins. Lyrically he had more in common with Cole Porter and Irving Berlin than contemporary lyricists (with the exception of Vic Godard and Pete Shelley), and Collins's vocal tones were also original. James Kirk served as John Cale to Edwyn's Lou Reed; Kirk's lead guitar was part Velvets and part Memphis soul, and he would soon make his defining statement on the next Orange Juice single. Josef K were a different proposition: dark shadows in dark suits with a penchant for existential ennui. They combined European literary influences with the more abrasive and angular guitar aspects of a New York and East Coast USA aesthetic. The

Go-Betweens fell somewhere in between Orange Juice and Josef K, unashamed of their Dylanesque lyrical and musical influences but with enough pop chops to pique Beserkley Records' interest in them.

EDWYN COLLINS: Some of my influences were Jonathan Richman's first album, some Byrds, Subway Sect, Velvet Underground. James is the country and western influence in Orange Juice; if James wasn't in the group we'd be like the Bunnymen or something. I think James's guitar solos are fantastic. The way he arranges is so apt, he's not a technical musician. James is the member of the group who improvises, he's the one that makes it either a great version of a song or a bad one, just like in jazz. A lot depends on James — he can uplift a song and make it really exhilarating instead of ordinary.

GARETH SAGER: I heard that Orange Juice stated they wanted to be a cross between 'She Is beyond Good and Evil' and the Chic Organization, especially 'Spacer' by Sheila B. Devotion, and I think they did a pretty good job of it.

MALCOLM ROSS: The building blocks we used for creating the Josef K sound were moving away from distorted guitars. A lot of the punk music in '77, '78 was using fuzzboxes, so we didn't use them — we wanted a very clean guitar sound, which was more like Television. Of all those bands who came out in 1977, Television were my favourite and I know Paul really liked Television as well. We were taking that clean trebly guitar sound and trying to take it to the extreme in some other way, making it angular and jagged. However, Josef K were all very interested in the rhythmic aspects of music, probably more rhythm guitarists than lead guitarists — we didn't build up great complex lead guitar solos or anything like that. I think the rhythm guitar was more important. We were interested in expressionism, art and modernism. Josef K were modernist in outlook, we wanted to be moving forward, we didn't want to be repeating music from the past. I think it was a major difference between us and Orange Juice. Orange Juice looked back — if you asked Edwyn which bands he wanted to be like he would probably have said the Byrds, Creedence Clearwater Revival, Buffalo Springfield, bands like that. Whereas Josef K wanted to be associated with Joy Division, Television, Pere Ubu — forward-looking bands. I think it just so happened our favourite groups were American, but we also liked the Subway Sect, Magazine and Joy Division.

MARK STEWART: Speaking to people from Orange Juice, Josef K, Fire Engines, a lot of them came to see the Pop Group and the Slits when we played Tiffany's in Glasgow and a lot of them were inspired to start their group after seeing us, in much the same way the Pop Group were inspired after seeing the Pistols and the Clash.

EDWYN COLLINS: Orange Juice were the first post-punk group to start incorporating elements of sixties music to punk that we liked, for example Buzzcocks. We liked the West Coast sound of the Byrds' astringent twelve-string guitar and Buffalo Springfield, which we married to the frenetic punk rhythm section, and we had quite an unusual lyrical slant. Orange Juice had our own aesthetic and looked different. It all added up to a strong identity which was easy for people to assimilate. It's been well documented that Postcard's label manager and Svengali Alan Horne wanted to push the Velvet Underground aspect because he had an Andy Warhol fixation.

ROBERT FORSTER: We used to rehearse with Steven Daly on drums and then Orange Juice would come into the practice room and take over. The recording session at Castlesound was like that too. We recorded our two songs very quickly and then Orange Juice started on the same day. We had done two singles previously in Brisbane, and there was definitely a seventies vibe to the studio we recorded in there, which was the best studio in town. Castlesound was futuristic in comparison. Everything we played sounded crisp and big and contemporary. A huge sonic shift and a great choice of studio to record in. Postcard wanted to be taken seriously with this round of singles, so there had to be a sonic jump.

With the three new Postcard singles freshly recorded at Castle-sound, Alan Horne and Edwyn Collins made the journey down to London to play Geoff Travis the tapes of the three Postcard groups' singles. Rough Trade had decided to work with Postcard after the critical success of 'Falling and Laughing', but Travis was unhappy that Horne had refused to press up more copies to satisfy demand for the record. The meeting at Rough Trade did not go well, and after listening to the singles by Orange Juice, Josef K and the Go-Betweens, Travis pronounced the singles were too polished and reneged on his promise of a Rough Trade manufacturing and distribution deal for Postcard. This caused considerable alarm for Alan Horne, as all Postcard's finances had been used to record the three singles on the understanding that Rough Trade would pay for the manufacture of the singles. It was unclear how Postcard could continue as a label if they had to pay for the three singles.

EDWYN COLLINS: Alan and I went down to London to try and arrange a deal for Postcard through Rough Trade, but when we saw Geoff Travis he told us that the songs fell in between punk and professional pop and that he didn't think Rough Trade could become involved. We left the offices very downhearted and Alan seemed to go into a crazed depression and started wandering about in the middle of the road saying, 'Let them run me over, let them kill me.' I said, 'Look Alan, give me the masters, I'll phone around some of the major record companies and see if I can get us a deal that way.' So Alan said, 'Take the masters. Betray me. But that'll cost you £25,000.' He was insane.

Paisley had retained its position as the venue for west coast gigs, something it had held on to since the Glasgow District Council's punk ban. The concerts no longer took place in the 'punk rock hotel', the Silver Thread, but in a small dark pub called the Bungalow Bar, where touring groups (including Echo and the Bunnymen, Wah! Heat, Associates, the Psychedelic Furs) would perform in the absence of gigs in Glasgow. It was at a Teardrop Explodes concert at the Bungalow Bar in Paisley on 19 May that Julian Cope led the group onstage and announced Zoo had heard from their Factory friends earlier that day – Ian Curtis had committed suicide the previous evening. Cope then dedicated the first song in their set, 'Sleeping Gas', to Curtis; a member of the stunned audience went out onto the street and from a BT phone box called John Peel at the BBC to inform him of the sad news. Peel announced Curtis's death to his Radio 1 listeners during his show, and the news spread from there. Curtis's suicide seemed to signal the end of something; the finality of it was compounded when Joy Division had a posthumous hit single with 'Love Will Tear Us Apart', followed by their second and final album *Closer*. The long mac brigade had lost their figurehead, and a dark gloom permeated the independent movement. For fans, artists and labels who had been associated with the more serious aspects of post-punk, it felt like the sands had shifted with a realisation that perhaps the heavy atmosphere needed a brighter contrast. The Bungalow would in time host performances by Fast- and Postcard-related groups like Scars, Restricted Code, Orange Juice and Josef K.

A solution was found to the challenge of paying for the manufacture and release of the Postcard singles recorded at Castlesound at the end of April. It was decided to hold the Go-Betweens single until November, and thanks to further borrowing there was enough money to release the Orange Juice and Josef K singles. Lack of funds also dictated that both singles would share the same fold-around sleeve, folded to present an Orange Juice single cover on one side and Josef K on the other. Ingenious.

MALCOLM ROSS: In August it was decided that Postcard would release 'Blue Boy' and 'Radio Drill Time' at the same time, with a fold-around sleeve that was used for both singles. Postcard was like a sort of cottage industry, part of the ethos was 'do it yourself'. Those shared sleeves was a cheap way to do it, and then they were hand-coloured. The sleeves were printed in black and white, Alan bought lots of felt pens and got the people who used to hang about in the Postcard flat to colour in the sleeves — various art student types. Alan liked to think it was like a wee Warhol Factory scene.

JILL BRYSON: We were helping at 185 when we were individually colouring the second Orange Juice single, 'Blue Boy', which took ages. Alan had a good attitude and really brought attention to Glasgow with Postcard. It became a burgeoning music scene with rehearsal studios like the Hellfire Club, and Glasgow suddenly became something instead of being a dead place. The success of Postcard resulted in major labels coming up to Glasgow to sign groups.

ROSE MCDOWELL: Orange Juice were fantastic, they were just so inspiring for a lot of people. Orange Juice would be singing songs like 'Felicity' which was just that wee bit of glitter, it was just really nice to have that and to not just have everything really dreary. We used to hang out at the Postcard flat with Alan and Edwyn and just have a laugh, and I remember folding the Orange Juice 'Blue Boy' singles and drawing on them.

ALLAN CAMPBELL: I would only go through to Glasgow occasionally to see Alan Horne about Postcard/Josef K business. Alan always moved in slightly mysterious, cloaked ways, but again it was exciting. You had all these big London magazines and newspapers writing about Postcard, but as Horne famously said, Postcard was basically a wardrobe in his flat in 185 West Princes Street. There was that nice feeling of a cheeky-chappy, up-and-at-'em attitude, and maybe upsetting the balance of things in a very positive way

JAINE HENDERSON: Glasgow and Postcard — it was everything. It was art and music and theatre. It was a strong community. I don't know if we were lucky, it was as if we were captured and somehow placed there. We didn't have much money but even if we had we would rather have bought something from Paddy's Market than a Vivienne Westwood.

The Go-Betweens: Robert Forster

The Go-Betweens left Glasgow after they played the Funky Glasgow Now concerts, with Grant travelling to New York and Robert returning to Australia. Their stay had been short and sweet; they made friends in their wake and impressed everyone who saw them live.

ROBERT FORSTER: We played the two shows with Orange Juice and Josef K and we were petrified, particularly the first show at the Edinburgh Nite Club where we were headlining. The second show at Glasgow Tech a few weeks later was better, because we played first, which was the right place for us. Both bands were more accomplished and ready than us. Grant and I were in a period of musical transition — our time would come with *Before Hollywood* two years later — whereas Josef K and Orange Juice were ready and had everything worked out, music- and image-wise. Orange Juice were a revelation. Still the best forty minutes of rock 'n' roll I have seen. They'd put out one single at the time, and were the best band in the UK.

MALCOLM FISHER: The Go-Betweens were two very relaxed guys and I remember they came round to my place for scones and tea and a chat, books left outside the door of course. I definitely feel their priority was to get through as many books as possible during their stay in Glasgow at our friends' flat and writing songs was an optional, an occasional pastime. There was one time where we had a Postcard football kick-about in Kelvingrove Park. I think Steven Daly was good but the rest of us were pretty awful, as you can imagine, with Paul Quinn avoiding the ball so his chaps wouldn't get dirty. The Go-Betweens were nice guys and I have fond memories of spending time with them. We never saw one another again and the rest is history.

August saw Postcard Records release singles two and three simultaneously — 'Blue Boy' by Orange Juice and 'Radio Drill Time' by

Josef K. Alan Horne's idea to have Josef K on the label to represent Edinburgh and counterbalance Orange Juice representing Glasgow was inspired. Josef K seemed to be everything Orange Juice weren't (and vice versa) – opposites that attracted an excitement in Glasgow hitherto unknown. Postcard presented a new Glasgow, poles apart from the No Mean City image and more like a camp union of Isherwood's *Cabaret* and Warhol's Factory.

Geoff Travis's change of heart about Rough Trade distributing and manufacturing Postcard was a hammer blow that resulted in further money being borrowed from family members to pay to manufacture the singles. Another visit to London was undertaken by Alan Horne and Edwyn Collins to distribute the two Postcard singles, with the same approach taken as before to their ad hoc promotional blitz of the music papers. The media fell head over heels for Orange Juice and Postcard – 'Blue Boy' in particular captured the zeitgeist perfectly. It was an astounding record; the production by Alex Fergusson really brought out the positive tension in the group. James Kirk's guitar solo captured the essence of Postcard and Orange Juice. It was the moment when the new decade of independent music announced itself – camp cowboy imagery merged with speed-injected Velvets' 'I Heard Her Call My Name' lead guitar noise.

EDWYN COLLINS: I was seventeen when I wrote 'Blue Boy'. I thought it was crude – I was thinking, 'I'm seventeen, I need to get better than this.' Alex Fergusson was quite a character, his production got the whole song in perspective and suggested a lot of things regarding producing 'Blue Boy' that we'd never thought of.

There had been a culture of fanzines in Scotland that circulated around all the record shops. The punk period was probably best served by *Ripped and Torn*, but the pre-eminent fanzine that documented the nascent Postcard scene was Robert Hodgens's *Ten Commandments*. By the time Orange Juice featured on the cover *Ten Commandments* had a writer (Kirsty McNeill) and photographer (Robert Sharp) in tow. The writing and photography in the Orange Juice article was brilliant, a high watershed moment that went a long way towards positioning Orange Juice and Postcard as the pre-eminent figures of Scottish underground pop. The *NME* picked up Kirsty McNeill and Robert Sharp as their Scottish reviewer and photographer.

ROBERT HODGENS: I was going to a lot of gigs on my own to the punk rock hotel aka the Silver Thread Hotel in Paisley. I saw *Fumes* fanzine, and after finding the address of the person that produced it knocked on his door and asked him how to do a fanzine. He told me all you really needed was a photocopier. I knew I could get into gigs for free if I was running a fanzine, so it seemed like a good idea. I then met Robert Sharp and Kirsty McNeill at the Spaghetti Factory and really liked them. Robert was a great photographer and Kirsty was a great writer, so we started working together on my *Ten Commandments* fanzine. I met Orange Juice and Alan Horne told me they had lots of flexi-discs of 'Felicity', so he gave me lots to give away with *Ten Commandments*. Once I met Alan and Orange Juice, I started hanging out at the Postcard flat at 185 on a daily basis, just around the period 'Blue Boy' was released.

ALAN HORNE: There are hundreds of groups in Glasgow, but apart from Orange Juice none of them are good enough. 'Blue Boy' is really strong and clear, it's a great record. Edwyn may not like it, but it's still the best record that's ever come out of Scotland.

STEFAN KASSEL: I just loved everything about Orange Juice, starting with the band name. The first song I ever heard by them was 'Blue Boy', played by John Peel on BFBS on German radio, and it blew my mind. Yes! That was *my* band. They had a great look, great songs, great lyrics and a cool attitude. They were new and different, the ultimate band for me. They were characters, just like in the Beatles — you knew every band member.

EDWYN COLLINS: 'Blue Boy' is a well-produced record. I don't think it's a very strong song, but I think I've got songs that could be hit singles. The saving grace of 'Blue Boy' is James's guitar solo.

ALAN HORNE: Apart from Orange Juice, the only other group doing anything interesting in Glasgow are the Fun 4. However, it's not depressing in Glasgow: what other city in Britain has a group like Orange Juice?

The two music press writers who celebrated the post-punk movement and championed the new breed of independent labels were Dave McCullough at *Sounds* and Paul Morley at *NME*. Both were smitten with the Postcard drumming kitten, with McCullough first in the queue to buy his plane ticket from London to Glasgow to interview the Postcard posse. These features resulted in further music press articles, all of which helped establish Postcard as the main shape-shifter of the independent sector. This didn't go unnoticed by Geoff Travis, who contacted Alan Horne and informed him Rough Trade would be interested in doing a manufacturing and distribution deal after all.

EDWYN COLLINS: Dave McCullough from *Sounds* had written a big double-page spread on Postcard, and when Geoff Travis saw it he miraculously changed his mind. So we got our manufacturing and distribution deal for Postcard with Rough Trade.

Horne had Travis where he wanted him and managed to extract an extremely generous 85 per cent/15 per cent agreement from Rough

Trade to give them exclusive rights to distribute future Postcard releases. The contract meant Rough Trade would pay for all recording and manufacturing costs, which, once recouped, would result in Postcard receiving 85 per cent of profits, an arrangement that delighted Horne. Travis's remarkable volte-face characterised the antagonistic relationship between the two men: Horne's one-up-manship would be a constant thorn in Travis's side for the duration of the Rough Trade contract with Postcard.

The music press acclaim for the Orange Juice and Josef K singles saw a ramping up of awareness of Postcard, which resulted in significant sales of both singles and high positions in the 'alternative' charts as featured in the music press. Alan Horne revelled in being feted by the music press big hitters McCullough and Morley, and duly gave good copy.

GEOFF TRAVIS: Whilst we didn't really reach an agreement over 'Falling and Laughing', we did over 'Blue Boy'. 'Falling and Laughing' was OK, but 'Blue Boy' was the one that really sparks. It had also helped us because 'Blue Boy' was single of the week in all the music press. So that does influence you to think, well, there must be something good here. We did make a deal with Postcard for manufacturing and distribution of their releases, and I think Alan felt that he'd won some tremendous battle by getting the best distribution deal in the history of distribution deals. And after that, of course, we loved Orange Juice, so it wasn't a problem.

ALAN HORNE: Music should always aim for the widest possible market, and the charts are there, that's where you need to be. Postcard was not really that well organised, it was in the back of my mind that the punk ideals had failed and dropped away. Groups like the Buzzcocks, who started off on their label New Hormones, knew the importance of getting into the charts, and could have been so powerful, so strong, and could have led the way for other groups. They didn't. Dexy's called it right when they mentioned brown-rice independents, and that's true, that whole hippy attitude, and while you can't fault the Fall, their attitude sucks. I consider that Postcard is the only punk independent because we are the only ones doing it who are young. Everybody else has come from the back of a record shop or are businessmen. We started Postcard with no money and just built it up from Orange Juice's first single. We want to get our records out as we want them, cut out the majors, all the old middlemen, it will be totally independent. That will be the ultimate achievement.

EDWYN COLLINS: When we talk to people in the music business they don't take us seriously because we're so young. We're not interested in Postcard being a trendy independent label, a cult esoteric joke. We want Postcard to be a popular label with a young audience.

CAESAR: I missed the release of 'Falling and Laughing' somehow. Now it's an all-time favourite. Not long after, Clare Grogan and I were going by a record shop, probably Listen in Renfield Street in Glasgow, presumably after an Altered Images rehearsal, and she wanted to buy the next Orange Juice single, 'Blue Boy'/'Lovesick'. I think it's fair to say, if not diplomatic, there was an unwritten rule in Altered Images, certainly amongst the male contingent, that you mustn't like Orange Juice, but Clare kept her own counsel regarding that, and I happened to remain neutral. So, although I knew Orange Juice by reputation already, Clare definitely encouraged me to buy a copy of 'Blue Boy'. Once I saw the name of Alternative TV's Alex Fergusson as producer on the cover, there was no question in my mind. I thought both tracks were great, much to the annoyance of the other Altered Images guys at the time. But you have to acknowledge when something sounds original, don't you?

The intense media scrutiny focused on Postcard was the stuff of dreams for avid music press disciples Horne and Collins, but it wasn't long before Horne's ambivalence towards Josef K was being voiced in the press.

ALAN HORNE: I still didn't like them much, but Josef K always seemed to be playing concerts at this time, on their own or supporting touring groups like the Clash, Adam and the Ants, Psychedelic Furs, Magazine, Echo and the Bunnymen and others I've forgotten. The best one I saw was at the City Hall in Glasgow with the Cure. The guitars were way up in the mix and really trebly, the audience hated them but they were brilliant. I wanted Postcard to have the best Edinburgh group and the best Glasgow group, I wanted something that would look solid. I knew how good Orange Juice were and Josef K were the group I chose from Edinburgh.

MALCOLM ROSS: Alan Horne didn't like 'Radio Drill Time', but put the single out to help establish Postcard, and to give him his due he didn't want the label to be all Orange Juice. I suppose you could say Orange Juice and the Go-Betweens are similar, and Josef K is the Postcard punk band.

PAUL HAIG: Alan Horne was never keen on our angular sound at all; he appreciated the softer west coast aspects of Orange Juice. He used to say that we were the Velvet Underground of Postcard, and Orange Juice were like the Byrds.

Dave McCullough and Paul Morley did separate articles on Postcard, Orange Juice and Josef K. Horne's caustic tongue and disregard for any of Postcard's contemporaries made good reading, as did Collins's articulacy. However, Josef K had great difficulty communicating with journalists and initially preferred their manager Allan Campbell to do the talking for them. Paul Morley described Josef

K as 'four shadows in search of a sunny day' for the headline of his *NME* article on the group.

PAUL MORLEY: In the late seventies as it hit 1980, it was an incredibly transformative moment in music, because it was that stage beyond punk that was given the name – possibly by me – post-punk. Punk splattered the idea that music could come from anywhere around the country, so suddenly you started paying attention to other areas of the UK. I was working for the *NME* at that point, and what excited me was I'd receive cassettes through the post from around the country that suddenly sounded tremendous. This was a new thing, as prior to '76/'77 it was assumed that music based from outwith the centre, i.e. London, wouldn't be very good or would sound like a copycat of something else. However, around '79/'80, because of the encouragement provided by punk, you'd receive tapes through the post from around the country that would contain fantastic music. Because of the stuff I wrote about in the *NME* (Echo and the Bunnymen, Joy Division, Gang of Four), I became the person at the *NME* that a certain sort of music would be sent to. This was unbelievably thrilling and exciting – in fact the very first thing I wrote about Josef K was because I'd been sent something extraordinary by them through the post. Josef K came to London and came to the *NME*, and were incredibly shy when I interviewed them.

ALLAN CAMPBELL: When Josef K and Orange Juice released their two singles at the same time, there seemed to be a genuine upsurge of interest in Postcard. It was a very exciting time – if leading writers like Paul Morley (who loved Postcard) decided to patronise these bands from Glasgow and Edinburgh, then he really would be indulged. So it was fantastic, you'd have other good writers like Dave McCullough of *Sounds* covering Postcard and the whole thing mushroomed. But having said that, Postcard was justifiably getting these write-ups and the whole thing snowballed pretty quickly.

PAUL HAIG: The music press then got interested. I noticed a difference after Dave McCullough came up and did a big Josef K/Postcard feature for *Sounds*. Scotland became a major point of interest for the press, but I think you can't take that attention too seriously because if you did it'd either go to your head or it would drive you nuts. You just have to laugh at it — there were some outrageous things said about me, like 'Is this man too cool to live?' Paul Morley at the *NME* was a big supporter, using very wordy, flowery language, and it became a real thing at the time wondering what Morley was going to say next. It was nice having that kind of exposure in the music press, but it can't be taken too seriously.

Any misgivings John Peel may have had about being accosted by Alan Horne outside the BBC earlier in the year had evidently evaporated in light of the collective excitement surrounding 'Blue Boy', which he played several times on his radio show. He also invited Orange Juice to record their first Peel session, which was broadcast in October. Orange Juice and Josef K played concerts throughout the UK, including prestigious support slots in London. However, unity at Postcard was being tested by Alan Horne's repeated negative comments in the press about Josef K.

ALAN HORNE: Josef K aren't really my cup of tea, but I really like them as people. One out of ten times I see them live I think they're great.

MALCOLM ROSS: Alan Horne doesn't really like Josef K, he never has done.

ALLAN CAMPBELL: I don't know if there's a traditional east versus west rivalry between Glasgow and Edinburgh groups, but they seemed to fall into different kinds of musical categories. As a general sweeping statement I think it was proven that Edinburgh bands very often had better ideas, more lateral thinking and were more interesting musically but couldn't get it together at a business level to get signed and promote themselves. Unkindly maybe, but on the west coast you've got the impression there was less musical talent but a real driving urge to make the best of that and get signed and be commercially successful.

MALCOLM ROSS: I think beneath the surface there was a rivalry between Orange Juice and Josef K; it would rear its head every now and then. I think people of that young age are competitive, but we wanted to help each other — I mean it was like a family rivalry thing, I suppose. Orange Juice and Josef K would present a united front to any bands outwith Postcard. Orange Juice would organise gigs in Glasgow as they knew more people there, with Josef K supporting at the gigs they organised. It would be the same in Edinburgh — we'd organise gigs and headline, with Orange Juice in support.

Postcard kept their foot on the pedal and recorded another two singles by Orange Juice and Josef K at Castlesound: Orange Juice recorded 'Simply Thrilled Honey' with Malcolm Ross helping out on production and, with Josef K, recording 'It's Kinda Funny'. Both singles were released in tandem with the Go-Betweens single that had been held over after Geoff Travis's about-turn.

EDWYN COLLINS: I remember that we were getting phenomenally good press at this time, and when Orange Juice went on tour supporting the Undertones things were starting to go well. There were major record labels hovering about, but we didn't really see any point in signing.

Rough Trade financed Postcard's three singles by Orange Juice, Josef K and the Go-Betweens, then financed the recording of the debut album by Josef K at Castlesound. The euphoric media response to the Orange Juice and Josef K singles continued to fuel the rise of Postcard, as did the Go-Betweens going public as the label's new addition. Robert Forster and Grant McLennan were now back in Australia with a permanent drummer in the group, Lindy Morrison, as the positive reviews of 'I Need Two Heads' b/w 'Stop Before You Say It' filtered through to them.

ROBERT FORSTER: Everyone was a character in or near Postcard. That's all there was − I never met a dull person during my stay in Glasgow. It was an astonishing collection of people around the label. There was a particular 1950s sense to things that I had never encountered before. The sixties were in vogue, as they always are, but the fifties not so much − the way Postcard people dressed and carried themselves, there was an early fifties feel to it. Malcolm Fisher was like a bohemian or churchgoer from 1952. Edwyn and David had a skiffle kind of look. The couple I lived with in my time there, Anne Hogarth and Robbie Kelly, were like late-fifties New Yorkers − perfume, cigarettes, dressing up to go out. Jazzy. They'd be the only people on the dance floor at an Orange Juice show. Doing the twist before the bandstand. It was perfect.

ROBERT HODGENS: I remember the Go-Betweens coming to Glasgow, and I featured them in my *Ten Commandments* fanzines. I already had the 'Lee Remick' and 'People Say' records − they were great records − then of course their Postcard single produced by Alex Fergusson.

PAUL HAIG: Our first single on Postcard, 'Radio Drill Time', brought attention to Josef K. Our next Postcard single was 'It's Kinda Funny', which is one of the quickest songs I've ever written − I think it took about twenty minutes. It was a song about the human condition, but it was an inspired moment as it's very rare for me to pull a song together so quickly, to have something that appeared somehow from nowhere.

Bob Last and Hilary Morrison had continued to develop pop:aural and signed Glasgow group Restricted Code to join the Flowers and Boots for Dancing on the label. The media success of Postcard had resulted in pop:aural being usurped as the dominant sound of independent Scotland. 'From the Top' and 'First Night On' received joint billing on the debut Restricted Code single for the label, both tracks produced by Last.

TOM CANNAVAN: I don't think Bob ever sat Restricted Code down and laid out a philosophy or grand plan for the label. We knew 'modern music for radio and dancing', was a slogan, and we were totally into that. Frank [Quadrelli] and I loved Tamla, soul, funk and a bit of reggae almost as much as punk and new wave, and having commercial success was definitely on our radar, not so much for fame and fortune, just to keep pushing us ahead and to allow us to keep doing what we loved, and to be heard more widely. Fast Product was very much the avant-garde, subversive art project, whereas with pop:aural there did seem to be more genuine chart and commercial ambitions. Whether Bob had a master plan for the bands to go on to major labels with him still managing, the way he had done with the Human League, I don't know, but we certainly felt pop:aural was having a crack at commercial success, albeit in an idiosyncratic way. There wasn't a lot of money about for anything like promotion and record plugging, but I guess we believed chart success was possible on pop:aural, and their team was tuned in to what was needed to achieve it.

FRANK QUADRELLI: Bob had been so impressed by the four songs on the demo — 'Love to Meet You', 'From the Top', 'Then There Was You' and 'First Night On' — that he wanted to use all four songs. Initially, we were not sure of the format, but we did all agree that 'Love to Meet You' should be the second single. Bob wanted to attract attention with the first release, 'From the Top' b/w 'First

Night On', and then release the more radio-friendly 'Love to Meet You' secondly, which the band totally agreed with.

KENNY BLYTHE: Bob Last had a vision of Restricted Code records being played on the radio to the masses, right from our first meeting with him when he came to watch us in the Assembly Rooms in Edinburgh. Bob was enthusiastic about signing us up for his pop:aural label. We all loved the Fast Product singles by Gang of Four, Human League, Scars, so we were overjoyed at the prospect of Bob being our manager and producer.

pop:aural also released a second single by Boots for Dancing, 'The Rain Song', which continued to build their momentum. Jo Callis took on guitar duties with the group and their ascent seemed assured when the NME offered the group a front cover and Last secured slots for Boots for Dancing to support Talking Heads and the Human League in London.

DAVE CARSON: The line-up for Boots for Dancing was always changing; our second single involved Jo Callis from the Rezillos. He was an amazing person to work with, a great songwriter who was involved in the writing with Boots for Dancing. When our second single came out on pop:aural we did a lot of promotion, including opening for Talking Heads and the Human League in London. The press didn't really understand us — we were doing punk-funk and were slightly ahead of the game.

JO CALLIS: Boots for Dancing was very much Dave's vision and it was a completely twisted version of James Brown, a punky funk kind of thing, quite scratchy and left field. Former Thursdays guitarist Michael Barclay was also in Boots for Dancing and had been involved with Fast Product as he had been in the Thursdays, so we started gigging in London and parts of England and getting a bit of a buzz going. Then the *NME* were interested in doing a cover feature on us so we did a photo session with them in London. A couple of weeks later we were coming back down to London for another gig and were going to do the *NME* interview for their cover story, but Dave bottled out. He was worried his punk mates wouldn't talk to him, think he'd sold out or something like that. So we didn't do the *NME* interview, we didn't get the *NME* cover story, and Boots for Dancing faded away.

Boots for Dancing: Jamo Stewart, Jo Callis, Dave Carson, Mike Barclay and Douglas Barrie

DAVE CARSON: We recorded a third single, but I wasn't really happy with it and it didn't come out. I had personal loyalty to some of the people in Boots for Dancing, but I was being encouraged to get rid of them which I wasn't comfortable with. I stated my case about this and affirmed my discomfort with this suggestion, and the relationship between pop:aural and me stopped at that point. I didn't play the game, but I'm proud I didn't play the game.

Moving on from the fallout of Boots for Dancing and taking on management duties for Restricted Code proved to be an easier task for Last than keeping the internal tensions within the Human League from boiling over. Phil Oakey and Martyn Ware found life together in the League somewhat claustrophobic, as Oakey wanted to move in a more pop direction. The fracture was inevitable, but Martyn Ware was blind to the internal manoeuvres going on between his manager and Simon Draper at Virgin Records.

BOB LAST: I loved those first two Human League albums, but it didn't feel to me that it could go on. However, there were a lot of tensions. I thought we were going to get dropped by Virgin and I guess the project part of me couldn't accept that. I talked to Simon Draper at the label, and I did conclude that Martyn Ware being in a different entity was part of the solution.

MARTYN WARE: Bob presented the concept of a production company to me and helped put BEF together and negotiated the deal with Virgin.

BOB LAST: It took a lot of pushing and shoving, and I had to sort of buy off both sides with deals to make them do it. To be honest, they would have split anyway — I just figured if we seized the initiative I had an idea that we could unlock something in both sides. They both wanted the same thing, they wanted to have hits, but they frustrated each other way too much, and I was sure the split was going to happen anyway so I chose to accelerate the process substantially.

Last had discussed the creative fissure within the Human League with Virgin at some length, and it was decided that the group would split in half. Phil Oakey and Adrian Wright would retain the group name, but at a cost — an override percentage on future Human League income would be paid to the ousted original members Martyn Ware and Ian Craig Marsh (Oakey and Wright also carried forward the not inconsiderable Human League debt for unearned royalties that was owed to Virgin). Ergo, not only did Last manage the Human League on Virgin, but he also managed the new Ware and Craig Marsh project (which was also bankrolled by Virgin). Last was a partner in the new production company created by Ware and Craig Marsh, the British Electric Foundation, the key component of which was a group project, Heaven 17 (featuring Ware, Craig Marsh and vocalist Glenn Gregory).

The Human League were due to start a European tour shortly, and were down to a vocalist and a projectionist. Oakey's solution to the change of personnel was to replace the two departed musicians with two schoolgirls he'd seen dancing in the Crazy Daisy nightclub in Sheffield. Susan Sulley and Joanne Catherall had no professional dancing or singing background, but after Oakey and Wright visited the girls' parents to assure them they'd be looked after, they both joined the Human League for the imminent tour.

BOB LAST: When Phil told me he had found Sue and Joanne, I was not at all sure, and then when they made 'The Sound of the Crowd', I was not at all sure about where the Human League were going. I didn't like 'The Sound of the Crowd'. It was difficult for me to get my head round what Phil was doing, but on the other hand once I had engineered the split of the original Human League, I felt that Phil had some instinct about the popular audience, about how far they would go in terms of how he presented himself. Somehow he knew it would engage that audience and not freak people out. I would not have necessarily known that. I was prepared to trust Phil's judgement, which oft times I found mind-bogglingly difficult. It was quite a tense start.

Fire Engines made their live debut earlier in the year and worked to a high-intensity, high-treble and high-concept ethos. Angus Groovy managed and packaged the group artwork, though there was a collectivist and co-operative approach to their Codex Communications operation. 'Get Up and Use Me' b/w 'Everything's Roses' was released on 7-inch and only available via mail order. It was a single that instantly enthused media and public alike.

GEOFF TRAVIS: 'Get Up and Use Me' was great.

INNES REEKIE: Fire Engines' live debut on 16 March 1980 in Leith Community Centre had them looking like the Subway Sect's scruffier younger brothers. Their sound was all lacerating guitars, primal Moe Tucker drumming and Richard Hell/James Chance screams and yelps, with lyrics adopting Burroughs's cut-up method. It was kinda unsettling, bravely new and utterly compelling to watch.

ANGUS GROOVY: I think if the packaging had an impact it was in how it complemented the music. If Fast was about disrupting the music industry I wanted Codex to communicate something a bit more generally disruptive. I had of course absorbed some of Bob's graphic style, and that of Linder Sterling who did the Buzzcocks covers. The 1930s artist John Heartfield was a shared reference. Like many others I had picked up on situationism from reading interviews with Malcolm McLaren, and took from it that we should annoy people out of slothful complacency through entertainment. I'd also been reading about discordianism through the Illuminati novels (hence the song 'Discord'). There was a bit of camp humour thrown into that mix, some New York no-wave edge and a love of playing with images of mundane objects from our everyday lives. All of that went into both the 'Get Up and Use Me' packaging and the music.

GRAHAM MAIN: We worked hard and did our first gig in Leith. We played three songs, we were raw and in your face. Bob Last had shown faint interest in the Dirty Reds but he was more intrigued by what the Fire Engines were going to produce.

INNES REEKIE: Fire Engines' short, sharp, fifteen-minute performances were bristling with electric energy — it was nothing short of exhilarating. Many people, especially Bob Last, were taking notice.

Postcard Records had become the self-styled Sound of Young Scotland and repurposed Tamla Motown slogans to their own ends. As 1980 drew to a close the label accepted an offer from Les Disques du Crépuscule to close the year out with an Orange Juice and Josef K concert in Brussels on New Year's Eve. There were also whispers that Postcard would expand the label with a new signing, with rumours running rife in Glasgow that one of the following would sign to the label: James King, Altered Images, Fire Engines, Article 58, Strawberry Switchblade, Aztec Camera or Robert Hodgens's new group, the Bluebells.

ROBERT HODGENS: I was already friendly with Altered Images as I had gone to school with some of them, and their manager Gerry McElhone suggested I start a group. When I told Edwyn Collins I planned on doing this he pointed out I needed to write some songs, as I'd only written one song at that point, called 'She Hates Travel'. I used to go round to Edwyn's house and he tried to show me how to write songs, and eventually I got a short set together. I had been inventing groups to interview and write articles about in my fanzine, so used an idea from that for my first gig with other musicians — we called ourselves the Oxfam Warriors. We played at the Vic Café in the Art School in Glasgow, and Edwyn, Alan Horne and *Ten Commandments* photographer Robert Sharp came along and sat at a table near the front of the stage with 'hit' or 'miss' signs they'd made. Of course everything was a 'miss' and they were laughing at us, but Alan said I had some not bad songs but the band were no good and that they were neds. They were not neds, of course, but they were from the south side, and as I was impressionable and Alan was very enigmatic, I went along with his suggestion and decided to get a new band.

JAMES KING: After the Fun 4 split I recorded a track with Steven Daly on drums, 'Back from the Dead', which Steven passed on to Brian Superstar who was Alan Horne's flatmate at 185. Alan then phoned me to ask me if I wanted to put the single out on Postcard, but by then I'd promised another label, Cuba Libre, that they could release the track as a solo single by me, but I could have been signed to Postcard Records.

CAESAR: Altered Images signing to Postcard was a possibility in the sense that a meeting took place at the Postcard flat with a view to working together. I attended along with our manager to represent the group. There was an obvious rivalry between the two sides; not on my part, I genuinely wanted to do something, anything, with Postcard, and I imagine Clare probably felt the same. However, the majority of our group, following the manager's lead, weren't convinced it was the right path to take. Looking back, I guess Alan Horne was simply checking out the local competition at close quarters and may not have been sincere about collaborating anyhow. I'm not even certain there was ever any serious offer from Postcard on the table, creatively speaking. Anyway, it became very clear that Orange Juice were the main consideration at the label and I suppose we'd always have played second fiddle to them, if not taking third, fourth or fifth place behind Josef K, Aztec Camera and the Go-Betweens. So it could be argued it was better the deal didn't go anywhere. In another scenario, I would've loved 'Dead Pop Stars' to come out on the label though, and believe we might have recorded an even better, more relaxed-sounding version in Scotland, but it just wasn't to be. Above all, I remember spending most of the day at West Princes Street talking to Orange Juice drummer Steven Daly about all the latest Rough Trade releases, as Alan and our manager battled it out for supremacy in the Postcard living room.

Altered Images: Clare Grogan and Caesar

ALLAN CAMPBELL: I remember when I was looking after the Delmontes after I'd set up Rational Records and released their debut single, we went down to Richard Boon's club in Manchester. Richard Boon was the guy who managed the Buzzcocks, and Aztec Camera hadn't been signed by a label yet but everybody knew they were an interesting group. Roddy Frame was only sixteen and we drove from Edinburgh to East Kilbride, picked up Roddy and drove down to Manchester. I think it was the first time he'd ever been in England, I'm not sure, but certainly the first time he'd ever been to Manchester and he was overawed by it, but he was fantastic. We did a great show and then drove all the way back the same day to East Kilbride and then back to Edinburgh, and already at that point people knew that Aztec Camera were doing something interesting. Malcolm Ross was a big fan.

ROBERT HODGENS: I met Roddy when he was still in Neutral Blue, just before Aztec Camera. I interviewed them for *Ten Commandments*, and I remember playing their early demo tape to Alan Horne, who didn't like them and thought they sounded like Joy Division.

Alan Horne and Malcolm Ross visited South Lanarkshire again in late December when they returned to Emblem Sound in Strathaven to produce two groups from the county, Article 58 and Aztec Camera. In some respects Article 58 felt like a perfect amalgam of Scars and Josef K and this was their first experience in a recording studio, while Aztec Camera had developed their sound away from their previous post-Joy Division demo recordings. They had evolved, influenced by Arthur Lee and Love, into something altogether more Postcard.

CAMPBELL OWENS: Aztec Camera made an initial demo at Sirocco studio in Kilmarnock. We recorded 'Green Jacket Grey', 'We Can Send Letters' and 'Lost Outside the Tunnel' on that demo and we could hear that something was happening. We sent it off to Zoo in Liverpool, who asked us to support the Teardrop Explodes; we also sent it to Allan Campbell's new label in Edinburgh, Rational Records. But we didn't send a demo off to Postcard. I can't remember why we didn't because they were right on our doorstep. I think maybe Roddy aligned himself more with Teardrop Explodes and Zoo. Josef K guitarist Malcolm Ross got a hold of the demo, probably through Allan Campbell, and Malcolm spoke to Alan Horne. Alan came to see Aztec Camera playing in the Bungalow Bar in Paisley along with Malcolm and Edwyn from Orange Juice. Straight away they recognised that something really special was going on and Alan spoke to us at the end of the gig. It was the first time we had met the three of them; we became instant friends with Malcolm and Edwyn.

GERRI MCLAUGHLIN: I was a fan of Alternative TV, PiL, and saw Subway Sect at the [Glasgow] Apollo shortly before my eighteenth birthday in 1978 — they supported the Buzzcocks. I rated the Buzzcocks very highly and had been talking to Pete Shelley in the foyer that afternoon — as was the way in those days you hung out at the gigs hoping to meet the bands or guest-list it. He said get in early, it's going to be a great night. I remember thinking that Vic Godard was quite the beatnik onstage and I liked his voice, delivery and style — a kind of punk Jack Kerouac. I'm pretty sure I already had 'Nobody's Scared' and 'Ambition' by the time of this gig as I hoovered up every single that came out at that time. At the Apollo I thought Subway Sect were chaotic in a way I liked. Vic's voice always spoke to me, Subway Sect were a big influence on Article 58. We sent an Article 58 demo to Postcard and Alan Horne wrote back to us telling us one track was crap and sounded like a bad rip-off of a Teardrop Explodes B-side on Zoo. However, he went on to say he thought the other track, 'Event to Come', was great and offered to come to Emblem Sound in Strathaven with Malcolm Ross to produce a single. I remember being pretty nervous meeting the Postcard cats, but calmed down after seeing how normal they were. I remember thinking that Malcolm got things done, he had sound and vision, he always seemed to me to have a quiet and confident personality, but a driving force of being good at what he did. Recording with Alan and Malcolm was an enjoyable experience, especially for someone like me who lacked confidence. I had the feeling with them producing Article 58 that I could get my vocal parts done and done decently.

EWAN MACLENNAN: Going into the studio with Alan Horne and Malcolm Ross was all about trying to capture the naive intensity Article 58 had as a live band and hoping to get that down on tape. It was exciting, building the tracks up, adding overdubs, hearing the songs come alive. The time spent working on getting guitars and drums sounding good was time well spent — the songs came together and everything just fell into place. The band was tight going into the studio; I think we managed to capture that. It was clear from the start of the session that Malcolm knew the kind of sound he was looking for. He spent time working on getting the perfect attack from the track and came up with a lot of ideas to build the sound — adding overdubs, giving the track a wilder sound. A great experience.

Les Disques du Crépuscule was a label/organisation founded in Brussels by Michel Duval and Annik Honoré in 1980. Crépuscule promoted art events and concerts at Plan K, a large venue in the city. Duval and Honoré had ties with Factory and worked with artists as diverse as Tuxedomoon, Gavin Bryers and Michael Nyman, and obviously had their antenna tuned to the glowing reports of Postcard releases throughout 1980. Crépuscule invited Postcard's twin attack of Orange Juice and Josef K to perform a New Year's Eve concert at Plan K, an event that left a lasting mark on Paul Haig in particular.

ALAN HORNE: Postcard ended 1980 in Brussels with Orange Juice and Josef K performing at the invitation of Les Disques du Crépuscule. Plan K was five floors of magic shows, transvestites, boxing, silent films and silent freaks, with two thousand people in attendance and the concert broadcast live on the radio. Josef K recorded a single of 'Sorry for Laughing' and 'Revelation' for Crépuscule before returning to London to play the ICA.

ALLAN CAMPBELL: Crépuscule Records was a label run in Belgium by a guy called Michel Duval; it was a very arty label, really beautifully made sleeves, and he would very often cherry-pick good British acts that were doing interesting things, like Cabaret Voltaire or Orange Juice. Crépuscule did a lot of really interesting compilations, and Josef K in particular had a good rapport with him. I think maybe Alan Horne's nose was slightly put out of joint when Duval invited Josef K to record a single in Brussels while they were over for the Postcard Plan K gig.

PAUL HAIG: Crépuscule were the first people to invite Josef K to play live in Belgium, and while we were there Michel Duval from the label suggested we record a single, which was 'Sorry for Laughing'. We were all really happy with the single. I don't think Alan Horne was too happy about our relationship with Crépuscule, but for us it was nice to have a European release.

The sound and fury captured in the Brussels studio by Josef K for their Crépuscule single highlighted to the group something they had been avoiding confronting — that something was missing from their recently recorded album, *Sorry for Laughing*, due for release on Postcard in a matter of weeks.

Nineteen eighty ended with Postcard now the hippest cats in the yard, with three Orange Juice singles, two Josef K singles and a solitary single by the Go-Betweens that all left an indelible mark on the year. The independent sector aesthetic had changed too: fans at Orange Juice and Josef K concerts now dressed like Orange Juice and Josef K. The new groups that had emerged throughout the UK displayed their Postcardian influences in both sound and lyrical approach.

While 1980 had seen the prodigious ascent of Postcard putting Glasgow on the map, Bob Last wasn't going to roll over and let Alan Horne steal his crown. Fast Product had mutated into a splinter label aimed at interactions with the pop charts — pop:aural — and was preparing to attack.

CHAPTER 5

1981 – Chasing the Chimera

Fire Engines: Russell Burn, Davy Henderson, Graham Main
and Murray Slade

ALAN HORNE: I'd love Postcard to be the level of a Fast Product or Factory, to have that kind of power. Although I think both these labels have been pathetic.

BOB LAST: Alan Horne? Stroppy little bugger. It was very tribal for whatever reason; my impression was that right from the get-go part of what energised Postcard was not being Fast Product. Fire Engines signing to Postcard was never going to happen.

DAVY HENDERSON: Bob had asked us if we wanted to be on his new label pop:aural. He maybe thought we were going to sign to Postcard or something like that. Does it really matter? I don't care.

The fact Fire Engines were coveted by both Alan Horne and Bob Last spoke volumes about the group's importance and the excitement generated on the back of their 'Get Up and Use Me' single on the Codex Communications outlet set up by their manager Angus Groovy. Last's confidence in calling in the last of the Keir Street gang to sign to his pop:aural label was well placed. The Fast Product incubator zone at the Keir Street flat had already helped form the teenage mindset of Scars, Thursdays, the Flowers and Boots for Dancing; it was only Fire Engines remaining. It could be argued that they absorbed the most Fast information; they regurgitated their cultural diet to create the perfect Fast product. Bob Last's overture to Fire Engines was to allow him to use and package them to provide 'background beat for active people' and 'improvised noisy beat' in the form of *Lubricate Your Living Room*. In many ways this was the ultimate Fast Product concept: Last recorded Fire Engines' fury and packaged it as speed muzak for youthquakers. The record was hard to categorise — neither 12-inch single nor EP, it was (erroneously) regarded by most consumers as an album. Bob Last's vision was to use Fire Engines and deconstruct their songs by removing most of the vocals. His production of *Lubricate Your Living Room* seemed to exist as a remix of an album that did not yet exist; in other words, pretty high concept. It was released on Accessory, which seemed to be a subsidiary label of pop:aural, which in itself was a subsidiary of Fast Product. The record came in its own plastic bag. Everything about the release felt new and forward-looking; its timing was perfect as media interest in Scottish underground pop was on an upward trajectory. Postcard had taken pole position as bearers of the 1980 Scottish pop mantle, while pop:aural had struggled to gain attention. However, as new signings Fire Engines and Restricted Code led the charge, Bob Last was ready to examine how far he could take it with pop:aural as an independent interloper. Alan Horne's stated ambition for Postcard was to become commercially successful and gain chart success for Orange Juice from an independent base. In stark contrast, Bob Last implored all Fast Product artists to sign to major labels and infiltrate the mainstream.

ALAN HORNE: The future is completely open, we'll just see what happens, see how many Postcard singles we sell. I think it's either a case of signing a licensing deal with a major or go it alone, which is what I'd like to do provided we have the money. I think that cult independent thing has been the problem with a lot of the small labels, it's held them back.

BOB LAST: I don't recall being bothered by Postcard's media success because one of our things that I was always very proud of was that Fast Product's success was UK-wide and international. That to me was the point of being based in Scotland — it wasn't to be narrowly Scottish, it was to say Scotland stands up there with everybody else. It's as good a place as any, it's got as many interesting ideas to feed into that global flow of ideas and cultural content. So I was quite happy to let Postcard occupy that space and to utilise that parochial sense of Scottishness as their brand, and I don't mean this to sound as judgemental as it does. We'd never sought to set out that kind of stall and also I was too busy at that time to get too bothered, because I was also managing the Human League by that time, which was starting to be quite a big thing.

GRACE FAIRLEY: I got the impression that Bob Last put a lot of thought into whether he was going to focus on Edinburgh-based groups for pop:aural because he always said that Fast wasn't an Edinburgh label in the way that Postcard was a Glasgow label. But he did release Scars, the Flowers, Boots for Dancing, Thursdays, the Prats and of course Fire Engines, and he really did have a lot of input in their development.

GRAHAM MAIN: Alan Horne was dead keen to have the Fire Engines on Postcard; we were big pals with Josef K who were from Edinburgh and on the label. We did a gig in Glasgow with Orange Juice and Alan hoped by osmosis we would sign to Postcard. Alan was offering us a good opportunity, but Bob had some proposals that interested us, so we went with him as his pop:aural artistic angle interested us more.

BOB LAST: Postcard didn't really register with me – to my mind they didn't have that multidimensional thing that was interesting to me. That was seen as a provocation.

DAVY HENDERSON: We'd played with Orange Juice so often it was maybe implied, or assumed, we'd also be on Postcard.

Fire Engines had their attack perfected and ready to launch; they could back up their slogans like 'Boredom or Fire Engines, you can't have both' with actions. Their idea of having two fifteen-minute sets as part of an evening programmed by the group seemed revolutionary, and in many ways it was. Bob Last packaged, produced and released *Lubricate Your Living Room* to mass acclaim — Paul Morley kick-started 1981 by interviewing the group for a two-page *NME* feature. 'Get Up and Use Me' was awarded the coveted single of the week, an accolade also accorded by Dave McCullough in *Sounds*. The Fire Engines gang now lived together in James Oliva's flat in Sciennes along with manager Angus Groovy; the Codex Communications crew continued their community conceptualisation.

DAVY HENDERSON: Fire Engines loved the Slits, Buzzcocks, Subway Sect, the Fall, Richard Hell and the Voidoids, Contortions, James White and the Blacks, the Velvet Underground, Television, the Pop Group, PiL, Johnny Thunders, Snatch. Girl singers and primitive drums turned us on, as did boys who wanted to be girl singers with primitive drums. To me Mark E. Smith is a soul singer. Bob Last asked us if we'd do extended instrumental versions of Fire Engines tracks, instead of putting out a traditional LP of our set. When he said he was going to release them in plastic bags we were thinking an album with a plastic bag is really Buzzcocks, let's do it. That swung it for us, the fact that he had plastic bags as part of the Accessories series, so we concurred and went into the studio, because the idea of not doing a traditional record appealed to us. With *Lubricate Your Living Room*, Bob had this idea loosely mimicking Eno's ambient output on Obscure Records, which was connected to Island Records and gave Eno carte blanche to put out what he wanted to release — music by Michael Nyman and Penguin Café. Eno had been doing his *(No Pussyfooting)* in the seventies with Robert Fripp, and I think Bob had an idea to create this exciting wallpaper music with Fire Engines.

GRAHAM MAIN: Bob was interested at this time in releasing a mini album of upbeat, instrumental ambient music and we liked the concept. Muzak to wind up to – it was active music. These were Bob Last's ideas   he was an ideas man and believed in form, probably from his architectural background.

RUSSELL BURN: Bob wanted to produce a dub instrumental version of the Fire Engines, as background action music. Fire Engines never recorded an album in the conventional sense of recording the songs we played in our live set.

MURRAY SLADE: I think the collaboration with Fire Engines and Bob Last reached its peak with *Lubricate Your Living Room*, the format of which confused media and public alike. Part of the reason was the way it was manufactured and packaged by Bob – is it an album, is it a 12-inch remix, or what? I would say that *Lubricate Your Living Room* was all of those things.

BOB LAST: *Lubricate Your Living Room* was absolutely about being a perverse lifestyle accessory. I was inspired by a company who made most of the elevator music at the time. This company very carefully analysed modularities and frequency spectrums that would be calming. *Lubricate Your Living Room* was a functional lifestyle accessory for a certain kind of wired young person, that was the model, and the point of that model was by Fire Engines adopting that strategy, it allowed them to musically do something that they otherwise wouldn't have done.

FRASER SUTHERLAND: Fire Engines and Bob Last had known each other for a good while before the pop:aural records of course, and the single the group brought out on Codex Communications had a fair bit of attention, which Bob hadn't been involved with. I thought the idea behind *Lubricate Your Living Room* was a great fit.

STEFAN KASSEL: When I first heard them on John Peel's show, Fire Engines just blew me away. Totally unique. The best music ever in ninety seconds. Concise. To the point. After those ninety seconds everything was said and told and done. Great slogans, great song titles and great artwork. Bob Last's artwork and packaging was unique, you just wanted to have those records. They looked great, they sounded great. They were different.

INNES REEKIE: *Lubricate Your Living Room* was an 8-track album of discordant, funky, improvised pieces of muzak. Music to go out to, to put you in the mood for 'action and fun'. The concept was Bob Last's. The release had more in common with the instrumental dub albums coming out of Jamaica and the extended instrumental disco mixes coming out of clubs like Danceteria in downtown Manhattan. *Lubricate Your Living Room* sounded like nothing else — Fire Engines were occupying a completely different hemisphere to that of their contemporaries.

PAUL MORLEY: Fire Engines beseech you through a music that has the anarchic application, derelict discipline and self-centred concentrated militancy. It takes your breath away, it turns you on. *Lubricate Your Living Room*, recorded and released by pop:aural on their Accessory label, is described as background muzak for active people. Music contrived to calm the listener invariably irritates. Noise as stimulant is far more effective and useful.

DAVY HENDERSON: *Lubricate Your Living Room* is not the first Fire Engines LP; it is our songs with the words taken away and the lengths extended. It was Bob Last's idea and we were into being used in this type of way. It's an amalgamation between pop:aural and Codex Communications using the Fire Engines and it's brilliant. Bob wanted to create a series of exciting, ambient records, he was asking Fire Engines to be the medium for his idea, which was really appealing to us. It was the total opposite of making a definitive album of your first set of songs. The way we saw it was that this was not really a Fire Engines record — it was Bob's record for pop:aural in which he was using our set to communicate his ideas.

MURRAY SLADE: Bob had these ideas that music could be something other than the standard album, single, tour type thing. It was his suggestion to extend the riffs of the songs we already had, adding to them and leaving out the vocals. So you had a record you could stick on and not analyse — you could either dance to it, or, ideally, do your housework to it. Active background music rather than laid-back background muzak.

Fire Engines had put down a beginning-of-year marker with *Lubricate Your Living Room*, which garnered critical kudos and sold well. Their debut John Peel session featured the group at a crossroads between their Codex Communications and pop:aural incarnations. The session included a song disliked by the group but earmarked by Bob Last as a single ('Candyskin'). They also premiered '(We Don't Need This) Fascist Groove Thang', a future single by the Last-managed Heaven 17 but as yet unreleased. However, the Codex aesthetic was fully evidenced in the two other songs in the session, 'Discord' and 'The Untitled One'.

GRAHAM MAIN: The Peel session in February 1981 was a good experience and we were very happy with it. Bob Last had just been through the Human League split and was also managing Heaven 17. We were doing a recording session at Castlesound and he played us a demo version of the Heaven 17 song '(We Don't Need This) Fascist Groove Thang', which we thought would be great to record for our forthcoming Peel session.

ANGUS GROOVY: Most of the early songs that featured in the John Peel sessions and the *Lubricate Your Living Room* album were conceived around the same Codex period. I think they achieved a blending of musical and stylistic influences that added quite a distinctive layer to British punk. They were hardly unique in importing New York sounds, as the Fall and others did that, but there was more of a jazz-punk-funk edge in Fire Engines. I suppose you could call the first eighteen months or so of Fire Engines the Codex period. The creative influence I had diminished pretty quickly after *Lubricate Your Living Room*. Although that was a pop:aural release I would still count it as Codex Communication in the creative sense, but by that time it had become clear that I had little aptitude for being a 'rock band manager'. I was content to let Fast take those things on, but pretty quickly Bob started to exercise more creative direction and nurture Davy's pop star ambitions.

The independent market thrived as Factory, Mute and Rough Trade stamped their mark on the year. Several other smaller independent/ self-release labels also broke through. At exactly the same time as Fire Engines gained success with what the public perceived as their debut album, Josef K and Alan Horne decided to scrap the debut Josef K album, *Sorry for Laughing*, prior to its release. Rough Trade had financed the album as part of their deal with Postcard, so yet again Geoff Travis was less than happy with Alan Horne.

ALAN HORNE: The Belgian single on Les Disques du Crépuscule has the sound Josef K have been looking for all along, so much so that their first studio LP has been scrapped.

MALCOLM ROSS: We recorded the first aborted album, *Sorry for Laughing*, at Castlesound studios, which is where all the Postcard singles were recorded, apart from 'Falling and Laughing'. I think our attention span was short, so we decided when we recorded the album we wouldn't listen to it until it came out. Then when Alan Horne got the test pressings it unfortunately coincided with

Alan having a confidence crisis about Postcard. He started sowing the seeds of doubt about the *Sorry for Laughing* album, saying he didn't think it sounded very good and that the drums were mixed too loud. Probably the sound of Josef K had changed a bit too, so when we listened to the album we were also disappointed. Alan started saying if we weren't happy with the album we didn't have to put it out. He said he'd talk to Rough Trade, who manufactured and distributed the Postcard releases, and we'd either remix or rerecord the album. However, Rough Trade were aghast, because they'd put up quite a substantial budget for it, in relative terms. So we didn't put the album out and instead went back to a studio in Belgium and recorded the scratchy, difficult debut album, *The Only Fun in Town*. Again, it was art, not commerce.

PAUL HAIG: We went in to record our album, which was going to be the first album on Postcard. We recorded it in Castlesound studios, and every morning I would drive us there. Alan would be in the back of the car ranting all the way to the studio, and as we were all tired from recording there was a real temptation to ask him just to shut up. During the recording we had more scope to try different things with production and instruments, we felt the recording was going pretty well. However, once we'd finished and listened to the test pressing, it felt really flat, like something had happened at the cut. In the studio the album had an edge to it, but when we heard the cut it sounded blanded out. So we didn't release the album because it didn't seem to capture the sound of Josef K, and Alan went along with our decision. Les Disques du Crépuscule had asked us if we wanted to do a single and that's how the recording and release of the 'Sorry for Laughing' single came out on Crépuscule, much to Alan Horne's disgust. No, he wasn't too happy — I think he felt that it was one of our most commercial songs and he really wanted it to come out on Postcard.

ALLAN CAMPBELL: There's a lot of argument about what happened to the first Josef K album. I think the prosaic version probably was just they weren't happy with the sound of the album. Josef K in many respects regarded themselves as a live band. That you had to be at a gig, to get the guitars, the feeling, the immensity of it all and that wasn't something you necessarily got out of a little record player. I suspect maybe there was an attempt to try and capture that live feeling on record. Seeing Josef K live was the thing, more than anything else, because the hairs would stand up on the back of your neck. It's an idea now that just seems antediluvian and everybody just wants to make and sell recordings. Josef K had to create an exciting moment in time, they were talking about just doing one album then that's it. The idea that when it became a job and it became predictable and they had to record album two and album three went against the idea of creating a flash of excitement. That is not a commercial idea, it's totally artistic, and these are the kind of ideas that are being forgotten, I think. Better a fifteen-minute set that's fantastic than a one-and-a-half-hour set that is OK.

Josef K returned to Belgium to have another stab at recording a debut album, while positive Postcard news revolved around the signing of a new group, East Kilbride's Aztec Camera, who centred around the prodigious sixteen-year-old talents of mercurial song-writer, vocalist and guitarist Roddy Frame. With Campbell Owens on bass and David Mulholland on drums, the trio had already recorded 'We Could Send Letters' for inclusion on the Rough Trade/ *NME* cassette, *C81*, and were sent to Castlesound to record another version of the song as the B-side of their first single, 'Just Like Gold'. January also saw Orange Juice record their fourth Postcard single, 'Poor Old Soul', so consolidation was the Postcard plan. East Kilbride new town loomed large in the Aztec Camera psyche and informed the poetic lyricism of Frame's teenage existentialism.

Alan Horne was delighted he had signed another group he could believe in and hoped they would share his Postcard/Orange Juice melodic vision.

ALAN HORNE: It was like stumbling into Max's [Kansas City] to find the Velvet Underground, but this Lou Reed was sixteen and the audience was sixty-one. We had all been proven wrong — there was another group in Glasgow apart from Orange Juice.

RODDY FRAME: East Kilbride was a bit bleak, but it was all right. I started hanging out with people that were like-minded during the punk revolution of 1977/'78. I was only about thirteen, so I'd hang around the local record shop, called Impulse. I started writing songs during the punk period, but they weren't very good so we'd end up playing Clash covers most of the time. My taste broadened. I was into Alternative TV then I started listening to sixties stuff when I saw a photo of Mark Perry surrounded by Zappa and Love albums. Bowie was where I learned about Nietzsche and Andy Warhol, then I was inspired by the Banshees and Joy Division. I'm inspired by attitude, people like Neil Young. I've got a really eclectic record collection, artists like Wes Montgomery, and I wear my influences on my sleeve. I spent a lot of time at home in East Kilbride practising along to my favourite records, that's how I learned to play guitar.

CAMPBELL OWENS: I was a young teenager in the mid-seventies and very much into music — it was the driving force of my life. I was not interested in anyone other than early seventies T. Rex. I played their records constantly. I didn't play sport, didn't hang out with musically minded people. T. Rex progressed on to Bowie and Roxy Music. I met someone at high school who was very knowledgeable about music, and around about 1975 he started playing me records by the Velvet Underground, Lou Reed, New

York Dolls, MC5, proto-punk bands. Growing up in an overspill new town, East Kilbride, also shaped me. The sense of being apart, alienation, no future, punk rock, chimed neatly with that and I think that's why it spread out from London into the provinces and really took a hold.

RODDY FRAME: Tamla Motown was what people listened to all the time. There was always a big country and western and soul thing, particularly in Glasgow. East Kilbride was built for what was charmingly termed 'the Glasgow overspill'. My friend said, 'We're not Glaswegians, we're a social experiment.' It was all new and modern, quite concrete, but that's all right, concrete's not always bad. There were strips of grass and football pitches and a youth club. My parents didn't like it because they came from Glasgow and missed the sense of community, the warmth of the tenements. But then my dad would remind my mum, 'Remember when you were pacing the block waiting for me to come home because there was a rat in the room?'

CAMPBELL OWENS: New towns — no character, very bland, nothing to do unless you're into sport. A separate identity from Glasgow, definitely. My parents came from Glasgow, but living in EK there was definitely a sense of not being part of Glasgow. EK definitely shaped Aztec Camera, the early songs were all steeped in EK. Teenagers living in places like EK understood the whole punk movement better than anybody, because we had nothing and lacked the vibrancy of a city like Glasgow. We were true punks, and the post-punk bands like Joy Division became extremely popular in EK, more so than in many other towns. I founded EK's first punk rock band, horrifically named the Dole. I wasn't happy with the band and I wanted to move things on. A chap in my class said that his neighbour was a brilliant guitarist, a guy called Roddy. I was seventeen the first time I met Roddy, at the local EK youth centre, the Key. I remember he was this

David Bowie lookalike, plastic sandals and spiky hair. I was playing 'White Riot' by the Clash, showing him how to play it. I gave the guitar to Roddy and as soon as he played it my jaw hit the deck. I thought, 'This lad is going to be a star.' Amazing. We were into hardcore punk but also into singer-songwriters like Don McLean, Paul Simon, Bob Dylan, which you kept quiet about at the time. Roddy played with his friend's band for a wee while, called Neutral Blue, and I was playing bass in a band called the Stilettos. Roddy and I used to hang out a lot, usually at a café in the town centre that we called the Kafka Café. We'd spend our whole day sitting with one cup of coffee. I told Roddy I was fed up and was leaving EK. I had been accepted for Dundee University, but I didn't want to go, I just wanted to get out of EK. When I got home, practically as soon as I shut the door of the house, the phone rang and it was Roddy, saying, 'Listen, rather than going to Dundee Uni, leave your band, and join mine.' It took about a proverbial nano-second to reply in the affirmative, that's how I joined Aztec Camera.

The first song I heard from Roddy was when he was fourteen and it was way beyond his years. He was musically and lyrically the best thing I had heard, and he was fourteen. The first version of Aztec Camera was after he split with Neutral Blue and he wanted to start up and lead his own band. For a while they called themselves Pink Triangle, so you can see the similarities here and where it was going. It was dreadful. They changed briefly to Aztec Camera just before I came in and Roddy, being the musical mercenary that he is, was looking to surround himself with the best musicians possible. Alan Welsh was a lovely guy and looked the part, but he wasn't really a great bass player. David Mulholland was a brilliant drummer however and I was fairly handy on the bass and that's when Roddy changed the line-up and brought me in. That was a great band, the line-up when we made our first recordings with Postcard.

Once signed to Postcard the media stamp of approval for Aztec Camera was immediate. *Sounds* writer Dave McCullough flew up to Glasgow to write a feature about the group before they'd released a note of music. High anticipation awaited whoever signed to Postcard next and Aztec Camera fitted the label aesthetic perfectly. Dave McCullough's article documented a new puritan ideal (as he saw it), and the tenderness of Aztec Camera chimed perfectly with McCullough's vision of Postcard.

RODDY FRAME: I hate being thought of as a child prodigy, because I don't feel that young. I think things should be better. I think there should be a better place. I don't think anyone should be bored. I think it's just that people lose touch and fall into boredom. I used to be bored at school, but then I left and discovered interesting things like reading. I like gentle music, and there's the fact that I do most of my writing at about four in the morning, so I can only use an acoustic guitar in case I annoy people.

The *Sounds* article had people primed for the debut Aztec Camera single, which was as close to Postcard perfection as it was possible to get. Aztec Camera echoed the past but reinterpreted it to sound new. That a sixteen-year-old wrote in such a literary manner and played a twelve-string acoustic guitar was a big statement; it felt like the complete antithesis of the austere values of Factory and Joy Division (although Aztec Camera noted their debt to Joy Division). 'Just Like Gold' b/w 'We Could Send Letters' was another forward gear change by Postcard.

CAMPBELL OWENS: I remember recording at Castlesound, the engineer Callum Malcolm was friendly and easy to work with. 'Just Like Gold' was to be our first release so that was exciting, I remember really enjoying the session and being pleased by the result. It was also the only record we ever did with original drummer David

Mulholland, who is an excellent musician. In terms of production ideas, we all chipped in. We got on really well with Malcolm Ross so production collaboration at Castlesound was natural. It was Malc who brought Aztec Camera to the attention of Alan and Edwyn, so we've got him to thank/blame for us being on Postcard.

pop:aural was also on the up. Fire Engines signing to the label was a major coup, and the success of *Lubricate Your Living Room* was a significant statement of intent. Personnel changes took place within Restricted Code prior to their next single being recorded at Castlesound, when drummer Robert McCormick's work commitments proved too difficult to juggle with his role in the group. Robert left Restricted Code to be replaced by Article 58 drummer Stephen Lironi, who had started working for Bob Last on a work placement at Fast Product's distribution wing. Article 58 had signed to Josef K manager Allan Campbell's label Rational Records, and kept things incestuous by replacing Lironi with Robert McCormick.

Bob Last co-ordinated a new pop:aural strategy that involved new singles and a tour by Fire Engines and Restricted Code, while his management manipulations of the Human League resulted in Jo Callis joining the group. Last produced two pop:aural singles he believed could compete beyond the independent marketplace and elevate Fire Engines and Restricted Code to a higher level. The first Restricted Code single had been well received and all signals were on red in anticipation of their new single. There was a sense of forward momentum in the air with lots of positivity towards Restricted Code and Fire Engines — the timing felt perfect for pop:aural to capitalise on the media interest in the Scottish independent pop underground movement. Restricted Code were now a sleeker, more rhythmic machine with new drummer Stephen Lironi in their ranks.

Restricted Code: Kenny Blythe, Tom Cannavan, Frank Quadrelli and
Stephen Lironi

FRANK QUADRELLI: We have always been grateful that we had two excellent drummers in the band. Robert was an absolute power-house and we would have been delighted if he had stayed with the band, but the more dates we played, the more difficult it became for him to keep his job so he had to leave the group. Tom and I were both students so it was less of a problem for us. For Kenny it was more difficult, using up all of his holiday allowance to play with the band. I'm not sure how we found out about Stephen, but we were certainly impressed by him and he was interested right away and before too long he was in the band. Stephen was a lot younger than the rest of us, and did not really impose himself too much, certainly not at first. Tom and I always had strong ideas about how our songs should sound and be arranged. Robert, also much younger than us, would generally accommodate and go along with our suggestions, but Stephen, with much more confidence, would suggest other ways of doing it, and he would generally be correct. He did offer to help Tom and I with songwriting, but we didn't take him up on it, which is ironic, given that he went on to co-write huge-selling hits.

TOM CANNAVAN: On our second pop:aural single, 'Love to Meet You', a review in *Sounds* or *Melody Maker* praised it for being driven along with 'plenty of African percussion', but it was just Stephen on his standard kit. Stephen was a serious musician and had ideas on arrangements and so on. Basically, however, the band continued very much as before.

Restricted Code had their John Peel session broadcast on 17 March and were tipped by Paul Morley at the *NME* — all signs augured well for a second single. It felt like a lot was at stake for Bob Last, pop:aural and Restricted Code with the second single.

TOM CANNAVAN: The second single took the 'lavish and indulgent' to an even greater level. I recall being told we had the longest time in the studio of any single Bob had produced. Those were creative and happy days in Castlesound studios, and a lot of effort went into the production. However, soon after when bands like ABC and Heaven 17 started releasing records with incredibly glossy, room-filling and sonically brilliant productions, I thought we'd been let down a little by the sound on our records with pop:aural. We were by then a much less punky/scratchy band, and we were writing more complex, slightly funky songs which we thought had real commercial potential, but which the sound of our records didn't fully capture.

FRANK QUADRELLI: Stephen's funkier drumming sensibilities were perfect for 'Love to Meet You', and Bob Last was quite happy to spend the time and money involved. I don't remember anyone having to talk anyone else into it, we all thought it was the best thing to do.

TOM CANNAVAN: 'Love to Meet You' was still a little bit DIY and might have benefitted from a bigger production. I believe the extra time in the studio was an effort to get that, though I am not sure it was achieved. It would have needed a Martin Rushent or Tony Visconti to give it the extra polish, but somehow I don't think the pop:aural budget would have stretched to that.

Postcard had been well represented on the recent *C81* cassette, a joint release by Rough Trade and the *NME*, on which Alan Horne described the Postcard groups as various editions of the Velvet Underground. Josef K's contribution was 'Endless Soul', taken from their scrapped debut album. Aztec Camera provided the acoustic guitar-led version of 'We Could Send Letters' recorded at Emblem Sound, while Orange Juice donated their second single, 'Blue Boy'. March also saw the release of a trio of Postcard singles with the

Aztec Camera debut and the fourth single by Orange Juice, 'Poor Old Soul', both contained in a new Postcard house bag to replace the cowboy record sleeves used for previous singles. The new black die-cut covers featured drawings of Scottish landed gentry in kilts and tweeds and were designed by Horne's 185 flatmate Krysia Klasicki. The back cover included planned Postcard singles; among those listed was catalogue number 81-6, 'Wan Light' by Orange Juice (which was never released). The third March single issued was 'Sorry for Laughing' by Josef K, released on Les Disques du Crépuscule and given the simultaneous catalogue numbers 81-4 (Postcard) and TWI 023. The cover was put together by Crépuscule's esteemed designer Benoît Hennebert, with no mention of Postcard on the sleeve. These three new Postcard-related singles had the media excited. All three records were of the highest quality and Orange Juice in particular hoped to make strides towards the charts.

RODDY FRAME: I made the first Postcard record, 'Just Like Gold', when I was seventeen or eighteen. I couldn't believe when we got our first fan mail, a letter from America. I thought it was amazing that a song written in my bedroom had gone out there into the world — I thought it was a great form of communication.

CAMPBELL OWENS: The press was pro-Aztec Camera even before we'd released anything. Signing to Postcard resulted in a big three-page spread in *Sounds* by Dave McCullough. I was amazed at the press prior to releasing anything, but when our first single came out, 'Just Like Gold', it really delivered, I thought it was wonderful.

RODDY FRAME: I don't think I could improve 'Just Like Gold' in any way. I spent a long time trying to sound unclichéd. There's no chorus in it, nothing is repeated.

CAMPBELL OWENS: Regarding the Postcard imagery, the twee middle-class Scottish thing was Alan Horne and Orange Juice, it definitely was not Aztec Camera — we weren't middle class for a start and I don't think we were twee. I didn't like the tweed jackets or the kilts on the Postcard house-design sleeves for the singles.

EDWYN COLLINS: We thought 'Poor Old Soul' was a bit like a Chic song. I really saw it as a chart contender, and there were arguments with Rough Trade over whether or not we should use a strike force to help promote it. They had this hippy mentality and said no, but Alan was very ruthless and had no scruples about bribery or corruption. Alan was still behaving very eccentrically — he would go around with huge cat's whiskers painted on his face saying, 'I'm catman and I make purrrfect records.' What we were doing with Orange Juice and Postcard was so strong, and because it was so strong it was widely copied, and I think what followed in our wake was diluted Orange Juice. Our ideal was to get someone like the Chic Organization or John Fogerty to produce the debut Orange Juice album; we were aware where our Postcard singles fell short, which was the production.

BILLY SLOAN: Glasgow was really exciting around the period Postcard were releasing singles. We had some great record shops like Listen, Graffiti, Blogs, places you could go and congregate and meet like-minded people, it was a classic case of interaction. Nowadays you're a click away on a computer from finding the most obscure record you might be interested in, but back in the early eighties you'd have people like Roddy Frame getting the bus from East Kilbride into Killermont Street bus station to make his way to the Glasgow record shops to meet like-minded people.

Scars finally had their *Author! Author!* album released, and the stars seemed to be aligned in the form of potential hit single 'All about You'. The production on the album was more coherent than the Pre Records singles, though still lacked the bite of the Fast production style of Bob Last. Their image also had an *i-D* (London fashion magazine) makeover — it felt a bit more London and New Romantic and a bit less Edinburgh and 'droog' — but their songs remained intact. Robert King was an *NME* cover star and it looked like Scars' boat was going to come in.

FRASER SUTHERLAND: The signing of the band to Pre seemed to take an age. Things tended to happen really quickly around then, and perhaps my memory doesn't serve me well, but it seemed to drag on forever. It was a real shame that a second single for Fast didn't happen — I think it might have captured a moment that had gone by the time the recordings for Pre happened.

ROBERT KING: It was tremendously exciting to suddenly see yourself on the front page of the *NME* and posters advertising the Scars album, the reviews of which were nothing but good.

JOHN MACKIE: We needed to make an album and exorcise it, get it out there. We all knew nothing lasts forever. Everything has a lifespan, and our creative relationship with Fast had a lifespan as well and when it was over we knew it.

PAUL RESEARCH: We made our base in London. It seemed to make sense because we were touring a lot in different countries and we wanted to be close to the record company. When we toured with the Human League, typically the record company would have to fork out a few thousand quid to get a band on tour as a support act. In 1980 we released the single 'Love Song' and in order to push that we went out on the road in the UK with the Human League, who were already friends from the early days but of course now we had a bigger label. Bob Last was managing the Human League and managed to extract some money out of our label to make the support slot happen for the Scars. Neither of the Pre singles were that great — we didn't really click in the studio and by that time I'd got so fearful that I was almost reluctant to do the album, because it seemed that every time we recorded we somehow neutered the sound. We were playing some really good gigs, quite ferocious gigs sometimes — and we just couldn't get that sound to translate in the studio. We didn't have the right sympathetic kind of ears that we had when we recorded 'Horrorshow' and 'Adult/ery'.

JOHN MACKIE: I think signing to a major label results in everything becoming much more impersonal. At that time the majors were experimenting with this whole new music scene and they weren't quite sure how much they should invest in promoting brand-new artists versus the massive money-making machines they already had on the boil.

PAUL RESEARCH: It suddenly felt like a bit of a roller coaster ride when our album came out. Paul Morley interviewed us for *NME*. He was very interested in what we were doing and then later on when the album came out, we got a very good review in *Sounds* by Dave McCullough, who gave it five stars. Then Paul Morley turned up on our tour and came with us to Berlin, and I said to him, 'Have you seen the review in *Sounds*, it's fantastic.' He said, 'That's nothing, wait until you see my review.' I just thought, 'Oh my God, this is great.' We never seemed to have any trouble getting good press, I don't know why, but in the early days we caught the imagination of the press much more than the public.

JOHN MACKIE: When we made *Author! Author!*, Pre immediately loved it and they started investing and promoting it. That was quite refreshing actually and we felt vindicated for signing to a major as we had been playing a lot of the material on the record around gigs for the previous couple of years.

PAUL RESEARCH: *Author! Author!* is actually a collection of songs that we'd been writing for many years. Some of those songs go back to the very, very early days. During the recording of *Author! Author!* there was a bit of conflict in the band. We were all moving in different circles and meeting a lot of new people since our move to London. We didn't think it was going to be the last album Scars made, but from a songwriting point of view I did wonder how we were going to actually get another full album worth of songs together. The recording of *Author! Author!* was definitely a peak and then we had used up all of our material just to create those twelve songs. However, it seemed that the band softened and lost a little bit of the edge that we had previously, and we endured a bit of criticism for that. To go from a position of being very well received and always praised to being thought of as going off the boil and perhaps not the coming thing any more, is actually quite an uncomfortable situation to be in.

KEN MCCLUSKEY: I think maybe the groups were a bit darker in Edinburgh, more menacing, with Scars, Josef K and Fire Engines, they seemed more art school than Glasgow, a more angular approach. When Scars played Glasgow their singer Bobby King wore ladies' high-heel shoes and earrings, he had a totally confrontational approach towards the audience. He had total conviction, and managed to turn audience hostility around, which I saw when Scars supported the Banshees in Tiffany's — he faced the audience down through his strength of personality, it was brilliant. Scars were the real deal in the same way as Suicide were. *Author! Author!* was a fantastic album, but by then Scars were dressed up in New Romantic clothes on the cover.

JOHN MACKIE: The clothes we were wearing when we did *The Old Grey Whistle Test* to promote *Author! Author!* were designed by Glen Matlock's wife, Celia, who was an embryonic fashion designer at the time. It hasn't worn the test of time but at the time we thought it was brilliant.

ROBERT KING: I suppose I do see myself as a pioneer and influence on the Fire Engines and Josef K, but at the same time I just ignore that kind of element of the whole thing, because on the one hand they're friends but on the other hand I do recognise that Scars' existence helped them. It never created them, but in some ways I suppose our influence was positive in the sense that we were happy to be friends with anybody that was similarly minded.

GEOFF TRAVIS: In Edinburgh there was the Fire Engines and the Scars, and the Prats, who we did a single with, there were lots of good things happening. I didn't know Scars really, but they didn't seem as important as the first wave of Postcard bands, and they went to a new Pre imprint on Charisma. I suppose the Bob Last trajectory was quite popular and maybe people were following Bob's lead, along with the manager of Gang of Four, Rob Warr, who thought they should go to a major, to take the money.

The Postcard movement accelerated at a swift pace. The debut Josef K album, now called *The Only Fun in Town*, had been recorded in Belgium and was being prepared for summer release. Postcard donated four songs from the abandoned Josef K album to BBC Radio 1 for a John Peel session, and interest in the self-styled Sound of Young Scotland was intense. Postcard was the hippest label in the UK and selling significant amounts of singles. Demos arrived at Postcard HQ from all over the world from bands that wanted to be on the label. Local bands were also eager to impress.

EDWYN COLLINS: Postcard was getting hundreds of tapes sent in by all the would-be hopefuls at that stage, and there were always the same characters hanging around. Robert Hodgens from the Bluebells was always trying to impress Alan in the hope they'd get signed up, but Alan would just play him along.

Alan Horne concentrated on managing Aztec Camera's career and developed ideas for the next releases by Orange Juice and Josef K. However, internal conversations within Orange Juice began to question how far they could take the group within the confines of independence and Postcard. Bob Last prepared an east coast assault with a UK tour that highlighted pop:aural's new singles by Fire Engines and Restricted Code. Last had also finally been involved in a hit single: the Human League reached number 12 in the charts with 'The Sound of the Crowd', which was co-written by vocalist Phil Oakey and new member Ian Burden (who had previously appeared on *Earcom 1* as a member of Graph). This was a major breakthrough and consolidated the new League line-up and their relationship with producer Martin Rushent, who had previously produced successful albums with punk-era groups the Stranglers and Buzzcocks. Virgin Records were extremely keen to get an album recorded with the new line-up, and the songwriting contributions of Burden and Jo Callis were noted by the label, who now venerated Last's contribution and guidance to both the Human League and their former group members, the British Electronic Foundation/Heaven 17 (which Last had incorporated as a production company). Another key component of the Fast empire was their distribution company (in cahoots with the Cartel), which was headed up by former Flowers drummer Simon Best.

SIMON BEST: I concentrated on building the new Fast business, essentially our regional independent wholesaling operation in Scotland.

SANDY MCLEAN: It was really interesting dealing with the distributors because those were the really formative years of independent distribution. There was no one place that you could get everything from. At retail we had to cherry-pick from some of these smaller distribution companies, then we started buying from Rough Trade's distribution company, which evolved into the Cartel, a national independent distribution network. Distribution started becoming much more professional. Rough Trade knew and respected Bob Last from his label activities so Fast became the Scottish distributor. Each member of the Cartel would bring in label product from their area and put it into a central pool, the central pot, and we would move product around and not charge each other for about two months.

GEOFF TRAVIS: Rough Trade distribution was in place when Bob started putting out the Fast records, and when Alan started putting out his Postcard records. The Cartel distribution expanded so quickly, and we started having hit records. It grew and grew and grew.

STEPHEN LIRONI: After Article 58 I was playing drums with Restricted Code, who were signed to Bob's label after Fast, pop:aural. I was doing a business degree that required me to take an industry placement for a year, so I worked for Bob as part of the Fast Product distribution wing.

April saw the release of the Alan Horne- and Malcolm Ross-produced single by Article 58 on Josef K manager Allan Campbell's label, Rational. The single, 'Event to Come', received a warm reception from the music weeklies and radio, with John Peel being particularly taken with the record. Rational had already released singles by Delmontes (who Campbell was managing) and Visitors, both of which had made an impact. However, inhabiting the giant shadows cast by Fast Product/pop:aural and Postcard made it difficult to attain the same degree of interest for Rational. Perhaps Rational would have gained more cultural capital if they hadn't been based in Edinburgh at that particular time (but of course it was that same time period and being based in Scotland that influenced Rational creatively).

Article 58: Gerri McLaughlin, Ewan MacLennan, Douglas MacIntyre and Robert McCormick

ALLAN CAMPBELL: In Henderson Row there was a small record shop called Gutter Music and I worked in there (I'd previously been working as a teacher and I'd had it with teaching). The guy that ran Gutter Music was a kind of slightly eccentric ex-actor type. He was very into music and let me base Rational Records there. He put a bit of money into it as well. So that was really how the Rational label started, with groups like the Delmontes, Visitors, Article 58, Mark, James and Julie, and Rhythm of Life.

EWAN MACLENNAN: Alan Horne gave us a lot of good advice, particularly when Article 58 were offered the recording contract by Rational Records. Article 58 played in Glasgow at the Rock Garden and Alan came along with Edwyn Collins. Edwyn was more interested in talking to Douglas about the Baldwin guitar he was playing at the gig, while Alan chatted to us about the business side of things. He looked over the Rational contract we had been given to sign and offered us advice, suggesting possible changes we should consider, which we did. Basically he was saying take control, and if it goes wrong you've no one else to blame.

ALLAN CAMPBELL: There was a very pronounced group of people, all revolving around band members or satellites around the bands. Josef K knew and respected the Associates, ditto for the Fire Engines with people like Paul Reekie and the Thursdays. There was a whole group of people who were all on the same wavelength in many ways, with a certain idealism as regards music. A lot of those people have stayed in contact with each other, which I think is indicative of the strength of feeling from that era that lingers on.

April also saw a great leap forward by pop:aural, with new singles released by Fire Engines and Restricted Code. The label had not made the impact it had hoped for during 1980, but the three uninspired singles released by Drinking Electricity may have contributed to that. The Flowers and Boots for Dancing were no longer part of the pop:aural plan, but Fire Engines and Restricted Code most certainly were. As usual, both groups' singles were produced and packaged by Bob Last and a pop:aural tour with both groups on the same bill was scheduled. This was the moment of truth, an orchestrated strategy that had been carefully planned by Last, who had the ear of every major UK label on the back of the Human League chart success. His management manipulations also began to bear fruit with the original League founders Martyn Ware and Ian Craig Marsh, who had prepped their first project under the aegis of their BEF production company. Heaven 17 were made up of Ware, Craig Marsh and vocalist Glenn Gregory, who was part of the same Sheffield electronic scene. Their debut single '(We Don't Need This) Fascist Groove Thang' was released to pave the way for their *Penthouse and Pavement* album, and another strategic ploy by Last had already secured the song's premiere when he persuaded Fire Engines to cover 'Fascist Groove Thang' on their first BBC session for John Peel on 23 February.

BOB LAST: I remember when 'Fascist Groove Thang' was being recorded by Heaven 17, I was blown away by the boldness of making something that funky and cool. I saw 'Fascist Groove Thang' as a more complicated piece because it had resonance.

MARTYN WARE: There was a lot of confidence with Virgin, and Bob from a management perspective, that 'Fascist Groove Thang' was amazing and was going to be a top 20 hit.

The pop:aural singles by Fire Engines and Restricted Code were 'Candyskin' and 'Love to Meet You' respectively. The production of the Restricted Code single 'Love to Meet You' had been reasonably straightforward, ditto the packaging which used a painting by Tom Cannavan on the front cover (along with Bob's design).

TOM CANNAVAN: The front covers are my paintings, Bob was totally happy to use them as I recall, as were the band. Neither was painted specifically to be the cover of the records, but we felt they worked, being slightly exotic and mysterious, both featuring main characters who stared out from the cover directly at the viewer. With 'Love to Meet You' in particular we hoped the slight sense of loss or alienation came through. Bob's team came up with the graphics and the slogans ('modern music for radio and dancing').

FRANK QUADRELLI: The artwork was Tom's — he had been at Glasgow School of Art and I had always loved his work. There was no real concept with the artwork, but somehow the Afghan men with guns and the camel seemed to work with the first single, despite the fact that the emotional drama of 'First Night On' was, content-wise, a million miles away. The exotic girl on the cover of 'Love to Meet You' was more obviously fitting.

Things were less straightforward with the Fire Engines' single, 'Candyskin', which was not a song the group loved. Bob Last followed a similar concept to *Lubricate Your Living Room* in that he wanted to use Fire Engines to sculpt and produce a pop song that could possibly be a hit single. Fire Engines were happy to be used by Bob, though happier still to represent their own vision with the song that was recorded for the B-side, 'Meat Whiplash', which ended up being the only pop:aural track by Fire Engines that reflected their Codex Communications sound.

INNES REEKIE: 'Candyskin' was a radical departure from their Codex debut. Henderson's trademark shouts and screams were replaced by a more orthodox vocal, and Keir Street regular, Simon Best, was employed to provide a string arrangement which did much to disguise any discordant guitar work still evident. That said, it was by no means a conventional single, and remains possibly their best-known work, peaking at number 2 in the *NME*'s alternative chart. It was Last's decision to release 'Candyskin' as the A-side, whereas the B-side, 'Meat Whiplash', was possibly the band's best recording as [regards] their trademark sound.

BOB LAST: We did 'Candyskin' and it was probably the closest we got throughout any of that time to something that was recognisable to other people as being pop. I'm not sure whether Davy's forgiven me for 'Candyskin' — he's ambivalent about it for sure, still — but it was a great bit of pop. BBC Radio 1 at the time had a review show in prime time where the week's new releases would be reviewed and it was the first thing we'd done that had ever got on that. 'Candyskin' was roundly dismissed as the worst-produced record that anyone had ever heard, interestingly enough, but I think it was a great bit of outsider pop and remains so.

DAVY HENDERSON: 'Candyskin' in some ways is the antithesis of 'Get Up and Use Me', and so we regarded it as a joke, humorous, literally a joke. We were playing it as we were rehearsing 'Meat Whiplash', which we were keen to record as the single thinking that it sounded like something off Captain Beefheart's *Safe As Milk*. Bob liked 'Meat Whiplash' as well. He came to the Fire Engines' rehearsals and as he walked in we were going through 'Candyskin', which we thought of as an Elvis pastiche, being fans of Vivian Stanshall etc. Bob responded to it right away, saying we should record it. It was Bob that put 'Candyskin' together and along with Simon Best from the Flowers, they came up with the strings, which is the best thing about it for me. They also came up with the la la la la la la for the ending which I suppose they thought was a bit like 'The Passenger'. It wasn't until many years later that I wondered how they came up with that motif, then realised the motif is just the guitar part, so that was a songwriting lesson. Bob took 'Candyskin' seriously so we forced ourselves to take it seriously and went and recorded it with him. It is not my favourite Fire Engines moment.

GRAHAM MAIN: 'Candyskin' was our first pop:aural single, which we wrote and completed in an hour or so. We had a few good tunes and they were fairly quickly and enjoyably written.

MURRAY SLADE: Possibly through the success that was happening with the Human League, Bob wanted to make pop:aural different from what he had done with Fast Product. I think he had ambitions for pop:aural where all the acts had a certain kind of affinity, a pop-ness if you like, aiming at charts.

ANGUS GROOVY: I would say 'Candyskin' was the start of the pop:aural period. It was a very alluring sound, and produced with top 40 ambitions. It just made my skin crawl, especially the string section. If I had been more assertive I would have tried to give the production a darker edge, but by then I knew I was out. For context there were six of us sharing a small two-room flat, pooling our dole cheques and spending a fair amount of that on drugs to fuel a nocturnal existence as self-styled neo-beatniks. But I was going through a personal crisis, and was quite relieved to be asked to leave.

STEPHEN LIRONI: When 'Candyskin' came out we sold 10,000 records in the first week, which was amazing.

BOB LAST: I was always thinking strategically or tactically and in my mind the quid pro quo of doing the incredibly poppy 'Candyskin' (let's put some strings on it and make it into this beautiful pop song), with [the idea] in mind that we would make other kinds of Fire Engines records at the opposite extreme. We did this with the incredibly energetic noise of *Lubricate Your Living Room*, so the two were opposite sides of the same coin in my mind.

DAVY HENDERSON: I remember letting Alan Horne hear 'Candyskin'. He just walked away laughing, saying, 'My God.'

The pop:aural package tour went well, and both records received strong Radio 1 support on Peel. Fire Engines went onstage first doing their two fifteen-minute sets, followed by Restricted Code. The London concert at the Embassy Club in particular brought industry interest.

FRANK QUADRELLI: Fire Engines played before us every night on the tour, which would cause some confusion as some of the crowd would mistakenly think that we were the Fire Engines when we took to the stage. The Codes received good press attention and plenty of airplay, but this did not compare with the Fire Engines. The tour reached its climax in the Embassy Club in London — I remember that gig so well. Alan McGee was a big fan of both ourselves and the Fire Engines and we had put him on our guest list. He was living in London at the time in a squat with Andrew Innes and another member of the Laughing Apple, their band at the time. We had known Alan for years and I remember him walking about the Embassy Club, eyeing the formally dressed staff, loudly declaiming, 'This is not punk!' John Peel was there, Paul Morley, Gang of Four, Julian Cope, Pete Wylie, Blondie, Frank Zappa and some Sex Pistols.

ALAN MCGEE: I think Fire Engines were one of the best Scottish bands ever. 'Get Up and Use Me' with its yellow and black sleeve, I loved it to bits. It was just the fucking rawness of Fire Engines. Bob Last's packaging of Restricted Code and the Fire Engines was great — I loved the art side of Fast Product and pop:aural.

PAUL MORLEY: Alan McGee and Creation seemed very much like a descendant of Alan Horne. When I think of Alan McGee, who obviously penetrated the mainstream much more definitively later on with Oasis and Creation, I see a second-rate Alan Horne, a derivation of Alan Horne.

Fire Engines finished off this burst of live performances at the Roseland Ballroom in Glasgow on 22 April as special guests of Orange Juice. It was a coming-of-age event as both groups peaked in front of a sold-out audience (all of whom were dressed like the bands). Everyone in the audience was aware it was a special moment. Super 8 cameras were present, plus a Postcard colour pamphlet was available courtesy of Barbara Shores, an American super-fan of all things Postcard. Her fanzine featured Orange Juice on the A-side (front cover), then when flipped over you could read the Josef K section on the B-side (back cover) with great photographs and interviews. Shores managed Strawberry Switchblade and remained a Postcard confidante, eventually sharing a flat in Holyrood Quadrant in Glasgow's west end with Alan Horne and Paul Quinn (after Horne moved out of 185 West Princes Street). The Roseland Ballroom concert provided a meeting ground of east and west, pop:aural and Postcard. Residual tension still hung heavy in the air as pop:aural made up ground with Postcard due to their intelligent media campaign for Fire Engines and Restricted Code. The social and cultural divide between Edinburgh and Glasgow was still evident — perceived class wars raged in tandem with label rivalries.

ALLAN CAMPBELL: Alan always wanted Fire Engines on Postcard. I suspect probably if you asked Alan do you want Josef K or the Fire Engines he would have probably said Fire Engines. He always wanted to sign Fire Engines and was absolutely galled that Bob Last signed them to pop:aural. As two of the bigger fish in the pond, both Bob Last and Alan viewed each other very warily, circled each other and avoided contact.

MURRAY SLADE: I wouldn't say Bob Last was influenced by Postcard Records, certainly not in the way packaging and visuals looked. I think it was about both labels being fiercely independent.

TAM DEAN BURN: We looked on Glasgow with a bit of disdain really, they were just sort of floppy, Orange Juice and all that sort of thing. We didn't see them as punk really, I mean there was definitely a divide, a big difference between the bands that emerged in Glasgow and the ones that emerged in Edinburgh. I don't know with Glasgow how much they tied in with the art college, but the art school in Edinburgh was a big part of us and there seemed to be a lot of working-class students as well. Edinburgh art students were stylish and there was a pub, the Tap o' Lauriston, that we hung out in. Edinburgh had a lot of affinity for New York, the Velvets, James White and the Blacks, Lydia Lunch — that was the music we related to. Whereas I don't know what they were into in Glasgow but it did seem a bit more like it was west coast Scotland and the West Coast of the States, almost like they were into the fucking Beach Boys, I don't know. They were definitely much more melodic and middle class, and I don't know why that happened. It was just a bit darker in Edinburgh in that period.

ALLAN CAMPBELL: It's interesting there are a number of Edinburgh bands in this period that do seem to have that kind of New York, spiky, no-wave guitar sound. I'm not quite sure why that is. My only theory would be that the musicians knew each other. Josef K and Fire Engines palled around together, played together, occasionally lent each other guitars, and when you're listening to the same stuff and you're on the same wavelength then it comes out.

SANDY MCLEAN: I didn't really notice a big difference in the immediate short term between Postcard and Fast Product. I didn't notice a huge musical difference in the early days — I don't think it was an east versus west coast thing at that point.

TOM CANNAVAN: There was a genuine rivalry between Glasgow and Edinburgh, and that was accentuated during this period, with Alan Horne's Postcard in the Glasgow corner, and Bob Last's Fast and pop:aural opposite in the Edinburgh corner. A Glasgow band like Restricted Code signing to the Edinburgh label was pretty much a shock. It led to us perhaps drifting away from the Glasgow scene slightly, but at the same time we were never part of the Edinburgh scene either. We were only in Bob and Hilary's flat, or had a drink with them and other Edinburgh bands at the Tap o' Lauriston, a handful of times. We were not an Edinburgh band, and remained outsiders, never really fully embraced by the scene in the east.

FRASER SUTHERLAND: I'd known Josef K well since TV Art days, and was a big fan, helping with their backline at gigs when I could. I wasn't aware at all at the time of this so-called rivalry between Postcard and Fast, other than what was written in the music press, so I'm not sure to what degree it's been constructed.

INNES REEKIE: In Edinburgh we really dug the more angular sound of groups like the Contortions, Pere Ubu, the Voidoids and obviously the Velvets. I think Edinburgh with Fast and pop:aural was akin to the East Coast of the US, like New York, whereas Glasgow and Postcard was like the West Coast with the Byrds and twelve-string semi-acoustics and melody.

ALLAN CAMPBELL: Orange Juice, Alan Horne and Postcard were middle class. Maybe it's not right to say so, but it was far from being a tough working-class background. It was more art school, it's maybe having a slightly more comfortable lifestyle that resulted in a cheerier outlook. Postcard was very intelligent — Alan Horne knew how to deploy camp by putting the Scottish kilt on Postcard artwork, poking fun at it. Postcard took Scottishness and stood it on its head, and that takes a certain amount of wit and cleverness, which Alan had. Maybe it's partly coming from that different background.

BOB LAST: There was nothing more exciting at the time of Fast Product than discovering incredible sophistication where there appeared to be none. That's the real kick in it. Sometimes we would purposely obscure that sophistication, but to find somebody who had none of the cultural baggage of the self-styled middle-class cultural person playing with very specific sophisticated stuff, that was a real kick.

The Scottish underground pop movement finally went overground with a front-cover article in the *NME*, 'The New Flowers of Scotland'. It mentioned many of the new groups that were operational, the Edinburgh labels pop:aural and Rational, but mostly it focused on Postcard. The cover photograph of Edwyn Collins and Altered Images' vocalist Clare Grogan was taken by Clare's former co-worker at the Spaghetti Factory, Robert Sharp, and the article was written by Kirsty McNeill. That both Robert and Kirsty had been involved with Robert Hodgens's *Ten Commandments* fanzine around six months prior was evidence of how fast the scene was moving. Altered Images had built their own following over the previous year and had toured with Siouxsie and the Banshees and performed at the Futurama festival. There had been rumours that Altered Images were going to sign to Postcard, but after their first Peel session was broadcast in October 1980 the group's manager Gerry McElhone was being courted by major labels. Major record contracts were offered, and it was only a matter of time until they signed a financially lucrative deal.

CLARE GROGAN: Johnny McElhone started the band with some school friends and I joined after my sister Kate introduced me to them. We were all big music fans. We basically started from scratch in terms of ability, contacts, everything really. But it was everything to us.

CAESAR: Some of us only had a passing interest in the Pistols and other main players. I was more of a Buzzcocks addict. They had avant-garde elements in their songs and presentations as well as an idiosyncratic authenticity. Manager Richard Boon had created his New Hormones imprint early doors. The game-changing release of the *Spiral Scratch* EP, mixed with a belated rediscovery of the Velvet

Underground's enduring back catalogue ultimately became the starting point for much of what was about to pass as a cohesive scene in this neck of the woods. These are great role models. I played guitar and wrote songs in the original line-up of Altered Images from 1979 to 1981. During this spell, we were often to be seen making our individual ways via public transport to a rehearsal den next to, if not inside, a row of dilapidated buildings, or, in stark contrast, being chauffeured to a community hall in the cosy village of Carmunnock made available thanks to band connections.

ROBERT HODGENS: Altered Images were never going to fit into the Postcard scene but Alan wanted to have them on Postcard, so I took their manager Gerry to 185 to meet him. After the meeting Gerry said never in a million years would they sign to Postcard. Gerry had a vision for Altered Images from day one, getting them touring with the Banshees and doing John Peel sessions. They wanted hit singles and Clare was always going to be a star.

CAESAR: When nothing happened with Postcard it became clear to me the rest of the group preferred the major-label route. I remember being courted by Island as well as Epic, and there may have been other options, but I can't remember anything definite, apart from those two. I was keen on Island as it still seemed to be slightly more creative than corporate but, in the end, it was left to our manager to decide. He was the only one, as far as I'm aware, who knew all the details of what was actually on offer, so, to be fair, I'm sure he did what he thought was best for all concerned. It worked out all right for the group eventually once I left, so, arguably, it was the right thing to do.

CLARE GROGAN: Lots of labels were interested but we really liked Muff Winwood at Epic/CBS — he made us feel special and actually talented, I suppose.

Altered Images recorded the bulk of their first album with Ban-shees bassist Steve Severin producing. Their debut single, 'Dead Pop Stars', had been released in March and reached 67 in the charts, all of which raised the bar in terms of the ambitions of the Postcard and pop:aural groups. It didn't go unnoticed that signing to a major label had some advantages: you could work with producers in big studios, you could tap into substantial marketing/ promotional budgets and expertise, and you didn't need to sign on the dole because major-label advances meant a regular wage.

CAESAR: I only worked with Steve Severin on the first two singles, 'Dead Pop Stars' and 'A Day's Wait'. Those sessions took place at studios either owned or simply used regularly by CBS/Epic, quite nondescript locations in London. Steve was exactly what you wanted from a producer at that stage. His experience allowed us to trust in the process and we could concentrate on playing the songs as they sounded live. My main recollection is that he wanted to make interesting records, and enabled us to do that as far as was possible at that time, rather than worry about providing hits for the label, and there would surely have been pressure to achieve that.

It wasn't long after appearing on the front cover of the NME with Clare Grogan that Edwyn Collins got his dole money stopped after someone shopped him as a result of his prominent Orange Juice media profile. The chat within Orange Juice intensified; the merits of remaining independent with Postcard or talking to major labels were heatedly debated. It felt like Orange Juice had reached a ceiling: they had graced the upper echelons of the alternative chart and front pages of the music press, performed throughout the UK to bigger and bigger crowds, but were still skint. As a holding exercise it was decided to demo all their songs for possible producers or labels, which they recorded with David Henderson in the Hellfire Club.

ALAN HORNE: We've got these young bands, and we're young ourselves; the talent's there but we have no experience. We're up against people that have been doing this for twenty years, and then you find out that it isn't as simple as putting out a good record and thinking it will sell. You've got to get played and to do that you have to employ people to plug the record to get it played on the radio. So we're going to pay for pluggers to get it played on the radio.

EDWYN COLLINS: The major record companies have got that whole machinery to get played on the radio, but I was exceedingly naive and believed that a single stood or fell on its own merits. The Orange Juice songs, and the rest of the Postcard groups' records, were good enough to be contenders in the charts on their own merits. We didn't realise you need this whole machinery behind you, with the hypers and pluggers and what have you. We're going to have to hire pluggers and take it seriously, and compete with the majors on their own terms.

DAVID HENDERSON: We started the Hellfire Club with the most basic 4-track recording equipment, and had Postcard groups like Orange Juice, Aztec Camera, the Bluebells and Jazzateers rehearse and demo at the studio. With the Hellfire Club demos for the first Orange Juice album we realised there was something quite special that we captured in these recordings, a freshness. I'm really proud of that, I love those recordings.

STEVEN DALY: The sessions took place over a few days in May 1981 at the Hellfire Club, a 4-track studio/rehearsal room located in the basement of a Glasgow tenement building. The engineer was Hellfire proprietor David Henderson, who was a key figure in the emergence of the Glasgow scene. We laid down all the basic tracks live, all four of us playing together in a small room, with just the vocals and occasional overdubs added afterwards. Orange Juice got enough confidence to believe that stepping out of punk's anti-music shadow and embracing melodic eclecticism would not prevent us from developing a credible style of our own.

EDWYN COLLINS: Originally I was influenced by Nico and I used to try and copy her voice in a Germanic accent. I was really contrived and affected. I'm interested in all kinds of music — fifties, sixties, seventies, disco. I think the O'Jays' 'Love Train' is great. David is into Eno and Kraftwerk, who personally I can't stand. James likes jazz and country and western. When it comes to a group like Creedence, I can just tell intuitively that they are honest and passionate — they are an influence on Orange Juice as are the Velvets.

The Orange Juice album demos became known as *Ostrich Churchyard*, and the Hellfire Club recordings captured the wild innocence of the group. The eclectic nature of the group's catholic tastes allied to internal disquiet perhaps pointed to critical future disharmony, something they camouflaged during media interviews.

BILLY SLOAN: The music press got really excited about Scotland and Glasgow in particular, because after punk the thing that really united all the media were Scottish groups like Altered Images, the Associates, and particularly Orange Juice who were a dream for journalists because Edwyn was so quick-witted and intelligent. Orange Juice were so sharp. I interviewed them a lot and you'd have James Kirk staring into space, not looking at you or even acknowledging you were in the room, and David McClymont would sit footering about with something he was playing with. Steven Daly and Edwyn Collins were like a comedy double act — Steven would load the cannon and Edwyn would fire it off. Any time I interviewed Orange Juice it was always hilarious — they were a dream for music press journalists who came up to Glasgow from London en masse.

EDWYN COLLINS: There isn't any sort of group feeling in Orange Juice. James keeps himself to himself, the group doesn't get on particularly well socially. I've never met anyone else with a similar attitude to us. The fact is there is a lot of tension in Orange Juice.

MALCOLM ROSS: Orange Juice was really Edwyn's band, but there were a lot of personality clashes in Orange Juice all the time. I helped them record their first and third Postcard singles — they would ask me to go into the studio with them because I could get on with them all. I was never really particularly close to James, but I was friends with David, Edwyn and Steven. A lot of the time Orange Juice wouldn't be speaking to each other, so I could kind of lubricate it.

Orange Juice did not have a steady record company influence like Bob Last and their relationship with Alan Horne was easily frayed. He had fulfilled a management position with the group until Postcard took off and he needed to focus on the label. It became obvious the lack of an Orange Juice manager made unified progress more difficult. Steven Daly suggested a young manager, Mark Wilson, who was appointed.

ROBERT HODGENS: I met Mark Wilson in the Rock Garden when he was sixteen. I immediately asked him to manage the Bluebells; I thought he would be our Andrew Loog Oldham. Steven Daly was a great guy, he was really ambitious, and he asked me if Mark could also manage Orange Juice as he could see we were catching up with Orange Juice in terms of music press attention.

Steven was concerned that they'd maybe miss the bus, and you do sometimes find groups that come in the second wave can overtake the originators. So getting Mark Wilson to manage Orange Juice and take care of business made a lot of sense. Steven could see that the majors were keen to sign the Bluebells, so thought the time was right for Orange Juice to leave Postcard and sign to a major.

The Bluebells' gestation period had been fairly lengthy, but Robert Hodgens finally had the perfect gang to execute his pop vision. Songs like 'Everybody's Somebody's Fool', 'Some Sweet Day' and 'Happy Birthday' all sounded like future hits with a grounding in the past, a glorious amalgam of the Monkees, the Beatles, the Byrds, the Lovin' Spoonful, the Velvet Underground and Orange Juice.

ROBERT HODGENS: I recorded a song for the *Fumes* fanzine compilation tape called 'She Hates Travel'. I used the name 007, then Alan Horne heard the song and he encouraged me to start a band. I was friendly with Altered Images' manager Gerry McElhone, and he found some musicians for me and named us the Oxfam Warriors. Alan was keen for me to be involved on Postcard in some shape or form. I think he thought he could control me as a Svengali figure like Mickie Most or Jonathan King, and I could put together a manufactured group like the Monkees. Alan always wanted to have a group he could control. He couldn't do that with Orange Juice, Josef K or Aztec Camera, but he thought he could do it with the Bluebells. Alan also set me up with Malcolm Fisher in the French Impressionists, working on song ideas together.

KEN MCCLUSKEY: It wasn't really until 1979/'80 that you got a scene and a sound in Glasgow, and that really developed from Postcard Records. They were really well informed and influential on us. We tuned into groups like the Velvet Underground, so the Bluebells were looking back to move forward. Postcard was great because it helped reinvent Glasgow. They were anti-macho, which was an antidote to the perceived idea of Glasgow's razor gangs and being a town full of thugs and hard men. Postcard made it cool to be camp, and really went against the grain, and suddenly Glasgow had a scene through Postcard which was quite arty. It was a breath of fresh air. They had a different way of doing things and had a certain beauty. At 185 West Princes Street soul music was always playing on their record player. Alan Horne was a bit cheeky with a fierce cynicism, but really funny. He didn't like my brothel creepers, slagging them off as 'Johnny Rotten shoes' — they all preferred wearing sandals.

ROBERT HODGENS: The Bluebells were now coming together. I got David McCluskey in first, he was only fifteen and drumming with a punk band from Bothwell, Raw Deal. Then Lawrence Donegan from Harry Mercer's Jazzateers and Russell Irvine who worked in the Virgin Megastore and was a cool-looking guy. Lawrence was excited immediately once I mentioned Postcard was interested. He could see the bigger picture. I already knew David's brother Ken from interviewing their punk band for my *Ten Commandments* fanzine. Ken was living in London at the time, but would intermittently attend Bluebells rehearsals. I thought he looked and sounded great, a Gene Clark figure on tambourine and harmonica before he started singing lead, and he's an amazing singer. I didn't feel like a front guy — I felt more like James Kirk in the background, so it made sense for Ken to move front of stage to become lead singer. He's such an amazing singer, really emotional. Our first gigs went well and Alan Horne wanted to meet the band. Of course he said they were bigger neds than the previous band I had; however, the guys were definitely not! Alan then asked the Bluebells if we wanted to play with Orange Juice and we became affiliated with the Postcard groups, which led to lots of doors opening.

The Bluebells set was getting stronger with each outing as they honed their craft at low-key gigs out of the glare of the national media (which would soon be on their trail). The Bluebells headlined an end-of-term concert at Holy Cross School in Hamilton, at which David McCluskey was still a pupil. Interestingly, future Postcard stablemates Jazzateers played one of their first concerts at the same event.

RUSSELL IRVINE: I remember it being a lovely summer evening near the end of the school term. Ken and Dave had gone to that school and I think Dave was still a pupil. Doing a gig at a school was a great idea. I don't know why it doesn't happen more often – it's a win–win situation, great for the kids to see bands that they might not otherwise be able to see and great for the bands to play away from the cynical glare of the 'grown-up' world. You're pretty sure of getting an honest reaction and it's a good way to build up a fan base too. My main memory of the Jazzateers that night was hearing and borrowing the chord progression from their best song, 'Natural Progression', to open our set. I used to love that, we would come onstage one by one building up the chords which had a real drama to them and then go straight into 'Goodbye and Good Luck'.

KEN MCCLUSKEY: Holy Cross had a big stage for school assembly room – it was great to play at the school David and I had attended. It had a huge catchment area and 2000 pupils. The student committee had invited us to perform at what would now be called a 'prom'. As it was just before the summer holidays Robert had added a strapline to the poster: 'SCHOOL'S OUT' in big type, followed by 'Burn Your Books' in small type. We all had great fun and even had some locally made Tunnock's Caramel Wafers and Irn-Bru on the rider.

GERRI MCLAUGHLIN: From as early as their gig at Holy Cross I thought the Bluebells had something, both essentially Scottish and poppy enough to go far, which they did.

The Bluebells bided their time and honed their art in the rehearsal and recording environment of the Hellfire Club. As part of the expanded Postcard coterie they were invited to support Orange Juice at several high-profile concerts, which in turn resulted in Dave McCullough getting back on the plane from London to Glasgow to do a big feature on the Bluebells for *Sounds*. This was followed soon after by a *Melody Maker* front cover, a Radio 1 session for Kid Jensen, then a live-concert rave review in the *NME*.

KEN MCCLUSKEY: We played with Orange Juice and Aztec Camera quite a few times in Glasgow and Edinburgh, including one with Orange Juice at Valentino's, Edinburgh, where we got a fab review in the *NME* by Kirsty McNeill. All the early Bluebells demos were recorded with David Henderson in the Hellfire Club, a dunny in the basement of a run-down tenement in the west end. There weren't a lot of studios at the time in Glasgow, David and his sister Jaine had set up the Hellfire Club and were very supportive of young acts like ourselves. They were and still are super-cool people.

ROBERT HODGENS: We did our first demos with David Henderson. 'Everybody's Somebody's Fool' and 'Happy Birthday' were on the tape, and Alan thought 'Everybody's Somebody's Fool' was a hit. We were now doing lots of supports with Orange Juice at Postcard events in Glasgow, Edinburgh and London. They would allow us to use their guitars, which was such a great thing to do. I would get knocked by people on the scene for being a huge Orange Juice fan, which I find a really strange thing — I mean Jonathan Richman was a huge Velvet Underground fan.

Major record companies were extremely excited about the Sound of Young Scotland, but only the west coast Postcard variant. The Bluebells appeared on the front cover of *Melody Maker* without having released a record, which created a lot of major-label interest. The commercial possibilities of Postcard groups was recognised. Bob Last struggled to gain any meaningful traction for pop:aural shining stars Fire Engines and Restricted Code, while Edinburgh's Josef K attracted both major-label interest and major critical notices (in part due to being on Postcard).

MALCOLM ROSS: After Postcard released 'Radio Drill Time', the major labels became interested when they saw the press we were getting. The major labels didn't have a clue about what was selling then. I think that's why independent records managed to sell a lot of copies because the major labels didn't have people who understood these labels and groups. We liked being on Postcard Records, we liked to be independent. Allan Campbell informed us that Virgin Records had phoned him to say they liked our records and wanted to come up and meet us, come to a gig. We asked Allan not to encourage them, because we had no desire to sign to a major label.

ALLAN CAMPBELL: Onstage was where Josef K made most sense, they were now becoming formidable live performers, and Malcolm's lead playing in particular was inspiring. Fiery, committed and ringing, it was a key element in the group's sound. A flirtation with psychedelic shirts and the occasional kaftan were also indicators that Josef K weren't quite the serious young men they first appeared to be, and that writers like Dave McCullough and Paul Morley claimed they were.

The Scottish media had been slower to respond to Postcard and pop:aural than the national music press big hitters at *NME*, *Sounds* and *Melody Maker*. Billy Sloan at Radio Clyde had supported Postcard, as had Peter Easton at BBC Radio Scotland. Billy Sloan had Alan Horne and Edwyn Collins on his radio show being interviewed live about Postcard and Orange Juice.

BILLY SLOAN: The influences on the Postcard bands were West Coast oriented, groups like the Byrds, Creedence Clearwater Revival, with floppy fringes and lumberjack shirts merging with jangly guitars. I remember going to the 185 West Princes Street Postcard flat fairly early on and found it an incredibly intimidating place, because when you walked into the flat they were all there — Alan Horne and all of Orange Juice. Horne would play the same Chic record on a loop on his Dansette record player, again and again and again. I found the whole scene quite threatening but not in a violent way. Up until Postcard the Scottish rock scene had been people like Frankie Miller, Alex Harvey, or Dan McCafferty of Nazareth, guys who looked like they could hold their own in a fight, whereas Orange Juice and Horne's form of intimidation came in the form of contempt for everything that they didn't like. As soon as you mentioned artists like the Rolling Stones or Paul McCartney they would simply sneer and dismiss you out of hand, but if it was music they liked, be it Chic, Gram Parsons, CCR, Stax or Motown, they would have talked to you all day. So although Postcard was intimidating it was also incredibly exciting simply because in Scottish terms it was something that had never happened here before. I had a show on Radio Clyde on a Thursday night from midnight to 2 a.m., and the response from me playing records by Orange Juice, Aztec Camera, Altered Images, Associates etc. was colossal. I had Alan Horne and Edwyn Collins on the show being interviewed and they treated me with contempt on air for the entire two-hour show. The next morning my bosses at Radio Clyde hauled me into their office and told me in no uncertain terms that under no circumstances were Horne or Collins to be interviewed on my radio show again.

PAUL MORLEY: Postcard had this quality that it was local, but also international. You could recognise the markers: there was some Velvets in there, some Tamla, Chic, some Buzzcocks, but it was wholly itself and it was great. Horne's mission statement was there immediately — why isn't Postcard music on *Top of the Pops*? — and he was correct because the minute you heard Postcard singles it was obvious it was just great pop music. Postcard had a great identity, it was of itself. Independent labels had now been established, you had Fast Product in Edinburgh, Factory in Manchester, Zoo in Liverpool, and you could see Postcard were inspired by these other great labels. Postcard had a sense of humour, a sense of provocation and a sense of play, and a sense of seriousness as well, very much marking out territory. It had a style, personality and vocabulary of its own. There was a sense that Postcard was something you wanted to collect, you very quickly had trust in the label's sensibilities and releases (Orange Juice, Josef K, Aztec Camera, the Go-Betweens).

Postcard single 81-5 (Josef K — 'Chance Meeting' b/w 'Pictures of Cindy') was released in June, but mysteriously not 81-6 (Orange Juice — 'Wan Light' b/w 'You Old Eccentric'). 81-6 was essentially a James Kirk-fronted Orange Juice, as both songs were his compositions and the first time he would have been singing lead vocals on the A-side of an Orange Juice single.

STEVEN DALY: 'Wan Light' is another gem from the ineffably bashful James Kirk. When he initially played the song for us, he asked for a mid-tempo Stax-Volt feel — obviously we didn't possess those kind of chops, plus we always gravitated towards the brisk bpm count of the era. Still, even at this sprightly clip, 'Wan Light' shows James at his otherworldly best. Strange as it may seem, there was no discernible hint of the kind of rivalry you might expect within a band with two separate songwriters. In fact, everyone was so happy with 'Wan Light' that it was slated to be Postcard's follow-up to 'Poor Old Soul'. The label would not survive long enough to release that record, but that's another story.

EDWYN COLLINS: 'Wan Light' was set to become our fifth Postcard single but it never actually came out. Postcard now seems like a hobby that we became obsessive about — you would have to be either very foolish or very generous to call it a business. Postcard was run on loans up until after 'Blue Boy', then it was financed by Rough Trade.

Josef K had released their most accessible single, 'Chance Meeting', in advance of their delayed debut album. This was a completely different beast to the ponderous version that was originally released as their first single on Steven Daly's Absolute label at the tail end of 1979. Gone were the Fall-esque keyboards, and in their place was a trumpet motif played by Malcolm Ross's brother Alastair, with Malcolm himself playing autoharp on yet another Postcard single ('Just Like Gold' being the first). 'Chance Meeting' sounded like it could be a breakthrough record, and following on from other sterling singles 'It's Kinda Funny' and 'Sorry for Laughing' had laid the groundwork for their debut album to make a major impact. Things didn't quite work out as anticipated for the album though, as the Postcard/Josef K cheerleader journalists in the music press hated the abrasive production approach taken by the group for *The Only Fun in Town*. The vocals were mixed low, the guitars were mixed high and on maximum treble, and the reviews by Dave McCullough at *Sounds* and Paul Morley at the *NME* were extremely negative.

PAUL MORLEY: I thought Paul Haig was a pop star — I liked the enigma and his cryptic quality, the beauty of his voice and definitive nature of his appearance. He was my kind of pop star, who looked like he read Beckett but listened to Diana Ross and the Supremes, he seemed the perfect hybrid. However, my *NME* review of the debut Josef K album was unenthusiastic. I was disappointed the album didn't deliver on the excitement of their Postcard singles. It felt like I was the 'Postcard guy' at the *NME*, who was now scrawling all over the postcard!

PAUL HAIG: We recorded our debut album again in a studio in Belgium, and we were happy with that album as it captured the live sound of Josef K. The review we got from Paul Morley in the *NME* for *The Only Fun in Town* was a shocker. We really didn't expect that as he'd been a big supporter of the band, but it was the early days of shiny new pop which soon followed with artists like ABC, who had the production featuring the glitter and the gloss. *The Only Fun in Town* was a dark, scratchy album, and I don't think Paul Morley felt we were fulfilling the potential that he saw in us. It was almost like a betrayal to him and that we'd purposefully committed commercial suicide. It had quite an impact when we saw that *NME* review come out, we didn't expect it. I had wanted the vocals mixed lower on the album because we wanted it to sound like a live recording, to get the essence of our live performance onto vinyl.

MALCOLM ROSS: *The Only Fun in Town* got completely slated in the music press when it came out. Journalists who had championed us up until then were moving on so quickly and when the album came out the whole idea of bands like Heaven 17 and ABC had started to germinate. The idea of a musician as a businessman, with a suit and tie and briefcase going to business meetings and infiltrating capitalism and destroying it from the inside, was starting to float about. I can remember Paul Morley talking to me about it, saying how disappointed he'd been, how it was like a punk record and, you know, things should have moved on and we should have sounded like the Police. He was disappointed and Dave McCullough from *Sounds* was as well, but I really didn't care about the music press, didn't give a shit about getting good or bad reviews. I mean, we'd have rather had good ones, it's obviously nice to be complimented, but it didn't really bother us. I suppose the music was out on a limb so if there was someone that wanted to savage it, they could. We weren't that bothered and it sold, you know, we had a number 2 in the independent charts the first week it was out.

DAVID WEDDELL: Rough Trade said they'd try and fix up a tour for us, which is quite surprising because when Alan Horne took the tapes of our first Postcard single to Rough Trade originally they said Josef K were too professional-sounding and they didn't want to be involved. Then after a big Postcard article in *Sounds* they said they'd give us enough money to do an album. I'm not sure what difference all the reviews and hype make anyway. I mean the Fire Engines' *Lubricate Your Living Room* on pop:aural sold 11,000, while the Scars who had a huge major-label promotional campaign behind them sold 12,000. Josef K sold 10,000 in the first two days, and the promotional budget with Postcard is zero.

ALLAN CAMPBELL: I still love *The Only Fun in Town*, but what lives on having seen Josef K many times is being in a club and feeling that wave of guitar sound and rhythm. That's what I think lingers on at the back of your mind, much more so than perhaps the record. But the records are great — I think there are moments when that does happen, particularly on tracks like 'It's Kinda Funny' and 'Sorry for Laughing', those still sound fantastic, but some of the other tracks maybe don't have quite the effect that you felt live.

PAUL HAIG: When we recorded *The Only Fun in Town*, we wanted to keep our live sound as much as possible. We thrashed it out in a really short time, it only took six days, and on purpose we mixed the vocals low because we wanted to keep that live feel, which again in hindsight was stupid.

MALCOLM ROSS: Paul and I didn't sit down and write songs together really, I would present a guitar part and show it to Paul, or get it going with Ronnie and David. Then we'd just shove it on a cassette and Paul would take the cassette away and come up with the vocals on top of that. Once a song was written that was pretty much it, there wouldn't be much change, though we did rework 'Chance Meeting'. Paul used to cannibalise the lyrics once we got fed up with the song if he still liked the words — he would maybe take the words to a new tune, which happened with the words of 'Radio Drill Time' being repurposed for 'Heart of Song'.

In spite of negative reviews from disappointed supporters of Josef K within the music press, the album sold well and Rough Trade organised a UK tour on which the group were supported by Aztec Camera and Article 58. Josef K reached a performance high on the tour, which they captured on their second John Peel session in July, probably the best recordings of their career.

PAUL HAIG: I think what we're singing about is important. Literature was massively influential. I was reading an awful lot: Kafka, Albert Camus and Knut Hamsun. There was this recurring theme of alienation that ran through all of their books, and that had a big effect on my lyrics. When I first read *The Trial* I could relate and totally empathise with the character. I had the same kind of feelings, it was finding something that was there already. The absurdity of existence was another common theme in nearly all of their novels, and that also had an impact on our lyrics. I was always thinking about that too from an early age, so I suppose you could say we're a serious band. Most of the songs are influenced by books or something personal to me — we want to move people.

DAVID WEDDELL: I think it's really funny when people expect us to be dark and serious, which we're not at all. I always like to think of us as like the Velvet Underground in that we're quite unusual compared to the main flow, but hopefully write really good pop songs.

PAUL HAIG: I think Josef K is a very funny group. I'm always laughing onstage, putting myself in the position of being in the audience and watching us. I think it must look really silly, all those guys onstage with dark glasses on, it's absurd. I just can't bring myself to say anything onstage — we're there to play music, not to speak to the audience. I think it's much more interesting to use tapes to introduce our songs onstage.

GERRI MCLAUGHLIN: Being on tour in England supporting Josef K gave us the feeling of going somewhere with Article 58, even though my own head was already fairly messy by then. Josef K were the outstanding band of that time, musically, lyrically and stylistically. They pulled together so many threads of different bands I had listened to growing up from Bowie/Bolan through Lou Reed and the Television days of American punk. I always admired Paul's lyrics, he could express a time and place and transport you there through his songs. 'It's Kinda Funny' remains a pure pop classic with none of the clichés we associate with pop, a fitting tribute to a singer gone way too soon [Ian Curtis].

pop:aural's assault on the charts did not happen; however, Bob Last's major-label management interests were really beginning to deliver. The Human League reached number 3 with 'Love Action' in July followed by 'Open Your Heart' hitting number 6 in September, while original League members Martyn Ware and Ian Craig Marsh released their debut BEF album production by Heaven 17, *Penthouse and Pavement* (also released on Virgin Records). The Human League were now *Top of the Pops* regulars only two years on from releasing experimental electronic music on Fast Product. They now presented an aesthetic and sound that was more akin to ABBA than Philip Glass. The songwriting input and influence of Jo Callis on the new Human League vision cannot be underestimated.

SIMON BEST: Once they started recording *Dare* with producer Martin Rushent the excitement from the band and Bob was palpable. Jo Callis was still Edinburgh-based, so he gave me regular reports and was clearly loving the new challenge.

MARTYN WARE: Bob Last got Jo Callis to join the Human League. Bob knew Jo well from their Rezillos days, and Jo is an incredibly talented guy.

JO CALLIS: Boots for Dancing had run its course for me after Dave Carson lost his focus or confidence. Not long after that I started getting involved with Adrian Wright of the Human League doing a bit of songwriting. I always thought it was just me and Adrian that got that together ourselves, but Bob's always credited for it. Bob was probably wheeling away putting ideas into the Human League heads, weaving that situation and making sure it happened. I had a drum machine with the preset sounds, and I'd strum along with my guitar. When I went down to Sheffield for songwriting sessions, I'd take the drum machine with me and try transposing what I'd done on the guitar onto a keyboard. I'm not a keyboard player, but you know, I'd take myself back to that naive state where I didn't really know what you do. There's a great benefit in not knowing what the bloody hell you are doing, because by doing all this on a keyboard I ended up coming up with all these wonderful new ideas.

SIMON BEST: After the split occurred the key for both halves of the band in going forward was to bring in a new member with complementary skills. Heaven 17 needed a great singer and frontman whom they found in Glenn Gregory, whilst the League needed a great pop songwriter who Bob found for them in Jo Callis. The Human League had signed up for the European tour that I managed for them. I thought it was a smart but risky move under the circumstances; however, once the girls were onstage they rose to the challenge and the risk paid off.

Bob Last had found time to assemble another 'muzak' release for his pop:aural offshoot label, Accessory. *At Home!* featured accordionist Frank Hannaway and former Thursdays guitarist Michael Barclay and was the second (and final) Accessory release (a rather strange companion piece to Accessory 001, *Lubricate Your Living Room*). It felt like a pub accordion player doing cover versions of ABBA songs was an art joke too far.

DAVY HENDERSON: The other release in the Accessory series was an accordion player called Frank, who played with a drum machine in Hilary's mum and dad's hotel. Bob was amused by this idea and he got Michael Barclay from the Thursdays to play guitar. This was at the same time the [Lydia Lunch] *Queen of Siam* record had come out on ZE Records, which was fully orchestrated and had Robert Quine playing guitar along to Lydia Lunch's compositions with a full orchestra, and I think that had sparked something in Bob. So he had this idea for exciting wallpaper music with Frank, with his drum machine and accordion, along with Michael Barclay from the Thursdays/Boots for Dancing playing electric guitar on top of it.

GRAHAM MAIN: *At Home!* with Frank Hannaway and Michael Barclay was released by Bob as a partner release to our Fire Engines mini album. Frank played hits of the day on his Farfisa organ at Hilary's family hotel in Arrochar. Bob gave it to Michael to overdub some wild, phased guitar on 'Fernando' and 'I Have a Dream'. Frank was less than happy with the result — he thought it was to be an album of his Farfisa hits only.

FRASER SUTHERLAND: The two mini albums that Bob released on his Accessories sub-label were intended to be unsettling ambient music. I got what he was trying to achieve with Fire Engines' *Lubricate Your Living Room* and the record Mike Barclay made with the accordionist Frank Hannaway, *At Home!*

MICHAEL BARCLAY: That was one of Bob Last's conceptual pieces. I think, like a lot of what Bob did, he didn't let you in on the secret of what it was, but you became part of his project to baffle the world with different products. It's partly to do with my own naivety at the time. I had this opportunity to be part of this concept album with some old accordionist and dub guitar on top, but it was two of the most horrible days of my life. It was in a recording studio in West Lothian, Castlesound, with this horrible accordion music being played and me trying to make something of it. He would change key halfway through some ABBA song and I was trying to work out something melodic to add — it was brutal. I now realise, or I realised soon after, that it was some Dadaist project that Bob had, to throw things together, completely disparate things, and see what happened. It just gave me a headache. There were some quite lovely pieces in it but it was very disturbing. In a way I think I was used and abused as an artist, but it was nicely packaged, like all things that Bob had his hand in, with a nice carrier bag. I never met Frank — he was an accordionist who played hotel functions on the west coast and did meandering run-throughs of songs in the pop charts at the time, changing key and tempo, morphing ABBA into Neil Diamond. I spent two days with Frank in my headphones and me trying to make something of it. So it was interesting, everything was interesting about Fast.

While success in the real charts had finally been achieved by Bob Last with the Human League, Orange Juice decried their so-called success in the alternative chart published in the music papers, comparing it to a 'toytown' chart. Orange Juice and their new manager

Mark Wilson decided to record their debut album in London using Rough Trade finance (ostensibly for release on Postcard). Neither Alex Chilton nor John Fogerty was hired as producer as previously mooted, and instead Adam Kidron got the job (he produced the debut Scritti Politti album, *Songs to Remember*).

Scritti Politti had come a long way from their Marxist roots, speeding all night in a Kings Cross squat discussing Gramsci and cultural hegemony. They had changed their sound and focus from scratchy Peel fodder to a more luxurious, soulful sound. They relaunched the group on the Rough Trade/*NME C81* cassette at the beginning of the year with their Robert Wyatt-assisted 'The Sweetest Girl', which was a great record. Steven Daly had experienced working with Adam Kidron when he drummed on the new Aztec Camera single, 'Mattress of Wire', after David Mulholland had been dismissed from the drum stool.

CAMPBELL OWENS: David Mulholland played on the debut Postcard single 'Just Like Gold' and I think he is an unsung hero of the Postcard period of Aztec Camera. He's a very talented chap and it's unfortunate what happened to David in many, many ways. The reasons for David's departure from Aztec Camera was that he and Roddy just fundamentally didn't get on and eventually Roddy couldn't take it any more and that was the end of David and Aztec Camera.

'Mattress of Wire' featured an image sourced from Roddy's granny's *Collins Encyclopaedia* of a young androgynous ancient Roman with a laurel crown. The B-side was an older song that hailed from Neutral Blue days, 'Lost Outside the Tunnel'. The tracks featured twelve-string acoustic and while the single was not in the same league as 'Just Like Gold' b/w 'We Could Send Letters', 'Mattress of Wire' was greeted with approval by fans and critics alike (if not by Roddy and Campbell who were not impressed with Adam Kidron's production).

CAMPBELL OWENS: We released a second Postcard single, 'Mattress of Wire', with Steven Daly on drums. It was a very enjoyable session because Alan Horne and Steven were good craic together; however, the single production didn't turn out quite how we'd have liked, but it's a great song.

Postcard musicians and believers were still in awe of Aztec Camera, photographs of whom now only featured Roddy and Campbell. They now looked and sounded like early Neil Young or Arthur Lee and Love; traces of Vic Godard's new jazz-influenced material could also be detected.

RODDY FRAME: If I heard something like Wes Montgomery, that would influence me, or the Clash. I was finding my way on the guitar, that's why there are so many chords and lyrics that are flowery and abstract. I wanted to write like Howard Devoto.

ALLAN CAMPBELL: My memories of Roddy Frame as a sixteen-year-old are slightly vague, but he was charming, quiet, a bit cowboyish with the red neckerchief, and supremely talented. There was a three-song demo with a track they never released called 'Green Jacket Grey', which was great.

ROBERT HODGENS: Once Alan signed Aztec Camera to Postcard he really started influencing them, playing them Buffalo Springfield albums.

DAVID HENDERSON: Alan Horne had found Roddy and Campbell, Aztec Camera, and we did some acoustic-based recordings at the Hellfire Club. Edwyn came to help out with Aztec Camera. I also became aware of Paul Quinn around this period too as he was singing with the French Impressionists prior to joining the Jazzateers. Roddy was quite shy. Both him and Campbell were from East Kilbride which is where I went to school. You could tell right away Roddy was a real talent, and with Postcard he received great encouragement from Alan Horne. Alan really got the best out of people like Roddy, Edwyn and Paul Quinn, he was a guiding light and great at putting talented people together.

KEN MCCLUSKEY: Aztec Camera on Postcard were almost dreamlike — Campbell was doing jazz-influenced bass lines and Roddy's guitar was very influenced by jazz, but they were only sixteen or seventeen and had come out of punk. The first time I saw them was at the Nite Club in Edinburgh when they opened for Orange Juice at a Postcard night — we were there with the Bluebells. We saw Aztec Camera at the soundcheck, and Roddy came out with a jumbo acoustic guitar and started playing. Russell, from the Bluebells, turned round to me and said we may as well just go up the road and go home! Roddy was amazing, way above anything we could do with our jingle-jangle, he really was top of the class.

BBC Television broadcast a series of programmes that highlighted the history of Scottish rock and pop — the dreadfully named *Jock 'n' Roll*. B.A. Robertson interviewed Alan Horne and Edwyn Collins for the programme at Postcard HQ at 185 West Princes Street. The interview was an ordeal for Robertson, whose inane attempts at humour brought out the charged, sarcastic wit of Horne and Collins as they giggled their way through the interview. They dismissed Robertson with acid barbs until he called a halt to proceedings. During the interview Horne revealed Postcard had added three new groups to the roster: the Bluebells, Jazzateers and the French Impressionists.

No one at this juncture in August 1981 would have believed that 'Mattress of Wire' was the last release on Postcard. Externally it seemed like Alan Horne and Postcard were at the peak of their powers; however, there was soon to be a rapid unravelling of the label's crown jewels and original movers, Orange Juice and Josef K.

Orange Juice recorded their debut album, *You Can't Hide Your Love Forever*, in London, financed by Rough Trade. The recording sessions proved to be a disharmonious experience as tensions spilled over. Steven Daly felt the group should have stuck with the sound of the Postcard singles, something David McClymont admitted retrospectively when he stated Adam Kidron was the wrong producer (McClymont felt he lacked a sympathetic approach). Kidron brought in strings and backing singers to the Orange Juice sound once he discovered the group liked Al Green.

ROBERT HODGENS: The Bluebells manager Mark Wilson was also managing Orange Juice and we went down to the studio in London where they were recording *You Can't Hide Your Love Forever*, with Adam Kidron producing. The vibe in the studio was really bad. They were recording their Al Green cover, but I think Edwyn was under a lot of pressure.

DAVID HENDERSON: When the Orange Juice album was recorded for release on Polydor, I thought it was great to see a Glasgow band from round the corner that rehearsed and recorded at the Hellfire Club release an album on a major. However, to me *You Can't Hide Your Love Forever* was too produced — it had an eighties gloss, and I was slightly disappointed. I preferred the Orange Juice recordings from the Hellfire Club.

Orange Juice recorded a second John Peel session (broadcast on 10 August) on which they sounded at the top of their game, with great versions of perhaps Edwyn's greatest song for the group, 'Dying Day', and their cover of Vic Godard's 'Holiday Hymn'. The Peel session at Maida Vale brought out the strengths of the group — the sound of the four musicians recorded quickly. Adam Kidron's production of *You Can't Hide Your Love Forever* brought female backing vocalists, keyboards and a brass section into the frame, and resulted in a straightening of the edge that was in evidence in David Henderson's Hellfire Club *Ostrich Churchyard* demos for the album. The feeling in the camp regarding signing to a major label was changing. Geoff Travis had assumed the money fronted by Rough Trade to record the album was for the purpose of a Postcard release, but it was decided between the group and management to court the major label that had expressed an interest in signing Orange Juice. They were in a strong negotiating position, which was reflected when they agreed to a tape-lease deal with Polydor. Signing to a major label meant the group received an advance and therefore wages.

GEOFF TRAVIS: Rough Trade paid for the Orange Juice album to be made. I think we were assuming it would come out on Rough Trade, but then, I think, Alan and Edwyn ran off and sold it to Polydor. We didn't know that was going to happen. We just sort of went, OK, if that's what they want to do, that's what they want to do. I think we were quite naive in a way — what we should have done was say, yeah, you can take it away and sell it to Polydor, but give us an override [royalty], but we didn't. They just gave us the money back and that was the end of it, and they signed to Polydor. But that was a huge act of deception, pretty bad behaviour by Alan and Edwyn really. I don't know what Alan told Edwyn, though. Who knows? I'm not really sure what went on there, maybe they were paying me back for not loving 'Falling and Laughing' from day one.

EDWYN COLLINS: Postcard used to be a co-operative between members of Orange Juice and Alan Horne. Alan is a really good manipulator. But we decided to make the move to a major company. It was a mistake in retrospect, as we had these huge expectations from Polydor and nothing actually seemed to happen. My own motivation has never been money though, and I feel that if we'd stayed in the independent sector of the market we would have become much more important. We were naive then, and stupidly tempted by a major label. I know that Alan was very upset, although he tried to put a brave face on it.

MALCOLM ROSS: Orange Juice signed to Polydor but it was actually a tape-lease deal, so in the end Orange Juice always owned everything, which was a very clever business move by them. Orange Juice and Aztec Camera were both in the situation where they could write their own contract, because every major label wanted to sign them.

So it came to pass that Orange Juice left Postcard and signed to a major label. Mark Perry had bemoaned in 1977 through his *Sniffin' Glue* fanzine that punk died the day the Clash signed to CBS. Many felt Postcard Records died the day Orange Juice signed to Polydor. The other twin pillar to Postcard's initial thrust, Josef K, surprised everyone when they announced that their Glasgow concert at Maestro's on 23 August was to be the last. The Josef K split took everyone by surprise; even the group members were unaware that Paul Haig had decided their Glasgow gig would be the end. The group were at their artistic peak and still on fire, as evidenced by their recent second Peel session. They had a clutch of excellent songs ('Adoration', 'Heaven Sent', 'The Missionary') that could have taken Josef K to the next level if they had been recorded for a second album.

MALCOLM ROSS: Josef K split up. We'd been in each other's pockets for two years rehearsing and recording. We did a lot of gigging and David and I were quite happy just to go around Europe and Britain, we were really quite happy doing that, staying in wee B & Bs and cheap hotels, there was something romantic and appealing about that to me. However, Paul and Ronnie didn't like the travelling. The closeness in the band had gone; you just stop being a teenager. I'd got a girlfriend so I didn't just hang out with the rest of the band as much, I wanted to spend time with my girlfriend. We'd lost that gang feeling, and Paul and Ronnie would moan when I would book gigs, but David and I were now living in a flat, we had to pay the bills, we had to buy food, we weren't living with our mums any more so our income came from doing gigs. Then one day we were playing in Glasgow and I phoned just to check what time they were all coming through. That's when David told me Paul had said he's not doing any more gigs after Glasgow, this is going to be the last gig. I was just kind of like, well, so be it then, fine — you know I'm not going to argue about this. Paul and I had never intended Josef K to be a career, to be in Josef K when we're in our thirties. I think we were, surprisingly for eighteen-, nineteen-year-olds, quite aware of a group's timescale.

PAUL HAIG: There had been agreement within Josef K that we wouldn't carry on too long, and I guess we had recorded two albums, albeit the first one was shelved. I'd decided I'd had enough, it was the right time. When you start to drift apart and not socialise it becomes hard to get that intensity back onstage. In a sense it had become like a job, meeting up to perform onstage, it wasn't like it was in the early days, kind of us against the world. I just wasn't having fun any more and I got quite depressed, and I also felt I'd reached the end of my Josef K persona and I was getting into a dark place in my head. It was getting me down and I felt I couldn't do it any more, I wanted to stop. I wrote all the words, every track had a meaning for me and brought back memories, and not necessarily happy ones. The darkness and intensity of some of the tracks was a bit unbearable, I didn't want to hear them again for a very long time. I found it emotionally exhausting.

ALLAN CAMPBELL: Paul, for his own reasons, has never really liked playing live, ironically, and perhaps he'd felt he'd done everything he could with Josef K. For whatever reason Paul decided he was not going to do it any more, but I think there was a lot more there for Josef K to achieve.

STEFAN KASSEL: Josef K were the perfect band, everything about them: the look, the sound, the songs, Paul Haig's voice, that incredible white funkiness coupled with soul. No one sounded like them before or after, and they were named after a Franz Kafka character. I also love the fact that they split up after just one album. Shine bright, burn fast. Josef K certainly did that — their music still sounds so fresh today, like no one else.

MALCOLM ROSS: I was with Alan Horne and my girlfriend Susan on the day Josef K did our last gig. We'd stayed overnight at Alan's and we were walking to the gig to do the soundcheck, and we bumped into Edwyn. We told Edwyn it was going to be the last Josef K gig that night. Orange Juice had signed to Polydor Records, so Edwyn said, 'Well why don't you join Orange Juice?' I asked him if he was sure, and Edwyn mentioned he felt the group needed someone who could play guitar and keyboards because he didn't want to play as much guitar and wanted to concentrate on singing. So Edwyn asked me to join Orange Juice without consulting with the rest of the band. So by the time we got to the gig, I told Paul I was joining Orange Juice anyway.

Malcolm Ross joined Orange Juice as the group prepared for the release of their first single on Polydor, their version of Al Green's 'L.O.V.E.'. The artwork of the single featured a photo of the four original members of the group on the front and back covers, and the back cover also featured the Postcard cat logo. The single felt like the first Orange Juice misfire after the perfection and excitement of their four Postcard singles, and it was a pretty major misfire. 'L.O.V.E.' didn't trouble daytime radio or the charts any more than 'Poor Old Soul' had.

The group performed live a five-piece on BBC 2 Television's *Something Else*. Edwyn performed on vocals only (unencumbered by playing a guitar), and James, David and Malcolm all played more traditional Fender guitars (Stratocaster, Precision and Telecaster), with not one semi-acoustic Gretsch in sight. Malcolm's first televised performance as a member of Orange Juice would also be the last public performance featuring all four Orange Juice originals. The song they performed on *Something Else* was 'Falling and Laughing', which they'd recorded in Strathaven as their debut single two years earlier. Orange Juice Mk 1 ended where it began — 'Falling and Laughing'.

News soon broke that founder members James Kirk and Steven Daly had been sacked. The tensions within the group had been multiple: David McClymont felt Daly never really got on with him and regarded him as a hippy art student. McClymont also felt Edwyn's ambitions for the group to become more professional were not necessarily shared by James. The introduction of Ross as the fifth member of the group led to Kirk feeling intimidated by Ross's presence, which according to McClymont led to further withdrawal by Kirk. Daly considered the growing success of Orange Juice had brought out a certain perversity in Kirk's behaviour, which was partly why the rest of the group wanted to get rid of him.

Daly fought stoutly in defence of Kirk: he argued that James was a sensitive soul and that the group was most of what he had. Daly was duly called back by Edwyn Collins to be informed that not only was Kirk sacked from Orange Juice, but Daly was too. In the *Big Gold Dream* documentary McClymont states that Edwyn felt a certain guilt that he had betrayed Steven and James, but ultimately it was McClymont who was seen as the person that split up the original Orange Juice. However, David points out it was Edwyn who unilaterally brought Malcolm into the group, which unsettled James. In David's opinion Edwyn projected his dark side on to him (in Jungian terms), leaving McClymont as the evil, dark part of the group that broke it up, making him the Yoko Ono of Orange Juice.

Orange Juice: James Kirk and Edwyn Collins

EDWYN COLLINS: To a certain extent I really regret that James and Steven were used as scapegoats. When I listen to *You Can't Hide Your Love Forever*, I realise that James was a great guitarist, and I feel that Steven was right for the group at the time. I got caught up in that whole thing too, the Trevor Horn production-line pop where the groups come secondary to the producer. James was really losing confidence because he felt threatened because I had invited Malcolm in as a member of Orange Juice, and it affected his guitar playing. James is an intellectual, certainly the most intelligent person I've ever met. He'd tell me he was interested in the dichotomy between structuralism and semiotics. I'd say, 'Wha'??' You know, I couldn't fathom him out.

MALCOLM ROSS: Orange Juice splintered not long after I joined because David and Steven weren't getting on. David phoned me one day and he was particularly pissed off with something Steven had said or done, and I told David I was thinking of leaving anyway, I didn't think it was working and I wasn't enjoying it. David said he was going to leave too and suggested doing something together and then we thought maybe we should ask Edwyn if he wanted to be in with us, at least offer him that. We told him we were leaving but would carry on with him, but Steven and James would have to go.

As Orange Juice ripped themselves asunder, one of their Glasgow post-punk contemporaries achieved everything Orange Juice and Postcard had coveted most, a massive hit single. Altered Images had released their first album, *Happy Birthday*, largely produced by Steve Severin. During the recording process, founder member Gerard McInulty aka Caesar left the group to be replaced by Jim McKinven.

CAESAR: As soon as Altered Images got a major-label deal there was a considerable degree of A & R pressure to take the well-worn path to transient pop stardom. We quickly and naively went from supporting the likes of Siouxsie and the Banshees and the Cure in congenial surroundings, garnering empathic audiences, straight into opening pantomime-style matinees for Adam and the Ants in a west end theatre, rocking out in front of bewildered and uninterested infants chaperoned by their parents or au pairs. By the close of 1981, in defence of pure imagination, I had quit Altered Images to set up the Wake.

The Severin-produced songs like 'Dead Pop Stars' and 'A Day's Wait' were darker songs that displayed their debt to the Banshees. The title track had been recorded with Buzzcocks' producer Martin Rushent during a gap in his recording schedule producing the Human League album. 'Happy Birthday' was released as a single and contained a much brighter pop sensibility that felt more in tune with the colour and freshness that Orange Juice had brought to the Glasgow scene. Rushent's production highlighted a pop element within Altered Images that was a natural fit for daytime radio, and once they got in the charts and appeared on *Top of the Pops*, the natural pop star appeal of Clare Grogan did the rest.

CLARE GROGAN: Our first gigs were always really exciting and people actually came, with the Mars Bar, the Doune Castle and the Bungalow Bar among the first. We rehearsed twice a week in Carmunnock village hall and before we knew it we were on *Top of the Pops*! From the beginning we wanted to reach as big an audience as we could and Epic seemed to understand that. We wanted to be global, I guess. I think we thought we had written a song that could help us go to the next stage with 'Happy Birthday'.

Altered Images reached number 2 in the singles chart with 'Happy Birthday', which sold in serious amounts. They were proof positive that having the right manager (Gerry McElhone), being signed to the right major label (Epic), and recording with the right producer (Martin Rushent) could create the perfect symbiotic storm to blow success forward into the mainstream. Buoyed by the success of the single, Epic engaged Martin Rushent to produce further tracks at his Genetic studio in Reading, where he'd now finished production work on the Human League album. Epic brought out another Altered Images single, 'I Could Be Happy', which reached number 7 in December, placing the group in a perfect position to capitalise further on their success in 1982. The Human League were an example of Martin Rushent's production nous, which allied to a label that believed in them — Virgin — and Bob Last's creative tactical deployment had resulted in four top 10 singles from a defining album. *Dare* was a major success on all levels and it looked like a Fast Product project that had truly infiltrated the mainstream. The success of *Dare* was about to accelerate into hyperspace with the release of the fourth single from the album, 'Don't You Want Me'. The single would go on to become the Christmas number 1 in the UK, which in turn resulted in colossal sales of *Dare*.

BOB LAST: *Dare* having this massive number 1 hit single felt entirely right. I know it seems ridiculous and it wasn't as if one went around being arrogant at the time, but you felt, 'OK, yeah, sure, it's come together, bit of a long route.' I do remember very clearly there were arguments about 'Don't You Want Me', as to whether it should be a single, and I very clearly remember hearing the opening bars of it and thinking, 'This has got to be the big hit.' Phil Oakey, who could outdo me for being cantankerous and perverse, picked up on the fact that I knew it was a big hit and did his damnedest to persuade everyone it wasn't. Which I think in retrospect was just he and I having an arm-wrestle about who was the cleverest tactician, but he tried very hard for that not to be the big hit. Though inadvertently it seemed like a great plan to release 'Don't You Want Me' as the last single off *Dare*, and [it] becoming a number 1 single. The madness became a plan.

MARTYN WARE: I think Phil has always had an intuitive radar for being the common man, but he wanted to be obtuse as well, and that dichotomy really worked.

HILARY MORRISON: I can remember saying to the Human League, 'You have to get a pension plan.' This wasn't being boring, it was saying if this is the route you want to take then this is what you have to do, and if you don't do it, make enough money to do something else. Think about it, because this is how the world works, and it's not to be dull but to make people aware that they had to make choices. If they didn't make choices, they would end up victims because someone else would make the choice for them. They had to be thinking about these things, music wasn't just something that happened in a vacuum.

JO CALLIS: I think Bob's vision was definitely key. Phil would bang on about how he liked anything from Frank Zappa to Judas Priest and Adrian was a massive Ramones fan, so I was about linking all their eclectic interests, including ABBA. Phil was a great admirer of the quality of ABBA's very honed and commercial production, very pop, which obviously would've influenced getting Joanne and Sue involved. I think the ABBA influence was picked up on by Bob and he thought let's just have an art ABBA with the men wearing make-up. 'Open Your Heart' was one of the songs I initially started working out on a guitar, just the basic chords. I think the first time I went down and started playing about with ideas in their studio, I tried transposing it onto keyboard and that developed into 'Open Your Heart'.

MARTYN WARE: I think Jo's songwriting ability was a big part of why *Dare* was so successful.

BOB LAST: Jo Callis was a big part of *Dare* coming together. Jo almost had a producer-like role, he helped tease out the tracks. It wouldn't have been born if he had not been there, but that's not to say it was all him.

SIMON BEST: When *Dare* became a massive commercial success it was very exciting and rewarding, Phil had achieved everything that he'd been aiming for with the League since they mailed

Fast Product the carefully prepared demo of 'Being Boiled'. I was delighted for him. I was at the Edinburgh gig of the *Dare* tour and remember it as musically very professional and tight, with the only negative being I didn't think that they had quite yet optimised the new incarnation of Adrian's visuals.

PHIL OAKEY: Bob Last doesn't like groups. If you notice, he splits up all the groups he's involved with. I'm willing to bet Bob had a hell of a lot to do with the Rezillos breaking up, and look at the Flowers and the Human League, they all split up. He's got this belief that he can manipulate the talented parts of a group and make them work together on different projects. It's one of his new theories which I don't agree with. I like groups, but Bob wants 'non-permanent relationships'.

Bob Last now managed the number 1 group in the UK and *Dare* achieved that rare status of being both critically acclaimed and commercially successful. Apart from reaching these heights with the Human League, his role within the BEF production company had contributed to the success of the Heaven 17 album *Penthouse and Pavement* (on which Last was credited as 'executive manipulator'). Virgin Records had now worked with Last since the first Mekons album; his commercially successful stewardship of the Human League and Heaven 17 meant his standing in the company could not be any higher.

MARTYN WARE: Bob designed the logo for the British Electronic Foundation and continued to manage us as well as the new Human League line-up. We decided Heaven 17 would be the first project of BEF, and included our cities of operation on the cover, Sheffield/London/Edinburgh. However, after our first album we decided to look after our own affairs and manage ourselves — we didn't need a strategist taking 20 per cent of our income.

Last's publishing company Sound Diagrams continued to receive income from songwriting interests in the Human League, Dead Kennedys, Scars, Restricted Code and Fire Engines. pop:aural decided to invest in another Fire Engines single and booked the group back into Castlesound to try to produce a breakthrough hit single for the group.

BOB LAST: *NME* did this interview with Jerry Garcia from the Grateful Dead. Paul Morley spoke to him and was trying to explain about the Fire Engines doing a fifteen-minute set and that was it. Jerry Garcia could not compute this idea because he would do a guitar solo that was longer than an entire Fire Engines set. I recall the fifteen-minute set idea received a very positive reception and I think it was another example of the kind of brand expectation we'd created. We'd opened up a space where you could get away with something like that and people would actually, instead of dismissing it, think maybe that's great. We would not always be helpful regarding the playfulness of it, sometimes we'd say, 'Well, maybe it's not great, maybe it's a load of shite', and I think Davy in particular, probably more than the rest of the band, liked that playfulness and Fire Engines probably couldn't have played much longer anyway even if they'd wanted to. Their fifteen-minute sets were seen as a provocation as indeed it was, but again the question it was really asking, and it was a question we constantly asked, was where's the value in this? It was saying the value in what we do is the intensity of the moment we create. The value is not in whether or not you've had half an hour or forty-five minutes out of us, and it was an assertion of that kind of confidence. That's how I took it.

Fire Engines' sound had mutated through the course of 1981, best exemplified by listening to their first John Peel session broadcast in March and contrasting it with their second session broadcast in November. The four songs recorded for the latter session, 'The Big Wrong Time', 'Young Tongues Need Taste', 'Qualitamatic', 'Produced to Seduce To', have never been released commercially. The second Peel session was the sound of a group trying to develop and expand their sound and vision. The speed of life over the past twelve months since they signed to pop:aural and worked with Bob Last had been relentless, fast and furious. A lot was riding on the production of the new single and Bob Last again brought in Simon Best to help out at Castlesound.

SIMON BEST: I had been playing with Hilary's band, the Flowers, and worked with Fire Engines as their sound man. I wrote the string arrangements for 'Candyskin', and played keyboards on 'Big Gold Dream'.

BOB LAST: 'Big Gold Dream' was obviously a transition, it was an attempt to synthesise all the different ideas Fire Engines had played around with into a new and consistent pop model. Like many of the things we did, it turned out to be a bit more eccentric than we thought it would be. Some people loved it, some people didn't get it. That's all there is to be said about it except that it had a very big sleeve, lot of graphics — we liked that.

DAVY HENDERSON: We were really influenced by *Live at the Apollo* by James Brown and the Famous Flames, knowing full well that we could never get anywhere close to emulating anything like that. It's still one of my favourite albums. The idea for the 'Big Gold Dream' lyrics was stolen from a Dirk Bogarde interview on the television where he says, 'The plan is my survival alongside the big song of the bulldozer.'

HILARY MORRISON: I did the 'Big Gold Dream' photo session with the Fire Engines where they said, 'Right, we want to be commodi-fied, we're going to be half-naked, oiled up, with slabs of meat and boxes of soap powder, but we'll have one guy in a suit.' I did this photo session in my flat, it was very funny. I had had a break-in the week before, and in the middle of the photo session the doorbell goes, and it was the police about my break-in and I had all these half-naked, oiled-up boys on my sitting room floor.

INNES REEKIE: 'Big Gold Dream' was their most commercial offering. The only hint of the devilment of the past was the sleeve, depicting all four members lying bare-chested, glistening in baby oil and covered in raw meat. Apparently Hilary, who photographed the session, and Bob, their new-found mentor, had recently become vegetarian.

DAVY HENDERSON: 'Big Gold Dream' was more about being excited about the packaging again, it doesn't matter what it sounds like as long as it looks good. We were more into the idea of doing a photo shoot in the abattoir in Fountainbridge, take our clothes off, and hang out and get covered in baby oil. We also wanted the abattoir because we knew Hilary was going to be the photographer and she was a vegetarian, so that would wind her up as well. Sadly we couldn't get into the abattoir and we settled on buying about fifteen quid's worth of steaks from Safeway's supermarket. I remember it vividly.

HILARY MORRISON: The 'Big Gold Dream' cover was worked out with the band, but when I took those photographs to the *Face* magazine, I got thrown out. I was told they were disgusting and obscene. Now, go figure. You take a male thing, which the guys wanted to do, flip it, show the commodification of sex. I had the photographs thrown back at me.

DAVY HENDERSON: The pop:aural packaging was a big double-gatefold sleeve and we explained what we wanted to do with the front cover. I think the music was pretty much secondary at that point to Bob's packaging. We were literally more excited about what it looked like rather than what it sounded like.

GEOFF TRAVIS: I'm not sure what Bob was up to with pop:aural. The music seemed slightly less important than the concept, but we were fine with that. You have to be quite judgemental about music, and it's a shame in a way. Obviously everybody can make music and have fun with it, but you don't always have to inflict it on everybody else.

GRAHAM MAIN: 'Big Gold Dream' was more of a laboured production because we had a difficult time writing it. Along with one or two disastrous gigs (sound problems) we thought our time was coming to a productive end.

RUSSELL BURN: Bob was trying to get Fire Engines into the charts. He'd tried with the production of 'Candyskin', and 'Big Gold Dream' was another attempt to make a modern pop record. Bob's idea was to make the production more radio friendly, so we recorded it at Castlesound studios, but it was quite a strange session for me because all they asked me to play was the bass drum pattern for the song to a click track. Bob then asked me to record the snare drum individually, but I can't really play like that. Bob then borrowed the Human League's Linn drum machine and programmed it over the drums I'd played. They never told us this was going to happen and we turned up to the studio and Bob had been in and done it without asking us. Bob had also asked Stephen Lironi from Restricted Code, who were another pop:aural group, to play lots of drum fills over the chorus. 'Big Gold Dream' is my least favourite Fire Engines song.

STEPHEN LIRONI: Bob Last had brought the Human League drum machine from *Dare* along to the Fire Engines session for 'Big Gold Dream'. I was working at Fast Product, packing records to be distributed to shops, when Bob asked me to go along to the session in Castlesound studio because they needed someone to do the drum rolls on the track. It got me out of the Fast Product office for a couple of hours, then I had to get the bus back from the studio to Fast to get back to packing records. I was a fan of the Fire Engines, so it was nice to work with them in the studio.

'Big Gold Dream' failed to get any daytime radio play, though two songs were televised on the BBC 2 arts programme *Riverside*. Fire Engines' only television appearance involved them miming to 'Big Gold Dream' (with Hilary Morrison on backing vocals) and 'Meat Whiplash' – oiled up and topless à la the 'Big Gold Dream' sleeve. The packaging of 'Big Gold Dream' was a conceptual high point for pop:aural and Fire Engines, although the track was far removed from the essence of the group. Russell Burn's radical and unorthodox drumming was the heartbeat of Fire Engines and by replacing him with the Human League's drum machine, Bob Last redefined and irrevocably changed Fire Engines. The race for the prize seemed to have placed market saturation above artistic engagement – it appeared the Codex Communications soul of Fire Engines had been corrupted and deleted.

Scars followed *Author! Author!* with concentrated touring and appeared to have a hit single in waiting with 'All about You'. The group appeared on *The Old Grey Whistle Test*, which felt like another marker, and had recorded their second Peel session. Unfortunately none of this promotional activity resulted in the chart breakthrough both group and label were hoping for, and personal issues within the group were seriously impairing progress.

DAVY HENDERSON: Scars were incredible for young boys but then they got really massive and signed to a major, which was pretty bizarre as well, and I kind of lost touch around that time. The single they brought out on Fast was fantastic, then they got pretty big and were on the TV, man, things like that, it's just insane – our friends were on *The Old Grey Whistle Test*.

JOHN MACKIE: I loved *The Old Grey Whistle Test*, I used to watch it all the time back in those earlier days. There weren't that many television music shows that were showing bands actually playing live, so it was great for Scars to do.

PAUL RESEARCH: The Velvet Underground were a big influence and one day when we were doing a photo session in London, the photographer mentioned that he was sharing a flat with Nico, and Rab was really excited by that, so he became friends with her. I did a gig playing guitar for Nico, I think it was at North London Poly, but it was a disaster. She told me I was playing in the wrong key when we were actually halfway through the song. Too bad, that's show business.

Alan Horne was quoted in the *NME* news story that broke the news that Josef K had split up. He blamed the music press for the demise of the group. The *NME* also announced that Malcolm Ross had joined Orange Juice and that James Kirk and Steven Daly had been sacked. The question that was on everyone's lips was, where now, Postcard?

Les Disques du Crépuscule released a compilation album, *The Fruit of the Original Sin*, that featured contributions from Orange Juice (the *Ostrich Churchyard* version of Kirk's 'Three Cheers for Our Side'), a Paul Haig solo piece and the recorded debut of the French Impressionists, one of the groups mentioned by Horne as being a new Postcard signing on the BBC *Jock 'n' Roll* documentary. The French Impressionists was essentially a vehicle for eccentric pianist Malcolm Fisher, who resided in the flat above Postcard HQ. Fisher had worked on his own compositions and collaborated on songs with Robert Hodgens; they co-wrote their contribution to the Crépuscule album with vocalist Paul Quinn. The track was called 'My Guardian Angel', and felt more akin to Cole Porter than the glut of experimental tracks on

The Fruit of the Original Sin (the album is probably best remembered for the outstanding artwork and packaging by Benoît Hennebert). Paul Quinn was a school friend of Edwyn Collins from Dundee, who had moved down to Glasgow to study at university. He was similar in look and Postcard style to Edwyn, and had a languorous croon perfectly suited to the French Impressionists track, on which Roddy and Campbell from Aztec Camera also played.

MALCOLM FISHER: When Paul Quinn arrived in town from Dundee it was easy to put two and two together and propose a combination for the upcoming Crépuscule release, *The Fruit of the Original Sin*. So it was that Paul and I had to come up with a song asap for that album — he penned the words and I knocked out the tune. It was still my Gershwin phase and 'Guardian Angel' was born and immediately performed in the Spaghetti Factory with Edwyn sitting in on guitar, maybe never having heard the song before. The song was recorded by David Henderson in the Hellfire Club. Roddy and Campbell had come to my new flat in Hayburn Crescent, which was Alan Horne's idea, probably because Roddy was also a Wes Montgomery fan and could easily switch from jazz to rock at the drop of a hat. We rehearsed 'My Guardian Angel' and 'Boo Boo's Gone Mambo' one or two times and then straight into the Hellfire Club. The recording was chaotic, but then so were all early post-punk sessions at that time. I like 'My Guardian Angel', but I would have binned 'Boo Boo's Gone Mambo' — it was a revised jazzy version of a manic Kurt Weill piece I'd been working on.

CAMPBELL OWENS: Malcolm Fisher is unforgettable! I really enjoyed that time. I loved Malcolm's outlook, and working with Paul Quinn was great fun and always has been. The standout moment was when Malcolm told me he was allergic to water. He didn't do anything in half measures.

The post-Orange Juice/Josef K regrouping of Postcard involved two live performances in the run-up to Christmas, with Night Moves in Glasgow then the Nite Club in Edinburgh hosting the Postcard Event. Two concerts had taken place at the Venue in London earlier in the year in August, when Orange Juice headlined one night, with the Bluebells opening and Josef K headlining the other night with Aztec Camera on first. The Postcard Event Scottish concerts sent an important message that the Postcard label was still a going concern. Both concerts involved sets by all four groups: teenage veterans Aztec Camera, new signings the Bluebells and Jazzateers, and the live debut of Orange Juice Mk 2, who for these shows comprised Edwyn Collins, David McClymont, Malcolm Ross and Colin Auld on loan from Jazzateers on drums.

ROBERT HODGENS: It was great fun doing the Postcard gigs with Orange Juice, Aztec Camera, Jazzateers, but we were also getting offers to tour with other bands, and record companies were making offers, plus we were getting BBC Radio sessions and front covers in the music press. We were on the front cover of the *Melody Maker* after four gigs.

RUSSELL IRVINE: Doing earlier concerts like the Postcard Event at the Venue in London on 6 August opening for Orange Juice was exciting — taking the Sound of Young Scotland down south. At that time playing anywhere was great, I loved doing all the Postcard gigs. Although we were pretty much focusing on our own thing, the Postcard/Orange Juice gigs were always exciting, especially as we were all big Orange Juice/Aztec Camera fans. I can remember Edwyn coming through to Edinburgh with us in our van for the Valentino's gig earlier in the year. Robert, who was older than the rest of us, was already friends with Edwyn and Alan Horne, but for me this was pretty exciting. As exciting as meeting Joe Strummer years earlier.

CAMPBELL OWENS: I remember headlining the opening night of Night Moves when it opened as a venue earlier in the year, when Jazzateers supported us. The Postcard Event pre-Xmas concerts were mobbed, the dressing room was teeny, and I spent most of the night in a nearby pub. The only band I recall seeing was the Jazzateers.

ROBERT HODGENS: Alan was really helpful and supportive of the Bluebells, he encouraged the fuck out of us. I remember after the Postcard Event gig at Night Moves in Glasgow, we were sitting with members of Orange Juice, Aztec Camera, Jazzateers, and in front of everyone Alan harangued Edwyn, telling him Orange Juice were going to be overtaken by the Bluebells, that we were way ahead of Orange Juice and we were going to have a hit first. That was good for us to hear, but wasn't so good for Edwyn. Postcard was really about Edwyn's songs, ideas, clothes, aesthetic, but it was probably difficult for him when Orange Juice weren't the only group getting critical acclaim on Postcard.

RUSSELL IRVINE: The main vibe at Orange Juice and Postcard was happiness. Remember this was 1981 and we were just coming out of the punk years. The Postcard Event on 19 December 1981 at the Nite Club in Edinburgh with Orange Juice, Aztec Camera and Jazzateers was the Bluebells' last Postcard-related gig.

Aztec Camera released 'Mattress of Wire' (81-8) in August, when the following Postcard catalogue numbers appeared on Rough Trade's release sheets: (81-9) — the Go-Betweens, 'Your Turn, My Turn' 7-inch; (81-10) — Orange Juice, *Ostrich Churchyard* LP; (81-11) — the Secret Goldfish, 'Hey Mister' 7-inch; (81-12) — the Bluebells, 'Everybody's Somebody's Fool' 12-inch; (81-13) — Aztec Camera, *Green Jacket Grey* LP; and (81-14) — Jazzateers, 'Wasted' 7-inch. None of these records were released. The Postcard originals were no longer on the label, with the fissured Orange Juice departed to Polydor,

Josef K split up and the Go-Betweens back in Australia. That said, there remained more than enough talent for Postcard to progress. Aztec Camera, the Bluebells and Jazzateers had literary songwriting talent in Roddy Frame, Robert Hodgens and Ian Burgoyne, and with a roster of talent it looked like a positive future was more than possible for Postcard. The groups all shared a fashion sense, a musical and artistic aesthetic, and a fierce intelligence. All the major labels were keen to work with the man with the golden ears, Alan Horne.

Bob Last ended 1981 at the toppermost of the poppermost with the Human League having achieved a number 1 single with 'Don't You Want Me' and number 1 album with *Dare*. His successful Tunenoise management company had also delivered major-label success with Heaven 17, and his Sound Diagrams publishing and Fast distribution business also performed well. The one area of the Fast Product empire that was underperforming was pop:aural. Attempts to expand the roster with releases by Marching Girls and Jo Callis failed to connect with either critics or the public. The decision was made to stop the label. Fire Engines' 'Big Gold Dream' was the final release on pop:aural and the last statement made in the independent record market by Bob Last.

Fast Product's initial Edinburgh provocateurs, Scars, were fatally fractured when singer and Keir Street totem Robert King left the group. They found themselves without not only a singer but also a label as Pre dropped them from their record contract. Close friends of the group were worried that King's experimentation with heroin was getting out of control.

PAUL RESEARCH: Scars didn't really click in the London studios, compared to being produced by Bob in Rochdale for the Fast single. We didn't have the same sympathetic ears that we'd had when we recorded 'Adult/ery' and 'Horrorshow' with Bob. After the release of *Author! Author!* the band started to fragment. We never had the most stable of relationships and after we recorded the album we went on tour again. We'd been touring continuously for a couple of years, and by this time we were fed up living in each other's pockets. It meant that when we had down time we were spending time away from each other whenever we could, and that's not a good recipe for getting together and fighting back with the next album. So people started to go off, write songs on their own, and we couldn't follow up *Author! Author!* We did go back into the studio and recorded a couple of songs that had worked well in rehearsal and tried to do a single but it didn't sound great, and the record company started to rapidly lose interest and the loss of momentum essentially set us against each other. Robert left the band and we carried on, tried to find another singer, but it didn't work out.

JOHN MACKIE: The thing about playing in a band like the Scars is it's like being married — all the good and the bad compressed. You're touring with guys, you know everything about them, what you want to know and what you don't want to know, and that's quite a pressure cooker for four young guys. I think you get elation, then you get hubris, and then you get collapse. Scars had a beginning, a middle and an end, and that's the right thing.

Pre Records dropped Scars, but opted to sign Robert King to a solo deal. 'Paper Heart' was recorded and released as a single by Pre to a degree of expectation of a commercial return by Pre's funder, Charisma Records. King's worsening heroin addiction allied with his relationship with Nico meant it was difficult to focus on his career. He moved with Nico from London to Manchester then on to Edinburgh, where close friends like James Oliva offered support trying to help King get clean. This proved difficult with Nico in tow, but eventually after going cold turkey King managed to kick smack and ended his relationship with Nico. With money from his Pre Records advance, he moved to Spain to get cleaned up properly and began thinking about putting a group together to promote the 'Paper Heart' single.

Allan Campbell also decided to shut up shop at Rational Records after the release of their magazine/cassette/vinyl product, *Irrationale* (RATE 8). Conceptually similar in some respects to Fast Product's *Earcom* series, *Irrationale* featured a 7-inch from Delmontes and posters from the Psychotic Reaction gigs Campbell promoted at Valentino's. The magazine featured literary contributions from the Fall's Mark E. Smith and a previously unpublished interview with Jim Morrison, and the cassette featured tracks from Josef K's unreleased Postcard album *Sorry for Laughing*, alongside unreleased tracks by Associates and Article 58 (among others). Rational had also released a couple of singles by Paul Haig's post-Josef K project, Rhythm of Life, and can lay claim to releasing one of the great hidden 7-inch gems from the period, 'Compatibility' by Visitors. James Locke was a musician friend of Paul Haig's who had been involved with Rational, producing the Article 58 contribution to *Irrationale* and the *Golden Duets* EP as a member of Mark, James and Julie (featuring erstwhile Delmontes vocalist Julie Hepburn).

JAMES LOCKE: My first single was on Rational with Mark, James and Julie. Allan Campbell was great, lots of energy. Of course throughout the time I knew him he was managing Paul Haig, so I guess that was his priority. If you're an artist and someone is prepared to pay for manufacturing a record for you it's like a vote of confidence.

ALLAN CAMPBELL: It was an idealistic period. I worked with the Delmontes, managing them, and at one point Virgin wanted to sign them, as did Bill Drummond's Zoo Records. The Zoo contract was terrible — it wasn't worth signing it was so exploitative. Virgin basically wanted to sack a member of the band and get a better player in, but we made the decision that's not how we wanted the Delmontes to operate. We did some good demos produced by Alan Rankine of the Associates, and it was a more altruistic period with some people trying to do the right thing. We also released Paul Haig's solo things when he was calling himself Rhythm of Life. The second RoL single Rational released featured the artist Sebastian Horsley. So it was quite a mixed bag that came out of the Rational era.

The two groups who had generated much optimism for the possibility of pop:aural going overground, Restricted Code and Fire Engines, themselves questioned future progression. Restricted Code's Tom and Frank decided to halt proceedings and split up the group.

TOM CANNAVAN: Our relationship with Bob Last ended because the band decided to split up. We were in the middle of planning our third release with pop:aural, a 12-inch EP, so it is a source of great regret that we didn't take it further, but it was entirely our decision.

FRANK QUADRELLI: I can't blame the record company for Restricted Code splitting up. Perhaps we were disappointed by the fact that 'Love to Meet You' didn't do all we thought it would, we went through a few months of relative aimlessness in the summer of '81. We had all put a lot of effort into the preceding two years and perhaps it was taking its toll. pop:aural had spoken to us about the potential release of a 12-inch EP, but we seemed to have been in a state of limbo at the time and did not really follow it up. During that long summer we seemed to have become more distanced from one another than we ever had been beforehand; this was strange, given our relative success. Perhaps there was more of a feeling that we had to get it right — to impress Bob Last, John Peel and the writers we admired at the *NME*, who by then seemed intent on finding a brand-new 'movement' to get excited about on a weekly basis — and that had a stronger effect than we would ever have imagined it could have as little as a year previously, when pop:aural had signed us. When Kenny and Stephen left the band, probably frustrated by our relative inertia, Tom and I decided to pack it in too.

TOM CANNAVAN: The pop:aural tour with the Fire Engines to promote both of our singles was a great time. As was usual with pop:aural the budget was super tight, so we stayed in dodgy B & Bs, downmarket guest houses. One of the memories that still makes me laugh was getting the Fire Engines to cut our hair. We had pretty boring barber haircuts, theirs were spikey and wild, so before one show we took turns in a chair to have one of the Fire Engines attack our barnets with what I am sure were nail scissors. Maybe that was some sort of ritual bonding. We watched them most nights on that tour and it was unpredictable but always engrossing.

FRANK QUADRELLI: The John Peel and Richard Skinner sessions we recorded in London for BBC Radio 1 were blissful. The Peel session was brilliant, former Mott the Hoople drummer Dale Griffin produced the session and both he and his engineer were very helpful. We rattled through all four songs very quickly, including a version of the Jacksons' 'Shake Your Body'. We also decided to include a cover when we recorded the Richard Skinner BBC session, a version of 'Dancing in the Streets'.

TOM CANNAVAN: We'd always been very confident in our songwriting, performance and direction, but I think the confidence had started to waver after the second single failed to dent even the lower reaches of the charts. A lot of people had predicted great things for us, with *Sounds* declaring we played the 'Best Gig of 1981', Paul Morley in *NME* choosing us [as] one of his top three bands to look out for in 1981 and the *Face* devoting four pages to us. We were as critically acclaimed as just about any of our contemporaries, but the records didn't sell the way we hoped they would and pop:aural expected them to. I think we began to overthink things. It just got too much for us, and we couldn't see the wood for the trees. With hindsight, we could have sorted things out as everything was actually going well when viewed objectively, and the situation was nowhere near as dire as it felt at the time. I do regret it, but that's history.

Fire Engines' tenure as the most exciting and creative group of the Scottish independent underground sound came to an abrupt end. Bob Last called a meeting with Davy Henderson on the final day of 1981. In another scheming, Machiavellian manoeuvre reminiscent of his orchestrated fracture of the Human League, Last decided (without prior discussions with the group) that Fire Engines should discontinue. He decided that Henderson would be best served if he concentrated on writing songs for Sound Diagrams and teamed up with Hilary Morrison in a new project, Heartbeat.

DAVY HENDERSON: After 'Big Gold Dream' had been and gone, Bob invited me to go for something to eat in Habitat in the west end in Shandwick Place. It was New Year's Eve. I remember it being very dark and he told me he was going to be focusing on his Sound Diagrams publishing company and he wanted me to be one of the acts that he signed, but not the Fire Engines. It was either me on my own or not at all, and I went home and split the band up, told them I was leaving. It's one of the biggest regrets of my life, of which there are a few. I do wish it hadn't happened in the way it happened, because the people in the band were like my family, they were really close and I have very strong ties with them still. The people in the Fire Engines and the Dirty Reds are my brothers, and I feel like I let them down, I wish we'd had more faith in our own inabilities − we were inventive people, always looking for something. Eighteen months is such a short time, but it seemed gigantic, it was as big as the biggest bill poster, enormous, it was widescreen and you were a tiny part of that. But there were other things − Murray had to go to university, he'd taken a year out when things started getting played on the radio etc., he had to take a decision to leave university for a year.

GRAHAM MAIN: I think if we had taken time out − six months or so, to write and regroup to work again − then I think we could have continued for some time longer. We were at the age where we perceived media interest to be so fickle and fleeting that we would be forgotten if we dropped out of the scene, some other band would occupy the slot we had created.

MURRAY SLADE: After the pop:aural releases we were a bit disappointed with what we were coming up with. Instead of just carrying on as before, letting things emerge and only guiding the material slightly, we tried to produce something more structured, more musical, and that was probably a mistake on our part. Another factor was the distance between Edinburgh and Dundee, where I was studying. I think Bob was trying to tempt Davy away as a solo artist, and the combination of these two scenarios fractured Fire Engines. Russell phoned me on New Year's Day 1982, and said that's it, it's finished, Davy has left the band. We were over and that was that, so it wasn't like we'd fallen out and started fighting, it was just we'd come to a crossroads and couldn't decide which road to take. In the end we didn't take any road, and that was it. It stopped.

RUSSELL BURN: Murray had decided to take time out to go to university, so it felt like we were losing it a bit. We did a second session for John Peel, and we tried other changes — I started using a hi-hat for the first time to try something different. Then Bob offered Davy a publishing contract and put him together with Hilary Morrison in a new project, Heartbeat, writing pop music. We were all still friends, but Fire Engines fizzled out.

GRAHAM MAIN: When we finished Fire Engines we left a beautiful corpse, we burned fast and bright. Bob Last had been working his Machiavellian ways and wanted Davy but not the rest of us. He offered Davy a deal, which Davy took. We were all young and impulsive, we could have taken time and regrouped but we felt the pressure was on when we should have taken a couple of months off to get ourselves inspired. The Fall continued for years and years, reinventing, which perhaps Fire Engines could have also done. It wasn't inevitable for Fire Engines to finish, I think we gave up too quickly. Bob had ideas with his partner Hilary, who had done backing vocals with Fire Engines on our BBC Television performance of 'Big Gold Dream'. Hilary was casing the joint, she and Bob had ideas for working with Davy on his own. Bob was also managing Scritti and the Human League at the time, so he felt Davy could be utilised in a better way by working with Hilary. There were no histrionics when we split, it was obviously sad, but we felt the Fire Engines was the four of us. Davy has said on several occasions that he regretted his decision to leave the band and that Bob made him an offer he should have refused. Nineteen eighty-two — I woke up and sold my Fire Engines 1965 semi-acoustic Baldwin bass, something I regret to this day. I went to work with Bob Last on the distribution side of his Fast business, I did backline with Orange Juice, then did tour managing with Tangerine Dream.

FRASER SUTHERLAND: Fire Engines had known each other for a good while before the pop:aural records of course, and the single they brought out on Codex Communications had a fair bit of attention, which Bob hadn't been involved with. I thought the idea behind *Lubricate Your Living Room* was a great fit, but I was less keen on the singles — I don't think the scaled-up productions worked that well for them. I know Bob was of the view that they couldn't continue to do these short punchy live sets for much longer before people got bored, but I think he was wrong to bring about their demise. I was with them at the gig in Newcastle which turned out to be their last show, and it was brilliant, the best I'd seen them. I think if they'd been given the space to develop they could have offered much more. Aside from that, the worst thing for me was that they were first and foremost a bunch of mates, before they'd even formed a band, sharing flats and living in each other's pockets. It was a pretty shabby thing to do, I think, to split them up like that just to further a plan.

BOB LAST: Why did the Fire Engines implode? They had originally set out on a course of doing really exciting, interesting things and you need to take it somewhere else. But just doing amazing fifteen-minute sets until people are bored or until it's become a kind of convention is surely not what Fire Engines were about, and I was very clear about that. I think partly because of this pressure I put on them, they couldn't answer that question and so I think that's why they imploded. I would expect it was that in large part, because Davy in particular would have wanted to answer that question. He didn't want to turn into the Grateful Dead of post-punk, and I certainly wasn't about to help them do that.

MURRAY SLADE: We'd always said if we didn't come up with another song by a certain time we should think about splitting up, but it was a combination of factors. I got a phone call from Russell on New Year's Day, 1982, saying Davy had left. Bob Last dragged him away to form Heartbeat, I think he saw him as a source of lyrics, music and attitude.

DAVY HENDERSON: Everything that Bob touched around that period was so successful, from his music publishing arm Sound Diagrams or his management interests in the Human League, Heaven 17, ABC, Scritti Politti. When he asked me to break up the band that I'd been involved in for what at that time seemed like a really big part of my life, that I'd dedicated twenty-four hours each day of my life to for a long time, his success indicated that it seemed like the right thing to do. I've heard Bob saying that with the Fire Engines we were just getting less of the same, but that's just some sort of pithy comment to make about somebody else's life. Fire Engines was my life and we should have had the courage to take six months, a year or five years, to actually learn how to play what we wanted to play. Fire Engines' whole career was incredibly short, about eighteen months. Interpretation of time and the way one perceives time now is completely different; being in the Fire Engines was a huge vast panoramic nothing, it didn't seem like it went quickly. One of the ideas was not to put a record out — I think that would have been a pretty exciting path to follow, to just perform live. I think that's where our strengths were and the virtue of non-playing was all in the performance, and Russell's adrenaline. I wish we had not released a record.

INNES REEKIE: Davy mentioned he thought the group should have trusted their internal magnets and their inability. Fire Engines finally ran out of steam and, as with shooting stars burning twice as bright and all that jazz, it was hardly surprising. They were light years ahead of their time, musically, attitude-wise and perhaps even culturally. Fire Engines carved out their own niche, nobody has come close to replicating their glorious, nihilistic no-wave sound of complete exhilarating abandon.

The Scottish independent pop movement looked like it had run out of steam by the end of 1981. The list of groups associated with Fast Product/pop:aural, Postcard and Rational that had split up was long: Scars, the Flowers, Boots for Dancing, Thursdays, Fire Engines, Restricted Code, Josef K, Orange Juice Mk 1, Visitors, Article 58 and Delmontes — none of these groups would release any further records. The movement that started with the original Fast Keir Street flat gang and was followed by the original Postcard gang of Orange Juice and Josef K failed to cross the finishing line in the race for the prize (which now seemed to be chart success). The movement that was started by Bob Last and Hilary Morrison in January 1978 with the release of FAST 1, 'Never Been in a Riot', looked to have finally crashed on the rocks. The independent dream was over. It was acknowledged by Last and Morrison that something special had happened during the Fast Product and pop:aural period. The intelligence of Robert King and Davy Henderson in particular helped create something truly special with their cohorts in Scars and Fire Engines.

BOB LAST: With pop:aural I was enjoying footering around in the studio, I was amping up the contradictions of trying to make poppy records on the one hand, and more extremely odd records on the other, like the record I made with accordionist Frank Hannaway and guitarist Michael Barclay, which was probably the most out-there thing we did sonically. At the same time we were trying to make things that sounded more like hits, like 'Candyskin' by the Fire Engines, which almost got on the Radio 1 playlist until it got reviewed on the station and was described as the worst-produced record of all time. I produced that record.

HILARY MORRISON: I moved on from the Flowers — I didn't like being the only girl in an all-boy band, and I brought in another girl, Trash from the Ettes, but I just felt things had become a bit stale, in the way that bands do. I mucked around for a bit after that trying to do an all-girl group, and we did lots of demos for people. But back then, to put it bluntly, there wasn't a lot of interest in all-girl groups. Some of the things that were said to us when we did demos were really quite disturbing and exploitative. I just thought, I don't like this.

It should be noted that the all-girl groups in Scotland that gained media attention — Twin Sets and Ettes from Edinburgh, Sophisticated Boom Boom in Glasgow — never signed recording contracts or released records during this period. These artists were endorsed by the local scenes and John Peel, but to reiterate Hilary Morrison's comment, there didn't seem to be a lot of industry interest in all-girl groups. However, Morrison's contribution to and influence on the Scottish post-punk movement and Fast Product remained a beacon and inspiration for girls (and boys) who were interested in communicating ideas.

HILARY MORRISON: Fast Product — it was unimaginable, but it happened. I was a wee bit older than everyone else and I had a flat, so it's all back to Keir Street and we would talk about films, books, we did a bit of art, endlessly sharing records. Collage was very influential, we used ready-made materials and magazines, cutting it up, mixing in a bit of drawing as well. Anyone could be an artist.

BOB LAST: Hilary's big contribution was she bought me a copy of *Spiral Scratch*, and that was absolutely the thing that made me think, OK, this thing that's going on in music, punk, is a great thing to do with this art project. In that sense she had a really crucial role in what we were doing. She did the photography and of course she had her own band, the Flowers, which I think was an underrated group.

HILARY MORRISON: pop:aural went by the by, Human League management took over, which is a twenty-four-hour, seven-days-a-week thing when major-label success comes along — not a lot else can fit in with it. We were saying to people we didn't want pop:aural to become a major record label, that was never the intention. We said to artists, 'Look, if you want to keep doing this you can either go and do your own record label, know how it works, or go and get a major deal, but get a deal with your eyes open.' pop:aural became very time consuming for not much in return, and as you get older you have to make decisions — you start to think, hang on. When the Human League originally split, nobody knew that *Dare* was going to be as big as it became, and it was a whole different proposition. Things change. Life changes.

BOB LAST: It's important to understand how tribal things were at that point, particularly locally. There were lots of people making music who thought that the label should release their music and were deeply offended that we didn't, and at that time I was not unfamiliar with violence about that. There were street fights about Fast; people cared, this stuff mattered and you were dealing with people who didn't necessarily respect or have access to any dispute-resolution procedure. So, these were really tribal things, very intensely felt and experienced. Fast Product did cause outrage but the whole point of that was about being fast, about being intense. It's your problem if you've not caught up, so it was a provocation — everything we did was a combination of provocation, strategy and expedience.

FRASER SUTHERLAND: I was quite close to both Boots for Dancing and Fire Engines — I used to roadie for both and also Josef K, when I wasn't doing gigs myself with the Flowers. I loved the Boots 12-inch on pop:aural, which really captured how good a band they could be live, but there were other releases on pop:aural which were disparate and pretty forgettable — Drinking Electricity for instance. By that time, of course, there were loads of independent records vying for attention. It was kind of ironic, I think, that Factory Records, who had learned so much about branding from the early Fast releases, were much more successful in taking that forward.

BOB LAST: Davy Henderson of the Fire Engines and Rab King of the Scars were particularly strong figures. They were both incredibly intelligent, articulate and completely untainted by any formal cultural expectation or education. We wanted to transgress any idea of what was formally considered good or intelligent or clever, because my view was that lots of mainstream, apparently formal high art and culture was actually pretty fucking dim-witted, and that was my starting point. So we had a bunch of kids and people around Fast Product who would bring me sparks of insight and intelligence that outshone anything you would find in the academies at the time. I think what Fast and its presence in the city had done at that point was enabled people like Rab or Davy and others to believe in themselves in a way that they may not have done otherwise. pop:aural was much more straightforward on one level in that it was just about, 'Well, we always thought this was about pop music, let's see if we can make some pop music.' It turned out a) we couldn't and b) we'd been so corrupted by what we did at Fast Product that we thought that Davy Henderson was a pop star, which was obviously a fatally flawed idea.

There may well have been bad blood between label bosses Bob Last and Alan Horne, but these tensions largely didn't exist between the artists and managers (most of whom had a real warmth towards each other).

ALLAN CAMPBELL: Fire Engines were one of the most inspiring bands I've seen and Davy Henderson is a star. Davy wasn't technically a great guitar player but he was a very effective one, he had a great line and lyrics, kind of half-pinched I guess from T. Rex. Musically they were spiky, challenging, interesting; their slightly skewed musical take was rooted by Russell's drumming style — he didn't use cymbals. Fire Engines were an interesting mixture, an undeniable power, and when Paul Morley started writing about them in the *NME* they really took off.

ROBERT KING: Scars possibly influenced Fire Engines; maybe they would have sounded different if we'd never met. Having an influence on people is good, but not something that should be taken lightly and feasted upon. It should really be ignored because generally you're too busy thinking about people that have an influence on you to notice your influence on other people, especially when you're just a teenager.

JOHN MACKIE: I thought Fire Engines were a great band. They flew under the banner of no compromise, they weren't interested in polishing their sound. It seemed like they just wanted to drive forward at full tilt, all other considerations were secondary. They were kind of funky as well, they had a sort of jangly raw funk about them.

PAUL RESEARCH: I used to know Edwyn pretty well in the very early days when Orange Juice did their first gig in Edinburgh. I made a cassette tape of the gig and we used to listen to it every single day. I thought they were the most fantastic band.

DAVY HENDERSON: Murray Slade was friends with David Weddell, the bass player from Josef K, and that's how we got to know Josef K. There was a bit of acrimony between us initially because they were so great and we were jealous — well, I was. They could play anything, and when they played at the Wig and Pen with the Scars we exchanged unpleasantries. I think there might have been some fists involved, very small ones, teenage fists. But then we became great friends after that through a shared interest in Lucky Strike cigarettes and other American tobaccos.

PAUL RESEARCH: It's fantastic that Josef K and the Fire Engines have such fond memories of those days because I do as well. I remember our second gig was with TV Art, who then subsequently changed their name to Josef K, and we thought they were a great band. Fire Engines as well, obviously, and prior to that the Dirty Reds — they're still our mates and when I see them today we'll give each other a big hug. People go off and do things in the world and then when they get back together again you've just got so much in common with those guys. Those were the best of times and it's so nice to see everybody's still there, all those guys are still interested in music and they're all still doing very valid and interesting stuff. The people who were there know what went on in 1977, so we'll always have punk.

CHAPTER 6

1982 – Split Up the Money

Hilary Morrison

BOB LAST: For me the Human League being UK Christmas number 1 then number 1 in the States with 'Don't You Want Me' — for me that was the upshot of everybody's collective work at Fast Product to date. Funnily enough it went all the way back to listening to Parliament. It had that amazing bass riff and opening line — it's interesting how these resonances crop up again in funny ways.

It had been three short and action-packed years since the FAST 1 mission statement 'Never Been in a Riot' was released, when Hilary Morrison had to break into a cottage in the Scottish Borders to record that epochal debut single by the Mekons. Bob Last and Hilary Morrison had now developed the Fast Product negative into Kodachrome colour with the Human League at the top of the pop charts. *Dare* had furnished hit after hit, with all of Last's management strategies viewed by the mainstream music industry as nothing short of business genius. His guidance resulted in success not only for the Human League, but also for League founders Martyn Ware and Ian Craig Marsh with Heaven 17 (albeit not to the same stratospheric level as *Dare*). Ware and Craig Marsh would soon remove Last from his managerial position with Heaven 17.

HILARY MORRISON: Starting from the first Fast release by the Mekons, we worked out what was needed, then persuaded Traverse Theatre to lend us a 2-track tape recorder. Tim Pearce showed us how we could bounce tracks on a 2-track machine to make it 4-track, and then 8-track, which was the way the earliest Beatles recordings were made. We begged or borrowed everything else we needed like mics etc., then it was just a learning curve from there. We had a preparedness always to be learning. If you've come the autodidact route, I think everything's just something new to learn. Nothing seems impossible. We learned the whole process, through mastering, pressing etc., which was fascinating. The most difficult aspects were marketing, and of course distribution, which was the most controlled element and where all the mark-ups occur.

Fast Product and pop:aural were now closed down, meaning Last's full attention was focused on management, distribution and his publishing company (Sound Diagrams). Apart from their residual Fast Product and pop:aural publishing interests, Sound Diagrams were actively working with songwriters Jo Callis, Hilary Morrison, James Locke and Davy Henderson.

DAVY HENDERSON: Around that time, everything Bob was involved in was enormous. Decisions that he'd made and engineered, like the break-up of the original Human League to create Heaven 17 and the Human League Mk 2, were on paper the right decisions. I don't think he was provoking these situations but you could see he was astute and perceptive. He had so much success with Fast Product and pop:aural — Gang of Four, the Mekons, Scars, the Human League. David Bowie played the Mekons single on his BBC Radio 1 show that he had in 1978. As a kid, there was no way you could perceive being on the BBC — the idea that your records got played, that you had some impact on these huge traditional institutions. Even Fire Engines being asked to go to the BBC to record a Peel session was like being dropped into the set of *Doctor Who*.

JAMES LOCKE: In 1979 I'd heard Human League's 'Being Boiled', seen the Flowers play, had heard of Bob and I think Hilary ran a club night, Danceteria at J.J.s. But for me the Scars were pretty dull, Flowers seemed messy, the Fire Engines were magnificent and I loved Boots for Dancing. The last two had some kind of taut creative energy and both lead singers were charismatic.

Sound Diagrams generated considerable income, largely on the back of the publishing share from *Dare*. Jo Callis made a massive impact on the songwriting approach to *Dare*; he had the pop nous that helped take the group from cult status to international mainstream pop success.

JO CALLIS: The success of *Dare* took everyone by surprise. I don't think anyone quite knew what to think, we were just expecting to follow the same route as the previous albums *Reproduction* and *Travelogue* – respectable sales for what was an electronic group. I joined a cult band that were doing new electronic music, though there was support from the New Romantic following that had built up, but it was all brand new as far as the mainstream public were concerned. I think we were expecting *Dare* would sell a few hundred thousand albums and it would hopefully be a step on from *Reproduction* and *Travelogue*, so it was a complete surprise that it went stratospheric – a bit like you've launched your space capsule to orbit the earth but ended up landing on the moon.

The final single to be lifted from *Dare* – 'Don't You Want Me' – was an international number 1 and generated considerable income for Sound Diagrams publishing (Jo Callis was a co-writer of the song). The choice of the single and the Brecht-influenced video were Bob Last's ideas, which from a Virgin Records perspective was further evidence of his Midas pop touch.

JO CALLIS: We never had a clue that 'Don't You Want Me' would be a massive success – for us it wasn't anything more than a filler track on the album. We were thinking that we were more of a dark, heavy band, our focus was on tracks like 'Seconds'. Phil

Oakey would have very, very set views about things and didn't want the track released as a single — that was all Bob's idea.

After being lured by Last to sign as a writer with Sound Diagrams (which precipitated the demise of Fire Engines), Davy Henderson teamed up with Hilary Morrison and James Locke and worked on a new project, Heartbeat. It was assumed that Last would procure a major-label deal for the project once they'd recorded some demos.

DAVY HENDERSON: Once I'd left the Fire Engines, Bob wanted me to be part of his Sound Diagrams publishing roster along with writers like Jo Callis. It probably appealed to the ludicrous part of the industry that Bob enjoyed. I suppose I was part of a Sound Diagrams songwriting stable. Hilary Morrison was in there too. Hilary was writing pop songs after the end of the Flowers, and I think the idea was courting the charts in the sense of 'let's try and play the game'.

HILARY MORRISON: We did bring out a Heartbeat track for an *NME* cassette, but I just really didn't like the nitty-gritty of the music business. At that time it was not a place that was sympathetic or interested in women unless they were being told what to do.

JAMES LOCKE: I'm guessing it was through the nights that Hilary ran that I played at with the Macnaires that she approached me. The Fire Engines lived in Sciennes in Edinburgh at that time, which was on my walk home after clubbing. Davy Henderson and I had some common ground in terms of musical influences — he's an inspirational guy. I was offered a publishing deal by Bob Last and it seemed a good direction to go in. However, it wasn't for me, it was fairly contrived and controlled. I guess Bob thought that would work.

DAVY HENDERSON: Heartbeat was formed with the idea of having pop success, and I was going to be the boy in the band. Heartbeat were established and Hilary was working with James Locke at the time. James was pretty talented, a great drummer and could play. He's got an aptitude for musical instruments and that was pretty rare at the time, so Hilary was utilising his talents and trying to write sophisticated pop songs and I was invited to be the boy in the band and contribute my take on it.

GRAHAM MAIN: With Heartbeat it didn't take too long before the cardiac arrest occurred! Bob saw Davy as the one he wanted to concentrate his energies and ideas on and suggested he left the Fire Engines and work with Hilary on the Heartbeat project. I didn't think Davy was ever happy working on Heartbeat with Hilary — it just didn't gel for him. Hilary was the leader of Heartbeat; I don't think Davy was happy taking a following role.

While Bob Last basked in the glow of international major-label pop success, Alan Horne had released his last record on Postcard with Aztec Camera's 'Mattress of Wire' and was plotting his next post-Orange Juice move. The schedule of forthcoming Postcard releases that appeared in the Rough Trade catalogue included planned singles by the Go-Betweens, the Bluebells, Jazzateers and the debut album by Aztec Camera (*Green Jacket Grey*) — these would never appear. The poor press reception for the Josef K album the previous year was the first time in its short existence that Postcard had received negative energy from the music press. At a crucial time in the label's history, Alan Horne had lost faith in Josef K, Orange Juice, Postcard and himself. Orange Juice had signed to Polydor and Josef K had split up. David McClymont's view is that Postcard was really all about Orange Juice and Edwyn Collins for Horne, and that he never really liked Josef K or the Go-Betweens. So what now for Postcard's boy wonder?

MALCOLM ROSS: Alan Horne didn't like the negative reviews for the Josef K album, he liked to get good press, and the whole Postcard thing had started to disintegrate. Alan lost confidence, started to doubt himself and the bands. The plan for Postcard Records was to release Orange Juice and Aztec Camera albums. If he'd done that and just ridden it out for a couple of years, Postcard Records could have gone on to be one of the most successful independent labels. If he'd put out the first Orange Juice album and the first Aztec Camera album, Postcard would have sold tens of thousands.

Alan Horne percolated a new idea, Postcard International. This idea seemed to revolve around the management, recording and licensing of albums by Aztec Camera and Jazzateers to major labels — the independent Postcard ideal was now officially dead. Horne expertly co-ordinated a media campaign announcing Jazzateers being the new wave of Postcard, and *NME*, *Sounds* and *Melody Maker* all ran articles and interviews with Horne and the group. The general consensus was Jazzateers inhabited a place where the gentler shadings of the Velvet Underground met the bossa nova appeal of Antônio Carlos Jobim, all under the managerial control of Alan Horne. As Postcard's newest signing it was only a matter of timing for Jazzateers to go national. They had been kept under wraps and played restaurants and Glasgow west end cocktail bars (Spaghetti Factory, Toffs, Bensons). Jazzateers performed at obscure Postcard-themed evenings called Après-Ski and Bourgie Bourgie, and supported Orange Juice and the Bluebells. Along with the French Impressionists and Aztec Camera, Jazzateers seemed to be taking the Postcard sound in a more jazz-influenced direction akin to Vic Godard in his Club Left persona. The group featured the fragile, honeyed vocals of Alison Gourlay (who mixed the cold aura of Nico with the distant warmth of Astrud Gilberto), combined with the prodigious songwriting talents of Ian Burgoyne and Keith Band.

Jazzateers: Colin Auld, Alison Gourlay, Keith Band and Ian Burgoyne

IAN BURGOYNE: I remember at school really liking the Beach Boys, but everyone else regarded them as a joke, everyone laughed at you for liking the Beach Boys. Now of course everyone loves the Beach Boys, but nobody in Glasgow believed me in the seventies when I said Brian Wilson was a pop genius. Edwyn Collins didn't believe me, Alan Horne didn't believe me, they said the Beach Boys were rubbish, but it's all turned on its head now. I was drawn to the Beach Boys because I've always loved tunes — I was a big Burt Bacharach fan growing up. I remember hearing 'Sail On, Sailor' on the radio and thought it was one of the best things

I'd ever heard. Then a friend at school gave me the *Wild Honey* LP because he thought it was terrible and after I listened to it I couldn't believe how good it was. I went into a record shop in Paisley called Cuthbertson's, around 1977/'78 and punk, and I used to see a copy of *Pet Sounds* sitting in the shop. No one bought it. I went to the record shop regularly after school with future Jazzateers bassist Keith Band, and no one had bought this copy of *Pet Sounds*. I saved and saved until one Saturday I finally bought *Pet Sounds*. I got home and listened to it and without a doubt it was life-changing. I became evangelical about the album, but no one listened — even Keith didn't like the Beach Boys. It was actually Douglas MacIntyre, who was staying in my house at the time in the early eighties, who listened to it in my house and loved it — that was the first person who really got *Pet Sounds*. So, I suppose what I'm trying to say is that *Pet Sounds* was a massive influence on the Jazzateers.

KEITH BAND: I was friends with Ian Burgoyne at school long before we considered being musicians. We were totally into music; prior to punk we both liked Neil Young, Bob Dylan, Joni Mitchell, as well as glam artists like Bowie and Roxy. Ian was a massive Beach Boys fan — no one liked the Beach Boys back then. He also liked the Beatles and was the first person I knew who liked Nick Drake. After the initial excitement of punk wore off because it had become so derivative, we became more interested in starting a group that involved melodic music that fitted with our basic level of musicianship. We were really into the Subway Sect and Buzzcocks. Ian and I lived in Paisley, so were fortunate in that we could go to see groups at the Bungalow Bar, groups like Echo and the Bunnymen and the Teardrop Explodes. However, the groups that made a big impression on me were the Postcard groups, Josef K and, in particular, Orange Juice. They seemed very sophisticated, but with a primitive energy that we related to, and we felt we could be in a similar group at that point.

When we started playing music, it was just Ian and I with guitars in a bedroom. We reacted against contemporary music. Shortly after we started we got booked for a gig in the Rock Garden in Queen Street and we had no original material so we quickly wrote six songs. Ian was singing, but decided the songs were better suited to a girl singer, and my brother recommended Alison. We knew she worked in the Café Gandolfi and we liked her and thought she looked good, so offered her the job of singer in the Jazzateers without having heard her sing. We were influenced by Bacharach and the first song we practised with Alison was 'The Look of Love' — not the easiest song to sing or play. Our first concert with Alison was at the Spaghetti Factory.

ALISON GOURLAY: Prior to punk I was into disco, and Bowie and Lou Reed. I was good friends with David Band, who I knew from hanging around clubs at Glasgow School of Art, and through him I met his younger brother Keith, who was in a group called Jazzateers. They invited me to the Hellfire Club to rehearse and hear their songs, and that's how I became the singer in the Jazzateers. I had never been in a band before, and that was my introduction to Postcard. I was aware of Orange Juice, but I wasn't really into groups associated with that scene, like Josef K and Fire Engines, but I was from East Kilbride so I knew Aztec Camera.

IAN BURGOYNE: Keith loved punk, and because he was my best friend a lot of his influences rubbed off on me, but I still preferred Dionne Warwick. We would lie about our ages and after school go to the Bungalow Bar in Paisley where we saw Altered Images, Orange Juice, Josef K. I thought Orange Juice were really good, they had tunes. That was a formative moment, seeing another group who were interested in melody which is what Jazzateers were trying to do. There just wasn't enough melody in groups like the Pop Group or the Gang of Four for my tastes.

I never had any aspirations to form a band at all, it was completely accidental, which I think made us different in many ways. Jazzateers' whole career was a series of accidents. Keith and I always liked to play guitar together but we didn't have any ambition to be in a band. Keith's older brother, David, was having his twenty-first birthday party in 1980 at the Rock Garden in Queen Street, and for some reason we got roped in and said we would play at his party as our present to him. So we got together with two friends who were at Glasgow Uni with us – Colin Auld on drums and Lawrence Donegan on bass – and played at David's twenty-first. People liked what we were doing and encouraged us to keep going, but we viewed it very much as a hobby, something fun to do on a Sunday afternoon. The Bluebells were around at the same time, and Lawrence left us and joined them, so Keith picked up the bass. We started rehearsing at the Hellfire Club. I was writing more songs using major sevenths and jazz chords. However, journalists started writing about Jazzateers and assuming I was listening to Astrud Gilberto, but in fact during the early Jazzateers period I was listening constantly to side two of *The Beach Boys Today!*

Jazzateers were purely hobbyists – we were students and were focused on our studies at Glasgow Uni. We recorded a demo with David Henderson at the Hellfire Club, and he did a really great job as we were rubbish musicians, we didn't have the technical ability to play the jazz-infused songs we had written. People dismissed us as MOR or easy listening, which didn't bother us. Two of the tracks on the demo were good, but what happened next was Keith's brother David was working behind the bar at the Rock Garden and had played our Hellfire Club demo in the bar, and people seemed to like it. Then, through that, we were approached by Alan Horne and he wanted to sign us to Postcard and manage us.

KEITH BAND: I had been to meet Alan Horne as he'd asked me about doing bookkeeping for Postcard (which didn't go any further), and I gave him our new tape which we'd recorded with Alison at the Hellfire Club. He really liked our tape and asked to manage us, everything seemed very easy, and then we were on Postcard which was the sum of our ambition at the time. Alan was Mr Postcard – he was God at the time in terms of music press hip quota – and he was great at controlling the media, with guys like Dave McCullough at *Sounds* and Paul Morley at *NME* taking him very seriously. Alan wasn't a traditional manager in that managers are meant to be organised and look after their bands, but Alan was more focused on ideas and was disorganised. His way of trying to motivate us was playing a record in the Postcard flat, probably the Velvet Underground, Chic or Diana Ross, and tell us Jazzateers had to be as good as these artists and write songs that compared. We always wanted to please him, but didn't quite know how to do it.

ALISON GOURLAY: David Band was managing Jazzateers initially then Alan Horne came on board as manager once we were on Postcard, and he used to give me Dusty Springfield and Blondie albums for direction. It was slightly intimidating being in the Postcard flat. Alan and Edwyn were incredibly smart and effete, rather foppish, and people like Malcolm Fisher would be around playing piano – his group featured Paul Quinn on vocals and were called the French Impressionists. I seem to remember lots of references to musicals and people like Jacques Brel.

After he'd licked his wounds in the aftermath of Orange Juice leaving Postcard for Polydor, February saw Alan Horne round up his press corps commandos, all of whom totally bought into his excitement about Jazzateers, Aztec Camera and the newly christened Postcard International. His influence on Jazzateers was manifest and was the first time he could exert total control over a Postcard group. Despite the obvious quality of Jazzateers' songs, Horne chose the Donna Summer track 'Wasted' (written by Giorgio Moroder and Pete Bellotte) to be recorded as their debut single, produced by Edwyn Collins. In a sign of things to come for Jazzateers, the track was never released. Horne used the Jazzateers articles in the music papers to launch the Postcard International concept, and, in much the same way Malcolm McLaren did with Sex Pistols' press interviews, placed himself centre stage.

ALAN HORNE: The ideas and attitudes within Postcard, especially these days, are more and more at odds with the pedantic and misguided would-be trend setters within the music press. It's tiresome to play down to these people when the rewards are so petty. The only groups I want to work with these days are working in a traditional vein — groups that are influenced by jazz or soul or folk or whatever — and are based around a songwriter. Everything is geared towards the song. The link-up with publishing companies I consider to be as important, if not more so, than the record companies we license Postcard International through. The main strength of Postcard is the songwriters: Edwyn Collins, Roddy Frame and Ian Burgoyne.

STEFAN KASSEL: Postcard moved into a different phase with Aztec Camera and Jazzateers incorporating jazz and bossa nova structures in their songs, which was a 'natural progression', to quote the Jazzateers. I loved it wholeheartedly — melodies make your heart jump, and they had great melodies.

In Dave McCullough's feature in *Sounds*, Horne discussed his master plan for Jazzateers. This included 'Wasted' being licensed to a major label followed by a sixteen-song debut album, and 'a full-length feature film with Alfred Hitchcock undertones' called *Après-Ski*. While this was fanciful in the extreme, McCullough was on point when he identified Jazzateers as being successors to an eclectic range of artists: Pentangle, John Prine, Jimmy Webb, Judee Sill and Neil Young. Glenn Gibson's feature in the *Face* about Postcard International stated Horne's intention to work with songwriters like Ian Burgoyne. Gibson also regarded Burgoyne as being capable of writing timeless classics and portrayed Jazzateers as the Velvet Underground with Dionne Warwick on vocals. *NME* and *Melody Maker* followed suit in praise of Burgoyne's songwriting talent and bought into Horne's mantra as regards Postcard International kicking against the post-punk pricks with the talented Jazzateers and Aztec Camera.

IAN BURGOYNE: Punk was really good, we were all into it at the time and it was really exciting, but nothing of interest happened since then. People were listening to bands like Echo and the Bunnymen; I wanted Jazzateers to appeal to the younger sisters of this sort of people.

KEITH BAND: Our music was really back to basics; a good [analogy] to use is that Picasso had to learn to draw before he could come up with paintings of people with three eyes, whereas too many people today start drawing the three eyes before they even learn the basics.

IAN BURGOYNE: Because we were so young, we were impressed by Alan as he was older and seemed to have a depth and breadth of knowledge about the music business. He informed us about things like *Nuggets*, and US West Coast bands. We were just really happy that someone had taken an interest in what we were doing with the Jazzateers, so when he asked to manage us we agreed to it. We got involved with Postcard just after the release of the 'Poor Old Soul', 'Chance Meeting', 'Just Like Gold' singles. We recorded a version of Donna Summer's 'Wasted', which was scheduled as a Postcard 7-inch release but we never really knew if the single would come out. However, Orange Juice had signed to a major label, Polydor, and I'm not sure if Postcard was repositioning or just breaking completely apart.

Alan wasn't a good manager. He had lots of good ideas about management, and in terms of the music press and radio he could make things happen, but as far as the creative process was concerned I didn't find him particularly encouraging — in fact he was quite dismissive. Alan was not a musician and he didn't understand that we were rubbish musicians, so he was frustrated in his aspirations for us to be like Chic, because we were poor musicians, apart from Colin, who also drummed with both Orange Juice and Aztec Camera. There was no way our musicianship would allow us to aspire to the ambitions that Alan had for us.

KEITH BAND: Ian was a very melodic songwriter — he'd take a guitar chord book and pick the most difficult-looking chords to play, and write a song around them. He was our main songwriter. Alan felt that a cover of 'Wasted' by Donna Summer would be a good idea, so Edwyn played guitar on it and produced the track.

ALISON GOURLAY: We played an early gig at the Spaghetti Factory, which was a restaurant that Orange Juice played in, and we played with the French Impressionists. The sound of the Jazzateers was influenced by bossa nova, maybe Velvet Underground's more gentle songs, but we weren't the most popular Postcard band — when we played supporting Orange Juice or Aztec Camera, a lot of beer would get thrown at us. We toured with Aztec Camera, all of us travelling in the van together. We got on well with Roddy and Campbell. Edwyn was friendly too, playing guitar and producing on some of our recordings. Ian wrote a lot of material and would present handwritten lyrics for all the songs, but we were so naive and inexperienced and the group played the songs in the key Ian wrote them in, which was a different key to my singing voice. Alan Horne was a big influence in that he loved torch singers and wanted to highlight having a girl singer out front.

ROBERT HODGENS: Ian from the Jazzateers wanted hit singles, they didn't want to be an albums band. He was a fantastic songwriter — the Bluebells used to do a live cover of Jazzateers' 'Natural Progression'. I always thought when Alison was singing in the Jazzateers that they were like what Altered Images would sound like if they'd signed to Postcard and were under Alan Horne's influence. The version Jazzateers did of Donna Summer's 'Wasted' with Edwyn producing sounded amazing.

The Bluebells had now moved on from Postcard associations and courted major record labels. Their manager, Mark Wilson, had also managed Orange Juice until he was sacked along with Steven Daly and James Kirk. The experience he gained from managing Orange Juice proved useful as he guided the Bluebells through the shark-infested pools of the major labels (most of whom wanted to sign the group). The group were now regularly being written about in the music press (including a front cover of *Melody Maker*), and recorded prestigious BBC Radio sessions. The icing on the cake came when they were booked as the first unsigned group on BBC Television's *Old Grey Whistle Test* and performed three songs live. All of which stoked up major-label interest in signing them.

The Bluebells: David McCluskey, Robert Hodgens, Ken McCluskey,
Russell Irvine and Lawrence Donegan

KEN MCCLUSKEY: The Bluebells were going to make a record for Postcard. We made some demos at the Hellfire Club with David Henderson, but at that time Orange Juice had flown the nest, so Postcard wasn't really there as it had been. When we were associated with Postcard we did lots of gigs with the other groups on the label — Orange Juice, Aztec Camera, the Jazzateers — and there were a lot of photographers connected to the label who photographed the groups, guys like Harry Papadopoulos, Robert Sharp, Peter McArthur. People like James Kirk from Orange Juice were unsung heroes and very important to the whole Postcard aesthetic. Although he took a back seat with Postcard, which was really run by Alan Horne and Edwyn Collins, it was James's guitar playing that gave Orange Juice their sound. Alan Horne got the idea that he would license groups to major labels. He realised that although Postcard was selling a lot of records, because they were doing independent distribution through Rough Trade they couldn't progress in terms of the charts.

ROBERT HODGENS: The Bluebells would have come out on Postcard — there were plans for a 12-inch single of 'Everybody's Somebody's Fool' — but we were offered a UK tour supporting Haircut 100, who were massive at the time. Nick Heyward had seen a photo and review in the *NME* and had written to me offering the Bluebells the support tour on the basis of liking the Hofner semi-acoustic guitar I was playing in the *NME* review. I told Alan Horne and he told me we couldn't do it, we weren't ready, it was too soon for the Bluebells, and that I should write back to Nick Heyward and tell him Aztec Camera would do the Haircut 100 tour instead. Alan told me if the Bluebells did the Haircut 100 tour we were finished with Postcard, so we did the Haircut 100 tour. We met Elvis Costello soon afterwards when we played the ICA in London, which always feels to me like the end of the Postcard period for us. The Bluebells were all wearing blue cord jackets, and he thought we were like the Byrds, he loved us. Elvis wanted to produce us, and within days we were in Nick Lowe's studio in London working with him, and by that point we knew the Bluebells were going to be offered deals by major labels. People should take into account that Alan never really got anything out of Postcard financially — when the groups signed to majors Alan never received a penny. He's a great artist, his visual eye and design ideas were fantastic. I think Alan Horne would have loved to have managed the Bluebells or Orange Juice when major deals were signed, get paid to be in the music industry.

RUSSELL IRVINE: Performing on *The Old Grey Whistle Test* was amazing, I absolutely loved it. When I watch it now I'm amazed at how blindly confident I was, and considering our first rehearsal was only a year and a half earlier it's pretty staggering. We were perfectly aware that a lot of the interest in the Bluebells at the start came from Robert's close connection with media friends like music journalist Kirsty McNeill and photographer Harry Papadopoulos, but there's nothing wrong with a little push-start. Pretty soon all the music press was covering us, even when they were slagging us off for being ramshackle, twee, jingle-jangly, like the Monkees. None of that bothered me because generally what they were saying was right, and we liked being all those things. When Robert was on the cover of *Melody Maker* we hadn't even signed a deal at that point — I don't know if anyone had ever done that before. At that point our upward trajectory was pretty phenomenal, we pretty much had it on a plate. Robert had everything mapped out in his head before it all happened — it's incredible really. I don't remember any setbacks. It was all up, up and away!

CAESAR: A track such as 'Everybody's Somebody's Fool' I just couldn't resist, and I get the same thrill hearing the guitar intro today. It takes me directly to a period when Glasgow's optimism in the face of economic adversity shone like floodlights from Hampden Park — a sight I witnessed from the back bedroom window of the house I grew up in — and I was often listening to demos by the Bluebells in the moment.

As the majors circled the Bluebells and the music press frothed over the recharged Postcard International concept with Aztec Camera and Jazzateers, February saw the release of the debut Orange Juice album on Polydor, *You Can't Hide Your Love Forever*. The LP artwork featured the original Postcard incarnation of the group and the album was warmly received by the London media. However, the Glasgow cognoscenti agreed with Steven Daly's assertion that the production seemed to be more of a calling card for producer Adam Kidron, and that the visceral excitement captured on the Postcard singles was absent from the album. Another single was released, James Kirk's 'Felicity'; however, like the ill-judged version of 'L.O.V.E.', it failed to reach the charts. Orange Juice regrouped with new drummer Zeke Manyika and guitarist Malcolm Ross, settling in to life in London as major-label recording artists.

Altered Images followed their two top 10 hit singles with a number 11 hit with 'See Those Eyes', which highlighted their pre-eminent position as the most successful group from the Postcard period. Altered Images had achieved everything to which Postcard aspired, with successful singles success and daytime radio play, highlighting the benefits of being on a major label. CBS had afforded the group the opportunity to work with the hottest producer in the UK, Martin Rushent, who had succeeded in transforming the Human League from a cult electronic group to an internationally successful pop group. The new Altered Images album, *Pinky Blue*, reached number 12 in the UK which resulted in headline touring status for the group (who took Vic Godard and the Subway Sect and the Bluebells on tour with them).

CLARE GROGAN: We adored the Human League and the Buzzcocks so going to Martin's place in the country to record our second album was exactly what we wanted. Pete Shelley was staying there as well but I was too shy to talk to him. John Peel came down and did backing vocals on 'Song Sung Blue'. It was all slightly surreal. Martin was a genius; his son told me after he passed that 'See Those Eyes' was his favourite production ever.

Associates: Billy MacKenzie and Alan Rankine

Associates were another group that initially orbited the Fast Product and Postcard galaxies; however, from an early stage they always felt their natural home needed to be a major label. They had saved 'Party Fears Two' (which became their first chart hit) until they signed with a major. The angelic vocal presence of Billy MacKenzie and the compositional prowess and musicianship of Alan Rankine were showcased on the first Associates album on Fiction, the Cure's label. Limited touring took place with the Cure's original bassist Michael Dempsey in tow, including 'A Tribute to Frank Sinatra' at Valentino's in Edinburgh with Scars, Josef K and Fire Engines (who had now all split up). The studio was MacKenzie and Rankine's forte and natural environment, and after they extracted themselves from their unsatisfactory Fiction deal, the group released a series of brilliant 12-inch singles on Beggars Banquet sub-label Situation 2. These singles were collected and released as an album, *Fourth Drawer Down*, and the media clamour that ensued resulted in significant major-label interest. Associates signed to Warner Brothers in the UK.

ALAN RANKINE: Bill and I had a flat in Edinburgh that was our base of operations. We were offered a record deal by Fiction Records, run by Chris Parry. It was a bloody awful deal. We also signed an awful publishing with him — we had no legal representation, it was a bit shambolic, but frankly, no one else was interested. We moved from Edinburgh to London and got Fiction to pay for this nice flat with a white baby grand piano in St John's Wood, six months in advance, and Bill and I recorded our first album *The Affectionate Punch* in the spring of 1980. We very quickly got a band together, bringing in Mike Dempsey, who'd exited the Cure due to musical differences, and we got this Australian drummer called Murphy. Despite everything appearing to be shambolic we had a plan and the plan was, let's ditch Fiction, who were basically financed by Polydor. To our surprise we got Fiction to release us from their recording contract, but Chris Parry wanted to keep the publishing, to which we reluctantly agreed. So we were free agents with no money living in a nice flat in St John's Wood. We planned our next move knowing we had to manoeuvre ourselves into a position where we became desirable to a major label. We proposed a series of 12-inch singles to Beggars Banquet, to be released on their Situation 2 sub-label, as we could see that Gary Numan was signed to Beggars but they had the distribution muscle of an agreement with Warner Brothers behind him. So we signed to Beggars Banquet and let the music papers know that we were going to release a 12-inch single every six weeks, a run that included 'Tell Me Easter's on a Friday', 'Q Quarters', 'White Car in Germany', etc. We did that and we got Record of the Week every single time and compiled them as an album, *Fourth Drawer Down*.

As Associates became a priority signing to Warner Brothers, Billy MacKenzie was heard extolling the vocal virtues of Paul Haig on BBC Television, where he named him as his favourite vocalist. After the abrupt and sudden decision by Paul Haig to disband Josef K at their peak, there was considerable interest in what Paul would do next. His new concept, Rhythm of Life, seemed very Thomas Jerome Newton/World Enterprises Corporation in nature and promised much in the way of multimedia activity. His first RoL release was a collaboration with Stephen Harrison (formerly of Metropak), which came out as a 7-inch on Rational Records, followed by another RoL 7-inch on Rational in collaboration with artist Sebastian Horsley (who in later years staged his crucifixion in the Philippines — he eventually died of a heroin overdose). Paul Haig had worked on tracks, some of which were released under his own name on Crépuscule. The material veered stylistically from Sinatra croons to electronic feedback manipulation — RoL provided an umbrella for a more eclectic, relaxed approach by Haig (Josef K could never be accused of being relaxed). This was a new beginning.

PAUL HAIG: After Josef K split up, I did a solo tour in Belgium and decided to live in Brussels. Crépuscule put me on a monthly retainer and I did a lot of recording there for about six months. Michel at Crépuscule suggested my first solo single should be a cover of 'Running Away' by Sly and the Family Stone, which I recorded in Belgium using an 808 drum machine with me playing all the instruments. I was only twenty-one so it was great to be living in Brussels in an art deco flat; it was a good experience spending a lot of time in the studio there recording tracks that were the basis of getting the deal with Island Records. I had seen David Bowie in *The Man Who Fell to Earth*, and read the Walter Tevis book, so had a fascination with the fact that this alien arrives and starts developing patents and massive conglomerate businesses, and I thought it would be interesting to do something like that – RoL tinned peaches or something as silly as that. RoL was really a banner under which I could do stuff; I liked the idea of my name not being the focal point, and would have liked to have been like Thomas Jerome Newton and hide behind the concept of a corporation, but unfortunately it doesn't work out like that once you sign major record deals. I dabbled with the idea of film-making at certain times, but mostly RoL was intended to be an umbrella organisation under which I could work with other artists, to write and produce other artists. But I'm definitely not a businessman – I make music and that's my focus.

ALLAN CAMPBELL: Crépuscule was a great label, it was a real labour of love. When Paul Haig signed with them they just let him just get on with it. At that point it was to your credit if you got a Crépuscule single out – you wouldn't sell a lot but it was a real tick in the margins indicating you were a creative act. I also think the thing about Crépuscule was that post-punk period was an era in which musicians looked less to New York and America for cultural influence; instead they looked to Europe. The idea of a modern Europe and a new modernity, there was a feeling that this was the new future in some kind of musical way. After Josef K split up I went back to work with Paul. I'd already put out a couple of Rhythm of Life singles on Rational before Michel Duval came back on the scene and signed Paul to Crépuscule and got a deal with Island. So I managed Paul in that period, but I was always friends with Paul and kept in contact. We were on the same wavelength.

Allan Campbell

JAMES LOCKE: I have great memories of touring with Paul Haig in Europe and Japan in the early eighties. We had such a laugh but Paul began to become very self-conscious about playing live, which changed everything. At one point we were playing an outdoors gig near the sea in Belgium. I still have the tape — he couldn't look at the audience and just berated them. Working with Crépuscule was a fantastic experience in terms of their hospitality — there were many bar tabs, guest lists and good meals. Saying that, I'm not really sure if I ever got paid for any of these gigs and never saw any royalties.

The wind had been blowing in a different direction for some time, perhaps ever since Orange Juice questioned why their final Postcard single 'Poor Old Soul' had not been a hit single in the real charts. While this presumption displayed business naiveté, it also highlighted their ambition to move beyond the confines of Peel sessions and music press acclaim. Orange Juice derided these markers of success and stated that the music press alternative chart listings for independent record sales were the 'toytown charts'. Alan Horne realised that if major success was to be achieved, a major label was required. Orange Juice signed to Polydor, Josef K split up, the Bluebells decided they needed to sign to a major, all decisions that heralded Postcard's transmogrification into Postcard International. Alan Horne intended to manage and license Aztec Camera and Jazzateers to major labels under the auspices of Postcard International. Horne played to his strengths and reeled in the press and media, who all still danced to his tune. His press release regarding Postcard International and Jazzateers was compelling; however, the reality was at odds with the rhetoric.

Alan Horne, taken from 'A Jazzateers Biography of Sorts' press release:

It is a period of transition at Postcard and Alan is becoming increasingly bored and restless with his lifestyle and sees the Jazzateers as an endless sea of possibilities to go drowning in. After six months of paddling, the group have wet their feet on a few stages and studios. Soon the Spring will be here and the Jazzateers will have recorded their debut single for the new Postcard International, a production company set up by Alan for Aztec Camera and the Jazzateers. Some lucky record company will secure the licensing and then people will begin to understand those Jazzateers more, and as our story continues 'Wasted' will be playing over the radio and our four players will be looking out from the covers of magazines throughout the land.

In the real world and the real charts Altered Images had led the way with massive chart success; Associates signed to Warner Brothers, and Paul Haig signed to Island, and followed in the footsteps of Orange Juice.

ALAN RANKINE: We signed to Warners and made *Sulk* with Mike Hedges co-producing. I played everything on the album — it just seemed to work better that way. The studio was an adventure with nothing laid out in front of you, but the other elements of being signed to a major involved us having to constantly do interviews and promotion. That's why Bill didn't like touring because suddenly our lives were planned nine months in advance, and that turned him off. Bill just couldn't stand becoming part of that machine.

Associates became part of the music industry machine. The *Sulk* recording sessions yielded three top 30 hits and appearances on *Top of the Pops*. Altered Images were still *TOTP* regulars too as 'Pinky Blue' joined their previous three hit singles and charted. Their second album (also called *Pinky Blue*) highlighted their instincts were spot on when they hired Martin Rushent as producer. The pressures of success led to a fissure in Altered Images with their drummer and a guitarist leaving. They were replaced by Fast Product employee and former Article 58 and Restricted Code member Stephen Lironi, who played guitar and drums in the group. *Top of the Pops* and *Smash Hits* were now the environment the post-punk Scottish visionaries wanted to inhabit; they'd done John Peel and the *NME* and wanted more. Associates and Altered Images inhabited that rarefied airspace where they were darlings of the *NME* intelligentsia like Paul Morley, and also made substantial inroads into the pop market. They were good-looking boys with more than a glint of mischief, allied to which they made the most modern-sounding music on daytime radio in much the same way Bowie had done in the 1970s. Their mimed performances on *Top of the Pops* were works of art.

ALAN RANKINE: The chocolate guitars. God, that was for '18 Carat Love Affair'. Well, it's a pretty long and boring day at the *Top of the Pops* studio, so Bill and I got thinking about how we could have some fun. I decided for the filming I would come on in a fencing suit with some chopsticks through my hair, and play a banjo even though there's no banjo on the record. Why not? Bill was engaging with the camera and, in his own way, he was laughing at it. I don't know why I came up with the chocolate guitar idea, I think it was because '18 Carat Love Affair' was probably the sugariest, sweetest sound we'd recorded. We wrote that song back in 1978, so I thought, OK, let's have some chocolate, so we got the chocolate guitar made at Harrods with three different types and colours of chocolate. During our performance I broke the chocolate guitar up and fed it to the audience — they just ate it all up. For our *Top of the Pops* performance of 'Club Country' we had Martha from the Muffins miming on keyboards — she was like a foil for Bill. Bill wanted the pink pound but he didn't want to alienate everyone else, so it was brilliant to have the heterosexual element with Martha.

Bob Last continued to reap the rewards of his management strategies with the ongoing success of *Dare* which was still selling in considerable quantities internationally. Last's perceived business-art approach was highlighted when he took on the management of ABC, who developed from the same Sheffield electronic milieu that bore the Human League and Cabaret Voltaire. ABC had previously been Vice Versa, but in vocalist Martin Fry ABC had a pop visionary who wanted interaction with the mass market. They did this in cahoots with producer Trevor Horn, who helped ABC create a pop masterpiece, *The Lexicon of Love*, that sold over a million albums worldwide. On the other hand, Last gained zero traction with Heartbeat, the project he created with Hilary Morrison and Davy Henderson. The group released one track on an *NME* cassette; however, Last could not attract interest from majors.

DAVY HENDERSON: Heartbeat did loads of demos and there was a lot of courting of record labels by Bob, but I wasn't really committed to it. It appealed to my vanity to be asked to be a member and it was very kind and thoughtful. I appreciated it at the time because I was pretty lost really.

JAMES LOCKE: I guess the aim with Heartbeat was to sign with a major. I can remember we did a BBC Radio 1 session which wasn't entirely successful. There was a debrief afterwards and I think that was the end. Some of the songs we'd worked on were used by Davy Henderson's next group, Win.

HILARY MORRISON: We'd moved into music publishing and artist management after Fast Product and pop:aural, and I stayed working on that, but I can't say I liked it. We did take on some other bands to manage, but it was very, very, very stressful work.

Fast Product's distribution wing had been a central player in the upsurge of independent distribution due to their role as the northern outpost in the Cartel. Simon Best, James Oliva and Stephen Lironi had all worked for the Fast distribution business, but as it expanded in tandem with the sales growth of the Cartel, Fast approached Sandy McLean to head up distribution. McLean had first-hand retail experience of a number of years – he learned the ropes from Bruce Findlay through Bruce's Records before working at Virgin's record shop in Edinburgh.

SANDY MCLEAN: Simon Best did the headhunting for Bob Last and approached me to work for them. Simon, who was also in the Flowers with Hilary, dealt with the shops and I was behind the counter at Virgin Records in Princes Street at this point. Bob was busy with the Human League and Heaven 17, so Fast basically came to the Virgin store and headhunted me to go run Fast distribution. Within a month or so I'd been taken to Rough Trade in Notting Hill to meet Geoff Travis and Richard Scott. When I joined in 1982, the name Fast Product hadn't been used on a record for a few years, but it's still a great name for a distribution company – get product into shops fast.

As Bob Last's business empire continued its successful upward surge, Alan Horne's Postcard International concept with Aztec Camera and Jazzateers hit the buffers after an initially impressive media launch. Jazzateers' Edwyn Collins-produced version of 'Wasted' and the press publicity resulted in an opportunity to record the song again with its co-writer (as it transpired, an opportunity they should have refused). Giorgio Moroder and Pete

Bellotte had achieved massive worldwide sales of their songs on Donna Summer albums, and when Pete Bellotte offered to produce a version of 'Wasted' with the group, naturally Horne and the group thought it was a good idea. It wasn't; it broke up the group.

ALISON GOURLAY: We went to London to record the track with Bellotte, but it didn't really work; we were a bit too shambolic.

KEITH BAND: Alan Horne's thinking was it could either be a single or used as a calling card for major record companies. Alan really liked the idea of working with a producer — in fact he wrote to Elton John asking if he'd be interested in producing Aztec Camera. Pete Bellotte was really unhappy with Jazzateers' musical proficiency; he wanted to program the drums, asked me to play slap bass, didn't like Alison's vocals — all of which Alan took really badly. We thought we were finished.

COLIN AULD: With Jazzateers, particularly at the start, the direction was all Ian and Keith, with me chipping in arrangements, supplying Ian with fags etc. The musical direction was definitely Ian and Keith. It was a new band so we were much looser with nothing to lose.

IAN BURGOYNE: We demoed songs for an album with Alison, but everything fell apart. I think we all loved Alison in the band in the first Jazzateers line-up. She didn't take any of it too seriously. I was such a shitty musician that I didn't even think of changing the key of some of these songs — they were all in keys that suited me — we just didn't have the knowledge to work that one out until much later.

It was a period of transition for Aztec Camera, who'd had enough of the Postcard International inertia and decided to sign with Horne's nemesis at Rough Trade, Geoff Travis. It was a sweet moment for Travis after financing the debut Orange Juice album only for the group to license it to Polydor instead. Aztec Camera had only been playing live sporadically recently, with Roddy and Campbell using Jazzateers' Colin Auld to stand in on drums.

COLIN AULD: I really liked drumming with the other Postcard groups. Orange Juice were well established and had played loads more gigs over a longer time and were more professional than Jazzateers. James and Steven had gone, so it was Malcolm Ross on guitar and me standing in on drums. From what I remember in rehearsals, Orange Juice wanted to sound like Chic, but were always too raw. They still sounded really great though. Aztec Camera were my favourite of the two. It was obvious Roddy was the real deal musically – he ran the show. Playing in a three-piece was cool; I played far more gigs with Aztec Camera than with Orange Juice. Aztec Camera were developing new songs, which was interesting to see. Roddy would come into rehearsals with more or less an arrangement in his head, whereas Jazzateers was a lot more collaborative. That apart, I don't think there were that many differences in the way the bands operated.

RODDY FRAME: Postcard was brilliant. A real scene. It just didn't work out in the end and we moved directly to Rough Trade. Postcard went through them anyway, so there was co-ordination. I wanted to move to London; I thought everything should change, it's bad to get too settled.

CAMPBELL OWENS: I don't know if Alan knew what to do with Aztec Camera, but with Roddy he couldn't really argue with that level of talent. I wanted to get away from Postcard after we released our second single, 'Mattress of Wire', as we were going nowhere. Roddy kinda hung on with Postcard until eventually I persuaded him to move on and go somewhere else. I think Postcard existed mainly to release Orange Juice records.

ALLAN CAMPBELL: I think in fairness, when Aztec Camera and Orange Juice got signed to bigger record labels it was the best thing for them. They wanted better studios, better promotion, and while I know that's not very exciting or creative, they needed that to go on to the next stage. I think they got what they needed — I mean Aztec Camera did great stuff when they signed to Rough Trade.

Jazzateers Mk 1 never recovered from the debacle of working with Pete Bellotte, which resulted in Alison being manoeuvred out of the group. This left Alan Horne's Postcard International concept in tatters, with Aztec Camera leaving to sign to Rough Trade and Jazzateers minus a vocalist.

KEITH BAND: Edwyn's friend Paul Quinn had moved down to Glasgow from Dundee to stay with Alan, and when Alan discovered Paul was a good singer he encouraged us to get Paul in the Jazzateers on vocals instead of Alison, which we did. Paul had been singing with the French Impressionists, a piano-led group with pianist Malcolm Fisher, and they released a song Malcolm wrote with Edwyn called 'My Guardian Angel' on a Les Disques du Crépuscule compilation album. Alan suggested Paul sing with Jazzateers to which we agreed because we generally agreed with everything Alan asked us to do. We'd seen Paul sing with the French Impressionists when they supported Jazzateers at the Rock Garden, and could see he was a good singer. Alan was always looking for people he could control, and he obviously couldn't control Josef K, Orange Juice or Aztec Camera, and I think Jazzateers were the most pliable group of people that he'd found. We were happy to go along with him as we realised we wouldn't get any press on our own, and the extent of our ambitions at that point was simply to be on Postcard Records.

IAN BURGOYNE: Alan brought Paul down to a Jazzateers rehearsal and he started singing with us. We thought this could be interesting for Jazzateers; he had a Bowie influence which was something we were also interested in.

Jazzateers regrouped with three new vocalists: Deirdre and Louise Rutkowski, and Paul Quinn. During the summer Jazzateers entered the studio with Alan Horne to record an album that was meant to finally launch Postcard International. With Horne taking the producer role, an album was recorded (*Lee*), which has thus far remained unreleased in the Postcard vault. The album contained original material by Ian Burgoyne and Keith Band, plus two covers — Mike Nesmith's 'Different Drum' (originally a hit for Linda Ronstadt and refashioned on *Lee* à la Staple Singers) and Dan Penn and Spooner Oldham's 'Hey Mister' (best-known version by Sandy Posey). The recording of *Lee* summed up where most of the critical fault lines were drawn with the Postcard International concept.

IAN BURGOYNE: We eventually recorded an album with Alan Horne producing, the album was called *Lee*, and was recorded with the second version of the group with the Rutkowski sisters and Paul Quinn on vocals. I really liked the Rutkowski sisters, they had that Everly Brothers thing, but I think Paul's Bowie influence confused this. We recorded *Lee* in a studio owned by Middle of the Road, who'd had a big number 1 single in the early seventies, 'Chirpy Chirpy, Cheep Cheep'. However, the *Lee* studio experience was a vortex of awfulness.

KEITH BAND: When Paul joined Jazzateers we started writing more country-influenced songs, and Deirdre and Louise Rutkowski sang our earlier jazzy Bacharach-influenced songs. It seemed like a good idea to record an album with the new singers, so we went into the studio for three weeks with the intention to release it through Postcard International, which was a mythical label Alan had developed.

However, once we recorded the album, Alan decided it wasn't good enough. We didn't really know what we were doing or what we wanted Jazzateers to sound like; it ended up very raw-sounding and really needed some kind of production. Alan ended up taking the best tracks on the album and playing them to major labels as demos, as the feeling was the independent route was limited and majors were getting it together. Alan's idea was to get some money from the majors. Our idea was always to make the best record possible, and we really needed the finance of a major to do that.

COLIN AULD: Alan Horne was managing Jazzateers full time and, to my mind, there was a major element of overthinking things, paralysis by analysis. This came mainly from Alan but we were all guilty of it. I've always thought the songs were basically really good songs, but rather than finding a groove and sticking with it, we'd chop and change styles, frequently reworking songs multiple times (some Staple Singers, a bit of Hank Williams, a bit of Bacharach — there's not a lot of room for the Jazzateers once that lot get in the room!). We had already recorded about an album's worth of unreleased stuff and were probably more self-conscious. Alan was constantly keeping us in check with our musical tastes — a bit Stalinist in that respect. Paul, Ian, Keith rehearsed at the Hellfire Club prior to going in to record the album. Rehearsals were without the girls initially, then Deirdre and Louise would turn up and Ian and Paul would work on harmonies with them. Of course, all of these vocal arrangements had to go through the Horne filter!

IAN BURGOYNE: Jazzateers Mk 2 had three great singers but it wasn't fun. It was a drag. Horne would always be moping about at the back of the rehearsal room. It was only when we tried some of the country tunes that the band started to sound pretty good. But who the hell wanted to hear country tunes from Jazzateers? Answer: no one.

KEITH BAND: There was no attempt to match the singer to the song that I can remember. Ian generally came up with the music and I arranged [the songs] and added bits. Jazzateers' influences were Bacharach, Jobim and Jonathan Richman for the straight-world attitude. Also, the prevalent Postcard attitude of being in opposition to everything else that was current. Any chord sequence that was obvious, i.e. commercial, was usually rejected, and Horne regarded anything angular as being 'too Rough Trade', which is ironic as both Postcard International groups (Aztec Camera and Jazzateers) ended up signing to Rough Trade on Postcard's demise. Our songs had lots of jazzy fifths and diminished piano chords, no funk. Basically we didn't want to pretend that we were anything other than middle-class white boys.

COLIN AULD: The studio dynamic when recording Lee was fairly relaxed, though I recall Alan was always slagging Keith off for his bass playing being too laid back. Wee things like that would creep into an otherwise good day.

IAN BURGOYNE: My memory of Lee was that it was a very undy-namic dynamic. Colin said that there was always some woman knitting in the studio control room, which, if true, is about the only interesting thing that happened. My memory is that Lee was going to be a Postcard album that Alan would license to a major label. A couple of major labels really liked it, but I think the nature of the Jazzateers was that it was a big mess, and I didn't really care. It was all happening so quickly, and our influences at that point were a jumble of stuff: country, jazz and some chaotic external influences.

Horne decided not to release the Jazzateers album, which effec-tively was the end of the Postcard International concept. After playing tracks to major labels it quickly became apparent none were prepared to offer a recording contract.

KEITH BAND: I think it was Horney's idea not to release *Lee* to launch Postcard International. He did suggest compiling the best tracks on one side and recording some Lou Reed covers for the other, but obviously that never happened. Operation Twilight/Les Disques du Crépuscule wanted to release it, but that was vetoed with the classic Horne comment — 'It's not as good as "White Lines"'! Jazzateers Mk 2 had more country influences when recording *Lee*. I don't think that version of the group lasted longer than a couple of months, but at that time, with the Postcard association, it was easy to get press and major-label interest.

IAN BURGOYNE: God knows what Postcard International was all about. The only person who understood the Postcard International concept was Alan Horne — we didn't have a clue. You have to remember that we had no ambition to do anything really; we saw getting a record contract as a good idea as it kept us off the dole. I think the intention was to release *Lee* through Postcard International, but it got lost on the road to Bourgie Bourgie. When we first started working with Paul Quinn, we discovered that he could sing falsetto really well. Keith loved this record by Dee Clark called 'Ride a Wild Horse' and was always wanting us to cover it. I think Horne must have come into a rehearsal and heard us playing the song and started going on about us being a soul band. That was the craziness of the Jazzateers. When your manager is five years older than you are, is checked in the *NME* and has released some great records on his label, you trust he knows better than you. But he wasn't a musician and he couldn't understand why we didn't sound as good as Chic.

Alan Horne's decision to regroup Jazzateers as a soul-influenced group involved ditching the name Jazzateers only months after the music press had been raving about the group being the Second

Coming of Postcard. Jazzateers became Bourgie Bourgie Mk 1 with Paul Quinn as sole vocalist. The Rutkowski sisters left to become vocalists in Sunset Gun, signing to CBS, before working with This Mortal Coil and 4AD. Postcard International was abandoned, heralding the end of Postcard. Horne focused on managing Bourgie Bourgie with the singular aim of signing a major record deal. The Horne independent ideal was dead.

Former head boys at Postcard, Orange Juice, found life on a major label difficult. Their debut album had done reasonably well commercially and received praise from the press, something Orange Juice had grown accustomed to from their debut single onwards. The new line-up released their first single as a fully integrated group on a major label; however, the double A-side of 'Two Hearts Together' and 'Hokoyo' was another misfire. The opening four singles on Postcard were so assured, yet their major-label singles 'L.O.V.E.' and now 'Two Hearts Together' were confusing releases — only James Kirk's 'Felicity' felt like an authentic Orange Juice single. For a group that had redefined the possibilities of life after punk in tandem with Postcard, Orange Juice now seemed to be further away than ever from the rationale that had propelled them into the arms of Polydor — gaining access to the pop charts. Scottish groups that emerged from punk who went on to major-label chart success like the Skids and Simple Minds had proved it was possible to be successful on a major, though the Skids had now split up after several hit singles while Simple Minds' move to Virgin Records had resulted in hit singles and album success. Altered Images and Associates still graced the pop charts too, and as Orange Juice recorded their new album pressure was building to have a hit single, both from within the group and within Polydor.

Altered Images took the opportunity to work with producer Mike Chapman in LA to record tracks for a new album with their new line-up. Chapman had produced Blondie to international success, and had earned his production chops through the 1970s writing and producing the Chinnichap hits for Sweet, Suzi Quatro, Mud and the like. Altered Images working with the man who produced 'Heart of Glass' was a natural fit.

STEPHEN LIRONI: I remember Restricted Code being in a feature in the *NME* with ABC, and shortly afterwards ABC made the transition to a pop approach and became legitimate pop stars. Going from Restricted Code and Fast Product to joining Altered Images on CBS coincided with all the bands from the independent scene discovering pop, the big gold dream. When I joined Altered Images just after their 'Happy Birthday' period, it seemed like bands rooted in post-punk were discovering pop. To me that was interesting. Altered Images were teenagers making pop for teenagers, making it up as we went along and selling half a million copies of 'Happy Birthday'. It was an exciting process.

However, the pressure of success was proving difficult for Associates after their run of hit singles and hit album. Sire Records offered a contract for the group's recording rights for the US that essentially allowed Associates to name their price.

ALAN RANKINE: After the success of *Sulk*, Seymour Stein came over to London hoping to sign Associates to Sire for the US. He took us to Langan's brasserie for a meal and to talk contracts. He was clear that he expected Associates to tour the States to promote the album, and told us he'd give Bill and me £400,000 each, but then Bill said he didn't want to tour or want Associates to get into any label debt. I could see Seymour choking on his quail's eggs and the meeting went downhill from there, and consequently so did Associates' fortunes.

On the eve of Associates' UK tour (due to open in Edinburgh), Billy MacKenzie walked out, which subsequently caused Alan Rankine's departure from Associates as he knew full well US labels would only commit to working with an artist if they were prepared to spend time touring through the various states. Billy's walkout proved to be the straw that broke Associates' back.

ALAN RANKINE: Bill walked out on our UK tour on the back of the success of *Sulk*. It was everything I'd worked for since I was eleven years old and Bill just fucked it up, so it was just downhill from then. Bill was doing music because he loved making records and singing, but he didn't want this massive world tour thing and all the pressure that would be brought to bear on him and everyone else around him. If you're the singer everyone's looking at the frontman, no one's looking at the drummer or the bassist or the guitarist, so all the responsibility is on the frontman. Apart from that, when you're doing sustained touring, you're just rehashing what you've already done every night, and I think Bill didn't fancy that. He wanted to keep being creative and it's very difficult to do that if you are doing a world tour.

Alan Horne worked Bourgie Bourgie through their paces, writing, rehearsing and demoing for major-label consideration. While there remained residual interest, no record contracts were forthcoming. Bourgie Bourgie and Horne remained outside the major-label industry. Former comrades Orange Juice, Paul Haig and the Bluebells were all now reaping the financial benefits of being signed to majors, something that had happened largely through being associated with Postcard. By contrast Bob Last and Hilary Morrison's empire and interactions within the music business continued to expand and deliver success, with a management roster (the Human League, ABC, Scritti Politti) that delivered both commercial and critical success, alongside the successful Fast publishing and distribution businesses. In spite of Last's best efforts to tempt major labels to sign Heartbeat, labels felt the group lacked songs. Heartbeat disbanded and Hilary joined Bob in focusing on the Fast management company (Tunenoise).

HILARY MORRISON: Part of our management ethos was imploring artists to go and get music publishing. Some artists didn't understand the importance of having a good accountant or having pension plans.

BOB LAST: I was managing the Human League and then we set up a management company, Tunenoise, and subsequently managed ABC and Scritti Politti, and that was the focus of my attention.

Last's management interests brought with it financial rewards and the business confidence to do international deals with the multinational music industry. He still retained a sense of mischief, and selected an unorthodox opening artist for the Human League's European tour in support of *Dare*. Morrison's former Heartbeat cohort James Locke (along with Nigel Sleaford and Callum McNair) performed 1940s Kurt Weill songs under the name the Macnaires — the perfect support for an ultra-modern group like the Human League.

JAMES LOCKE: I was playing with Callum McNair and Nigel Sleaford in many different line-ups throughout this time, including the live debut of Paul Haig's Rhythm of Life at Valentino's. The Macnaires was a concept band put together for an evening at the Danceteria. I came in for a week around England supporting the Human League in the UK and the subsequent *Dare* European tour. The concerts were great. I don't really think most of the Human League's audience was ready for 1940s tunes by Kurt Weill being played by three young Scots, but some were. We travelled around Europe by Interrail, mostly independent from the League, staying in pensions and hostels. In Milan the audience threw money at us, which the crew collected, so that bought us some drinks.

Postcard had created a big impression throughout the UK, with groups in various cities who sounded and looked like Orange Juice. Ironically the group within Postcard that Alan Horne had seemed most antipathetic towards, the Bluebells, were the group that looked most likely to capitalise commercially on the Postcard aesthetic. They had the look and they had the songs, and after receiving offers from several major labels decided to sign to London Records, and began recording with Elvis Costello producing.

ROBERT HODGENS: We were going to do a single on Postcard, but when Orange Juice went to a major it was hard to see how Postcard would progress as Edwyn had a lot of control over the label, and Alan didn't seem to like the other groups — I think he only really liked Orange Juice. Then we were the first unsigned band on *The Old Grey Whistle Test*; I think people felt we were the more commercial aspect of Postcard. The thing that really moved us away from Postcard was meeting Elvis Costello, who really wanted to produce us.

KEN MCCLUSKEY: When Aztec Camera and Orange Juice moved on to Rough Trade and Polydor respectively there was a feeling that Postcard had maybe had its time. We therefore had to widen our horizons and think about the other offers which started to come in. It would have been great to put out 'Everybody's Somebody's Fool' as planned on Postcard but it was going to take at least six months and we needed a wage. Postcard paid in street cred and good vibes only. Major labels and publishers were courting us from maybe our third gig. There were journalists from *NME*, *Sounds*, *Melody Maker* and *Record Mirror* up in Glasgow every week and the A & R teams followed. We enjoyed being dined out in some very fine eateries ordering dishes we had never come across before. Lobster thermidor anyone?

RUSSELL IRVINE: As far as I remember we had actually decided to go with CBS, probably because of the Clash, but an hour after deciding that we all changed our minds and went for London Records. I didn't get involved in it very much — all I was interested in was, have they got a cool office and how many gold records were on the wall. I didn't care for record companies much, I was a guy in a band, not a businessman!

ROBERT HODGENS: The media and record companies thought the Bluebells had hits, kinda like the Monkees. I'd bump into the head of London Records Roger Ames socially, and he'd be asking why we were thinking of going with CBS. I told him we thought their head of A & R Muff Winwood was a great guy, and that our friends Altered Images were doing well on CBS, and that they'd offered us a big advance. Roger would immediately offer us substantially more if we would sign to London Records, so our manager Mark went to see London Records and set up a deal with Roger Ames.

The Bluebells' recording sessions with Elvis Costello seemed like a match made in heaven. Both parties were song-oriented and liked the idea of group recordings that didn't rely too much on modern studio technology. However, the debut single by the Bluebells, 'Forevermore', ended up being produced by Robin Millar and Colin Farley, with the Elvis-produced 'Aim in Life' being the B-side.

ROBERT HODGENS: Elvis was great with us; we weren't great musicians and Elvis would send us tapes all the time with tracks he thought we'd like. In the studio he'd show us how to use mics for vocals and how to hold the guitar properly, which he did with great affection, and Elvis ended up taking the Bluebells on tour as his support. We kept recording with Elvis producing, but the thing we realised when we signed to a major is that it was going to be really disappointing. We did our first single, 'Forevermore', at George Martin's Air studio in Oxford Circus with a different producer, but it was a really stale experience. I wish we'd recorded that track with Elvis producing.

KEN MCCLUSKEY: Elvis Costello first came to see us at the ICA. We all liked his music anyway and respected him as an artist, which was a good start. He had just released *Almost Blue*, his country album, which was so great. We had a couple of meetings where he asked us all individually to make cassette tapes of our favourite music to try and find what we were into at that time. He listened to our tapes and gave feedback and then reciprocated by handing us bespoke tapes of music which he thought we should listen to. Top man.

RUSSELL IRVINE: Elvis was a different character from the skinny, spiky, angry Elvis. He was a bit heavier now, vegan and pretty laid back. Ken has said before about how much Elvis helped him with vocal and mic techniques; it was the same for me on guitar. I wasn't a versatile player at the time − when we went into the studio I would have my parts worked out and rehearsed. So when it came to changing the part or doing something different it wasn't easy for me, but Elvis was very patient with me and took his time suggesting and showing me additional parts. He had great little tips and loads of little Beatles-type tricks. We put a lovely harmonic note on the end of the solo on 'All I Ever Said' straight out of

'Nowhere Man'. He could have played all these parts in minutes but he understood that we were a band and that it was important for me to play the parts.

Aztec Camera's departure to London and Rough Trade re-energised their momentum, with a single being quickly recorded and released. 'Pillar to Post' saw former Ruts drummer Dave Ruffy take over drumming duties, with organ and keyboard supplied by Bernie Clark. Rough Trade only featured Roddy and Campbell in promotional photographs — the vibes were Simon and Garfunkel, Dylan and Neil Young. 'Pillar to Post' was an excellent calling card and shifted Aztec Camera to a higher gear, as they worked on their debut album. Geoff Travis was a major fan of Roddy's songwriting and regarded the group as a priority for Rough Trade, who as a label were now keen to engage more vigorously with concepts like promotion and marketing that they previously viewed as being somewhat tawdry.

CAMPBELL OWENS: We decided to leave Postcard and we knew Geoff Travis from Rough Trade, as they distributed Postcard Records, so there was that connection. We moved down to London in 1982 and spoke to Rough Trade, who were more than happy to take us on. We thought we could sign to whatever label we wanted but I think we stayed a bit too long with Postcard. I never lost faith in Roddy and he never lost faith in himself at all. We went to Rough Trade and they were going to make an album with us. They introduced us to a lot of people — musicians, most notably Dave Ruffy who became our drummer. Rough Trade was a really good time, the best time for Aztec Camera.

GEOFF TRAVIS: I don't think Alan Horne really had any aspirations to grow Postcard at that point. I think those singles were perfect, and I think that's what he wanted. Alan probably thought he was

Andy Warhol; the idea was just to have a set of absolutely perfect artefacts, which would gain him immortality, and that's probably exactly what's happened.

Paul Haig's relationship with Les Disques du Crépuscule resulted in Island Records bankrolling his Rhythm of Life concept, and it was obvious big commerce was interested in the stir created by these post-punk urchins from Scotland who were talking the talk. The new ambition driving the original Postcard cats resulted in Paul recording a highly polished album in New York with Grace Jones's producer, Alex Sadkin.

PAUL HAIG: When I signed to Island the discussions quickly moved to where I wanted to record the album. They suggested the Caribbean, but I wanted to go to New York where it was winter and freezing, I thought it'd be more edgy. I went to see producer Arthur Baker in New York. I was hoping to work with him, but worked instead with Grace Jones's producer Alex Sadkin. I lived in New York for a period. It was great going to clubs in New York in the early eighties, hearing the sounds, beats, production, and soaking it all up. Coming from Postcard to having Island discussing spending a quarter of a million pounds on an album – it was a culture shock being on a major. When I was growing up I always looked on Island as being one of the best labels because they had Roxy Music, and I thought they might be more artist-oriented than other major labels, and in some respects they were. There was more pressure, however, to recoup label investment, and there were a few conflicting episodes. The music I wanted to make after Josef K wasn't really orientated towards a band set-up; I was interested in using drum machines and synths. I was called the face and sound of 1982 by Paul Morley, who only the previous year had savaged the debut Josef K album in the *NME*.

JAMES LOCKE: I first met Paul Haig when we were going to the same clubs in Edinburgh, and at some point I think he asked me if I would put some drums on a tune for him. This was after Josef K obviously and our collaboration became the foundation for his *Rhythm of Life* album. The album that was released was really a rerecording of what Paul and I had produced in Edinburgh at Palladium studios, and when Paul signed to Island I was in expectation of joining him to complete the album. Of course that never happened. I've never met Alex Sadkin, but had the great pleasure of meeting, working with and becoming a friend of the legendary Bernie Worrell of Parliament and Funkadelic, who played on Paul's album.

The influence of the Grace Jones albums (*Warm Leatherette*, *Nightclubbing*, *Living My Life*) on the Sound of Young Scotland protagonists was substantial and is somewhat underappreciated. Fire Engines had also been infatuated by Grace Jones, especially the theatrical *A One Man Show* live event in London, created in association with artist Jean-Paul Goude. This had an impact on Fire Engines' ambitions and desire to move forward from their initial Codex Communications and Bob Last-packaged vision. Sonically, their attempts to progress can be heard on their final John Peel session, though tellingly Fire Engines have never allowed these tracks to be released — they sound like a bridge to a place that didn't exist.

Crépuscule's Michel Duval had not only been a supporter of Paul Haig, but also signed Postcard associate Malcolm Fisher's group, the French Impressionists (after Alan Horne squired Paul Quinn away to work with Jazzateers/Bourgie Bourgie).

PAUL HAIG: Michel Duval met Chris Blackwell at a party, and mentioned me, so Island became interested in signing me. It all seemed to happen so quickly, moving from Crépuscule to Island.

The French Impressionists: Malcolm Fisher

MALCOLM FISHER: The French Impressionists were definitely not Postcard material – no yellow banana, instead we were *café au lait* and Gershwin croissant, therefore fitted easily in the arty Crépuscule scene.

Haig's erstwhile Josef K colleagues David Weddell and Ronnie Torrance joined the Happy Family, a group fronted by Nick Currie and signed to 4AD who released their album, *The Man on Your Street* (Nick Currie would later go on to record as Momus). Haig's co-guitarist in Josef K (Malcolm Ross) was about to release his first album as a member of Orange Juice. *Rip It Up* contained a more disco-fied Orange Juice, where the influence of records by George McCrae, KC and the Sunshine Band and Chic all merged with the continuing influence of Al Green. When Steven Daly was relieved of his drumming duties and the group were auditioning drummers, they asked prospective candidates to drum along to side one of Bowie's *Low* album, which Zeke Manyika did with added funky groove. However, the release of the first single 'I Can't Help Myself' failed again to reach the charts and stalled at number 42. The reviews for November's release of the *Rip It Up* album were uniformly bad.

MALCOLM ROSS: Orange Juice had been striving for a hit from before I joined — I mean the great holy grail for Orange Juice and Postcard Records was to have a hit single. Edwyn was very disappointed how media reacted to the new album — our reviews in the music press were bad. All through Postcard Edwyn got nothing but good press; Orange Juice were press darlings, flavour of the month. Then when the *Rip It Up* album came out we were rehearsing to go on tour, and I remember going into the rehearsal rooms and Edwyn was sitting on the floor and he had *Melody Maker*, *NME*, *Sounds*, all laid out open at the page of the reviews and was sitting there like, 'Woe is me, look what's happened, we've got bad reviews.' I remember David and I had been thinking there's nothing we can do about it, so let's practise, but Edwyn was saying, 'I don't know if you understand how important the press is.' We argued a bit about that because my attitude was you can't have a career of making music to try and get good reviews. Those bad reviews for the *Rip It Up* album hit Edwyn quite hard.

Nineteen eighty-two ended where it began, with Orange Juice releasing an album. *You Can't Hide Your Love Forever* contained the songs honed over their Postcard years and epitomised what was described as the Sound of Young Scotland — literate, melodic and jangly. Their *Rip It Up* album owed more to Bowie's 'plastic soul' masterpiece, *Young Americans.* Paul Quinn's soulful backing vocals accompanied Edwyn on some tracks, but the predominance of Fender Rhodes electric piano and sax solos on *Rip It Up* were anathema to the Postcard fans who had lapped up the debut album at the beginning of the year. Fans of the original Postcard iteration of Orange Juice regarded *Rip It Up* as bland major-label fodder. The mood music around Orange Juice was not promising, with the label starting to display concern about the lack of commercial success and Edwyn feeling demoralised by the poor reviews.

Alan Horne touted Bourgie Bourgie demos around major labels and hoped that Paul Quinn's prominent backing vocals on the new Orange Juice album would help his mission to get the group signed to a major. No majors wanted to sign Bourgie Bourgie, as managed by Alan Horne. The Bluebells' debut single had been a slight disappointment to the group, who were starting to realise how difficult being signed to a major could be. They continued recording tracks in preparation for releases in 1983, while both Paul Haig and Aztec Camera were finishing off their albums. This looked like being the year the main players of Postcard would attempt to go overground and achieve their much-vaunted chart success, something Bob Last had already managed with great aplomb. He had achieved his stated aim of infiltrating the mainstream with the substantial international success of the Human League and ABC (with Scritti Politti in the wings, preparing to leave Rough Trade and sign to Virgin). The Postcard alumni chase for the big gold dream was about to get serious.

CHAPTER 7

1983 – Empty Shell/ Make Me Sad

Aztec Camera: David Mulholland, Campbell Owens and Roddy Frame

JAMES KING: I think the worst thing that happened to Paul Quinn and Alan Horne was meeting. I think Alan wrecked Paul's career and Paul wrecked Alan's career.

January 1983 saw Alan Horne, Paul Quinn and Barbara Shores vacate their flat in Holyrood Quadrant in the west end of Glasgow to follow their friend and previous occupant of the flat, Edwyn Collins, who had already split for London. Barbara Shores was an American fan of Postcard who had produced the coveted colour Postcard fanzine; she also managed Strawberry Switchblade and Del Amitri. Horne had convinced Quinn to go solo, which brought about the demise of Bourgie Bourgie Mk 1.

IAN BURGOYNE: Paul was really influenced by Bowie and Roxy. Alan changed our name to Bourgie Bourgie after deciding to reposition Jazzateers as a vehicle for Paul's voice. After a period of writing and demoing as Bourgie Bourgie and being managed by Alan, I felt our relationship with Alan had broken down. The next we heard Paul was going solo and both him and Alan moved to London, which both Keith and I were glad about.

KEITH BAND: The next stage of Jazzateers was dictated by Paul leaving the band, which he was encouraged to do by Alan. I think his idea was that Alan would move with Paul to London and he would be a solo artist and Edwyn would write songs for him, although he had also approached Ian to continue writing for Paul, but we weren't interested in that.

Aztec Camera enjoyed being signed to Rough Trade and the belief shown in the group by Geoff Travis. The group followed their first single for the label, 'Pillar to Post', with a new single that was about to take the group to another level. 'Oblivious' was released in January to immediate acclaim; it sounded like it could, just possibly, be a hit single. It almost was, reaching number 47 in the singles chart, which was good going as independent distribution issues meant it was hard for labels like Rough Trade to attain mainstream chart success. Glasgow artist David Band designed Aztec Camera's covers and a visual aesthetic was developed for the group (something he had already succeeded in doing with Altered Images' artwork). David would soon provide artwork for his younger brother Keith's group when Jazzateers signed to Rough Trade. He also hooked up with fellow Glasgow School of Art alumnus Fraser Taylor and formed design company The Cloth (Fraser would go on to provide artwork for the Bluebells and Friends Again).

CAMPBELL OWENS: The first thing we did with Rough Trade was 'Pillar to Post' as a single — we recorded that with 'Queen's Tattoo' on the B-side. Things were changing and you could hear the difference between 'Just Like Gold' and 'Mattress of Wire' — we were achieving a much bigger studio sound, more poppy. A lot of the songs that made it into the *High Land, Hard Rain* album had been around for a while from East Kilbride days — in fact most. I think the only new songs written after moving to London were 'Down the Dip' and 'Back on Board'.

RODDY FRAME: *High Land, Hard Rain* was rehearsed for a week then recorded over three weeks. I wrote 'Oblivious' consciously as a pop song. I thought it was prime *Top of the Pops* material and it turned out to be a hit eventually. I knew *High Land, Hard Rain* was a great record.

EDWYN COLLINS: Roddy's really talented, especially as a lyricist. Alan Horne's been a massive influence on him, you know, all these things he cites like Buffalo Springfield and Neil Young. To his credit Roddy would admit that.

Aztec Camera were invited to perform live on the Channel 4 Television music programme, *The Tube*. 'Oblivious' was gaining lots of ground and preparation was ongoing for the release of their album. Aztec Camera asked Jazzateers guitarist Ian Burgoyne to perform with them on *The Tube* as second guitarist, which led to Jazzateers joining Aztec Camera in signing to Rough Trade.

IAN BURGOYNE: I'd been playing guitar with Aztec Camera, who'd also left Postcard. They'd signed to Rough Trade and I appeared with them on *The Tube* TV programme. Around that time we'd been in Rough Trade and had a meeting with Geoff Travis, who offered us money if we'd do a Jazzateers album for Rough Trade along the lines of our previous jazz-influenced songs.

KEITH BAND: Geoff Travis from Rough Trade got in touch because he'd heard the discarded album, *Lee*, and wanted us to record a new album exactly in the same vein but with a girl singer. So he gave Ian and I an advance for an album in this style, which we decided we didn't want to do, and instead made a Stooges/New York Dolls-type album with a new singer we'd seen performing, Grahame Skinner.

IAN BURGOYNE: David Band again came to our rescue — he was like our guardian angel. He introduced us to Grahame Skinner, who was vocalist in a group called Kites. We rehearsed with Skin and thought he was absolutely brilliant — like Iggy meets Lou.

Jazzateers joined fellow former Postcard groups Aztec Camera and the Go-Betweens in signing to Rough Trade. The label had licensed the first album by the Go-Betweens, *Send Me a Lullaby*, from Australian label Missing Link for release in 1982, and the group subsequently relocated from Brisbane to London and signed directly to Rough Trade. The Go-Betweens recorded their next album using the same producer and studio as Aztec Camera's recently recorded album and also hooked up with Aztec Camera's manager, Bob Johnston.

GEOFF TRAVIS: I think we probably just asked the Go-Betweens if they wanted to make a record on Rough Trade and it was the same as Roddy. I don't think we felt we were encroaching on Postcard, because there's an independent-label code of honour too, where you don't poach people from other labels.

Orange Juice followed up their *Rip It Up* album by releasing the title track as a single. It was a strange period for the group; once feted by the music press, they were now on the receiving end of critical negativity for the first time in their career.

MALCOLM ROSS: Orange Juice Mk 2 were meant to be slicker because we were meant to be finding a new style, funkier and based mostly on soul music. Zeke joining on drums was good for that and David was trying to play these dancey bass lines that were hip at the time. We used to listen to things like the Grace Jones albums from the period, with Sly and Robbie as the rhythm section. Edwyn and I were really good friends, but I found I didn't really like it when I joined Orange Juice. When we were rehearsing to go on tour and promote the album I realised my guitar style was just completely Josef K, and I was trying to play in a more traditional way to fit the Orange Juice guitar style.

To the surprise of many, Orange Juice finally became bona fide pop stars. To the delight of the group and Polydor Records, 'Rip It Up' became a top 10 hit and put the group where they'd always wanted to be, in the pop charts. After eighteen months of negotiating the murky waters and machinations of the multinational corporate machine, Orange Juice had finally cracked it. The 'Rip It Up' single was all over the radio and the group received the inevitable invitation that accompanied a chart position — an appearance on *Top of the Pops*. The group made two performances on the television chart programme, the second of which resulted in Orange Juice being banned for life from appearing on the programme again. The group had roped in experimental musician Jim Thirlwell (aka Foetus) to mime the sax solo on 'Rip It Up'. However, as the programme was going to be broadcast live it was a requirement for all artists to spend the whole day at the television studio. At the dress rehearsal, the *Top of the Pops* dancers had been choreographed to rip up paper while the group mimed their performance of 'Rip It Up'. The group requested this didn't happen (which the programme did not agree to), and by the afternoon some members of Orange Juice were drinking whiskey and gin, with Foetus providing some amphetamine sulphate to speed things up. This resulted in an increasingly wasted McClymont being abusive to the programme presenter, John Peel (who called McClymont a wanker on his BBC Radio 1 show the following week). There was a strange feeling within some quarters of the group that this performance on the biggest UK pop television programme was an opportunity to destroy everything that had been built up over Orange Juice's career. McClymont in particular stated he'd wanted to sabotage everything. He succeeded, knocking Foetus offstage onto a dancer during the live broadcast, before wandering off the stage to miss all his miming cues. *Top of the Pops* and the BBC were furious, which resulted in Orange Juice being hauled into Polydor Records' offices the following day to be told by the label that they had been banned by *Top of the Pops*. They were warned their shambolic television appearance would result in the single dropping down the charts. The following week it climbed into the top 10.

As Orange Juice enjoyed the fruits and vindication of chart success, fellow former Postcarders the Bluebells released a second single, 'Cath', a record that acknowledged the influence of folk rock filtered through the Faces. They had delivered a classic pop single. Despite having solid radio support, 'Cath' peaked at 65 in the charts while Orange Juice finally took the charts by storm. The first output of Altered Images' recordings in LA with Mike Chapman was the magnificent single 'Don't Talk to Me about Love', which went one better than Orange Juice in reaching number 7. Orange Juice and Altered Images shared the media spotlight for the first time since Edwyn and Clare appeared on the cover of *NME*. The Sound of Young Scotland had gone overground.

Alan Horne was now ensconced in London plotting solo success for Paul Quinn. Momentum built when a video for the Ian Burgoyne-penned 'I Gave You Love' appeared on BBC 2 Television culture programme, *The Oxford Road Show*. An article about Quinn appeared in the March edition of the *Face* and his voice was all over the radio as featured backing vocalist on Orange Juice's hit single. It felt the timing was perfect for Horne to finally get his foot in the door of the major music industry. Paul Quinn was a talent, the perfect synthesis of the Postcard aesthetic — he looked great and had a fantastic voice. Surely this was his moment? Quinn's influences (Bowie/Roxy merged with Al Green/Stax and Waylon Jennings/Willie Nelson) allied to his voice and looks suggested it was the time for Quinn and Horne to go overground and hit the mainstream. Paul Quinn was a much-loved figure in Glasgow, as much for his shy, sensitive and soulful personality as for his fantastic voice. He looked and sounded like a major star in the making.

ALISON GOURLAY: Paul Quinn epitomised Postcard in the same way that Edwyn did.

ALLAN CAMPBELL: Paul Quinn is one of these figures who'd always been around Postcard, waiting for his time, who made great music but was not particularly commercially successful. Paul had been a singer in the French Impressionists and then Jazzateers and Bourgie Bourgie. He had a lovely deep voice, really kind of mellow.

Paul Quinn

MALCOLM FISHER: The possibilities of that French Impressionists duo with Paul and I would have been endless.

CAMPBELL OWENS: I really enjoyed it when Roddy and I recorded with Malcolm and Paul Quinn on the French Impressionist recording of 'My Guardian Angel' for Crépuscule. I loved Malcolm's outlook and working with Paul was great fun, and always has been. I am a fan of the Great American Songbook so getting the opportunity to perform some of those songs with a singer of Paul's calibre when Aztec Camera backed him at Postcard events was wonderful.

KEN MCCLUSKEY: Paul Quinn was an enigma. He was amazing-looking, a tall, slim guy with an amazing deep voice. Paul was friends with Edwyn from when they were both in Dundee, and Edwyn and Alan both encouraged Paul [to] be a singer. He was a magnificent singer, something else, and was involved with Postcard through singing with the French Impressionists and Jazzateers.

GRAHAME SKINNER: Paul was an amazing vocalist. The first time I heard him singing was at a party when he was singing 'Golden Years'. He was handsome, a really lovely guy, but Alan Horne had a really big influence over Paul.

Rough Trade released *High Land, Hard Rain* to universal love for Aztec Camera from critics and public alike. Elvis Costello transferred his love of the Bluebells to Aztec Camera and invited the group to open for him on his US tour. David Band provided the artwork for *High Land, Hard Rain* and was lauded for his album design. 'Walk Out to Winter' was released as a single in May and continued the group's ascendancy, though there was the beginning of grumblings in the camp over the lack of chart positions. The Go-Betweens released their new album on Rough Trade in May;

predictably *Before Hollywood* received massive music press acclaim. Jazzateers were now also signed to Rough Trade – as they worked on an album with new vocalist Grahame Skinner, it finally felt that their moment was about to arrive.

STEFAN KASSEL: I think Aztec Camera, the Go-Betweens and Jazzateers releasing albums on Rough Trade was the logical next step, and they all released great albums after Postcard. *High Land, Hard Rain* stands out especially, a stone-cold classic that touched my heart back then and still does so today. Ditto the Orange Juice debut *You Can't Hide Your Love Forever* on Polydor. Adam Kidron did a great job producing it – the *Ostrich Churchyard* version of the album doesn't sound half as good. The official Polydor version is a masterpiece in my book. I even think that their version of 'L.O.V.E.' tops Al Green's original – it has more heartfelt soul and a killer vocal performance by Edwyn.

ROBERT FORSTER: We got to know Aztec Camera very well. 'We Could Send Letters' had sent me flying and then a year later we met Roddy and Campbell in the London Rough Trade offices. The Postcard connection pulled us together. It's a brotherhood, baby.

GRAHAME SKINNER: Orange Juice were the big influence on me, they were local and I loved the aesthetic of Postcard. Edwyn used to make curt comments and was really funny in his *NME* interviews. My ambitions were largely to be interviewed and lauded by the *NME* as opposed to making lots of money out of music. Fast Product and Postcard created an interest and shone a light on new music in Scotland, with people identifying with fashion, clubs, literature.

I went to see Jazzateers at the Spaghetti Factory when Alison was singing – they set themselves apart although you could see they were on Postcard. Paul Quinn had been the vocalist on the second album Jazzateers recorded for Postcard, *Lee*. It never got released, then Alan Horne rebranded Jazzateers as Bourgie Bourgie and tried to secure a major-label deal for the group. This didn't happen and Alan decided Paul should go solo and they both moved to London to pursue a deal. It was at this point Ian and Keith reactivated the Jazzateers name and signed to Rough Trade, inviting me to join the group as lead vocalist. My involvement with Jazzateers started when artist David Band and Altered Images manager Gerry McElhone asked me if I'd be interested in singing with the group on an album they were recording for Rough Trade. The new Jazzateers material was more along the lines of Lou Reed and Iggy Pop, which fitted me perfectly.

IAN BURGOYNE: So we decided to record the Jazzateers album in Park Lane studios in Glasgow with Skin on vocals, and it was a complete departure from what Jazzateers had done before in terms of songwriting and guitar playing. I was playing lead guitar influenced by the Stooges and Voidoids, groups I'd never really been interested in. We were really influenced by early Modern Lovers in our approach to the Rough Trade album.

GRAHAME SKINNER: Jazzateers had already recorded material for Postcard that wasn't released for various reasons, so when they followed Aztec Camera and Go-Betweens in signing with Rough Trade it was on the basis of the sound and material of these unreleased Postcard recordings that featured Alison, Paul and the Rutkowski sisters. However, both Ian and Keith decided for their own twisted reasons to record a Stooges-sounding album for Rough Trade, the complete opposite of what Rough Trade were looking for.

KEITH BAND: I remember Geoff Travis coming up to Glasgow to check on progress of the album and he wasn't very happy because it was a male singer, not a female vocalist as he'd expected, and he thought the album sounded, in his words, rockist. He didn't like the album and didn't want Rough Trade to promote it. The Rough Trade album was very much a project — it was really Ian and me as directors, with Grahame playing a part for which we wrote a new collection of songs.

GRAHAME SKINNER: Geoff Travis didn't like the album at all, though Rough Trade went on to release the Jazzateers album and it received lots of plaudits in the music press and singles of the week when 'Show Me the Door' was released as a 7-inch.

STEFAN KASSEL: Jazzateers' album for Rough Trade is just fantastic, another all-time classic in my book. The very best and shortest and most brutal guitar solos I've ever heard on record, great song-writing by Ian Burgoyne and Keith Band, killer vocals by Grahame Skinner, a perfect record sleeve by David Band. I always return to this album, and I'm always amazed how well it has aged, I love it. Up there with the Velvet Underground.

In spite of Geoff Travis's serious misgivings about the eponymously titled Jazzateers album, its release continued Rough Trade's run of positive media reaction. The former Postcard triumvirate that resided at Rough Trade were on the up; the profiles of Aztec Camera, the Go-Betweens and Jazzateers were at the forefront of literate independent pop and it seemed like Jazzateers' previous bad luck under the management of Alan Horne had turned. However, contrary to the last, Jazzateers were to prove they were adept at inflicting self-harm (which it could be argued they did by accepting Paul Quinn's request to rejoin the group).

KEITH BAND: During the recording of the Jazzateers album Paul moved back to Glasgow — in fact we managed to get Rough Trade to pay his train fare. I think he was literally starving in London, and he ended up singing backing vocals on the album. Paul was keen to rejoin the band, and Grahame was starting a new group with Douglas MacIntyre, the White Savages. All of this felt quite natural, and there was label interest in us working with Paul, but without Alan Horne being involved.

IAN BURGOYNE: After we had delivered the Jazzateers album to Rough Trade, we got a call from Paul Quinn who asked if he could rejoin the group, as he had left Alan Horne in London and was moving back to Glasgow. We thought at that point if Paul was interested in coming back then maybe we should see if we can get a major label interested. We also got another guitarist joining on lead guitar, Mick Slaven, and revamped the name Bourgie Bourgie for this new line-up.

GRAHAME SKINNER: I loved being involved with the making of the Jazzateers album. I learned so much as it was the first time I'd been in the studio making an album. The process was interesting, we had a great time and Paul Quinn sang backing vocals. I first met Douglas MacIntyre on his twenty-first birthday at a party at his flat in Holyrood Quadrant. We'd just received a white label of the Jazzateers album, so Ian, Keith, Paul and I went to Douglas's and played the album for the first time on his record player at the party. I hit it off with Douglas and we decided to start a new group, White Savages, which we named after a Contortions track, and which was sonically influenced by the Jazzateers album and New York loft groups.

Suddenly Jazzateers Mk 3 had a single and album in the independent chart garnering excellent reviews for Rough Trade, who also managed to get the group booked on a new live Channel 4 music show, *Switch*. Keith Band and Ian Burgoyne accepted the offer to appear live on television, but it would be as Bourgie Bourgie Mk

2, with Paul Quinn on vocals instead of Grahame Skinner. Bourgie Bourgie performed both songs featured on Jazzateers' single from the Rough Trade album, 'Show Me the Door' and 'Sixteen Reasons'. Bourgie Bourgie augmented their line-up when Mick Slaven joined on lead guitar.

KEITH BAND: We quickly went from mixing the Jazzateers album with Grahame on vocals for Rough Trade, to changing our name back to Bourgie Bourgie with Paul on vocals and recording demos for major labels. The timing was good, as on the back of the critical success of the Rough Trade album we got an offer for Jazzateers to appear on a music TV programme, *Switch*, which we accepted, but would appear with Paul on vocals as Bourgie Bourgie singing a couple of songs from the Jazzateers album. In retrospect bringing Paul back on vocals was obviously a big mistake; we should have continued working with Grahame.

All of which started a feeding frenzy by major labels to sign Bourgie Bourgie, and ironically it was the involvement of Rough Trade that created a platform for the group to attract label interest. This was something Alan Horne had singularly failed to do for Jazzateers Mks 1 and 2, Bourgie Bourgie Mk 1 and Paul Quinn as a solo artist. It looked like perhaps major labels did not want to deal with Alan Horne, who was now cast adrift in London on the outside of the music industry looking in.

Bob Last and Hilary Morrison's management empire continued to grow with ongoing success with the Human League and ABC, and Scritti Politti being lined up to record their first major-label album in the US with legendary producer Arif Mardin, with talk of Miles Davis guesting on trumpet.

BOB LAST: The kinds of management strategies that we had advocated, allied by a similar set of fascinations, had been carried out by the Human League, ABC and Scritti Politti and subsequently became successful strategies.

HILARY MORRISON: We always advised artists to get a good lawyer, a good accountant, and keep control. A lot of artists realised they needed management to steer that, and management for us was a fast track to learning an awful lot about the moneyed world, the line of money, the money trail, how that all worked. In artist management, it is not necessary for artists to always do exactly what they want, but to do more of what they want than a major record label wants them to do. The major label is controlling artists and that can work in a positive way or it can work in a very negative way, but it's about having that awareness.

Last also tried to diversify and start an actors' agency called Ricochet, which would be run by Tam Dean Burn. Last and Morrison had invested some of their management monies from *Dare* and bought properties to rent in Edinburgh. Bob, Tam and James Oliva set up in one of Last's vacant properties, with Last filming Burn doing a Steven Berkoff monologue on 16mm and Oliva doing the lighting. The Ricochet project failed to materialise, but it did highlight Last's abiding interest in developing film-related projects. While their management and publishing companies successfully expanded their business reach, Last decided it was time to pull the plug on his involvement with distribution. Fast Product's initial involvement in distribution and membership of the Cartel may have started along an altruistic path, but it ended with a hard-nosed business decision that led to staff unemployment.

SANDY MCLEAN: Bob got us to do a stock check and it turned out we had actually technically lost three grand that quarter or something similar. We lost money on one quarterly stock check, so technically we were insolvent and he pulled the plug on the company despite having bought a new warehouse a month before that. I think we could have battened down the hatches and gotten through that, but he just pulled the plug very quickly and, before we knew it, we were unemployed. I met my distribution colleagues at Rough Trade and Red Rhino, showed them the sale figures and the accounts, and they both agreed there was a viable business there. So Red Rhino agreed to set me up and continue, which got me an office and a phone line and wages. We found an office in Edinburgh, Alva Street, and I just thought, 'OK, Fast Product . . . Fast Forward.' Great name, easy, done. And within a few weeks we were started up and running in 28a Alva Street as Fast Forward Distribution, phoning up the shops in the morning, faxing the orders down to York and they were dispatched from the Red Rhino warehouse to the Scottish shops.

The photography and design aesthetic of Hilary Morrison, allied with the strategic deployment of consumerist packaging concepts by Bob Last, had stamped a cultural identity on Fast Product and pop:aural that had a reverberating influence over those that followed, particularly Factory Records. There seemed to be natural alignments with Fast and Factory, and to a lesser extent Zoo and Postcard; however, it can't be denied that the stylistic and musical presentation of Postcard and Orange Juice became the definitive template for what ultimately sired a genre: indie. While it's still a much-loathed word, the 'indie' fashion that exists to this day is a distillation of the *C86* distillation of Postcard. Edwyn Collins and Alan Horne are rightly acknowledged as Postcard's prime movers, but the input of James Kirk, Steven Daly and David McClymont was central to the development of the look and sound of the label. James Kirk in particular is the overlooked boy genius, but the cognoscenti knew then as they know now his pivotal importance in the Postcard movement.

The cultural and musical echoes of Postcard had already reverberated throughout the UK and beyond, as groups turned on to the naive charm, sound and image of the label. Nineteen eighty-two had seen several releases that felt like Postcard singles; perhaps they would have been Postcard singles if the label had thought about consolidating the market they had created. Zoo released the Wild Swans single 'The Revolutionary Spirit', and the Kitchenware organisation in Newcastle (who had booked gigs by the Postcard groups under their Soul Kitchen live promotion guise) had started releasing singles: Hurrah!, the Daintees and Prefab Sprout all released debut singles on Kitchenware during 1982.

EDWYN COLLINS: Kitchenware is completely a surrogate Postcard — they have the whole look down to a T. I don't know if it was the Daintees or Hurrah!, but they came to Glasgow when they were called the Green-Eyed Children and were fairly punky, but they must have seen us wearing all our floppy fringes. It's flattering in a way, but I don't like their music, though Prefab Sprout's Paddy McAloon seems pretty astute.

Groups from regional outposts like Norwich (the Farmer's Boys) and Leeds (the Wedding Present) muscled in on the John Peel action, and all the aforementioned groups were picked up by the music press. Perhaps the group that most synthesised the Postcard aesthetic was Liverpool's Love-obsessed Pale Fountains, who meshed Arthur Lee and Bacharach's melodic purity with a new puritan visual representation. The Pale Fountains' arrival was an example of right place, right time, but more importantly, in vocalist and songwriter Michael Head they had a figurehead for this new feeling. The group were signed by Rough Trade employee Patrick Moore to a new label, Operation Twilight, which he had set up in conjunction with Les Disques du Crépuscule's Michel Duval (shareholders included Cabaret Voltaire's Richard Kirk, Skids vocalist Richard Jobson and Alan Horne). Jazzateers' album *Lee* was a planned release on Operation Twilight as was Paul Haig's debut album (prior to him signing to Island). Malcolm Fisher's new configuration of the French Impressionists was also lined up to sign to Operation Twilight. The Pale Fountains were the perfect group for this period of major-label acquisition of artists from the independent sector. They had the look — Boy Scouts' hats and shorts — covered 'Walk On By' and had a trumpet player in the group, and were discussing approaching Alan Horne or Edwyn Collins to produce their debut single. They ended up recording their debut single 'Always on My Mind' themselves, which when released received praise from the *NME*, the *Face* and *Record Mirror*. They recorded a session for John Peel and major labels circled the group. Rough Trade's new confidence on the back of the commercial successes of the debut Aztec Camera and Scritti Politti albums resulted in a two-album deal being offered to the Pale Fountains by the label (which Alan Horne advised the group not to sign). They signed to Virgin Records for £130,000, a scenario unthinkable a year previously when Aztec Camera released the final Postcard single. This was proof positive that late 1982 was the period where the big gold dream had been realised in terms of finance — the majors wanted some of the action. While the Pale Fountains' major-label single, 'Thank You', failed to chart, it laid the pathway for the 1983 gold rush.

Strawberry Switchblade: Jill Bryson and Rose McDowell

Postcard comrades Strawberry Switchblade recorded BBC Radio 1 sessions (featuring James Kirk playing bass) for John Peel and Kid Jensen in October 1982. These sessions were heard by Zoo partners Bill Drummond and Dave Balfe, who through managing both the Teardrop Explodes and Echo and the Bunnymen already understood the major-label environment. Drummond and Balfe contacted Strawberry Switchblade and had soon usurped Barbara Shores as the group's managers. They arranged the release of a single, 'Trees and Flowers', on Bunnymen guitarist Will Sergeant's label 92 Happy Customers as a calling card for the group. Kitchenware released another trio of singles by Hurrah!, the Daintees and Prefab Sprout to continuing acclaim. But the city that was still feted as the centre of independent pop in 1983 was Glasgow, where the gold rush continued apace on the back of the chart success of Orange Juice and Altered Images. Major record labels and publishers regularly prowled Glasgow and hoped to unearth independent pop that could potentially cross over to a mainstream audience. The Kingfishers were formed after the demise of Article 58 and Restricted Code, with two members from each forming the new group. The Kingfishers were offered a publishing contract and put into Park Lane studio to record demos for CBS. The new group formed by James Kirk and Steven Daly, Cormorant (later to become Memphis), also attracted attention. Apart from looking after Cormorant, Barbara Shores now managed Del Amitri, whose 'Sense Sickness' 7-inch brought them to the attention of Geoff Travis who was keen to sign them.

The group that seemed most likely to succeed were Friends Again. Built on the twin attack of Chris Thomson's vocals and songs, in tandem with the country-picking guitar of James Grant, they signed a publishing deal with CBS affiliate April Songs. They financed a single, which in time became the modus operandi of publishers. Friends Again's single, 'Honey at the Core', was excellent, and tapped into the prevalent melodic mood of Postcard with literary lyrics that chimed with the times. Friends Again signed a major record deal with Phonogram and further singles were released ('State of Art' and 'Lucky Star'). Phonogram somehow failed to deliver chart success for the singles; 'State of Art' in particular is majestic, with sweeping strings arranged by Paul Buckmaster (who had arranged on tracks by Bowie). It wasn't to be for Friends Again, and the group would split on the release of their debut album *Trapped and Unwrapped*.

The Glasgow group that was garnering most interest from major labels was Bourgie Bourgie, with new groups Lloyd Cole and the Commotions and White Savages also attracting industry attention. The timing felt perfect for Bourgie Bourgie; they had the voice of Paul Quinn, and the songs of Ian Burgoyne and Keith Band — they even had a guitar hero in Mick Slaven. Their television appearance on *Switch* had upped the ante, with David Band continuing to manage the group (though he soon handed over management to Rough Trade employee Pat Bellis). It was obvious a major deal was coming; all the companies were bidding on the basis of a demo recorded at Park Lane (which featured what would be their first single, 'Breaking Point'). An audition rehearsal was scheduled in London at Nomis studios, at which every major label turned up to see the group go through their songs. Bourgie Bourgie were yet to play live in public, so to elicit such label interest was testimony to the songs and Paul Quinn's voice and potential star status.

KEITH BAND: The new Bourgie Bourgie demo resulted in a lot of major-label interest, and we decided to sign to MCA and they made us a priority act. They were very keen to break the band into international markets.

IAN BURGOYNE: We signed a major-label deal with MCA. It wasn't something I was particularly comfortable with, and the whole Bourgie Bourgie sound was quite pompous. I think Alan Horne had hoped Paul would get himself established with Bourgie Bourgie and then do something with Alan again, which I thought was quite cynical.

Aztec Camera also signed to a major. Warner Brothers signed a deal with Rough Trade whereby they reissued *High Land, Hard Rain* and pursued a hit single with 'Oblivious'. As a priority signing with Warners, Aztec Camera received the full might of the Warners promotional and marketing machine. This resulted in a number 18 hit single in November and appearances on *Top of the Pops*. Fellow associates of the Postcard camp, Strawberry Switchblade, also signed to Warner Brothers and made the move south to London.

RODDY FRAME: I'd been slagging Rough Trade off in some fanzine in Aberdeen and I remember someone from the record company taking me aside like some kind of headmaster. 'Here at Rough Trade we're not in the business of making stars,' and I said, 'I noticed.' I was quite a mouthy young person. I think our ideas were slightly ahead of theirs, if I might be so bold. We were pushing. Rough Trade finally got their act in gear with the Smiths. Then they understood what Alan Horne had been banging on about. They didn't realise that it was OK to go on *Top of the Pops* if you were clever. The two things weren't mutually exclusive.

ROSE MCDOWELL: Edwyn was saying nice things to industry people when Strawberry Switchblade supported Orange Juice on tour, so he was spreading our name about a wee bit. When we did the 1982 Peel session, John Peel actually phoned me up himself to ask if we wanted to do a session, and then the next day Kid Jensen's producer called and asked us to do a session. It was like there was a wee race between the two of them to see which one of them would get us on first. That was the trigger for Dave Balfe and Bill Drummond coming up to Glasgow. Then when Strawberry Switchblade signed to Warner Brothers, they put a fair amount of money into pushing us, which was insane.

JILL BRYSON: Bill and David produced and released a single, 'Trees and Flowers', and we ended up signing to Warner Brothers and moving to London, which neither of us really wanted to do. I hated travelling and was agoraphobic, so I found it all really difficult and it put a lot of pressure on us as a band. As soon as you go from a nurturing environment in Glasgow like Postcard and find yourself living in a hotel in London and being on a major label where you're viewed as a money-making machine, you become a cog in their money-making machine.

The new Glasgow groups recalibrated their ambitions to bypass the independent sector. They focused on following Bourgie Bourgie (who signed a major record deal with MCA). However, the independent ethos was being kept alive by the Pastels. The group originally existed around the fulcrum of vocalist/guitarist Stephen Pastel and guitarist (and flatmate of Alan Horne at 185 West Princes Street) Brian Superstar.

BRIAN SUPERSTAR: I was working in a record shop, and Stephen Pastel used to hang around and wanted to start a band, so I thought why not. We had a few line-ups but then settled with Martin on bass and Bernice on drums. Stephen's always been obsessed by music, so when we started the Pastels it seemed like a good idea — we were friends, but it was never a full-time preoccupation.

STEPHEN PASTEL: At the time Brian lived at 185. He'd a slightly antagonistic if mostly good-natured relationship with Alan Horne. They were kind of opposites. Alan was unbelievably uptight, Brian much less so. Alan was very pristine in a way — he was always editing his world to try to make it slightly more perfect for him. I remember he was chucking out a bunch of great singles including the TV Personalities' '14th Floor' which he told me just to take. There was never any serious thought of us being on Postcard; we were too raw and it really wasn't where we saw ourselves either. But both Steven and James were encouraging. Orange Juice and the Pastels didn't massively overlap in terms of time frame and we probably had more of a place in what came next.

The Pastels: Brian Superstar

ROBERT HODGENS: I'd sometimes go into Brian Superstar's room at 185 West Princes Street — I'd sometimes play guitar with the Pastels whilst in the other room you'd get the Postcard madness. Brian Superstar would answer the front door of 185 and ask if we wanted to go into the sane room with the Pastels, or the insane room with Alan and Postcard.

STEPHEN PASTEL: We had more than our share of beginner's luck. We managed to get Chris Gordon [who'd briefly played with Orange Juice] to join on drums and we booked a studio to make a demo. Maybe we'd played one show by then. Robert Hodgens played bass at a rehearsal but not on the recording — Michael Giudici agreed to join us. I sent it off to Whaam! [Dan from the TV Personalities' label] and Rough Trade — both were into it but Dan asked if he could put out a couple of songs as they were. That was 'Songs for Children'. It was really basic and childlike but it was exciting to have made a record so quickly. Another song on the demo was 'I Wonder Why', which we rerecorded for Rough Trade. I think we hoped it would be more than a one-off deal. I had an over-idealised view of them and was ready to sign up. Geoff Travis was a total adult and at the time I wasn't — I couldn't read him. It being Rough Trade, I thought it would be excellent to have a Mayo Thompson and Geoff Travis production but I don't even know if they were still working together in 1983. Years later Mayo told me he'd have loved to have worked with us. Geoff suggested he would help and we should use an engineer called Steve Parker. I think the drums were recorded in Glasgow and run through the [mixing] desk drum by drum, hit by hit in London. It wasn't subtle and it gave the single a slightly dislocated un-group sound. Making it wasn't the most brilliant experience, the whole vibe wasn't right for us and we felt a bit patronised. It was quite a long time until the single came out, but it was the first time Annabel (Aggi) and I worked on the artwork together and their production department were really helpful. There was other support too, especially from Richard Boon. Long after the single had sold out Richard loved bringing up the idea of a re-press at every monthly meeting.

DAVID HENDERSON: I enjoyed recording the Pastels, and struck up a really good rapport with Stephen that has remained to the present.

STEPHEN PASTEL: For a while we felt quite dismayed by how far short we were coming up compared to what we wanted to be. We weren't sure what to do next. David Henderson from the Hellfire Club had taken over new premises and he asked if we'd like to record something. The premises were really just a shell and his equipment was basic but he was super-intuitive and friendly, and he knew what he was doing. He didn't try to disguise what we were and tried to capture us in a good light. By then we were becoming more of a group, with Martin and Bernice permanent members. We recorded four songs including 'Something Going On' which was totally eureka – that was the first time we completely sounded like us. As we went on we still made mistakes but at least we'd done something we could refer back to.

ROSE MCDOWELL: We did backing vocals for the Pastels – we did it on record and live, that was fantastic. I love Stephen Pastel. He was just this little icon wandering around Glasgow with his duffle coat, always teasing his hair. He was one of those people that you could just watch, he was an interesting person to watch. Brian Superstar was totally opposite to Stephen, he was a big tall thing, but they were just really, really interesting people. Stephen had his *Juniper Beri-Beri* fanzine; everybody was really active, buzzing and full of life – great characters came out of that scene. The Pastels were even more avant-garde in that kinda way than Orange Juice were. Orange Juice could play all the stuff really well, they were bloody good musicians. The Pastels were kinda learning as they went, and that was what punk was like.

JILL BRYSON: I remember when the Pastels got going they signed a deal with Rough Trade. Rose and I sang backing vocals on their single, 'I Wonder Why', which was recorded in a studio in the south side with Geoff Travis producing.

Perhaps the label head that had learned most from Postcard was Alan Horne's former nemesis, Geoff Travis. He had kept Rough Trade independent and relevant but had slowly realised that the positive media responses to his trio of former Postcard acts (Aztec Camera, the Go-Betweens and Jazzateers) would not be enough to move Rough Trade to the next level. Slowly but surely, Travis realised that had Rough Trade engaged in orthodox industry practices like aggressive radio plugging and engaged press agents with clout, he might have kept Aztec Camera and Scritti Politti rather than lost them to major labels.

GEOFF TRAVIS: Rough Trade wasn't really in a place to compete, I don't think, until 1983 and the Smiths. Then it really reached a point in my mind where I felt we can do anything that a major could do and better. Which is the reason why Green [Gartside] left Rough Trade, and Roddy left Rough Trade, because they wanted to be commercially successful and to be able to compete in the mainstream, and we just didn't have those resources. Being a musician is a difficult thing to do well, and sometimes people only have a short musical life. So it's a big responsibility on those people that are working with them to have their lives and their careers in their hands, and make decisions that are correct. Who knows what would have happened if they'd both stayed at Rough Trade at that point? But certainly the money that Green needed to make those records were at the margin where we couldn't afford it.

In much the same manner that the Pale Fountains highlighted Liverpool's debt to Postcard, so the Smiths highlighted Manchester's. Rough Trade adapted their business practices and attempted to compete in the charts, and although the first single by the Smiths, 'Hand in Glove', failed to chart, their second single was a hit. 'This Charming Man' changed the landscape of independent music forever. It reached number 25 in the singles chart and was accompanied by an appearance on *Top of the Pops*. The Smiths seemed imbued with an aesthetic that occupied the same territory that Postcard had in its short history, except the Smiths and Rough Trade succeeded in achieving their aim of infiltrating the mainstream.

EDWYN COLLINS: The Smiths are good, you know. They're dabbling around in the same area as Orange Juice were, but I much prefer 'Simply Thrilled Honey' to 'This Charming Man' when it comes to twelve-string Byrds pastiches.

It must have been a strange feeling for Alan Horne at the end of 1983 to see the Smiths' successful chart incursion when they joined his former Postcard artists Orange Juice and Aztec Camera in the top 30. Added to which Paul Haig had released his debut album *Rhythm of Life* on Island, the Bluebells were still releasing singles on London Records, and his former charges Bourgie Bourgie were a major priority for MCA and being touted as the next big thing. Paul Quinn had finally found a platform for his outstanding voice, which existed at an intersection of Al Green and Bryan Ferry, with some Bowie thrown in for good measure. Bourgie Bourgie were on the cusp of following the Smiths into the charts and had already received a Dave McCullough feature in *Sounds* (the *NME* and *Melody Maker* also published major articles on the group). As journalists tried to unravel the complicated Bourgie Bourgie history (from Postcard to Jazzateers to Bourgie Bourgie to Jazzateers to Rough

Trade to Bourgie Bourgie to MCA), the group prepared themselves for the expected imminent success and explained their vision.

PAUL QUINN: Bourgie Bourgie isn't calculated. When we started rehearsing we were intent on becoming a soul group, though I think the influences in Bourgie Bourgie are still a real pot-pourri. My main influences are soul, but the Velvets are still an inspiration, though I don't think too many of our songs actually sound like the Velvets. When I first started singing everyone hated my voice, then when I had a little more experience they thought it was OK. It wasn't until Alan Horne heard me singing that I got some positive response.

IAN BURGOYNE: The good thing about Orange Juice was they had a really distinctive sound. The unfortunate thing was that within a year there were ten other groups doing the same thing. It was good that Orange Juice got away from that sound too, all those jangly guitars! We wanted to try something different with Bourgie Bourgie.

PAUL QUINN: Ian and Keith write the music, mostly I write the lyrics but sometimes Ian does. Mick's got a really distinctive guitar style, though mostly Ian is the more dominant driving force. That's what I like about Bourgie Bourgie — Ian's like John Fogerty and Mick's like Tom Verlaine, two of the best.

KEITH BAND: We tried to get Daryl Hall to produce us, but he said no. Before that we tried to get Arif Mardin because he produced Hall and Oates's *Abandoned Luncheonette*, but the money he wanted was space age.

PAUL QUINN: Alan Horne and I made a film we were going to call *Bourgie Bourgie*, but when we got the spools back something had gone wrong, so that particular application of the name never really came to anything. I think the time is right now for Alan's ideas.

EDWYN COLLINS: Paul Quinn is a great talent, a really nice guy, very introverted, quite shy. I can't think of a contemporary singer who's better than Paul at the moment. I don't know about his band, I think they're holding him back somewhat.

IAN BURGOYNE: We spent most of the first half of the year recording tracks for the Jazzateers album on Rough Trade, even though that group was no longer really in existence. But we're in no hurry, 1984 is going to be the year of Bourgie Bourgie.

As it transpired, 1984 wouldn't be the year of Bourgie Bourgie, and Paul Quinn's assertion that the time was right for Alan Horne's ideas proved to be prescient. Everyone was chasing the big gold dream of hit singles and TV appearances on *Top of the Pops*. Production values became the primary concern, with the hope being cultural resonance would merely be a complementary bedfellow to commercial appeal. However, it was far easier to extrapolate these concepts to sympathetic music press journalists in a pub than to multinational corporation record company executives in a boardroom. That said, the Sound of Young Scotland cohort created an environment where major labels were keen to sign anyone who walked down Byres Road with a semi-acoustic guitar in a tartan shirt and sporting a quiff. As is often the case, sometimes the originators are left with recognition as cultural arbiters but with empty pockets, while their ideas are looted for monetary gain. Major record companies were happy to sign groups from Glasgow who looked the part, and tried to fashion them into something they thought they could sell if they incorporated modern production techniques and session musicians. Ever was it thus.

Nineteen eighty-three was coming to an end and so were Altered Images. They split up after successful US and UK tours, leaving their Mike Chapman and Tony Visconti-produced *Bite* as their best album. It had four great singles, but after the first single released from the album ('Don't Talk to Me about Love') reached number 7 in the charts, the subsequent singles released from *Bite* achieved progressively lower chart positions.

STEPHEN LIRONI: When the independent scene in Scotland exploded in the early eighties, you'd have a group like Aztec Camera on Postcard then Rough Trade, which were great homes for the group as these labels were run by music fans. However, when they ended up on a bigger label like Warner Brothers, it can be difficult to stay focused solely on the music when there are so many other business-related aspects to think about. I think that situation is true of quite a few groups where you leave the closeted environment of a smaller label to sign to a large entertainment conglomerate. Artists can get confused and diluted by associating with corporate people who don't necessarily understand where you've come from or where you're going.

Orange Juice had followed their top 10 'Rip It Up' single with another single from the album, but 'Flesh of My Flesh' tantalisingly reached 41 in the chart. This resulted in a slow decline in the group's relationship with Polydor. The group decided on Dennis Bovell as the producer for what became *Texas Fever*.

EDWYN COLLINS: Alan Horne had always said the ultimate single to come out of punk was the Pop Group's 'She Is beyond Good and Evil', which was produced by Dennis Bovell. It's a great mixture of punk, funk and abrasion. It's brilliant, trebly, the lyrics are good, a bit Nietzschean, but that's not the reason we asked him to produce — it was because he'd done 'Silly Games' by Janet Kay, which is great. Obviously Dennis was prepared to take a fairly radical approach.

It wasn't just the label relations that had fractured; the group started to form a schism with Ross and McClymont on one side and Collins and Manyika on the other. An attempt at recording an album with all members contributing to the writing had resulted in tension, with Collins finding it difficult to write lyrics and top-line vocal melodies to the collaborative tracks. The completed tracks eventually appeared as the *Texas Fever* mini album early in 1984, by which time Ross and McClymont were no longer in Orange Juice. Their departure was exacerbated by their jaunt to Barbados with producer Dennis Bovell to record for a new project, Ape the Scientific. That they went to Barbados without telling Collins or Manyika caused a seismic fault line to occur in Orange Juice. To rub salt into their wound, the Ape the Scientific version of Can's 'I Want More' was never released.

EDWYN COLLINS: David had his own project, Ape the Scientific, and went off to Barbados to record with Dennis Bovell in Eddy Grant's studio. He came back a lot more assertive and confident in his approach in the studio, which clashed somewhat with mine, and that's when it fell into dissolution. There was just animosity between me and David — that hoary old chestnut, 'musical differences'.

MALCOLM ROSS: After the *Rip It Up* album Edwyn really wanted to get good reviews again with the *Texas Fever* album. It ended up coming out as a mini album, us trying to be arty again, in that arch-Orange Juice way. Halfway through recording *Texas Fever*, David and I left the band. Edwyn started work on another album that became known as *The Orange Juice*. I think it's his masterwork — it was the best Orange Juice album and the best thing Edwyn ever did with Orange Juice.

Orange Juice split apart and were reduced to a duo of Edwyn and Zeke, though in reality the final Orange Juice album was all but a solo album by Collins. His singular clarity of vision on *The Orange Juice* resulted in an epochal release, a fitting epitaph for Orange Juice. After the split from Orange Juice, Ross was invited to join Aztec Camera, and McClymont took the advice of Robert Forster and moved to Australia. Nineteen eighty-three ended with no Altered Images, Orange Juice on the slide, the Go-Betweens feeling unloved by Rough Trade (who were now in love with the Smiths) and the Bluebells losing founder members Russell Irvine and Lawrence Donegan. Island Records released the 'Heaven Sent' single and *Rhythm of Life* album Paul Haig recorded in New York with Grace Jones's team (including Alex Sadkin and Bernie Worrell); however, the expected chart success didn't materialise and Island dropped Haig. Davy Henderson reconnected with Fire Engines drummer Russell Burn and formed Win. Aztec Camera bucked this trend with the success of the Warner Brothers reissue of *High Land, Hard Rain*. Roddy's position as Warners' favourite son would see the group regarded as a multinational priority for the label.

GEOFF TRAVIS: I think Roddy had made up his mind he wanted to sign to a major, which I actively helped him do. I don't remember ever fighting to say no, don't do that, you're being a traitor to the independent scene, because I think the scene and the structure is really important, but only as long as people want to participate in it. I don't really believe in this Stalinist thing, that you're either in my little wing of the party, and if you're not, you're an enemy. I hate all that. It's rubbish. I didn't ever want to be part of something that appeared self-righteous. I grew up listening to Bob Dylan, Paul Butterfield Blues Band and Tim Buckley, and they're all on majors. So I was always quite forgiving of that, really, but my thing is that you have to know that you can do the best job for an artist with their work and do justice to it. That was really my thing, and we were still at a very early stage then. Rough Trade was evolving and we had no idea of the future, and whether we would be able to sustain the careers of people or what they could be. It wasn't really until the Smiths came along that we made the decision, OK, we have to be a little bit more grown-up now, we need to deliver for these guys because they are just so good. We have responsibility, and we have the resources to do it as well.

Bourgie Bourgie were poised to realise their industry hype with a single being recorded with Ian Broudie prior to recording an album with Associates' producer Mike Hedges. The other main next-wave Glasgow contenders experienced differing trajectories: former Jazzateers vocalist Grahame Skinner was also a former White Savages vocalist after they split up having supported Altered Images on their final tour, while Lloyd Cole and the Commotions had added former Bluebells bassist Lawrence to their ranks. This appointment coincided with a renewed vision and determination by the Commotions. Their sound morphed from a Stax-based soul sound to a distillation of Orange Juice and the Velvets. Cole was hitting his flow as a songwriter and the group equally upped their game. The quality of songs like 'Are You Ready to Be Heartbroken' and 'Forest Fire' were game changers for the group.

Bob Last and Hilary Morrison watched as their successful management and publishing companies continued to grow. Last brokered deals at the top tables of the music industry and disentangled Green from his Scritti Politti legal wrangles with Rough Trade. Green signed to Virgin and recorded in New York with production legend Arif Mardin. The original Fast Product ethos of mainstream infiltration continued to pay dividends; their business-as-art conceptualisation had become a reality as their market was now international. The only player not participating in this music industry success party was Alan Horne. However, that was about to change. The Postcard kitten was about to stalk the industry as a Swamplands panther.

EPILOGUES

1984 – Exit: No Return

Alan Horne and Jazzateers

(i)

Malcolm Ross joined Aztec Camera, which closed the circle that started when he suggested to Alan Horne that they should follow Orange Juice, Josef K and the Go-Betweens in being signed to Postcard. Aztec Camera were now a completely different proposition — they had toured the US, had a hit album and single, and received universal praise for the songs and precocious talent of Roddy Frame. They had enjoyed the creative freedom of being signed to Rough Trade and released an album on Warner Brothers produced by Mark Knopfler. This engagement with the multinational corporate music industry increased the pressure on the group.

MALCOLM ROSS: After the Orange Juice split I ended up joining Aztec Camera, which I didn't really enjoy that much as I don't think it suited my style of guitar playing. Roddy's a very good guitar player technically and he had very strong ideas. I think I'm the only person who's ever played guitar on a Roddy Frame or Aztec Camera album apart from him.

RODDY FRAME: I always wanted to work with Malcolm Ross. I was at the last Josef K gig but Malcolm joined Orange Juice when Josef K split. When Malcolm left Orange Juice I asked him to join Aztec Camera, so I got to work with him at last.

CAMPBELL OWENS: Malcolm Ross joined the band, but the conditions weren't right for us as a band to make a good second album, it just wasn't happening. After the success we had with *High Land, Hard Rain* on Rough Trade, we ended up signing with Warner Bros.

Being on Rough Trade was different from being on a major label for lots of reasons. First of all, our circumstances had changed by then and our expectations were different. On an independent label you do what you want, but with a much smaller budget and less expectations. Rough Trade were kind of 'hippy dippy', they were 'cool man', so we got to make *High Land, Hard Rain* under very pleasant conditions, as an unrushed experience. The songs had been around for a while so we were happy with the material and there was no pressure whatsoever. Then you have some success: first 'Oblivious' charted and we were on *Top of the Pops*, and then the major labels are interested all of a sudden, because they sniff profit. Rob Dickens was the chairman of Warner Bros and he signed us, so we were signed by the top guy.

RODDY FRAME: We'd been to America touring *High Land, Hard Rain* with Elvis Costello and the Attractions, so I went back to New Orleans to write some songs. I chose Mark Knopfler as producer of the second Aztec Camera album; apart from the fact it was quite contrary, I thought the soundtrack music he did for Bill Forsyth was fantastic. I never bought the idea that indie labels were more honest or genuine. I wanted some success, some recognition.

MALCOLM ROSS: The album I did with Aztec Camera was produced by Mark Knopfler. I mean it was recorded in the poshest studio in London, you know, you're playing *Asteroids* with Paul McCartney, things like that. Which was kind of all right but I didn't really feel like I was involved that much.

CAMPBELL OWENS: Money was getting flashed around and there were promises that we were going to be huge, break in the States, and you believe it. So we went into the studio with songs that were underdeveloped and a producer who didn't get what it was all about, and a songwriter who is getting madder and madder by the day. Roddy is a very intense person and he must have been under incredible pressure himself. When he moved to London he was eighteen, and he had all this fame and exposure from a very early age. He was very mature for his years, but the lifestyle on the road constantly was the same old rock 'n' roll story. How do you get through the day? You start drinking, you start taking drugs. These things aren't good for you and he was becoming more difficult to deal with — for me, anyway.

Aztec Camera released their second album *Knife* to mixed reviews. Both singles taken from the album failed to make the top 30 and the album peaked at number 14 in the chart. An intensive international touring schedule ultimately resulted in their group identity being fragmented. Future Aztec Camera albums would effectively be Roddy Frame solo albums using the group's brand. Roddy's biggest hit, 'Somewhere in My Heart', reached number 3 in the UK singles charts in 1987.

The Go-Betweens followed Aztec Camera in leaving Rough Trade when they signed to Warner Brothers' affiliate label Sire. They released a well-received album *Spring Hill Fair* and supported Aztec Camera on tour on which they played large venues that would have been unthinkable when both were signed to Postcard. The Go-Betweens would go on to release several more albums, and the literate songwriting of Robert Forster and Grant McLennan was revered by critics and public alike.

Paul Haig was dropped by Island Records; he returned to Crépuscule and released his second solo album.

PAUL HAIG: My second album was recorded with Alan Rankine producing, who I knew quite well as he was in my group when I toured my debut solo album. Alan played keyboards, and Malcolm played guitar, with David from Orange Juice on bass. Allan Campbell was managing me, and helped put the touring band together. I got the title for my second album by taking something from a Norman Mailer book, which I changed slightly to *The Warp of Pure Fun*. I then did some recording with Barney [Bernard Sumner] from New Order producing and Donald from A Certain Ratio playing drums. Crépuscule also suggested I record with Cabaret Voltaire at their Western Works studio in Sheffield, which was interesting as I'd been a fan since 1977, singles like 'Nag Nag Nag'.

While Paul Haig returned to an independent working environment that suited his temperament and a label that shared his aesthetic values, his former Postcard label mate Edwyn Collins worked largely on his own on what would be the final Orange Juice album, *The Orange Juice*. Nominally a duo with Zeke Manyika, the reality was Collins made the album on his own with Dennis Bovell, augmented by session musicians — Zeke only spent a few days in the studio when he recorded drums on the album. *The Orange Juice* album contained two singles, the superlative first single 'What Presence?' peaking at 47 while the follow-up 'Lean Period' stalled at 74. *The Orange Juice* didn't trouble the album charts, though many argue that the album is Edwyn's best work. He executed his vision unfettered by the chains of group democracy; however, it proved to be the final throw of the dice for Polydor and the Orange Juice name was retired after a benefit concert for striking miners.

Bourgie Bourgie also played their final gig in support of striking miners, at the Kelvin Hall in Glasgow, with Stephen Lironi on drums following the production work he did on the B-sides of the two singles the group released. However, all was not well in the camp.

Bourgie Bourgie: Keith Band, Ian Burgoyne, Paul Quinn and Mick Slaven

IAN BURGOYNE: We did our last gig, which was a benefit concert for the striking miners, but by that point I didn't really want to see Paul again.

KEITH BAND: The first single by Bourgie Bourgie was 'Breaking Point', which was almost a hit. We recorded it in a good studio, it was produced by Ian Broudie and the engineer was Flood. We then worked on an album with Mike Hedges producing, which we started in London before recording the bulk of it over a month in Bavaria. It was a bit indulgent — we had the Nuremberg Symphony Orchestra playing on a few songs, a jazz band playing on another track — it was all a bit out of hand really. We weren't happy with the album, we didn't think it sounded good at all, though it was partly our fault as probably half the songs weren't good enough.

IAN BURGOYNE: I just hate the Bourgie Bourgie recordings, especially our best-known song, 'Breaking Point'. It is the absolute opposite of everything I love in music, which is: understatement, low-key, melody. I think it was a complete and utter mess, the whole album is a travesty.

The Bourgie Bourgie story is imbued with pop heartbreak: a rollercoaster of apparent success, despondent failure, then further ups as heir apparent to the Postcard crown when they signed a dream deal with a major record label. They fell from grace in the most unfortunate manner. MCA regarded the group as their priority; their debut single was nearly a success but the follow-up, 'Careless', was a complete failure on all counts. The B-sides the group recorded quickly with Stephen Lironi producing at Park Lane studio in Glasgow were by far their best recordings. On the evidence of his production work on 'Après Ski' and 'Change of Attitude', Bourgie Bourgie would have realised their potential better under his guidance. Instead the label plumped for Mike Hedges to produce the album, which he did at great cost, mostly in Bavaria. While his overblown production of Associates' *Sulk* suited that album perfectly, it rendered the Bourgie Bourgie tracks pompous, and on the evidence of the Bavaria sessions, it's clear to see the group had lost control of the album. There was worse to come.

KEITH BAND: Bourgie Bourgie returned from Bavaria and then of course Paul Quinn left the group for the second time at that point. Alan Horne had set up Swamplands Records through London Records and had convinced MCA that he had recorded 'Pale Blue Eyes' with Paul and Edwyn prior to Bourgie Bourgie signing to MCA, so MCA let Swampland release 'Pale Blue Eyes' and shortly after that Paul officially left Bourgie Bourgie.

IAN BURGOYNE: After we returned from Bavaria it was such a relief when we heard Paul was going back to live in London with Alan and sign to his new Swamplands label. I was just glad that horrible MCA year for Bourgie Bourgie was over.

(ii)

Alan Horne was back in the game. He had been invited by London Records to set up a new label, Swamplands, with offices and finance provided by the major. The first release was a version of the Velvets' 'Pale Blue Eyes' recorded by Paul Quinn and Edwyn Collins, which had London Records convinced they had a hit on their hands. A BBC Radio 1 session was recorded and several music press features (including a front cover) and a superb television appearance all pointed to Horne and Quinn finally having connected with a mainstream audience. London Records' optimism was short lived when 'Pale Blue Eyes' stalled at 72 in the chart.

Polydor had lost faith in Edwyn Collins and Orange Juice, per-haps accelerated by the instant hit of their new pretenders, Lloyd Cole and the Commotions. They had learned lessons patiently while they'd waited in the wings as they perfected their aesthetic. They released a single financed by their publishers April Music (the same blueprint as Friends Again), then signed to Polydor. Cole had hit his flow as a songwriter, the Commotions had found their *Highway 61 Revisited* meets *Loaded* groove; in fact their timing was impeccable. The major-label debut single 'Perfect Skin' was a hit, reaching number 26, which afforded the group a *Top of the Pops* slot followed by an appearance on *The Old Grey Whistle Test* when their album was released. The second single by the Commotions, 'Forest Fire', was an absolute classic that didn't seem to halt the group's progress in spite of sticking at 41. *Rattlesnakes* was, arguably, the album that perfected the Postcard aesthetic, and along with the Smiths on Rough Trade took literate pop into the mainstream. The production on *Rattlesnakes* by Paul Hardiman was precise and sympathetic, building on his work with The The. String arrangements by Anne Dudley showed Cole's love of T. Rex. *Rattlesnakes* name-checked a plethora of cultural icons that resonated perfectly and connoted literature and pop in an intelligent manner that had journalists frothing: Simone de Beauvoir, Truman Capote, Leonard Cohen, Eva Marie Saint, Arthur Lee and Norman Mailer were just some of the names that were dropped on the album. Cole understood the importance of good hair, clothes, guitars and good record company politics, all of which gave the group a platform that resulted in *Rattlesnakes* reaching 13 in the album chart (it sold over 100,000 copies). He had developed into a great songwriter and had a group structure capable of delivering the goods, which they did.

Strawberry Switchblade lost the oboes and Velvet tones of their 'Trees and Flowers' independent single and fell foul of the eighties programmed production values of David Motion. Warner Brothers were happy though as the group hit number 5 with their 'Since Yesterday' single. The group went on to have major success in Japan, but the pressure ramped up and took its toll on the relationship between the duo. Strawberry Switchblade split up.

Though both groups had started as part of the 185 West Princes Street/Hellfire Club milieu, Strawberry Switchblade had followed a diametrically opposite pathway to the Pastels, who remained within the independent sector.

DAVID HENDERSON: Jill and Rose had a definite look and style. Alan and Edwyn were always encouraging them because they were interesting people who were trying to do something creatively. When Rose and Jill started writing together, they were simplistic songs that sounded great. James Kirk from Orange Juice had donated the name Strawberry Switchblade and Alan and Edwyn loved their songs. We demoed songs at the Hellfire Club, and then Bill Drummond got interested in them for Zoo.

Stephen Pastel

STEPHEN PASTEL: In Glasgow we always felt slightly isolated even when we were more connected than we realised. After Peter McArthur photographed us we became good friends with him and his partner, Jill Bryson. They lived just round the corner from 185 on West End Park Street. I met Rose through them — it was just a natural friendship, we all felt on the same side of things, trying to make melodic, interesting music that wasn't too muso. Strawberry Switchblade were focused, they had something special in their sights but all our lives felt really normal in a way. I was still living at home, as was Annabel, and we'd go round to theirs to just chat and maybe hear a new Strawberry Switchblade song. That's how *Juniper Beri-Beri*, our fanzine, came about — it seemed like something we could collectively do. It's actually a good document of a moment when one time becomes another. In the first issue Peter contributed a Postcard obituary while at the same time we were going all-out to make it seem like somehow Strawberry Switchblade and the Pastels, our small world, had taken over. It's got a kind of innocent ruthlessness to it, that's what we were like when we were young.

The Bluebells were now trimmed to a trio of primary songwriter Robert Hodgens and the McCluskey brothers, Ken and David, and finally delivered on their pop promise with a hit single at their fourth attempt when 'I'm Falling' reached number 11. 'Young at Heart' followed and reached number 8, and there were further appearances on *Top of the Pops* before a final top 40 hit with the reissue of 'Cath'. The album, *Sisters*, had been compiled by London Records from sessions recorded with various producers and reached a respectable 22. The group were signed by Seymour Stein to Sire for the US and toured the States. The promise of their early Postcard demos and tracks produced by Elvis Costello had now come to fruition as the group straddled chart success with critical praise, always a difficult trick to execute. The Bluebells would go on to become the most successful group of the Postcard associates when, years after splitting up, they were approached for permission to use 'Young at Heart' in a Volkswagen advert. The high profile of the adverts resulted in London Records reissuing 'Young at Heart' in 1993, and the single flew to number 1 in the pop charts where it stayed for a month. The original five members — Robert, Russell, Lawrence, David and Ken — appeared on *Top of the Pops* and the single embedded itself in the nation's psyche. London Records released *The Singles Collection* album and capitalised further.

Bob Last and Hilary Morrison continued to strike gold through their management and publishing interests. The Human League had two producers leave the follow-up album to *Dare* – Martin Rushent and Chris Thomas both walked before Hugh Padgham finally finished the album. The three-year gap between *Dare* and its follow-up *Hysteria* had seen the group lose momentum and creative stasis had kicked in. Last was tiring of dealing with the Human League.

BOB LAST: The obtuse nature of Phil Oakey created something special, but I finally got exhausted by it. My memory is I finally resigned from managing the Human League from a phone booth in Burbank airport. I remember thinking, I can't do this any more. I'd been staying in the Sunset Marquis in LA and Phil had called me and woken me up before breakfast because he was really annoyed about his leased car. I just thought, no, I can't do this any more. It was some point after the release of *Hysteria*, which was a really challenging experience for everyone. So that was the moment when I quit.

Last had worked with Rob Warr from when he had managed Gang of Four, and it fell to Warr to manage ABC as part of Last's Tunenoise management company. As with the Human League, ABC had difficulty when they followed the international success of *The Lexicon of Love*, and didn't have the involvement of producer Trevor Horn for its follow-up, *Beauty Stab*. The album jettisoned the sweeping strings of its predecessor in favour of a more guitar-oriented approach, and although viewed as a failure in some quarters the album still sold over 100,000. Bob Last's management focus was now on taking the Marxist-theory modern shiny pop of Scritti Politti into the mainstream. Scritti Politti were music press darlings; their *Songs to Remember* album on Rough Trade was still much loved, but leader Green and Last had a vision that embraced mainstream success at the highest level. This was achieved with the album *Cupid and Psyche '85*, an album that defined highly polished, state-of-the-art studio production (industry legend Arif Mardin was involved in the project). The album yielded international hit singles with 'Perfect Way' making its way into the US singles chart. What the young Bob Last (a massive fan of Miles Davis' *Bitches Brew* album) would have made of working with Miles on his future version of 'Perfect Way' for his his *Tutu* album, is not on record.

GEOFF TRAVIS: Green leaving Rough Trade to sign to Virgin wasn't really anything to do with me, because Bob Last took over at that point. One day we were working with Scritti, and the next we weren't, and that was it. They left without any bad blood from me, although I think probably other people at Rough Trade were very upset about it, but that was a whole new era for Scritti.

Eventually Bob Last would move away from artist management to pursue his interest in film, an art form that had always held more creative sway for him. His management portfolio with Tunenoise had successfully taken on the international mass market. Hilary Morrison had also had enough of artist management and wanted to move on.

BOB LAST: I was managing Scritti Politti and through my company, Tunenoise, Rob Warr was managing ABC. Not long after that I got out of managing; as a teenager I watched more films than I listened to music, I just thought now is the time to get involved in film, now is the time to do it. The thing that crystallised that decision to move away from management was I got a call about managing Elton John asking if I would do a meeting. At the time I thought, I didn't get into the music industry to end up managing Elton John.

HILARY MORRISON: As a woman, some of the shit I had to put up with was off the dial. I mean, we were young, and we were possibly quite naive, because once you get into the belly of the beast, you have to be awfully careful that the beast doesn't start pouring its digestive juices all over you. You have to think, OK, do I really want that, and what does that really mean? It gets a bit biblical, because people start offering you a lot of things, and it's a bit like selling your soul.

Alan Horne's Swamplands label gave a major-label platform to Davy Henderson's new group with Russell Burn and Ian Stoddart, Win. They released four sensational singles: 'Unamerican Broadcasting', 'Shampoo Tears' (co-written with Hilary Morrison from their Heartbeat period), 'Super Popoid Groove' and most notably 'You've Got the Power' – probably the biggest hit single that wasn't actually a hit (due to a marketing bungle at London Records). David Motion had been appointed their producer on the back of his success with Strawberry Switchblade, a union that pleased the group as he could technically deliver their wish to create pop as fizzy and sweet as the 1970 Coke advert that influenced them, 'I'd Like to Teach the World to Sing'.

DAVY HENDERSON: Alan had total carte blanche to do what he wanted — he was the sort of *enfant terrible* in the basement of London Records. Their offices were like glass box units for each department and sub-label, and Alan covered his glass wall with the day's edition of the *Sun* — I suppose to piss off the rarefied atmosphere in the rest of the corridor, he was just having a lot of fun. Swamplands had also signed Paul Quinn and Edwyn Collins. I don't know how all that came about but I think there were a lot of legalities — it was around the time of Paul and Bourgie Bourgie being signed to MCA. Paul was on Swamplands as a solo artist and he had Memphis, who were James Kirk and Steven Daly, so Swamplands was like a second-generation outfit — you know, two Fire Engines and two Orange Juices, please, and a Paul Quinn. He had James King and the Lone Wolves as well, so quite an eclectic but toxic Scottish collection of incendiary devices. We didn't know what the game was in any way whatsoever, but we wanted to release 'Unamerican Broadcasting' and Alan loved it, just the statement 'this is an Unamerican Broadcasting'. It was the period of Reaganomics and Thatcherism. 'Unamerican Broadcasting' was one of maybe two songs that I'd written in my two-year tenure at Sound Diagrams. I never made anything up because I couldn't play anything. When it came time for renewal of my publishing deal, Bob Last brought me into the office. I didn't know how to let him hear the songs, so I remember he said I should go away and sing them onto a tape, so he's got an a cappella version of me singing 'Unamerican Broadcasting' and 'Shampoo Tears', which were the only two songs I made up during that time. With Win our objective was, let's get a major deal and Alan responded with Swamplands after he heard the demo. Then it was, let's make a record, let's do a 12-inch, let's do the sticker, let's get an American flag on it, it'll be like the banana album with a sticker. London Records thought this was a complete joke, they actually sort of laughed at it. We found out quickly that at a major record label there are departments upon departments, needing to know who's releasing what, when and how it's going to be dressed and who's going to dress it, and how you are going to promote it. It was an incredible waste of energy being on a major. A lot of waste. It's weird calling it an industry because it's just so wasteful, but they just laughed at us, which I think Alan liked as well. 'Unamerican Broadcasting' got some press and all that, but London Records' ears pricked when we made a song called 'You've Got the Power', and they could not deny in any way whatsoever that this was a pop song that could get into the national charts. They suddenly took us pretty seriously, and Alan wanted us to go with a producer called David Motion, who'd worked on Strawberry Switchblade. Alan was friends with the girls and he thought it should be produced properly, and with David having chart success with Strawberry Switchblade he knew that was the right button to press with London Records. We wanted to get Prince to produce it and make it sound like 'Dirty Mind', like low-grade funk-pop. So it kind of became this exaggerated, overblown pop song that London Records could not ignore. But everybody else in the world did.

London Records had initially felt Paul Quinn and Edwyn Collins were the Swamplands ticket to the charts, but the undeniable charms of Win's 'You've Got the Power' convinced them that Win might be the group to break Swamplands in the charts. London did a good job and gained solid press and radio attention for Swamplands' acts, and although they may not have regarded Memphis and James King and the Lone Wolves as priority artists, they did succeed in getting the Lone Wolves on *The Old Grey Whistle Test*.

James King

JAMES KING: After Alan set up Swamplands with London Records, he came up to Glasgow a few times to discuss doing something with me and the Lone Wolves. He laid out his plans for Swamplands and who would be involved, including Patti Palladin, Jayne County, Johnny Thunders, with Paul Quinn and Edwyn Collins coming in later. Alan's original idea was starting off with Thunders and Palladin, then coming in with the Lone Wolves. However, the first release on Swamplands ended up being Paul and Edwyn's cover version of 'Pale Blue Eyes'. I thought the Lone Wolves signing to Swamplands was interesting. There was potentially a good storyline with Jayne County, Johnny Thunders, Patti Palladin, but these people drifted away once Thunders didn't sign. There was another interesting idea Alan had, a project called What Ever Happened to Baby Jane, which was basically Jayne County, Patti Palladin and a monkey – that was the band, which shows how far out Alan was at the time. Alan got Derek Jarman to shoot a video for the project, around the same time Jarman shot a video for the Orange Juice single 'What Presence'. So the Lone Wolves demoed and had trips to London, where we supported Orange Juice. We became aware Johnny Thunders was pulling out of the deal because he wanted money for an album deal, whereas London Records were only prepared to bankroll Swamplands to do a singles deal because of Johnny's reputation. The Thunders/Palladin single was a version of 'Crawfish', and it was given a catalogue number on Swamplands along with an unreleased Lone Wolves single, 'Flyaway', which we recorded in RAK studios with Phil Thornally producing (although Alan remixed 'Flyaway' without our knowledge). The Lone Wolves appeared on *The Old Grey Whistle Test* around the same time we were recording with John Cale. We also recorded with John Porter, who had produced the Smiths. We had suggested Dave Edmunds to produce the band, but that didn't happen. The label could have saved themselves a fortune if they'd let us record in a Glasgow studio like Park Lane instead of London studios and hotel costs. I also think the Lone Wolves would have been more stable in Glasgow rather than London, where it's soul-destroying living in hotels and people drink more than they should through boredom. Working with John Cale producing the Lone Wolves was good. We'd done pre-production in London at Nomis, and we usually rehearsed quietly, but the first thing Cale did was turn all our amps up to full volume because he wanted to hear the band play really loud whereas we weren't attuned to that level of noise. He had a lot of ideas. I remember when I arrived at the studio he'd be there reading *The Times* with one hand and playing the piano with his other. The Lone Wolves were big Stooges fans, so we'd be asking him lots of questions. He told us he thought Ron Asheton was a pretty poor guitarist. He'd talk about being in the Velvets and there was still a grudge regarding Lou Reed.

Alan Horne was in a great position to use the might of London Records' promotional and marketing machine to deliver commercial success. Paul Quinn was a star in waiting, as was Davy Henderson. James King and the Lone Wolves also had a song that had 'hit' written all over it, 'Flyaway'. Memphis had an abundance of great songs written by James Kirk (allied with Steven Daly's pop nous). All of which highlighted that there was no reason why Swamplands wouldn't succeed. But it didn't.

EDWYN COLLINS: James King is a real character, a definite talent. He is a rock 'n' roll legend, if you like, and he's going to come through OK, I'm sure. Hank Williams meets Iggy Pop!

ALAN HORNE: I'm interested in characters, in individuals with star potential. If a person excites me I want to work with them. James King and the Lone Wolves are like a legend in Glasgow, no one would sign them because of their reputation, which had nothing to do with the music. Basically they were naughty boys in the eyes of the record industry. The same mentality that was confused and shocked by the Sex Pistols is operating again, probably ten times worse than before punk. I'd been working with Paul Quinn on and off for years, I always thought he could be very successful and make great records. I manage Paul as well, it's a very important thing for me to make him successful on some level and make great records. I like to push myself as much as the bands; it's a bit obsessive, a bit of an ego problem, but I don't like to let things get out of my hands.

PAUL QUINN: I knew Alan personally, so reputations don't put you off or encourage you – everything he thought was worth listening to. Creative people are erratic, I'm erratic, everyone involved with Swamplands is erratic.

BOB LAST: I retained an involvement with Win through publishing. I was still interested in them and I liked what they were trying to do. I thought they came very close to cracking what they were trying to do. I was only involved peripherally, I don't quite know why it didn't fully work in the way it should have done. That had to in part be down to the record company. I mean they were with London and I don't think the label fully understood them. If you are going to work with the major labels it required a kind of business strength and resilience that they didn't have collectively. Davy is extremely dismissive of Win, but I think that's in part how he has had to digest the fact that it seemed so close to some big prize and was very disappointing that it didn't get there. I can understand why Davy and the others had to turn their back on it; otherwise you would live with some sense of injustice, which doesn't do any of us any good. They were on Swamplands but Alan wasn't the guy who could negotiate through that sort of more hardcore business world either.

ALLAN CAMPBELL: The story of Swamplands can be traced from the logo at Postcard, which is a little pussy cat banging a drum. At Swamplands, the pussy has become a big cat, a panther, and I think Alan inevitably realised that he had to grow up a bit and get muscle and do a deal with the devil, which in this case was London Records. Success was the name of the game for Alan — it's all very well having critically raved-over independent singles but you know people wanted to get into the top 10. I remember he had a dentist chair in the Swamplands office (which was an office within London Records), that you could pump up and down. I remember Alan once being quoted as saying 'We can pump you up like that, and we can let you down the minute we want to.' That was him being manipulative, but good luck to him because he signed acts that weren't necessarily always commercial. James King was a phenomenal artist, fantastic, but no other major would have signed James King. It was great that Alan took some of these artists onto what was effectively a major label. Alan also signed Davy Henderson's post-Fire Engines group Win to Swamplands. Davy had lots of ideas post-Fire Engines and was working with Bob Last, which helped generate ideas too. Win were a bit too far ahead of their time, with lots of good ideas.

GEOFF TRAVIS: Paul Quinn had a lovely voice and was a really talented singer, but perhaps didn't have the songs. I don't know if Alan recognised that or not, really. Also, to have American hit records and to go through all of that is a big strain. It's a big, big job, a huge ask, but the Human League and Scritti, they had the talent to do that, and they pulled it off, Bob Last did that. In terms of being a manager in rock 'n' roll history, that's a pretty amazing feat but maybe Bob was just a better communicator. Alan Horne was a more troubled, internal character, who wasn't really able to have the same empathy that drew people to his cause.

BILLY SLOAN: Swamplands promised a lot and the vibe coming back from London Records about the label was really strong as [Alan Horne] was making some inspired, Postcard-related signings. Horne had the basis of something really great at Swamplands, but then he missed an open goal with the opportunities he had. He had to start dealing with major record company people that he didn't like, and who didn't like him, viewing Horne as a necessary evil they had to put up with in order to get to sign the talent he was bringing into Swamplands. It was a great idea, Alan Horne working with major-label finance, but it didn't really happen. *The Old Grey Whistle Test* television programme on BBC asked me to interview Alan for a feature on Swamplands, their idea being to fly me down to London to interview the former Postcard guru about his new label. I interviewed Alan on location where he was doing a video for a song Edwyn had written for Paul Quinn as a Swamplands single, 'Ain't That Always the Way'. It was being filmed in a very ornate old Regency-style hotel in London near Buckingham Palace. So we spent a day there doing interviews with Alan, Edwyn and Paul for the *Whistle Test* feature about the making of the video. These extras were all walking around the ballroom while Paul mimed his singing, and in the background with his arms folded like Brain Epstein was Alan Horne. It was going to be a big television promotion was Paul's single and Swamplands, and then true to form at the eleventh hour, Alan pulled the plug because he didn't like the video. *Whistle Test* ran the item anyway, glibly noting that here was another Alan Horne record that you were never going to hear or be able to buy. James King recorded, with John Cale producing, but again these didn't come out – it really was the beginning of the end for Swamplands before it even got started. Swamplands launched like a rocket on Fireworks Night, then plummeted rapidly to earth.

Swamplands was a short-lived project that promised much but didn't deliver commercially. The artistic merits of the label are overlooked; some great records were released, but ultimately it felt destined to fail on the commercial terms it was set up under. London Records wanted hits and Alan Horne's long-stated desire to interact with the charts did not happen. Ironically the independent-label movement he was instrumental in establishing with Postcard had now delivered the chart success he craved. Horne had derided Rough Trade and their distribution for not being able to deliver Postcard hits for him, but they were now doing that with great success for the Smiths.

ALAN HORNE: Postcard ran for just over a year on an explosive fuel of anger, ego, hysteria and everyday insanity, although it can't have been total chaos because we got a lot done. My concept was, do a label for a short time, make something great and then completely destroy it, before it had time to stagnate. I was a fan of Orange Juice which I never was of any of the other groups. I thought Aztec Camera had some value but I never really liked them that much. Decisions would be based on an emotional response rather than business calculation. We were very young and made it up as we went along, there were no ground rules because we were inventing the rules. It was a pretty perverse vision and it was important not to let anyone's reality impinge — it seemed to me integral to maintain an almost fascist approach. So anyway, it was an instant success, Knickerbocker Glories every day, but with the sugar came pressure and those awful feelings of responsibility. Then the opportunists arrive, you get these people like Lloyd Cole who come along saying, 'What can we steal, what can we nick, what can we use?' That always happens. Little Richard turns into Cliff Richard.

GEOFF TRAVIS: Bob Last wasn't particularly interested in being the star himself. I think he worked his magic behind the scenes, but it was more like a collective enterprise, and it was about the art, and the artifice, and the packaging and the marketing. I don't know whether Alan Horne was interested in making albums with his artists. Maybe it was just a sort of phase Alan and Bob were going through with their labels, and they just wanted to do the small things, and that was satisfying enough for them. It was more about the action, and the imprint, and the art of it, rather than supporting musicians' careers and creating a livelihood for them.

The Scottish independent pop underground movement as seen through the prism of the London media was the story of Bob Last and Alan Horne. However, the massive contributions made by Hilary Morrison and Edwyn Collins are unheralded and should be given due prominence for their contribution at Fast Product and Postcard. The cognoscenti recognised the labels were under the direction of Bob and Hilary, or Alan and Edwyn, but the roles played by Rab King, Davy Henderson, James Oliva, Jo Callis, Malcolm Ross, Steven Daly, David McClymont and James Kirk (among others) in fermenting this short-lived pop pop-art explosion are largely overlooked by media and public alike. That short period in the late seventies and early eighties when youth, intelligence and ambition all coalesced, spurred on by the possibilities of punk and beyond, was as fleeting a moment as punk itself. Fast Product and Postcard coexisted and coincided with a confidence in being Scottish: literature, art, cinema, theatre and dance came to the fore without apologising for being Scottish. The influence exerted by these pioneers would resonate through the years and regenerate regularly; it was the first time the London media saw fit to leave the confines of their world and jump on a plane to Edinburgh and Glasgow.

BOB LAST: There was a lot of debate about if you should, as it were, sell out to major labels, which I never saw as a sell-out, hence I actively helped our bands go and sign up to major labels. I didn't have any idea that I was a manager in the conventional sense; I have no real idea where my ability to interact and edit other people's creativity came from. It's certainly not in my upbringing — I was brought up to be a scientist — so I just don't know where that came from, although I sometimes think there's a large number of people in the music business who came through architecture. I think with the architecture course, even though I dropped out, you learned how to work with creativity alongside real-world limitations at a very concrete level, so maybe there was something to do with that. You learned that you had to analyse the routes forward, so maybe some of that skill set was why I was able to plunge in.

Fast Product was a kind of art project that happened to use the appearance of a label, but it was an art project that everyone involved with the label was part of, albeit I might have brought a certain focus. At Fast I was not good at all dealing with the networking, and Hilary did a lot of work keeping an international network, through that whole fanzine world and fax world. There was a shitload of interesting music going on, and we made some perverse choices, which people found interesting. So that's the core difference, and that was always the driver of the project. At the time it was all very visceral — we were young and it was intense. The reason it didn't just become some stupid art thing was because it was also combined with the visceral enjoyment of the noise — you know, turn it up loud. Fast Product caused a certain outrage, the whole point of it was about being intense and being fast, so if you've not caught up it's your problem. So it was a provocation, everything we did was a combination of provocation, strategy and expedience.

ALAN HORNE: When we were starting out with Postcard I determined early on that we wouldn't go cap in hand to the London multinationals. What Orange Juice were doing was way ahead of London or anywhere else in the world at that time. The ambition of Postcard was to do it, to put out the singles by Orange Juice and see how far we could take it and then stop it. Postcard was not a reflection of Glasgow in 1980, it was a reflection of me. We literally dragged the London media up to Glasgow, and that had never been done before, so we turned the whole thing around. When you go out to open up a door that has been shut in your face then I think you have to be tough, and I think that was construed as me being difficult, arrogant, obnoxious. In fact I think we were all very vulnerable and our arrogance was probably our armoured plating at the time, but we were also kicking against this Scottish inferiority complex that suffocates us all in Scotland. We went out there with Postcard and said art is what matters, don't sell your soul.

(iii)

Bob Last/Hilary Morrison (Fast Product/pop:aural)

DAVY HENDERSON: Bob and Hilary, they were creative partners. I know the things that were getting made in the Fast flat and she was always in that house when they were getting made — they were collaborators, absolutely 100 per cent. I think there was loads of information around, staying up all night watching the Open University, that was good fun. Fast and Bob was similar to Warhol in that we were investigating our influences, like Iggy, then the Velvets' connection to Warhol. The Factory information was available and you could find that, it was just our investigative nature. Bob and Hilary created an environment that followed on from punk; it was autodidactic, it was anti-ignorance, that was the message — it was respect for people and respect for information and find out what you are.

RUSSELL BURN: Bob Last was always coming up with something new; rather than just continuing with more Fast Product tracks, he would change. Bob liked to freshen things up, which is what he did when he started pop:aural.

MURRAY SLADE: I didn't know Bob Last that well as a person but he seemed likeable enough and always seemed driven and could produce good artwork. Bob had some kind of angle which we liked, but as I say, as a person I didn't get to know him that well. I don't think anybody did, actually. I would say pop:aural was a vehicle for him to produce packaging designs, and there's nothing wrong with that, but I wasn't particularly interested in any of that. As long as our records looked good that was fine for me.

GRAHAM MAIN: We'd signed a contract with Bob before we recorded *Lubricate* and it was a poor deal for us, we're still tied in after forty years with no evidence of what the contract dealt with! We were on the dole and thought the fees for a lawyer to read and explain the contract's small print would cost hundreds of pounds so we decided to sign without legal advice. And anyway, Bob was a pal — he wouldn't shaft us. You can befriend a carnivorous animal but it will always see you as food! Bob was a business, man!

ANGUS GROOVY: I had a lot of respect for both Bob and Hilary and still do. I'm sure the impact of Fast was much greater than it seemed at the time. I think the aesthetic worked pretty well to communicate the ethos of the label. I believe it was aiming to go beyond a punk DIY philosophy towards disrupting the way the music industry worked. That style of cut-up collage of advertising and glossy-magazine lifestyle content communicated pretty well the ethos of the label, which I took to be 'this is commercial product, but we don't need big-label A & R or marketing to produce it'. The artwork rarely portrayed the bands at all, let alone any sexualised imagery of them. There was a feminist element to the aesthetic. That came from Hilary, and yes that has been overlooked, ironically. I think Bob had quite limited empathy for the musicians or understanding of what they wanted to do. He could be quite contemptuous of any artistic ambitions on their part. He was an architect by training, and by nature I think, and a skilled entrepreneur. There were others involved in Fast who made it work, especially Simon Best and James Oliva, as well as Hilary. I think Bob may also have been influenced by his acquaintance with Richard Branson. I'm not sure if that encouraged him to be more manipulative, or maybe 'interventionist' is a better word, in the creative careers of the musicians he worked with. I'm not entirely sure that this worked out as well for the Fire Engines as it might have done otherwise. But, on the whole, Fast Product helped make my life an adventure for a while, as it did for many others, and I'm hugely thankful for it.

FRASER SUTHERLAND: I know Bob was of the view that Fire Engines couldn't continue to do these short punchy live sets for much longer before people got bored, but I think he was wrong to bring about their demise. I was with them at the gig in Newcastle which turned out to be their last show, and it was brilliant — the best I'd seen them. I think if they'd been given the space to develop they could have offered much more. Aside from that, the worst thing for me was that they were first and foremost a bunch of mates, before they'd even formed a band, sharing flats and living in each other's pockets. It was a pretty shabby thing for Bob to do I think, to split them up like that just to further a plan.

TOM CANNAVAN: pop:aural had suggested a few things for Restricted Code, but didn't feel totally comfortable with what was happening. We'd always been so quietly confident and assured, but for the first time we were not running on instinct. Instead, we were struggling to know exactly where we were heading, and what we had to do to take the next step in commercial, rather than critical, success. We were living in an all-consuming, intense bubble.

FRANK QUADRELLI: Perhaps there was more of a feeling that we had to get it right to impress Bob Last. That had a stronger effect than we would ever have imagined it could have as little as a year previously, when pop:aural had signed us. Hilary and Bob took Tom and I to one of the swankier tailors in Edinburgh to buy suits that we would never have been able to afford otherwise. We might not have felt like a young Billy Fury or Tommy Steele with impresario Larry Parnes moulding us — we were too streetwise for that — but there was an element of that.

KENNY BLYTHE: As time went by I got the impression Bob was only interested in the songwriters and that he saw the rest of the band as expendable. He tried to change the image to a funk model and bought Tom and Frank suits and arranged for the photo shoot with the huge ghetto blaster that was used as flyers for the tour with the Fire Engines. I am sure he employed the same strategy with the Human League and was instrumental in breaking that band in two. Would the League have been so successful if they had stuck with the original line-up? Personally I think they would have made more interesting and less commercial music, but from a financial point of view Bob made the correct decision. Regarding the Restricted Code recordings, Bob Last insisted on the recording being mixed to sound best on a transistor radio. I found this rather bemusing given that most people had a decent home sound system and the likelihood was that the single would only be played on the John

Peel show. I am sure that Bob had a vision of it being played to the masses on daytime radio – how wrong he was!

STEPHEN LIRONI: I worked for Fast Product, which was useful for me as Restricted Code were touring and recording John Peel sessions for BBC Radio 1 in London. Being part of Fast Product and that scene was very informative for me; Bob had ideas, he had the Fast ethos, he was great at coming up with concepts. He didn't always come up with a good record but he made a great product, and it was Fast. Confusion is sometimes useful.

GEOFF TRAVIS: Fast Product was exciting. Hilary and Bob were doing exactly the kind of thing that Rough Trade wanted to encourage. Hilary was the first person we met from Fast Product, but she probably left Rough Trade disgruntled and went back to report what a bunch of wankers those people in London were when we didn't respond positively to the first Fast release by the Mekons. But we reached an accord and a distribution deal. Bob was slightly different. I mean, I think Bob was less passionate about music, and it was about ideas and perhaps his medium was really film. He did a brilliant job as a manager and with the label, but I don't remember talking to Bob about music that much, so I think he was more of an ideas man. I respected what [he] and Hilary were doing, although I didn't think it was any huge, big deal, to be honest with you. I mean, all that talk of situationism and interventionism, and changing the beast from within – I didn't really believe in it all that much. You know, I think the ideology and the sociology of music is much less interesting than the actual music and whether it's any good or not. Fast Product mattered because the Human League single and the Gang of Four *Damaged Goods* EP were two of the best records of the era. To me, that's the way I think about it, and it also galvanised the fact that you could come from Leeds, and you could come from Sheffield.

You didn't need to come from London. That was important — to make something that was world class.

ALLAN CAMPBELL: Bob Last was a really important figure, a giant in that late-seventies/early-eighties period. He was a conceptualist and was doing all these things with posters and artwork about consumerism and how we're all consumers. The kind of stuff that's absolutely accepted nowadays and isn't even thought twice about, but then it seemed quite unusual. He put out the *Earcom* compilations on Fast Product, which contained unreleased recordings by Joy Division, and gave Edinburgh's musicians a feeling that they were connected to a greater outside musical world. Bob was a mover and shaker and, you know, maybe if you got your head down and worked at it you could do some interesting things musically in the way that he had. Fire Engines very much got involved in that when they worked with Fast Product and Bob, I think sometimes to their detriment. Bob's concepts sometimes slightly dwarfed the band later on, but again, there was a real ferment of ideas and Bob was absolutely essential in all that.

(iv)

Alan Horne (Postcard/Swamplands)

EDWYN COLLINS: Alan's always been very perverse — he loves winding people up to get a reaction. He's never been accurately portrayed by the press, he's just a total eccentric who is very clever and thinks about things in a detached way. He's not an intellectual, he's just got a great insight. The idea of Scottishness is very appealing; we knew that we were the brightest people around, not in an intellectual sense, but we were really shining. We felt that nobody else could touch us, and that was largely down to Alan's incredible arrogance. When we came along we made a massive impact, by default, because Orange Juice and Postcard was such a contrast to what had gone immediately before. Because it was so strong it was widely copied, but I think a lot of what has followed in our wake is diluted Orange Juice, if you'll pardon the pun.

PAUL HAIG: Alan Horne had an opinion about everything, but I think he was prepared to keep putting out our records if they were going to be well received. I think he wanted Postcard to be like Motown, with big choruses and production, but we were certainly an antidote to the glossier side of things. Josef K were given a free rein by Postcard to do whatever we wanted to do. The only time he had a really strong opinion was about 'Chance Meeting', which he really believed could be turned into a commercial song – that is the only time I really remember him being involved in recording decisions.

MALCOLM ROSS: Alan Horne was a kind of larger-than-life character that used to hang around with Orange Juice. My first impression of Alan was he was kind of like girls at school who sort of fancied you but they really didn't want you to know that they did, and their way of communicating with you would be to insult you constantly and take the piss. So that was kind of what Alan was like – he could be very rude sometimes and he could be very funny, he was very witty, and you didn't really want to disagree with Alan. He was a strong character with a strong personality, and for a while it worked really well for Postcard Records – he really got people to sit up and take notice, though I suppose he did have a good product. Postcard finished really when Orange Juice signed to Polydor.

ROBERT FORSTER: Alan Horne was very intelligent and very sharp. Prone to making outrageous statements and then giggling on them. Bands in Brisbane didn't have managers, the scene was too small and disorganised and away from the world. So for a young band like Orange Juice to have a manager and label person was quite unusual for Grant and I. But then Alan was in no way a traditional person in those roles. He was very much like Orange Juice in personality and musical taste. More like a fifth member of the band. He was very generous to Grant and I and we liked him immensely. Memories of the Go-Betweens' period in Glasgow would be Alan telling me to just write 'classics'; Edwyn in long, very funny anecdotes being able to impersonate every member of Orange Juice; and Alan, leaving Grant and I laughing through tears. Creedence Clearwater Revival taken seriously. The London music scene despised. Label meetings in tea shops, where we were the only people under seventy. Grant and I had to sharpen up — we'd seen greatness, got very close to it, lived with it, hung out with it, and now we had to carry on and be great ourselves. Which took some time, but we got there.

RODDY FRAME: I owe Alan Horne a huge debt. He imbued me with confidence and a healthy cynicism — I picked up some of his contrariness. When I was thirteen I'd read NME from cover to cover. Alan was like my Andy Warhol and Julie Burchill rolled into one. He was very cynical, very stylish. Postcard was the perfect apprenticeship. We were seen as a bit gauche because we were very working class. I was still learning. I wore my influences on my sleeve.

CAMPBELL OWENS: Alan Horne was the Andy Warhol of the west end of Glasgow. Alan was one of these guys that is really focused. I wouldn't say Alan was my friend, I am a bit more neutral about it. I can see why people got rubbed up the wrong way by Alan, he's that kind of a personality. He can be a wee bit arrogant and his manners are a bit lacking. But at the same time he's very intelligent, fierce energy, somebody who makes things happen. I found him very condescending and dismissive of musicians, that kind of attitude that believes it's not the musicians that do great things, it's the people behind the scenes that manipulate musicians, people like him, like Warhol. He didn't give musicians the credit they deserved, he thought that they were just 'dumb fucks' but I don't know if he extended that attitude to Edwyn and Roddy. Alan's a very complicated chap, he's certainly not the easiest person to get on with. During the Aztec Camera period on Postcard you felt like punching his lights out. I don't know what really drove Alan, I don't know what his agenda was. He did a lot of things I didn't approve of, how he dealt with money for example — not everybody is happy with his dealings. Aztec Camera used to meet up often in Equi, an Italian café in Glasgow, and we'd sit there without tuppence to rub together watching Alan tuck into a big ice cream. He would never ask us, 'Can I get you something?' He had more money than us, but he would never do that. We used to go on tour and Alan would be our tour manager — he would be driving the bus in more ways than one. He'd be driving the transit van at 100 miles an hour up and down the M6, terrifying — out of his head on speed and madness.

ROBERT HODGENS: My main memory of Postcard was walking around Glasgow during the day, walking down to Paddy's Market, walking to 185 West Princes Street, to Equi's, then in the evening it would be walking to the Rock Garden and the Rogano. When the singles by Orange Juice and Josef K came out in August 1980, that's when I really became an acolyte of the Postcard scene. The people who lived in the flat were Alan, Brian Superstar from the Pastels and Krysia who did a lot of the artwork for Postcard. Brian was like the voice of reason in the flat, he was so mocking. When you went to see Alan it was like going to see the queen, but Brian would debunk and mock Alan with ruthless sarcasm, which Alan couldn't handle at all. Edwyn would be in 185 a lot, and he started calling me Bobby Bluebell after Joey Ramone. I was in a band because of Edwyn — he used to teach me guitar chords and was very encouraging. It was a bit hurtful when the Bluebells started getting media attention and Edwyn would sometimes slag us off in the press. I remember hearing 'Dying Day' just after he had written the song — I was so impressed with that song. The Bluebells didn't try to sound like Orange Juice, but Edwyn went through a phase of slagging groups off in the music papers — Haircut 100, Altered Images, Jazzateers, Josef K, Aztec Camera — everyone was getting it. I think because all the other groups were doing well, he went through this phase. One day Alan would tell you to fuck off then the next day he was on the phone apologising and asking you to come back round to the 185 flat or to go shopping down Paddy's Market. We'd often go to cafés or the Postcard flat; my memory is your sides would be splitting, it was a great laugh, really funny, then other times it would be so argumentative it would be really horrific. Alan would play music non-stop in 185 but he'd play the same record all day — it could be 'Do You Believe in Magic' all day or a northern soul record on repeat the next day. Alan was generally very kind to us and was always encouraging — he used to drive us around to gigs. Even when Alan was being really critical and tough with the Bluebells, you could learn from his comments.

KEN MCCLUSKEY: When we first met Alan Horne, I thought he was a funny guy, quite arch, and his humour was quite cynical. When we were first in the Postcard flat with the Bluebells, Alan asked us, 'Which part of Easterhouse are you neds from?' He was a really humorous, well-read young man, great fun to hang around with. Alan definitely modelled himself as an Andy Warhol figure, but he had great ideas, as did the guys from Orange Juice, such as not playing pubs but playing cafés and restaurants like the Spaghetti Factory, which is where Clare Grogan worked. We thought Alan Horne was peculiar and funny in a sarcastic way but always entertaining.

RUSSELL IRVINE: I liked Alan and I think in reality he was actually very fond of us. I think we were probably a refreshing break from the high-stake sarcasm of the Postcard crowd. He joked that we were a bunch of neds but I think he enjoyed being with us, was quite excited by the obvious growing interest in us in the press and record companies. I remember we got into a potentially violent altercation on our way out of Edinburgh one night (Alan was getting a lift back to Glasgow with us) when we all jumped out of the van to confront a gang of guys in a car and Alan jumped out with us. 'Now that *was* fun,' he said when we got back into the van, genuinely excited. He definitely was an Andy Warhol character, the joke being that he already had his Velvet Underground in Orange Juice, so we were his Monkees. That was cool with me, I loved the Monkees.

KEITH BAND: To me, Postcard is really just Orange Juice. Seeing them for the first time at the Bungalow was the equivalent of the Velvets at the Dom, or the Pistols at the Free Trade Hall. I think Alan thought that we were more malleable than the other Postcard groups, so he could have more influence over the Jazzateers' sound than he could with Orange Juice or Aztec Camera. He did think of himself as a Svengali — the missing link between Larry Parnes and Simon Cowell. There's no doubt he was good at getting display press, but he was too fickle and contrary, he tended to piss too many people around. Maybe he realised the more stuff he released, the more the Postcard legend would be diminished.

IAN BURGOYNE: I was never a big fan of Postcard. Horne was a terrible manager — really, really terrible — but he was a creative guy. Glasgow during the early 1980s was like the stone age, so you have to admire the fact that he managed to create something kind of remarkable in that environment.

JAMES KING: I'd often meet Alan for a cup of tea and he'd play me demo tapes by Aztec Camera or whoever. I always got on well with Alan, usually at the Postcard flat as he wasn't the kind of person that would go out drinking in pubs. You'd bump into Alan in the street, he'd always have gossip about who was leaving Orange Juice that week or who'd been thrown out; I remember meeting him at Charing Cross when he told me James and Steven had been tossed out of Orange Juice, which really surprised me. Once Edwyn moved to London after Orange Juice were signed to Polydor, Edwyn had helped Alan get his foot in the door with London Records, who gave Alan money and an office within London Records. However, if you look at any Swamplands press from that period it's not so much about the artists, the story is Alan Horne — the bands were secondary and really it should have been the other way about. Alan made the mistake of making himself too available to the media. Paul Quinn had a good thing going with Bourgie Bourgie, they were recording their debut album in Bavaria as a priority signing for a major label, MCA, but Alan seemed to have a lot of influence over Paul. There were legal issues when Paul left Bourgie Bourgie in the middle of them recording an album, MCA were not happy and were trying to block Paul signing to Swamplands, and I can see why MCA were quite miffed. If Alan had butted out and stopped whispering things in Paul's ear and devoted more time to the bands on Swamplands, I think it would have been better for both of them. Davy Henderson felt the same thing was happening with Win and Swamplands — everything was all about Paul with Alan. Paul Quinn was a good singer, but he wasn't a songwriter, he only sang songs Edwyn had written or cover versions. He sang on a track with Vince Clark, and it is the only release by Vince Clark that hasn't been a hit. I think Paul could have had a good career if he'd continued with Bourgie Bourgie and had a different manager, and the irony is Paul couldn't actually sign to Swamplands because of the legal issues with MCA. Alan Horne is a great ideas man who thinks up fabulous ideas, for example he had this movie concept he spent a lot of time on, *The Punk Rock Hotel*, but nothing was filmed. With the Lone Wolves, we had our own problems. We found out we were getting dropped by Swamplands at a party — Alan didn't have the manners or decency to actually tell us. A few months after being dropped the money started drying up for us, and that's really why the Lone Wolves split up.

GEOFF TRAVIS: Alan Horne was a very difficult character. As you grow older, you realise that people hide their insecurities behind a kind of attack-dog facade, and that was really what Alan was like, with a bit of charm, but certainly more aggressive than we were used to dealing with at Rough Trade on a daily basis when we were trying to help people. What makes a great group is not really the manager. A manager can be hugely helpful, but the musicians are really the most important people in that equation. Maybe Alan felt he was more important than the musicians.

DAVID HENDERSON: In retrospect it sometimes appears as if Postcard was like a dysfunctional family; however, I thought Alan Horne was doing a good job positioning and connecting people.

CAESAR: When I left Altered Images to start the Wake and we decamped to Manchester in 1982 to find our home from home at

Factory, we approached the nascent Postcard label with our first demo. Alan was genuine, considerate and encouraging about our demo, which was really quite bad, although we didn't think so at the time. In any case, it was completely unsuited to Postcard. But he made me feel OK about it by emphasising the positive elements and he didn't need to do that. It's no more than an impression but I think he's probably a very kind person, with incredible loyalty, and, as time has shown, an integrity and consistency of vision that's rare. There was a certain warmth to his personality if you could see beyond the slightly brittle surface.

ALLAN CAMPBELL: Alan Horne was very cheeky, egocentric, naughty, inspired, fuelled by negative punk energy. You know you define yourself partly by what you don't want to be and what you hate, so you make a point of rubbing people up the wrong way. Alan would define himself against other people, but he had great ideas and was a big part of Postcard, though obviously a big part of Postcard was Edwyn (which I think is slightly understated). You've got to remember with Alan and Josef K they were defining themselves against other bands, fakers and bad models, therefore they had to have that self-belief that they are the real thing. Postcard, Orange Juice and Josef K defined themselves as not just another band with a new haircut who are playing some rubbish of a different style than the previous month, which I think was healthy. That defined Horne, it defined Postcard. I liked him, but could you always trust him? Perhaps; perhaps not. I think Alan did see himself as the Scottish Andy Warhol. I mean you can see it with the Warhol spectacles, the blond hair. There's the famous picture on the Velvet Underground album cover of Warhol holding the tambourine and looking through it — there's a picture somewhere in the archive of Alan doing that, the pop moment is something Alan aspired to. The influence of Postcard could be seen in countless Glasgow bands that took Postcard's ideas and made [them] very commercially successful, but that's often the way, you know — the pioneers are never quite rewarded financially.

BILLY SLOAN: The whole Postcard Records thing was great for singles by Orange Juice, Josef K, the Go-Betweens and Aztec Camera, but Postcard was also great for Alan Horne. Horne was like a Scottish pop Svengali combination of Phil Spector, Brian Epstein, Colonel Tom Parker and, most of all, a manipulator like Malcolm McLaren. After Postcard had disintegrated, with Orange Juice going to Polydor and Aztec Camera, the Go-Betweens and Jazzateers all going to Rough Trade, all the major record companies were trying to woo Horne into running label for them, and eventually London Records waved a blank chequebook in front of Alan and he started Swamplands. So for the first time in his life Alan had a bag of money and a blank canvas, which meant he could do proper recording, promotion and marketing. I personally think he was better suited to working Postcard on an ad hoc, DIY, cottage-industry basis, where although there was no money it was creatively stronger.

PAUL MORLEY: Every label needs someone like Alan Horne to do the promotion, the selling, the hype, the persuasion, the amplification, someone who was a philosopher/huckster/entrepreneur/circus barker. Alan Horne was always there when Postcard groups came into view, and he understood a label needed a sound, whether that was via distressed guitars or vocals. You could hear the influences on Postcard, from the Velvet Underground through Buzzcocks and *Spiral Scratch* and sounds that set things on fire in terms of what you can do. Alan Horne had very much a bullying element; I remember him being very confident and convinced in a missionary and evangelical manner. There was a sense that Postcard was Alan Horne. I loved the personality of Postcard, it came out of its own world from the sleeves, the label, the design — everything about it could only have been Postcard. It was a huge influence on me, and these labels had a spokesperson — with Postcard it was Alan Horne, with Factory it was Tony Wilson, with Fast it was Bob Last. These labels had figureheads who were shaping the labels. The combination of Postcard receiving instant, enthusiastic and loving praise from the music press and radio support from John Peel, combined with Postcard's output, repositioned the idea of Scotland in my head. The Sound of Young Scotland, that whole sloganeering thing, created a new transfiguration. Although the activity of Postcard was encapsulated in a short time frame, I think that was somehow true to the spirit of pop. The idea of Postcard happening, making a statement, then disintegrating, perversely had a weird kind of glorious quality, an accelerated energy that couldn't sustain itself. Postcard and Fast Product were pioneers of the true spirit of what an independent label could represent.

Text Permissions

We would like to thank the following for kindly granting permission to quote from their text:

Steven Daly (liner notes) — *The Glasgow School* (Orange Juice compilation released on Domino in 2005).

Robert Hodgens — *Ten Commandments* fanzine.

Stephen Pastel and Robert Hodgens — *Yesterday Was Another Day* fanzine.

Innes Reekie — *State of Play* fanzine.

Fraser Sutherland — 'Permission to Disobey: The Emergence of DIY Culture in the Post-Punk Era, 1978 – 1982' (University of Birmingham MA thesis, 2016).

The majority of quotes featured in *Hungry Beat* are from interviews conducted with the following individuals for Grant McPhee's documentary film, *Big Gold Dream*, about the Fast Product and Postcard Records period:

Keith Band; Michael Barclay; Jill Bryson; Ian Burgoyne; Russell Burn; Tam Dean Burn; Jo Callis; Allan Campbell; Dave Carson; Grace Fairley; Fay Fife; Vic Godard; Alison Gourlay; Angus Groovy (Whyte); Paul Haig; David Henderson; Davy Henderson; Robert Hodgens; Peter Hook; James King; Robert King; Jon Langford; Bob Last; Stephen Lironi; John Mackie; Ken McCluskey; Rose McDowell; Alan McGee; Sandy McLean; Paul Morley; Hilary Morrison; Campbell Owens; Alan Rankine; Innes Reekie; Paul Research; Malcolm Ross; Gareth Sager; Grahame Skinner; Murray Slade; Billy Sloan; Mark Stewart; Brian Superstar (Taylor); Ronnie Torrance; Mark White.

Douglas MacIntyre conducted interviews with the following:

Colin Auld; Keith Band; Kenny Blythe; Jacquie Bradley; Ian Burgoyne; Caesar (Gerard McInulty); Tom Cannavan; Malcolm Fisher; Robert Forster; Clare Grogan; Robert Hodgens; Russell Irvine; Stefan Kassel; James Locke; Ewan MacLennan; Graham Main; Ken McCluskey; Gerri McLaughlin; Campbell Owens; Stephen Pastel (McRobbie); Frank Quadrelli; Fraser Sutherland.

Neil Cooper interviewed Geoff Travis for the book. He also had conversations with Bob Last and Hilary Morrison for further background information on Fast Product/pop:aural.

Sources

This is a selected list of publications used as source material. It does not aim to detail every source used to corroborate factual information or provide background material. Quotes attributed to Simon Best, Edwyn Collins, Ian Curtis, Roddy Frame, Alan Horne, Jon King, Phil Oakey, Paul Quinn and David Weddell are from the following sources:

NME, *Sounds*, *Melody Maker*, the *Face*, *Uncut*, the *Quietus*, *The Old Grey Whistle Test* (BBC Television), *Out There* (Scottish Television), Gary Crowley interview (Scottish Television), *Black Hit of Space*, *Ten Commandments*, the *List*, *Did Not Chart*, *Dig*, BBC Radio Blackburn.

Simon Best:
  Black Hit of Space

Edwyn Collins:
  NME
  The Old Grey Whistle Test
  Ten Commandments
  Uncut

Ian Curtis:
  BBC Radio Blackburn

Roddy Frame:
  Sounds
  The *Quietus*

Alan Horne:

NME

Sounds

Melody Maker

Ten Commandments

The Old Grey Whistle Test

Out There (Scottish Television)

Gary Crowley interview (Scottish Television)

The *List*

Did Not Chart

The *Face*

Extracts from 'A Jazzateers Biography of Sorts' (courtesy of Ian Burgoyne Archive)

Jon King:
Dig

Phil Oakey:
Black Hit of Space

Paul Quinn:
NME
Sounds
Melody Maker
The Old Grey Whistle Test

David Weddell:
Sounds
Melody Maker

Reading List

The music press of the period provided a rich research resource (especially Paul Morley and Dave McCullough), as did magazines from the era such as *ZigZag* and the *Face*. Internet research related to the post-punk period was also useful, though there are too many sites to list here. Notable blogs and social media sites that have covered Scottish post-punk include: Scottish Post-Punk, For Malcontents Only, Penny Black and Is This Music?, among others.

The following books have been inspirational over the years:

Viv Albertine, *Clothes Clothes Clothes, Music Music Music, Boys Boys Boys Boys* (London: Faber & Faber, 2014)

Mike Barnes, *Captain Beefheart: The Biography* (London: Quartet Books, 2000)

Michael Bracewell, *Re-make/Re-model* (London: Faber & Faber, 2007)

David Cavanagh, *The Creation Records Story: My Magpie Eyes Are Hungry for the Prize* (London: Virgin Books, 2000)

Julian Cope, *Head On* (London: Thorsons, 1999)

Robert Forster, *Grant and I* (London: Omnibus Press, 2017)

Richard Hell, *I Dreamed I Was a Very Clean Tramp* (New York: HarperCollins, 2013)

Clinton Heylin, *From the Velvets to the Voidoids* (Chicago: A Cappella Books, 2005)

Richard King, *How Soon Is Now? The Madmen and Mavericks Who Made Independent Music 1975–2005* (London: Faber & Faber, 2012)

READING LIST

Simon Reynolds, *Rip It Up and Start Again: Postpunk 1978–1984* (London: Faber & Faber, 2005)

Jon Savage, *England's Dreaming* (London: Faber & Faber, 1991)

Neil Taylor, *Document and Eyewitness: An Intimate History of Rough Trade* (London: Orion, 2010)

Thanks

Hungry Beat has been a labour of love that couldn't have happened without input from its cast of thousands. This includes all those interviewed, those who clarified details by phone, email or chance meetings, and those who were part of the original scenes in bands and at the gigs. It is these who inspired the documentary films *Big Gold Dream* and *Teenage Superstars*. *Hungry Beat* wouldn't be here without you.

Thanks to those who gave their time to be interviewed, rewinding on their past lives and all the incident and colour that came with them: Colin Auld; Keith Band; Michael Barclay; Kenny Blythe; Jacquie Bradley; Jill Bryson; Ian Burgoyne; Russell Burn; Tam Dean Burn; Caesar (Gerard McInulty); Jo Callis; Allan Campbell; Tom Cannavan; Dave Carson; Grace Fairley; Fay Fife; Malcolm Fisher; Robert Forster; Vic Godard; Alison Gourlay; Clare Grogan; Angus Groovy (Whyte); Paul Haig; David Henderson; Davy Henderson; Robert Hodgens; Peter Hook; Russell Irvine; Stefan Kassel; James King; Robert King; Jon Langford; Bob Last; Stephen Lironi; James Locke; John Mackie; Ewan MacLennan; Graham Main; Ken McCluskey; Rose McDowell; Alan McGee; Gerri McLaughlin; Sandy McLean; Paul Morley; Hilary Morrison; Campbell Owens; Stephen Pastel (McRobbie); Frank Quadrelli; Alan Rankine; Innes Reekie; Paul Research; Malcolm Ross; Gareth Sager; Grahame Skinner; Murray Slade; Billy Sloan; Mark Stewart; Brian Superstar (Taylor); Fraser Sutherland; Ronnie Torrance; Mark White.

Special thanks to Bob Last, Hilary Morrison and Geoff Travis for taking part in new interviews.

Thanks as well to all those whose input went beyond the call of duty in helping *Hungry Beat* relive its times: Colin Cassells; Zoë Howe; Gavin Fraser; Katy Lironi; Mike O'Connor; James Oliva; Peter Carr at Woodend Films; Dave Carson; Rachael Cloughton and all at Craigmillar Now; Colvin Cruikshank; Graham Dey; Malcolm Dickson, John Farrell and Ken McCluskey at Street Level Photoworks; Concubhar Ó Liatháin; Councillor Rob Munn and Jack Gillon at City of Edinburgh Council; Alistair Cant and Mark Stolarek at Lister Housing Co-operative and History Association; Malcolm Ross; Ben Watson.

Thanks to Vic Godard for chapter titles and inspiration.

Thanks to the photographers who were in the thick of things for allowing us to reproduce their images: Michael Barclay; Simon Clegg; Heather Findlay; Robin Gillanders; Alistair Littlejohn; Hilary Morrison; Carole Moss; Harry Papadopoulos; Paul Research; Peter Tainsh; Angus Whyte.

Thanks as well to those who kicked the whole thing off with *Big Gold Dream* and *Teenage Superstars*, especially Wendy Griffin, Angela Slaven, Erik Sandberg and Innes Reekie for co-producing the films.

Thanks also to Ian Ballantyne and all at Arteus; Rachel Bell; Gaye Bell; Krister Bladh; Natasha Brown; Jim Burns; Tim Cairns; Simon Clegg; Graham Drysdale; Bill Drummond; Douglas Fairgrieve; Bruce Findlay; Vic Galloway; Karen Gardner Dion; Paul Hartman; Tayba Hussain; Mani; Angus McPake; Davie Miller; Martin Parry; Nick Peacock; Bjorn Sandberg; Kle Savage; Patricia-Anne Stirton; Lucy Watt; Helen Whiteley-McPhee; Angus Whyte.

For legals: David Burgess at Reviewed & Cleared; Mark Stafford at Lee & Thompson LLP Solicitors; Katharine Otway at Kenren Media.

Thanks to Lee Brackstone and everyone at White Rabbit for keeping the faith in *Hungry Beat*.

Thanks

Finally, an extra-special thanks to Bob Last, Hilary Morrison and everyone who made Fast Product so vital; and to Edwyn Collins, Alan Horne and everyone who did likewise with Postcard Records of Scotland.

The Hungry Beat goes on.

Douglas MacIntyre, Grant McPhee, Neil Cooper,
February 2022

Index

Illustrations are denoted by the use of *italics*.

A Certain Ratio 100, 388
A Clockwork Orange 79, 85
ABBA 252, 253, 267
ABC 324, 334, 361−2, 395−6, 396
Absolute Records 138, 145, 146, 246
Accessory Records 198, 202, 252−3
Adam and the Ants 145
Adamson, Stuart xiii
Albertine, Viv 44, 162
Altered Images 187−9, *189*, 233−5, 264−5, 333−4
  Orange Juice and 175
  split 377
  Bite 377−8
  'Dead Pop Stars' 235
  'Don't Talk to Me about Love' 354, 378
  'Happy Birthday' 265, 334
  Happy Birthday 264
  Pinky Blue 315, 322
  'See Those Eyes' 315
Alternative TV (ATV) 100−1, 150, 156
Ames, Roger 338
Another Pretty Face, 146
Anti-Nazi League 41, 78−9
April Music label 367, 391
Article 58 190−2, 211, 222−4, *223*, 250, 280, 367
Asheton, Ron 402
Associates 316−18, *316*, 323, 333, 334−5
Au Pairs 127
Auld, Colin *303*, 306, 326−7, 330−1, *383*
Aztec Camera 190−1, 206−11, 254−6, 276−8, 325−8, 340−1, *347*, 350−2, 385−7
  Auld on 327
  Gourlay on 310−11
  Postcard International 302

success of 259
Warner Brothers 368
High Land, Hard Rain 350, 356, 365, 368−9, 380, 386
'Just Like Gold' 215
Knife 387
'Mattress of Wire' 254−6, 277, 301, 350
'Oblivious' 350−1, 368−9, 386
'Pillar to Post' 340, 350
'Somewhere in My Heart' 387

B-52s 63
Backstabbers, Rev Volting and the 134
Baker, Arthur 341
Balfe, Dave 366, 369
Band, David 305−7, 350, 356, 358, 368
Band, Keith 302−7, 309−10, 328−32, 358−61
  Bourgie Bourgie 368, 376, 389−90, *389*
  on Horne 326, 349, 419
  Jazzateers *303*, *383*
  Travis and 351
Barclay, Michael (Mike) 252−3
  Boots for Dancing 182, *183*
  on Fast Product 48, 56
  Thursdays xiv, 79, 88, 106−7, 111−12
Barrie, Douglas 130, *183*
Basczax 106
Bauhaus 162
Beach Boys 303−4, 306
BEF (British Electronic Foundation) 184, 225, 250, 268
Bellis, Pat 368
Bellotte, Pete 308, 326, 328
Best, Simon 61−2, 87−8, 251−2, 267−8

on *Earcom* series 111
Fast Product 221, 411
Fire Engines and 226, 270
on The Human League 56, 94, 99, 104
on Last 116, 119
McLean and 325
The Mekons and 41, 45
Big John 132
Bloomfield, Simon 104
Bluebells, The 187−8, 238−42, 277−8, 311−15, *312*, 337−9, 394−5
  Melody Maker cover 242
  members 306, 380
  singles 242, 345, 354
  Sisters 394
  'Young at Heart' 394, 395
Blythe, Kenny 182, *212*, 213, 282, 412
Boney M. 63
Boon, Richard 190, 233−4, 373
Boots for Dancing xiv, 81, 128, 182−4, *183*
Bourgie Bourgie 360−1, 370, 375−7, 381, 388−91, *389*
  Horne and 333, 335, 345, 349, 358
  'Breaking Point' 389−90
Bovell, Dennis 73, 74, 102, 378, 379, 388
Bower, Paul 58
Bowie, David 11, 62, 75, 131
Bradley, Jacquie 159
Branson, Richard 411
Brierley, John 129
British Electronic Foundation 221, 268
Broudie, Ian 381, 389
Bruce's Records 116−17, 119, 132, 325
Bryson, Jill 168, 369−70, 392−4
  on music scene 133, 157, 374
  Strawberry Switchblade 131, 141, 142, *366*
Buckmaster, Paul 367
Burchill, Julie 38
Burden, Ian 104, 221
Burgoyne, Ian 302−5, 309−10, 330−2, 389−91
  Aztec Camera 351
  Bourgie Bourgie 360−1, 368, 376, 377, *389*
  on Horne and Quinn 349, 420
  Jazzateers *303*, 326, 329, 358, *383*

Burn, Russell 41, 129, 410
  The Dirty Reds 23, *43*, 44, 45, 80, 90
  Fire Engines 91−3, *195*, 201, 272−3, 285
  Win 380, 397
Burn, Tam Dean 15−16, 44−6, 230−1
  Bourgie Bourgie 389
  Carson and 22, 23
  The Dirty Reds 43, 80
  Henderson on 89
  on music 18, 20
  on politics 78
  Ricochet project 362
Buzzcocks 12, 14−15, 165, 174, 191
  Spiral Scratch 11, 233−4, 289
Byrds, The 165, 375

Cabaret Voltaire 58, 70, 96, 130, 388
Caesar (Gerard McInulty) 150, 175, 188−9, *189*, 233−5, 264, 314−15, 421−2
Cale, John 401, 402, 405
Callis, Jo
  Boots for Dancing 182−3, *183*
  The Human League 211, 221, 250−1, 267, 299−300
  on Last 112−13
  The Rezillos 27, 28, 33
Campbell, Allan *320*
  Aztec Camera 190, 255−6, 328
  on bands 224, 231
  on Crépuscule Records 193, 319−20
  on Fire Engines 291−2
  gigs 143, 146, 147−8
  Haig and 260−1, 388
  on Horne 162, 168, 230, 232, 422−3
  interviews 176, 177
  on Josef K 153, 158−9, 206, 243
  on Last 414
  on *The Only Fun in Town* 248
  on Quinn 355
  Rational Records 191, 223, 280, 280−1
  on rivalry 178−9
  on Swamplands 404
Cannavan, Tom 181, *212*, 213−14, 225, 231−2, 281−3, 412
Cargo Records 82, 84
Carson, Dave 16, 44, 129
  Boots for Dancing 130, 182−3, *183*, 184

Index

The Dirty Reds 22−3, *43*, 44, 87
Cartel (distribution network) 114, 115−16, 117, 221−2, 325
Catherall, Joanne 185, 252
CBGB music club 63, 117
CBS/Epic Records 234, 235, 259, 265
Chance, James 91, 92−3, 101
Chapman, Mike 333−4, 354
Charm, Bobby 46
Chic 63, 164, 244
Chilton, Alex 115, 254
Chiswick Records 134
Clark, Bernie 340
Clash, The 75, 133, 150, 259
  influence 115, 209
  White Riot tour 9, 10, 11−12, 13−14, 34
Codex Communications 186, 197, 200−4, 226
Cole, Lloyd 381, 391−2
Collins, Edwyn 134−43, 236−8, 258−9, 261−4, 275−7, 377−9
  and Aztec Camera 191
  on 'Blue Boy' 171, 173
  on Frame 351
  Haig and 401
  Hodgens and 187−8, 418
  on Horne 216, 414−15
  Horne and 131, 148−9, 151, 156−7, 166
  influences 163−4
  interviews 256
  James King and 402, 420−1
  Jazzateers and 325
  on Kitchenware 364
  MacLennan on 224
  NME cover 233, 235
  Orange Juice 122, *123*, *139*, 165, 179, 180, *263*
  on Postcard 175, 220
  Quinn and 391, 405
  Sloan on 244
  on The Smiths 375
  on 'Wan Light' 246
Contortions, James Chance and the 92−3, 101
Cope, Julian 166−7
Copland, Andy 22, 23, *43*, 44
Corrigan, Andy 33, *35*
Costello, Elvis 313−14, 337, 338−9, 356, 386
Craig Marsh, Ian *95*, 185, 225, 250

Cramps, The 56, 57, 63
Creation Records 229
Crépuscule Records 187, 192−3, 204−5, 215, 318−20, 341−2, 387−8
  The Fruit of the Original Sin 274−5, 328
Cure, The 176, 317
Currie, Nick 343−4
Curtis, Ian xii, 73, 97, 108, 167

DAF (Deutsch Amerikanische Freundschaft) 110−11
Daintees 364, 367
Daly, Steven 132, 134−5, 236−7, 238−9, 262−4
  Absolute Records 138, 145, 146
  Aztec Camera 255
  on The Bluebells 315
  Caesar and 189
  Cormorant 367
  drummer 140, 188
  Fun 4 137−8
  The Go-Betweens 158
  Memphis 398, 402
  Orange Juice *123*, 136, 140, 141, 143, 153, 257
  Ross and 145
  sacked 344
  on Subway Sect 155−6
  on 'Wan Light' 245
Damned, The 26, 34, 133
Dancing Pigs xiii, xvi
Davis, Miles 361
Dead Kennedys 102−3, 110, 118
Debord, Guy 10
Del Amitri 349, 367
Delmontes, The xiv, 190, 222, 280−1
Delta 5 34, 87−8, 127
Dempsey, Mike 317
Dexys Midnight Runners 174
Dickens, Rob 386
Dirty Reds, The 15, 20, 22−3, 31, *43*, 44−5, 81, 87, 90
Dr. Feelgood 65
Donegan, Lawrence 240, 306, *312*, 380, 381, 395
Draper, Simon 184
Drinking Electricity 224, 291
Drummond, Bill 73, 366, 369
Dudley, Anne 392
Durutti Column 70, 77

Duval, Michel 192−3, 320, 342, 365
Dylan, Bob 87

Earcom series (Fast Product) 104−12, 126, 148
Echo and the Bunnymen 73, 143, 149
Edmunds, Dave 401
Embassy Club, London 228−9
EMI Music 99, 118
Eno, Brian 19, 200
Erasmus, Alan 100

Factory Records 70, 73, 77, 100, 106−10, 117−21, 291, 363
Fairley, Grace 47, 49, 55, 56, 67, 81, 120, 199
Fall, The 101, 174, 285
Fast Forward 363
Fast Product Records 31−70, 82−8, 94−122, 125−30, 149−50, 197−9, 409−14
  bands and 19, 217, 272−3
  early days 9−11, 15
  McLean and 325
  success of xv, 73, 77, 81, 278, 297−8
Fergusson, Alex 156, 159, 171, 175, 180
Fiction Records 317
Fife, Fay 26, 27−8, *27*, 28, 62−3, 86
Findlay, Bruce xiv, 325
Fire Engines *195*, 197−204, 219−21, 224−31, 269−73, 282−8
  early days 45−7, 50, 81, 87, 89−94
  gigs 186−7, 229, 269, 282
  influence 76, 290−3
  Jones and 342
  Last and 412
  mini album 252−3
  Peel sessions 203, 225, 269−70, 298, 342
  pop:aural label 211, 243
  singles 224, 225, 226−8
  split 283
  'Big Gold Dream' 270−3, 278
  Lubricate Your Living Room 198, 200−4, 228, 248
First Year Plan, The (FAST 11) 118
Fisher, Malcolm 161−2, 274−5, 342−3
  Forster on 180
  The French Impressionists 307, 328, *343*, 356, 365

on The Go-Betweens 170
on Orange Juice 157
Flesh (Fast) 106
Flowers, The 44−5, 51, *105*, 127−30, *128*, 289
  early days 31, 81, 87, 88, 128
  Peel sessions 129−30
  singles 102, 125
  'After Dark' 105, 105−6, 125, 129
Foetus (Jim Thirlwell) 353
Forster, Robert 158, 169−70, 179−80, 416
  Aztec Camera and 357, 380
  The Go-Betweens 154, 161−2, *169*, 387
Frame, Roddy 207−10, 254−6, 385−7
  Aztec Camera 190, 191, 206, 327, *347*
  on *High Land, Hard Rain* 350
  on Horne 416
  on 'Just Like Gold' 215
  Rough Trade and 369, 374
  Warner Brothers 380
French Impressionists, The 274−5, 307, 328, 342−3, *343*, 355−6, 365
Friends Again 367
From Chorley 110
Fry, Martin 58, 324
Fumes fanzine 172, 239
Fun 3 137
Fun 4 137, 145, 146, 154

Gang of Four 34−6, 64−6, *98*
  Fast Records 42, 55, 69−70
  influence 77
  Peel sessions 73
  Travis on 99
  Damaged Goods 64, 69, 99, 413
  Entertainment 118
Garcia, Jerry 269
Gartside, Green 374, 381, 396
Gibson, Glenn 309
Gill, Andy 34, 35, *98*
Go-Betweens, The 161−2, 169−70, *169*, 278, 351−2
  Postcard Records 151, 154, 156, 158
  Rough Trade 179−80, 356−7, 380
  Warner Brothers 387
Godard, Vic 7, 14−15, 75, 86, 154−5, 191
Gourlay, Alison 302, *303*, 305−7, 310−11, 326, 355, 357−8, *383*

Graffiti record shop 132, 159
Grant, James 367
Greenhalgh, Tom 34, *35*
Gregory, Glenn 185, 225, 251
Gretton, Rob 97−8, 100, 107−8
Griffin, Dale 282
Grogan, Clare 175, 188, *189*, 233−4, 265, 316, 419
Groovy, Angus 13−14, 40−1, 85−6, 203−4
  on 'Candyskin' 228
  Codex Communications 197, 200
  on Davy Henderson 17
  on Fast Product 56, 57, 410−11
  Fire Engines 186−7
  orange peel and 120
  Talkovers 46, 49−50, *49*
Gutter Music 223

Haig, Paul 248−50, 259−60, 318−21, 341−4
  Collins and 401
  on Crépuscule Records 193, 387−8
  Horne and 151, 162, 176, 415
  Island Records 342
  Josef K 144−5, 148−9, *152*, 180, 205, 247
  Morley on 246
  on the music press 177−8
  Operation Twilight label 365
  Rhythm of Life 280−1, 318−19, 320, 336, 341, 342, 380
  solo piece 274
Haircut 100 313
Hall, Daryl 376
Hannaway, Frank 252−3
Hannett, Martin 100, 107
Happy Family, The 343−4
Hayward, Martin 370, 373
Head, Michael 364−5
Heartbeat 283, 285, 287, 300−1, 324, 336, 397
Heartbreakers, The 68
Heaven 17 221, 250−1, 278
  Penthouse and Pavement 225, 250, 268
  '(We Don't Need This) Fascist Groove Thang' 203, 225
Hedges, Mike 322, 381, 389, 390
Hell, Richard 48
Hellfire Club 159, 236−7, 242, 275, 305, 313
Henderson, David

The Bluebells and 242, 313
  on The Go-Betweens 159, 161
  Hellfire Club *160*, 236−7
  on Horne 421
  on Orange Juice 257
  on The Pastels 373
  on Strawberry Switchblade 392−3
Henderson, Davy 86−7, 202−3, 292−3
  on 'Candyskin' 226−7, 228
  character 47
  The Dirty Reds 44, 45−6, 80−1, 89
  Fast flat 52
  on Fast Product 55, 409−10
  Fire Engines 9, 91−4, *195*, 200, 270−1
  Heartbeat 300−1, 324
  on *At Home!* 252
  on The Human League 57
  on King 81−2
  Last and 54, 197, 283−5, 287, 291, 298
  The Mekons and 41
  on music 11−12, 16−17, 19
  Peel sessions 20−1
  on The Pop Group 76
  on Postcard 199
  Research and 68
  on Richard Hell 48
  Rough Trade and 112
  on Scars 273
  Slade on 90
  on Subway Sect 155
  Talkovers 49, *49*, 50−1
  Warm Jets 22, 44
  Win 380, 397−9, 403, 404
Henderson, Jaine 159, *160*, 168, 242
Hennebert, Benoît 215, 275
Heyward, Nick 313
Hodgens, Robert 238−40, 276−7, 338−9
  on Altered Images 234
  on Aztec Camera 190, 255
  The Bluebells 242, *312*, 313−14, 337, 394−5
  Fisher and 274
  Horne and 220, 417−18
  on Jazzateers 311
  on music 133
  on Orange Juice 257
  Oxfam Warriors 187−8
  on Superstar 372

Ten Commandments fanzine 156 – 7, 171 – 2, 180, 188, 190, 233
Honoré, Annik 192
Hook, Peter 109 – 9, 120
Horn, Trevor 324
Horne, Alan 173 – 5, 220 – 1, 274 – 8, 397 – 409, 414 – 24
   on Article 58 191 – 2
   and Aztec Camera 190, 207, 255 – 6
   on 'Blue Boy' 172
   Collins and 139
   on Crépuscule Records 193
   Fire Engines and 197 – 8
   on Glasgow scene 133
   on Godard 155
   Hodgens and 188, 220, 239
   interviews 256
   Jazzateers and 383
   Josef K and 175 – 6, 178, 204, 274
   King and 188, 349
   major labels and 361
   on Nu Sonics 135
   Orange Juice manager 136 – 7, 138, 142 – 3, 162, 165 – 6, 238
   Postcard Records xv, 131, 140, 151, 159, 188 – 9, 301 – 3, 307 – 14, 321 – 2, 325 – 32, 335, 337, 340 – 1, 345, 408 – 9
   Quinn and 354, 358, 376
   on radio play 149, 236
   Shores and 230
   Smiths and 375
   Swamplands Records 390 – 1
Horsley, Sebastian 281, 318
Hot Licks (record shop) 15 – 17, 21, 25
Human League, The 56 – 8, 95, 98 – 100, 184 – 6, 265 – 9, 297 – 300
   drum machine 272 – 3
   Peel sessions 62
   split 290
   success of 224 – 5, 250 – 2, 361 – 2
   support acts 182, 217
   tours 103, 336
   'Being Boiled' 56, 58, 59 – 61
   Dare 251, 265 – 8, 290, 324
   The Dignity of Labour 94 – 6
   'Don't You Want Me' 266, 278, 299, 413
   Hysteria 395
   Reproduction 118
   'The Sound of the Crowd' 185, 221
Hurrah! 364, 367

Innes, Andrew 229
Irvine, Russell 240 – 1, 276 – 7, *312*, 314, 338 – 40, 380, 395, 419
Island Records 200, 319, 341 – 2, 380

Jam, The 12, 14
James White and the Blacks 90, 101
Jarman, Derek 401
Jazzateers 240 – 1, 302 – 11, *303*, 321 – 2, 325 – 33, 349 – 51, 357 – 61, *383*
   Lee 329 – 32, 351, 357, 365, 377
   'Wasted' 308 – 10, 311, 322, 325
Jensen, Kid 369
Jock 'n' Roll (BBC) 256, 274
John, Elton 28, 326, 397
John Peel Show xiv, 11, 31, 41, 66, 149, 167, 178, 228, 365 – 6
John Peel's Music on BFBS 149, 172
Johnny and the Self Abusers 134, 137, 159
Johnny Thunders and the Heartbreakers 20, 64, 101
Johnson, Donald 388
Johnson, Martha 323 – 4
Johnston, Bob 352
Jones, Grace 341, 342, 352
Josef K 143 – 54, *152*, 158 – 70, 175 – 80, 245 – 50
   Crépuscule Records 193
   gigs xiv, 131, 193, 292 – 3
   Peel sessions 220
   singles 179, 215
   split 259 – 61, 274, 276
   'Chance Meeting' 138, 143, 145, 146, 245, 246, 415
   The Only Fun in Town 220, 247 – 9
   'Radio Drill Time' 159, 162, 167, 170, 176, 180
   Sorry for Laughing 193, 204 – 5, 280
Joy Division 70, 97 – 8, 106 – 11, 167
   Unknown Pleasures 100, 107, 109
Juniper Beri-Beri fanzine 373, 394

Kassel, Stefan 149, 172, 201 – 2, 261, 308, 357, 359
Kidron, Adam 254, 257, 315, 357
King, James 137 – 8, 398 – 402, *400*
   The Backstabbers 134
   on fanzines 132
   Fun 4 145
   Horne and 131, 402, 420 – 1

Index

Last on 404
Sloan on 405
solo 188
King, Jon 64−5, *98*, 99
King, Robert (Rab) 19−22, 24−6, 56−7, 67−8, 279−80
on bands 220
debut single 43
on Fast Product 53
gigs 78−9, 219
on Last 83, 119
Last on 291
NME cover 217
on Quinn and Horne 349
Scars xiv, 15−16, *71*, 82, 278, 292
on singles 84−5
Talkovers 46, 49
Kingfishers, The 367
Kirk, James 141−2, 262−4, *263*, 363−4
Bryson on 142
Collins and 163
Cormorant 367
'Felicity' 315
McCluskey on 313
Memphis 398, 402
music and 138, 237
Nu Sonics 134
Orange Juice 122, *123*, 136, 158, 160, 171, 245
Strawberry Switchblade 366
Kitchenware 364, 366−7
Klasicki, Krysia 131, 141, 215
Knopfler, Mark 385, 386

Langford, Jon 33, 34−5
Last, Bob xv, 17−18, *29*, 31−62, 82−4, 94−110, 112−22, 125−31, 197−205, 251−3, 266−73, 283−91, 298−301, 395−7, 409−14
assaulted 78
bands and 361−3
Best and 88
on 'Candyskin' 226−8
Cannavan on 181
Davy Henderson and 398, 403
on Fast Product 10−11, 68−9, 76−7, 232−3, 407−8
Heaven 17 185, 225
on The Human League 184−6, 297
influence 363
on James King 138

on politics 66
pop:aural label 211, 221, 230
Restricted Code 214
The Rezillos and 28
Scars and 15, 25
success of Fast 73, 278, 324−5, 335−6
Laughing Apple 229
Levene, Keith 154
Lironi, Stephen
Altered Images 323, 334
Bourgie Bourgie 388, 390
on 'Candyskin' 228
Fire Engines and 272−3
on labels 378
Last and 211, 413
Restricted Code *212*, 213−14, 282
Listen record shop 132
Lloyd Cole and the Commotions 368, 381, 391−2
Locke, James 280, 298−9, 300−1, 321, 324, 336−7, 342
London Records 337−9, 375, 390−1, 394−5, 397−9, 401−9
Lone Wolves, James King and the 398, 399, 401−3, 421
Lunch, Lydia 91, 252

McArthur, Peter 140, 142, 313, 393
McCluskey, David 240, 241, *312*, 394−5
McCluskey, Ken
on Aztec Camera 256
on bands 133, 219
The Bluebells 239−42, *312*, 313, 337−9, 394−5
on Horne 418−19
on Quinn 356
McClymont, David 257, 262−3, 352−3, 379, 380, 387
Orange Juice *123*, 136, 157, 180, 237
Postcard Records 138, 141, 301
McCormick, Robert 211, 213, *223*
McCullough, Dave
Aztec Camera and 210, 215
The Bluebells and 242
Fire Engines and 200
Jazzateers and 309
Josef K and 243, 246
Postcard Records 173, 176, 177
McDowell, Rose
on Glasgow scene 131, 133−4

Index

going to gigs 156
on Horne 373—4
on Orange Juice 168
The Pastels 392—4
The Poems 158
Strawberry Switchblade 141, *366*, 369
McElhone, Gerry 187, 234, 239, 265, 358
McElhone, Johnny 233
McGee, Alan 229
MacIntyre, Douglas *223*, 304, 360
MacKay, Calumn 21, *71*, 82
MacKenzie, Billy 316—18, *316*, 322—4, 335
Mackie, John
  Fast Product and 43, 50—1, 54, 83
  on Fire Engines 292
  on music scene 19, 24, 26
  on The Pop Group 75
  Scars 15, 21, *71*, 74, 82, 217—19, 274, 279
Mackie, Paul 15, 74, 82
McKinven, Jim 264
McLaren, Malcolm 10, 14, 60, 115, 308
McLaughlin, Gerri 191—2, 241, 250
McLean, Sandy 116—17, 119, 221—2, 231, 325, 362—3
MacLennan, Ewan 192, *223*, 224
McLennan, Grant 154, 158, 179, 387, 416
McNair, Callum 336
Macnaires 300, 336—7
McNeill, Kirsty 171—2, 233, 242, 314
Magazine 162
Main, Graham 48—9, 51—2, 200—1, 284—5
  on 'Big Gold Dream' shoot 272
  The Dirty Reds 44, 45, 80
  Fire Engines 90, 187, *195*, 203, 227
  on Hannaway 252
  on Heartbeat 301
  on Last 199, 410
  on Scars 84
Malcolm, Callum 210
Manicured Noise 101
Manyika, Zeke 315, 344, 352, 379, 388
Mardin, Arif 361, 376, 381, 396
Mark, James and Julie 280
Matlock, Celia 219
MCA Records 154, 368, 390—1
Mekons, The 33—42, *35*, 64—5

albums 103, 413
Best and 41, 45
The Clash and 150
Fast Product 32, 67
The Flowers and 129
Peel sessions 59
support acts 41
'Never Been in a Riot' 31, 36, 38, 40, 41, 59, 119
The Quality of Mercy Is Not Strnen 118
'Where Were You?' 65
Memphis 398, 399, 402
Métal Urbain 41—2, 113
Middle Class 110, 111
Miles Davis 396
Miller, Daniel 70
Morley, Paul 176—8, 244—5, 423—4
  on Creation 229
  Fire Engines and 200, 292
  Josef K and 243, 246—7
  on labels 173, 424
  on *Lubricate* 202
  'post-punk' 41
  Restricted Code 213, 283
  Scars and 218
Moroder, Giorgio 61, 308, 325
Morrison, Hilary 31—57, 67—9, 125—7, 288—90, *295*, 409—14
  bands and 10—11, 180—1, 361—3
  'Big Gold Dream' and 270—1, 273, 285
  The Flowers 23, 79—80, 105—6, *105*
  Garcia and 269
  Haig and 341
  Heartbeat 300—1, 324—5
  on The Human League 61, 266—7
  influence 363
  Joy Division and 108
  The Mekons and 297—8
  on music industry xv, 18, 397
  places and 25
  Scars and 15—16, 22
  success of 335—6
  on Thursdays 88
  Warm Jets and 17, 87
Morrison, Jim 280
Morrison, Lindy 179
Motion, David 392, 397, 399
Mulholland, David 206, 209, 211, 254, *347*
Mute Records 73, 109, 117
Myers, Paul 7

Index

Neutral Blue 190, 209
Nico 79, 87, 274, 279–80
92 Happy Customers 366
Noh Mercy 110
Nu Sonics 131, 134, 135–6

Oakey, Philip 94, *95*, 104, 184–6, 221, 266–8, 300, 395
Obscure Records 200
Old Grey Whistle Test, The 17–18, 82, 219, 273–4, 311, 314, 399, 401, 405
Oliva, James
  bands and 41, 82, 111, 200
  Fast Product 69, 112, 362, 411
  Rab King and 25, 279
Operation Twilight label 365
Orange Juice *123*, 136–43, 145–7, 153–80, 242–5, 256–65, *263*, 378–80
  album demos 235–8
  Auld on 327
  Band on 304–5
  Burgoyne on 376
  gigs 143, 149, 193, 229, 276–7, 292
  Gourlay on 310–11
  Josef K and 151, 187, 189, 193–4
  Mk 2 276, 352
  Ostrich Churchyard 357
  Peel sessions 155, 178, 257
  Polydor Records 333
  singles 179, 206, 352–3
  Sloan on 237–8
  support acts 242
  'Blue Boy' 159, 162, 167–8, 170–5, 178
  'Falling and Laughing' 122, 131, 138, 140, 141, 143, 146, 149–50, 154, 157
  'Felicity' 140, 141, 333
  'L.O.V.E.' 261, 357
  The Orange Juice 379, 380, 388
  Ostrich Churchyard 237, 258
  'Poor Old Soul' 215, 321
  Rip It Up 344–5
  Texas Fever 379
  You Can't Hide Your Love Forever 253–4, 257–8, 263, 315, 345, 357
Owens, Campbell 206–11, 215–16, 385–7
  Aztec Camera 190–1, 254–5, *347*
  on The French Impressionists 356
  on Horne 327, 416–17
  Postcard Event 275, 277

  on Rough Trade 340, 350
Oxfam Warriors 188, 239

Paddy's Market, Glasgow 140, 142
Padgham, Hugh 395
Pale Fountains 364–5, 375
Palladin, Patti 401
Papadopoulos, Harry 313, 314
Parry, Chris 317
Parsons, Tony 38
Pastel, Stephen 132, 134–5, 142, 370–3, 393–4, *393*
Pastels, The 370–4, *371*
Pearce, Tim 56
Peel, John 61, 62, 105, 113, 149, 222, 316, 353, 369
Pere Ubu 115
Perry, Mark 100–1, 259
Phonogram 367
Pierce, Tim 104
Poems 158
Polydor Records 257–9, 261, 315, 317, 327, 333, 352–3, 391
Pop Group, The 73–7, 74, 101, 101–2, 137
Pop, Iggy 103–4
pop:aural label 125–30, 180–2, 224–8, 271–2, 281–3, 288–91, 409–14
  Fire Engines 197, 202–3, 211, 221
  Restricted Code 211, 221
  underperforming 250, 278
Porter, John 401
Postcard International 301–2, 307–15, 321–2, 326–33
Postcard Records 138–62, 165–81, 187–94, 197–9, 204–11, 214–16, 220–2, 230–6, 238–48, 254–9, 274–8, 340–5, 414–24
  The Bluebells and 337
  influence xv, 9, 363
  Josef K 288
  Orange Juice and 261, 288, 337, 344–5
  Prats, The 104–5, 111
  Pre Records 216–18, 279–80
  Prefab Sprout 364, 367
  Public Image Ltd 31

Quadrelli, Frank 229, 412
  Restricted Code 181, *212*, 213, 214, 226, 281–2

Quality of Life fanzine 52−4, 60, 70, 106, 111, 118, 125
Quinn, Paul 274−5, 328−30, 354−61, *355*
  Bourgie Bourgie 333, 368, 376−7, *389*, 390−1
  Collins and 345, 391, 405
  The French Impressionists 307
  Horne and 230, 376, 403
  James King on 349, 421

Radar label 73
Radio Clyde 243−4
Raincoats, The 65
Ramones, The 23, 63, 117, 133
Rankin, Ian xiii−xvi
Rankine, Alan *316*, 317−18, 322−4, 334−5, 387
Rational Records 190, 191, 211, 222, 280, 320
record shops 15−17
Red Rhino 363
Reed, Lou 86−7, 402
Reekie, Innes
  on bands 232
  on 'Candyskin' 226
  on Fast Product 55
  Fire Engines 186, 187, 202, 271, 287
  on Henderson 53−4
Reekie, Paul 47, 51, 79, 88, 112, 130
Reid, Jamie 10
Research, Paul 217−19, 278−9, 292−3
  on Fast Product 51, 81
  on Glam 19, 24
  guitarist 21, 84
  on King
  on Last 42, 85
  letter to Siouxsie Sioux 68
  on Nico 274
  Scars 15, 25, *71*, 79, 82−3
Restricted Code 180−2, *212*, 229, 334
  Last and 184, 211, 221, 412−13
  Peel session 213, 282
  singles 224, 225
  split 281−3, 367
Reynolds, Eugene 63
Rezillos, The 26−8, 32−3, 62−3
  Fife and *27*, 86
  gigs 112
  hit single 52
  roadies 56

support acts 23, 32, 35, 109
Rhodes, Bernie 10, 14, 115, 154−5
Richman, Jonathan 242
Ricochet project 362−3
Ripped and Torn fanzine 132, 171
Robertson, B.A. 256
Rooney, Mickey 132
Ross, Alastair 246
Ross, Malcolm 140−1, 143−6, 204−5, 248−9
  and Article 58 192
  and Aztec Camera 190, 191, 211, 380, 385
  on Campbell 148
  on Collins 379
  Haig and 387
  on Horne 153, 167−8, 176, 178, 301−2, 415
  Josef K *152*, 164, 243, 246, 247−8, 259−60
  on Orange Juice 238, 259, 352
  Orange Juice 138, 261−2, 264, 315, 344, 379
  on rivalry 178−9
Rotten, Johnny 62
Rough Trade Records 37−9, 41−3, 113−14, 149−51, 221−2, 350−2, 356−61, 372−5, 380−1, 396−7
  bands and 98, 105, 331, 363
  C81 214
  Gartside and 381
  Josef K 248
  The Mekons and 65
  Postcard and 165−6, 171, 173−4, 179, 204−5, 240
  profit split 109
  Subway Sect 154−5
Roxy Music 82−3
Ruffy, Dave 340
Rushent, Martin 221, 265−6, 315−16, 323, 395
Rutkowski, Deirdre and Louise 329, 333, 358

Sadkin, Alex 341, 342, 380
Sager, Gareth 73−7, *74*, 83, 86−7, 101−2, 164
Saville, Peter 70, 100
Scars 20−2, 24−6, 81−6, 278−9
  Barclay on 88
  early days 15
  influence xiv, 76, 292

King on 119
punk explosion 31
singles 43, 63, 84−5, 103
Sutherland on 51
'All about You' 216, 273
Author! Author! 216−20, 248
'Horrorshow' 84−6, 150
Scott, Richard 114
Scritti Politti 42, 254, 361−2, 365, 381, 396−7
Sensational Alex Harvey Band, The 19
Sensible Records 27, 112
Severin, Steve 235, 264
Sex Pistols 10, 16, 31, 34, 115, 134
SeXex (FAST 6) 70, 106, 111
Sharp, Robert 171−2, 233, 239, 313
Shelley, Pete 191, 316
Shores, Barbara 230, 349, 366, 367
Simonon, Paul 75
Simple Minds 137, 159, 333
Simpson, Bernice 370, 373
Siouxsie and the Banshees 20, 68, 219, 264−5
Sire Records 27−8, 63, 112, 394
Situation 2 Records 317−18
Skids xiii, 333
Skinner, Grahame 351, 356, 357−60, 381
Slade, Murray 89−90, 227−8, 286−7
Fire Engines 91−3, *195*, 201, 284
Josef K and 292
on Last 203, 230, 410
Slaven, Mick 368, 376, *389*
Sleaford, Nigel 336
Slits, The *13*, 20, 67, 102, 128, 162
White Riot tour 9, 10, 12, 14
Sloan, Billy 216, 237−8, 243−4, 405, 423
Smith, Mark E. 112, 200, 280
Smith, Patti 74
Smiths, The 375
Sniffin' Glue fanzine 259
Something Else (BBC) 262
Sordide Sentimental label 109
Sound Diagrams (Fast) 103, 269, 278, 283, 298−300, 398
Spaghetti Factory, Glasgow 172, 233, 275, 305, 310, 357, 419
Station 6 89
Steel Pulse 135
Stein, Seymour 28, 63, 112, 334, 394
Stewart, Jamo *183*

Stewart, Mark 73−5, *74*, 77, 101−2, 164−5
Stiff Little Fingers 65, 114
Stoddart, Ian 397
Stooges, The 37, 90
Stranglers, The 134
Strawberry Switchblade 131, 141, 142, 230, 366, *366*, 369, 392−4, 399
Strolch 46
Strummer, Joe 12
Stupid Babies 110
Subway Sect 7
gigs 154, 191
influence 75, 86
Peel sessions 20, 154
singles 136
White Riot tour 10, 12, 14−15, 135, 155
What's the Matter Boy? 9, 154−5
Suicide 58, 133
Sulley, Susan 185, 252
Summer, Donna 61, 308, 310−11, 326
Sumner, Bernard 388
Superstar, Brian 131−2, 138, 141−2, 188, 370, *371*, 372−3
Sutherland, Fraser 129−31, 143−4, 252−3, 290−1
on bands 51, 83−4, 232
on Fire Engines 201, 286
The Flowers *105*, *128*, 130
on Last 411
on Pre Records 217
Swamplands Records 390−1, 397−406, 414−24
Switch (Ch4) 360
Symmons, Rob 7, 14

T. Rex 18−19, 133, 395
Talking Heads 63, 182
Talkovers 41, 46, 49−50, *49*
Tap o' Lauriston, Edinburgh 50, 51, 130, 231
Taylor, Fraser 350
Teardrop Explodes, The 73, 143, 166−7, 191
Television 89, 114−15, 148, 164
Ten Commandments fanzine 156−7, 171−2, 180, 188, 190, 233
Thomas, Chris 395
Thompson, Mayo 65, 372
Thomson, Chris 367
Thornally, Phil 401

Index

Throbbing Gristle 130
Thunders, Johnny 401
Thursdays xiv, 81, 87, 88, 102, 106–7, 111–12
Top of the Pops 17, 62–3, 353, 375, 395
Torrance, Ronnie 144–5, 148, *152*, 153, 259–60, 343
Trash 77 fanzine 132
Travis, Geoff 37–8, *39*, 41–2, 69–70, 97–9, 113–15, 340–1, 350–2
    on bands 186, 220, 396
    on Cartel 222
    on Collins 258
    on distribution 117
    on Frame 380
    on Horne 151, 166, 258, 406–7, 421
    Jazzateers and 358–9
    on Last 166, 413–14
    The Mekons and 65
    Pastel on 372
    on pop:aural 272
    Postcard Records 171, 173–4
    on Quinn and Horne 404
    on Rough Trade 374
Tube, The (Ch4) 351
Tunenoise management 278, 336, 395
TV Art 131, 138, 143–4, 146–7
2.3 42, 58, 59

Undertones, The 179
Up, Ari 12, *13*

Vega, Alan 133
Velvet Underground 37, 86, 87, 135, 142, 162, 165, 274
Vice Versa 58, 324
Vicious, Sid 44, 154
Virgin Records 15–16, 50–1, 103–4
    bands and 243, 281, 333, 365
    The Human League 99, 185, 221
    Last and 268
    shops 22, 325
Voidoids, Richard Hell and the 48, 89, 155

Wake 421–2
Waller, Johnny 148
Ware, Martyn 57–60, 103–4
    on Callis 251, 267
    Fast Product Records 62, 69
    Heaven 17 225, 250
    The Human League 95, *95*, 185, 225

    on Last 184, 268
    on Oakey 266
    on Virgin 100
Warhol, Andy 58, 62, 86, 142, 416–17, 419, 422
Warm Jets 17, 22, 50, 87
Warner Brothers 317–18, 322, 368–9, 380, 385–6, 392
Warr, Rob 395
Warsaw 107, 109
Weddell, David 144–5, *152*, 248, 249, 259–60, 264, 292, 343
Welsh, Alan 209
Whaam! Records 372
What Ever Happened to Baby Jane project 401
White, Mark 'Chalkie' 33, 34, *35*
White Savages 360, 368, 381
Wig and Pen pub 46–7, 49, 82, 292
Wilson, Mark 238–9, 257, 311
Wilson, Tony 70, 97, 100, 109–10, 120, 254
Win 380, 397–9, 403–4
Winwood, Muff 234, 338
Worrell, Bernie 342, 380
Wright, Adrian 61–2, *95*, 185, 251, 267–8
Wright, Annabel (Aggi) 372–3, 394

ZE Records 101, 252
Zoo Records 73, 138, 143, 166, 191, 281, 363